KIRI
HER UNSUNG STORY

STEPHEN D'ANTAL is a British journalist contributing to magazines and newspapers in the UK, Australia and New Zealand. He lives with his family in Auckland, New Zealand.

GARRY JENKINS is a former *Daily Mail* journalist and the author of biographies of the actors Daniel Day-Lewis and Harrison Ford. He lives with his wife and children in Blackheath, London.

KIRI

HER UNSUNG STORY

Garry Jenkins
& Stephen d'Antal

HarperCollins*Entertainment*
An Imprint of HarperCollinsPublishers

HarperCollins*Entertainment*
An Imprint of HarperCollins*Publishers*
77–85 Fulham Palace Road,
Hammersmith, London W6 8JB

www.**fire**and**water**.com

This paperback edition 1999
1 3 5 7 9 8 6 4 2

First published in Great Britain by
HarperCollins*Publishers* 1998
Copyright © Garry Jenkins and Stephen d'Antal 1998

The Authors assert the moral right to
be identified as the authors of this work

ISBN 0 00 653061 3

Printed and bound in Great Britain by
Clays Ltd, St Ives plc

CONTENTS

LIST OF ILLUSTRATIONS

For Eva and Gabriella

PROLOGUE

Shortly before noon on Wednesday, 29 July 1981, the anxiety that had been etched on the features of Charles, Prince of Wales for most of an eventful morning finally gave way to a faraway smile.

The heir to the throne of the United Kingdom was in the midst of the most solemn moment of his thirty-two-year-old life. Dressed in the full uniform of a Commander of Her Majesty's Royal Navy he was positioned behind a large desk in the Dean's Aisle in London's St Paul's Cathedral. He had, in the presence of his mother, Queen Elizabeth II, just signed the wedding certificate confirming the vows he had taken moments earlier in the main hall of Sir Christopher Wren's imperious basilica. Sitting next to him, cocooned in a sea of ivory silk, was his new wife, the twenty-year-old Lady Diana Spencer, now the Princess of Wales.

For both Charles and Diana, the intimacy and privacy of the moment had helped lift the tensions of the previous few hours. The atmosphere inside the chapel, where they were congratulated by their families and the man who had just officiated over the wedding, the Archbishop of Canterbury, Dr Robert Runcie, was one of joyous relief.

For all the happiness Charles was sharing with his radiant bride at that moment, however, it was another woman who was responsible for his most spontaneous smile. Some fifty metres away, back in the north transept and out of his view, her familiar voice had begun delivering the opening stanzas of one of his favourite arias, 'Let the Bright Seraphim' from Handel's *Samson*. Suddenly, Charles admitted later, he found himself strangely disconnected from the tumultuous events unfolding around him. Instead, he said, his head was filled with nothing but the blissful sound of 'this marvellous, disembodied voice'.

If the divine soprano of Kiri Te Kanawa was instantly recognisable to the man at the centre of the most eagerly awaited Royal Wedding in living memory, it was less so to the vast majority of the 700 million or so people watching the spectacle on television around the world. At first the unannounced sight of her striking, statuesque form, dressed in a rainbow-hued outfit, a tiny, pillbox hat fixed loosely on her lustrous, russet red hair, had been something of a puzzle. Yet the moment her gorgeous operatic phrases began climbing towards the domed ceiling of St Paul's her right to a place in the proceedings was unmistakable.

Charles had wanted the occasion to be a festival as well as a fairytale wedding, in his own words, 'as much a musical event as an emotional one'. His bride had entered St Paul's to a rousing version of Purcell's Trumpet Voluntary. Sir David Willcocks, Director of the Royal College of Music, had conducted an inspired version of the National Anthem. A glorious version of Elgar's Pomp and Circumstance March no. 4 had been prepared to lead the newlyweds down the aisle. Yet it was the occasion's lone soloist who was providing its unquestioned highlight.

Since she emerged, a decade earlier, as a musical star of the greatest magnitude with her performance as the Countess in Mozart's *The Marriage of Figaro* at Covent Garden's Royal Opera House, Kiri Te Kanawa had grown accustomed to glamorous occasions on the world's great stages, from the New York Met to La Scala. The faces she saw assembled before her today, however, made up the most glittering audience she or indeed any other singer had ever encountered. Seated on row after row of gilted, Queen Anne chairs were not just the vast majority of the British Royal Family but Presidents Reagan of America and Mitterrand of France, Prince Rainier and Princess Grace of Monaco, the monarchs of Belgium, the Netherlands and Denmark, ex-King Constantine of Greece and the giant figure of the King of Tonga. Behind them sat crowned heads, presidents and prime ministers representing almost every nation on earth.

The soprano's emotions were, as usual, a mixture of fire and ice. Inside, she confessed later, she was a maelstrom of nerves. Yet her voice, unfaltering and flawless, betrayed none of her true feelings. It was as if she had been born for this moment and this place – as, indeed, many were sure she had been.

In the decade or so since her early stage triumphs, Kiri Te Kanawa had frequently been described as a member of aristocracy. Her father, people said, was descended from a great chief of the Maniapoto tribe, a member of the Maori nation of New Zealand. In truth, she did not know her true identity. She had no real idea whether she was a Maori princess or not. Among the hundreds of millions of people who watched her sing that day, only a tiny handful knew the truth. They sat 13,000 miles away, on the east coast of her homeland, their television sets tuned to the wedding being broadcast live at midnight Pacific time.

As the strains of Handel faded inside St Paul's Cathedral and the television commentators paid tribute to the singer who had so charmed the assembled kings and queens, they shook their heads quietly and a little mournfully. They knew Kiri Te Kanawa's true story was rather different from that which the world imagined. They knew, much like the wedding of Charles and Diana, it too was far from a fairytale.

PART ONE

When people ask you
To recite your pedigree
You must say,
'I am forgetful, a child,
But this is well-known,
Tainui, Te Arawa, Matatua,
Kura-haupo and Toko-maru,
Were the ancestral canoes
That crossed the great sea
Which lies here.'

Nga Moteatea, *Peou's Lament*

The Road to Gisborne

In the early months of 1944 in the remote New Zealand community of Tokomaru Bay, an auburn-haired, twenty-six-year-old woman, Noeleen Rawstron, walked out of the shabby, corrugated iron bungalow that had been her home. She loaded a few belongings into a taxi and began the fifty-mile drive south to the nearest major town, Gisborne, on the eastern Pacific coast.

The two hour journey she was about to make was an uncomfortable one at the best of times. Despite recent improvements, the road to Gisborne remained little more than a rutted dirt track. Given the fact she was heavily pregnant, however, she would have had even more reason to dread every pit and pothole that lay ahead of her.

The child she was expecting was her second. She had left her first son, James Patrick, inside the ramshackle house with her own mother, Thelma, with whose help she had raised him. Like any mother, her anguish at leaving her son ran deep. Yet, in truth she had no choice. Noeleen Rawstron had reached a crisis in her life. The child she was about to give birth to was the result of an affair that had scandalised the tight-knit community in which she had spent her entire life. She had climbed into her taxi that morning to escape.

Noeleen Rawstron had kept her condition a secret from almost all her family, no mean feat given she was one of six children, three boys and three girls, each of whom lived in the small community. Her flight from Tokomaru Bay was almost certainly precipitated by the fact that she had failed to hide the truth from the most powerful figure in that family, her mother.

Noeleen had inherited much from Thelma Rawstron. She too was copper-haired and steely-willed, fiercely independent and at times too

3

fiery for her own good. Now she would need to emulate another of her mother's characteristics – an instinct for survival.

Thelma's parents, Samuel and Gertrude Wittison, had fled Ireland at the turn of the century. After a spell farming land near Hobart in Australia, where Liza Thelma had been born in 1887, the Wittisons had sailed on to Napier in New Zealand. It was here, on 12 July 1909, that Thelma married Albert James Rawstron, the twenty-nine-year-old son of a police inspector who had emigrated to New Zealand from Bamber Bridge, Lancashire.

With his new bride, Albert, a carpenter, had soon moved to begin a new life along the coast in Tokomaru Bay. Thelma recalled to her children how she watched her possessions lowered on to the harbour in a wicker basket. To the eyes of later generations, Tokomaru Bay's setting, on one of the most brutally beautiful stretches of coastline on New Zealand's North Island, would conjure up images from New Zealand film director Jane Campion's Oscar-winning movie *The Piano*. However, to Thelma there was little or no romance to this bleak, windswept outpost. The town amounted to little more than a threadbare collection of homes and farms. In the 1930s the town had little street lighting or indeed electricity of any kind. Fifty miles of often impenetrable dirt track separated it from the nearest large community, Gisborne.

In summer, the so-called East Cape was the hottest, driest region of New Zealand. Yet in winter the cold, Pacific winds would cut into the town with a vengeance. Thelma soon discovered life itself could be no less callous.

At first her marriage was happy enough. Albert, like many of the town's population, had found work at the giant, meat freezing works that served the district's sheep-farming industry. Thelma had six children in rapid succession and the demands of his rapidly expanding household became an increasingly difficult burden for Albert to bear. Work at the freezing factory was seasonal. At times money was so tight, all eight of the family were forced to live in a tent near the meat works. Eventually, as the pressures of providing piled up, Albert told Thelma he had decided to leave the coast in search of better paid work in Auckland. He was never seen in Tokomaru Bay again.

Even by the standards of Tokomaru Bay, Thelma's life and that of her family became a grim and impoverished one. The community was spread out along the edge of the Pacific; the white, European immigrants concentrated in the more affluent part of the town, known as Toko, the indigenous, dark-skinned Maori in a shanty town called Waima. The Rawstrons were among the few white families forced to live in what most regarded as the wrong side of Tokomaru Bay.

In the aftermath of Albert's desertion, Thelma had kept a roof over the family's head by working as a cleaner. She would leave Waima each morning at five and walk five miles to a farmhouse owned by two elderly spinsters. She used the money she scraped together to move the family into a rented, corrugated iron bungalow. The home was pitiful – its floors were earth – but in comparison to the tent it seemed positively palatial to her children.

Of all her offspring, Noeleen seems to have been the one who inherited her mother's combination of inner strength and outgoing attractiveness. She had been born Mary Noeleen Rawstron on 15 October 1918, in Gisborne. A spirited girl, she was also blessed with striking good looks. By the time she had reached her teenage years, she had become an object of admiration for many of the area's menfolk.

Noeleen's first serious boyfriend was Jimmy Collier, a handsome Maori farm labourer who lived in Tokomaru Bay. The pair conducted their courtship far from the prying eyes of the local community, in the shadow of Mount Hikurangi and the parched hills overlooking the town. Their idyll was short-lived, however. Soon Noeleen had fallen pregnant. She gave birth to a son in 1938, naming him James Patrick after his father. If she had hoped the child would cement their relationship, she had been mistaken. Jimmy seemed frightened by the responsibility and the speed at which matters had progressed. Noeleen was left to raise Jimmy junior, or Ninna as he was nicknamed, at home with her mother. As Jimmy junior grew into a young boy, his father became less and less an influence in his life. By 1940 Collier had moved to Gisborne where he married another woman. Noeleen found the desertion hard to bear.

'Noeleen couldn't understand what Jimmy was doing with her,' recalled a friend, Ira Haig, a schoolteacher in the town. 'She knew she was much better looking than this girl and couldn't accept his rejection.'

In the aftermath of Collier's disappearance, Noeleen cast her eye around the male population for a man capable of bringing her new happiness. Three years after Collier left Tokomaru Bay, she thought she had found him.

As World War II brought Europe's economy to a standstill, Tokomaru Bay found itself entering one of the most prosperous periods in its history. With the rest of the world in desperate need of wool and mutton, the freezing factory was at full capacity. More than 2,000 men poured into the area to work, among them a twenty-five-year-old Maori butcher, Tieki 'Jack' Wawatai.

Jack had travelled down to Tokomaru from the village of Rangitukia, sixty miles to the north along the Pacific coast. As a Maori he could not be conscripted into the ANZAC forces now being dispatched by the New Zealand government. Instead, with little work available on the farms in his area, he headed south to the freezing factory where his skills with a knife had brought him work in previous seasons. Not for the first time in his life, Jack Wawatai arrived in Tokomaru in need of money. Back in Rangitukia a wife and a large family were depending on him.

Jack had been born and raised in Rangitukia. His father had died there when he was just thirteen. When his mother remarried he had been taken in by the community's Anglican minister, the Reverend Poihipi Kohere. Jack worked on the minister's farm where he made an instant impression on his employer's daughter, Apo. In November 1937, twenty-year-old Jack and eighteen-year-old Apo were married in the Reverend Kohere's home. By 1943 they had four children.

Jack was a good-looking man with piercing eyes and an engaging, happy-go-lucky personality. 'He could charm the birds from the trees,' said his schoolteacher wife. Blessed with a fine singing voice, his renditions of traditional Maori songs and Mario Lanza arias would often drift towards the farmhouse. 'I would hear him singing to the cows in the field in the middle of the night,' smiled Apo. In Tokomaru Bay, Jack whiled away the long evenings singing with a group of other, mostly Maori, men in a shop near the Rawstrons' home.

He had been introduced to the impromptu singalongs by Ira Haig, a friend of his family for years. 'At first he told me he couldn't go. He was married and these meetings were for single men only,' said Ira. 'But he loved to sing, he really did, and in the end he went. I took him there.' By 1943 Noeleen had landed herself a job working as a waitress in the meat works' canteen. It was there she first set her eye on the handsome newcomer. He reciprocated her interest and soon they were seeing each other discreetly. According to her sister, Donny, Noeleen may have assumed Jack was unmarried when she met him. If she had suspicions, they would have been deepened by his regular disappearance at weekends to return to Rangitukia and his family.

Whatever the truth, Noeleen felt the cut of her mother's Irish temper when Thelma found out what her daughter was up to. 'My mother kicked up a hell of a fuss,' recalled Donny. 'She didn't like Jack. One, because he was Maori – she didn't like the Maoris even though she lived surrounded by them – and two, because he was married.'

Disapproval may have been exactly what Thelma's most headstrong daughter was looking for, however. 'I saw them walking around town one Sunday afternoon and once I saw them at the pub. I spoke to Noeleen about it and I told her she should stop seeing Jack,' said Donny. 'But she told me it was none of my business. She had a strong will.'

Jack's wife Apo had suspected nothing of her husband's infidelity, even when he returned with little of his wages left. She put his shortage of money down to his weakness for drinking and gambling on a game called 'two up'. 'Jack was terrible with money,' she lamented. Soon, however, news of his relationship with another woman found its way back to the farm via relations in Tokomaru Bay. While her father, an introverted man, bottled up his fury, Apo packed her bags and headed south to confront her husband. 'It was a hell of a shock. I hadn't expected it,' she said.

When Noeleen got wind of Jack's wife's imminent arrival she prepared for the worst. 'She thought she was coming to knock her block off,' said Donny, to whom she confided news of the crisis. 'Maybe Jack warned her because Noeleen stayed well out of the way all weekend.'

Instead, however, Apo maintained a dignified silence. She moved in with Jack in Waima and let him know she intended staying until their marriage was once more on an even keel. When she eventually saw Noeleen on the street she simply ignored her. 'I couldn't help but pass Noeleen by – but I don't think I ever spoke to her,' she recalled.

Apo treated her husband's contrition with the scepticism it deserved. 'He was a naughty boy. Jack said he was sorry and wouldn't do it again.' In years to come Jack would confirm her suspicions by straying once more, this time for good. Yet by the end of the freezing season of 1943 the couple were able to make the journey back to Rangitukia with their marriage intact.

Unable to see or speak to Jack, Noeleen was powerless as the latest man in her life left Tokomaru Bay. Her pain was compounded by the fact that he did so oblivious to the reality she was left to face alone. She was pregnant once more.

During the early months of morning sickness, Noeleen managed to keep the news to herself. 'We never knew,' said her sister Donny. 'She never told me or anyone else.'

If she had a confidante, it was probably a woman from outside Tokomaru Bay and her family circle, Kura Beale, stepdaughter of the area's richest landowner, A.B. Williams, for whom Noeleen had worked as a cleaner in nearby Te Puia Springs. According to some, Kura Beale had herself fallen pregnant in unfortunate circumstances and had, apparently, given her child away for adoption. As Noeleen's condition became obvious, however, it seems her mother realised what had happened and was instrumental in Noeleen's decision to leave Tokomaru Bay. Noeleen decided to head for Gisborne, a town large enough and far away enough for her to have her baby in relative peace. When she left, her mother had prepared a cover story for her. 'I remember my mother telling me that Noeleen had gone away to work for a while,' said Donny.

The unhappiness she must have endured during the final weeks of her pregnancy can only be imagined. Her misery came to an end at the maternity annexe of the Cook Hospital, on 6 March, when she gave birth to a baby girl. She named the child Claire Mary Teresa Rawstron.

With Jack Wawatai once more reunited with his family and unlikely to have been aware of the birth, Noeleen had no choice but to leave the name of the girl's father blank on the birth certificate. Forced to remain in Gisborne and without an income, however, she could not leave matters as they were for long.

If Jack and Apo Wawatai had hoped the unpleasantness of the previous year had been put behind them, their wishes were shattered when a policeman arrived on the farm one day that autumn. The officer solemnly presented Jack with a summons to appear at the courthouse in Rotorua in the coming days. 'He had to go to Rotorua for a hearing about maintenance for the baby,' said his sister, Huka. 'That was the first we knew of it.' Shaken and confused, Jack once more turned to his wife in the hope she would be understanding. 'He said we should take her in as our own,' recalled Apo. This time, however, his wish was beyond even Apo's charity. 'I told him that was out of the question,' she said softly. 'Apart from anything, we had enough children already and couldn't afford it. Things were very hard at the time.'

It is unclear what decision the court in Rotorua came to when it heard the case against Jack Wawatai. Even if Noeleen had been able to prove he was the baby's father, any maintenance award would have been pitiful given his finances and other responsibilities. The court case only underlined the hopelessness of Noeleen's predicament. She knew she would eventually be forced to return to Tokomaru Bay and her mother. Yet she also knew that Thelma's hostility towards her – and the child of an adulterous affair with a Maori man – would be hard to bear.

A few weeks after baby Claire's birth, Noeleen – perhaps influenced by her friendship with Kura Beale – decided to put her up for adoption and headed back up to Tokomaru Bay where she picked up her life with her mother and her son Jimmy. There she maintained a steadfast silence about the dramas of that year for the rest of her life.

'The Boss'

Within weeks of Noeleen Rawstron's departure back to Tokomaru Bay, a member of Gisborne's social services staff took baby Claire to a house at 161 Grey Street, a short walk from the ocean. There the social worker introduced her to a Maori, Atama 'Tom' Te Kanawa, and his wife Nell.

The middle-aged couple had been married for four years. While Tom ran a successful trucking company, Nell was in the process of completing the purchase of the Grey Street property which she was already running as a thriving boarding house.

Approaching her forty-seventh birthday, Nell, the mother of two children from a previous marriage, was now too old to bear Tom a child. The couple had decided to adopt instead. According to their own account, passed on to their daughter later, Tom Te Kanawa was particularly keen to adopt a boy and rejected Claire on first meeting her. Unable to find another home for the baby, however, the social worker persisted. When Claire was taken to Grey Street for a second time Tom had been smitten by the dusky-skinned little girl with huge limpid eyes. He and Nell agreed to adopt her as their daughter.

As the legal formalities were completed Tom and Nell were asked to choose the child's new name. Nell had agreed with Tom's idea of calling the little girl Kiri, after Tom's father, a Maori name meaning 'bell' or 'skin of the tree', depending on the dialect. For her other names they chose Jeanette, one of Nell's own middle names, and Claire, the only name they had heard the social workers use when referring to the child. For decades to come, the name her birth mother had chosen for her would remain Kiri Jeanette Claire Te Kanawa's sole link with her troubled past.

As she handed her baby over to the town's social services, Noeleen Rawstron had accepted that she could have no say in choosing the family who would become Claire's parents. As she dwelled on her daughter's fate back in Tokomaru Bay, she would have hoped for a life filled with love and security. On a deeper level, her instincts may have wished for a home and a family background that fitted the little girl's own complex beginnings. In time Noeleen would come to discover the identity of the couple who had taken her daughter in, but she would never appreciate quite how alike Claire's real and adopted parents were.

In the course of a colourful and eventful life, the redoubtable Mrs Tom Te Kanawa had found herself addressed by any number of names, not all of them charitable. At birth on 14 October 1897, she had been christened Hellena Janet Leece. Since then she had been addressed at different times, and with varying degrees of happiness, as Mrs Alfred John Green and Mrs Stephen Whitehead. In electoral and postal directories around the North and South Islands of New Zealand, her unusual Christian name had been rearranged as Ellenor, Eleanor and even Heleanor. It was little wonder she insisted new friends simply call her Nell. To her family and the boarders she took in at her guest house there was little cause for confusion, however. To them she was The Boss – and she always would be.

A boisterous, ruddy-cheeked woman with a heart – and a temper – to match her oversized frame, Nell Te Kanawa cast her considerable shadow over every aspect of life at the house that became baby Claire Rawstron's new home. During the formative years of her new daughter's life she would be its dominant – and at times overwhelmingly domineering – force. She would not thank her for it until later in life. Yet without The Boss, it is unlikely Kiri Te Kanawa would have left the town of Gisborne, let alone the North Island of New Zealand.

Like Thelma and Noeleen Rawstron, Nell Te Kanawa had endured a life of early hardship. She was born in the gold-mining town of Waihi in the Bay of Plenty. Nell's mother, Emily Leece, née Sullivan, was the daugter of a miner, Jeremiah Sullivan. She was one of fifteen children Emily bore with her husband, another miner, John Alfred Leece, originally from Rushen on the Isle of Man. Like many men of his generation, John Leece dreamt of making a fortune at Australasia's

11

largest gold mine. Instead, however, his life seems to have disintegrated there. It is unclear whether Emily Leece was widowed or divorced her husband. What is certain is that when Hellena was a teenager her mother uprooted the family to the town of Nelson, at the northerly tip of the South Island, where she set up a new life without John Leece.

'Nell', as everyone called Hellena, was less than lucky in her own relationships with men. It was certainly not for the lack of trying.

She had wasted little time in finding a husband. She had been just eighteen when she married Alfred John Green, a twenty-year-old labourer from Hobart. Nell had been employed as a factory worker in the town and living with her mother, now re-married to a Nelson labourer called William John Staines. Emily and her new husband were the witnesses at the wedding, held at the town's Catholic Church on Manuka Street on Monday, 1 November 1915.

Within four years, the Greens had two children; Stan, born in 1916, and Nola, born three years later. Around the time of Nola's arrival in the world the family moved to a farm in the remote community of Waimangaroa, outside Westport on the stormy west coast of the South Island where Nell's parents had been married. Life on the land seems to have proven too hard and soon the family were living in the tiny village of Denniston, where Alfred had found work as a carpenter. The move was no less of a failure. With Stan and Nola, Nell left her husband and Denniston for Gisborne on the East Cape of the North Island. She and Alfred Green were divorced in October 1933.

The divorce inspired a new energy in Nell's life. In the years that followed, she often proclaimed that she had arrived in Gisborne with nothing but 'two suitcases and two kids'. With the determination that would characterise her later years, she began the process of building a more secure life for herself and her family.

With Stan and Nola and a relation of her mother's, Irene Beatrice Staines, she moved into a large boarding house at 161 Grey Street. It was while lodging here that, according to some, Nell began performing illegal abortions. Her services were much in demand in the busy coastal town where too many young women found themselves compromised by visiting sailors and other transient workers. As discreet as she was efficient, she apparently found much of her custom within members of the Gisborne's growing Greek and Italian immigrant population.

12

Nell had soon found herself a new husband too. Around the time her first marriage was dissolved she met Stephen Whitehead, a forty-eight-year-old widower from Gisborne. Nell and Whitehead, a bicycle dealer and mechanic, were married at the registrar's office in Gisborne on 8 August 1935. The marriage proved childless, short-lived and somewhat scandalous. It was Kiri herself who later suggested Nell's second marriage had left her in disgrace, both with her family and the Catholic Church. 'There had even been talk of excommunication,' she remembered. If the exact details of Nell's shame are unclear, it is not difficult to imagine the outrage her backstreet operations would have provoked if they had become known within the church.

From baby Claire's perspective, at least, there were more encouraging threads linking the lives of Nell Te Kanawa and Noeleen Rawstron. Of all the parallels, perhaps none would prove so significant as the fact that both Nell and Noeleen had found themselves involved in mixed-race relationships.

As her second marriage headed towards divorce, Nell had met and fallen in love with a soft-spoken, deeply reserved truck driver also lodging at Grey Street. In Atama 'Tom' Te Kanawa, it turned out, she had found the ideal man with whom to reinvent herself.

Tom Te Kanawa's family originated from the west coast of the North Island, near Kawhia Harbour and the community of Kinohaku. His bloodlines led directly back to a legendary Maori figure, Chief Te Kanawa of one of the Waikato tribes, the Maniapoto. Chief Te Kanawa's primary claim to a place in New Zealand's history rests on his exploits in the Maori wars of the 1820s. In 1826, Te Kanawa and another chieftain, Te Wherowhero, had ended the ambitions of the region's most feared warlord, Pomare-nui, by ambushing his canoe and murdering him. According to Maori folklore, the two chiefs had then cooked and eaten their vanquished rival. As the gruesome ritual had been carried out, strange, yellow granules had been found inside his stomach. Thus, corn is said to have arrived in the Waikato region.

Tom was one of thirteen children born to a farmer, Kiri Te Kanawa, and his wife Taongahuia Moerua. By the time Tom, his parents' fourth child and third son, arrived in the world in 1902, the Te Kanawa family had moved from Kawhia inland to the lush green hills above the small towns of Otorohanga and Waitomo. Tom spent the formative years of his childhood in a community built around the family meeting place, or marae, Pohatuiri. The community was a remote collection of earth-floored houses made from punga logs – the trunks of a native fern tree – set miles from the nearest roads. His early life there was rooted in a simple, self-sufficient lifestyle that had served the Maori people for centuries.

Tom's younger brother, Mita, later wrote of the Te Kanawas' way of life in a privately published history. He remembered Pohatuiri as a 'very busy community', and looked back with affection at 'the closeness, unity and warmth of everyone' who shared their world. The fertile land around Pohatuiri provided almost everything they needed. The families bought in only sugar, salt, flour, tobacco and alcohol to supplement their home-brewed supplies. Seafood was often provided by family members from Kawhia. In this land of milk and honey, the depression that afflicted the rest of the world in the 1930s passed almost unnoticed.

The highlights of each year were the *huis*, or feasts, prepared communally. 'Our family homestead was situated just above where the spring and the orchard trees were. Whenever there as a *hui* approaching, everyone planned on the preparation for the function,' Mita wrote. 'Each family group looked after certain duties, but we all helped each other. Fruit picking was done by all of us – we collected the fruit and our kuia [elder women] would be busy with the making of jams, pickles, sauces, preserves and homebrews.'

Both Tom's parents were God-fearing individuals. Taongahuia's family were staunch members of the Christian Ratana movement, named after its founder Bill Ratana, a farmer who had become convinced of his pastoral role after witnessing visions in 1919. Kiri was never slow to chastise younger members of the family overheard using bad language. It was a community steeped in the Maori language, and its tradition of passing its history on orally rather than the written word. According to the family, Kiri was the possessor of a fine singing voice. 'Kiri and his wife couldn't speak English at all. They didn't really have to up there,' said Kay Rowbottom, Tom's niece, the daughter of his sister Te Waamoana. 'They maybe could read a little but not speak it, perhaps just a few basic words.'

At school, however, Tom was introduced to the harsh realities of New Zealand life. Tom and his siblings were taught English as a second language and were banned by statute from any use of their native tongue. 'In that era they would have been beaten with a leather strap for speaking Maori,' said Kay Rowbottom.

Tom's childhood in the hills eventually came to an end when he was sent to a foster mother, Ngapawa Ormsby, in the town of Otorohanga. The arrangement was far from unusual. 'Kids were fostered out as workers,' said Kay Rowbottom. 'They were like slaves. In a lot of cases, the girls worked in the houses and the boys on the land.' Tom's unhappiness at the arrangement was soon obvious, however. 'I don't think Tom enjoyed his time down there. I remember people talking about it years later.'

Tom went to a local school for both Maori and European (or Pakeha) children but, like all but the offspring of the wealthy, had no option but to leave at the age of twelve. Forced to find his own way in the world, he became increasingly estranged from the Maori family in which he had been raised. The death of his parents and the end of the old lifestyle at Pohatuiri, where the old community was slowly reabsorbed into the bush from which it had grown, only added to the distance between him and his siblings.

While the Te Kanawa family moved to the Moerua family's marae at Te Korapatu, Tom decided to break away from his roots and move to Gisborne on the east coast. He arrived there in the late 1920s or early 1930s. It was while renting a room at 161 Grey Street that he met the formidable figure of Nell Whitehead.

On the face of it, at least, Tom and Nell made an unlikely couple. At the age of thirty-seven, Tom was five years Nell's junior. He was as taciturn as she was ebullient. She had been married twice before, he had seemingly formed few, if any, lasting relationships. Yet against all the odds they seem to have conducted a whirlwind romance. They were married in Gisborne on 14 July 1939, only twenty-four days after Nell had been granted a decree absolute dissolving her second marriage.

In many respects Tom and Nell Te Kanawa were older, wiser and, in Gisborne terms at least, more financially secure versions of Jack Wawatai and Noeleen Rawstron. From the very beginning, they devoted their lives to giving their only daughter Kiri everything she could possibly want in life.

Perhaps Tom's most significant gift was the name he chose for his baby girl. His choice of his father's name served a dual purpose. In the short term the name short-circuited any arguments within the family over the child's adoption into the Te Kanawa line. While fostering was a common practice among Maori, full adoption was rarer. Tom's relations, notably his younger brother Mita, believed the Te Kanawa name was reserved for blood family and adoption diluted that exclusivity. 'Mita didn't like adopting kids,' said Kay Rowbottom. 'His only daughter Collen was fostered by him and his wife but they never adopted her. She was always known as Collen Keepa, her birth surname, and she's no relation of the Te Kanawa family.'

Tom, who had been unhappy during his time as a foster child, was not about to condemn his only daughter to such limbo. Deliberately or otherwise, by handing on his father's Christian name, a gift Maori tradition dictates can only be given once in a generation, he signalled to Mita and the other members of his family that baby Kiri was his own child. 'They believed she was a blood daughter because Tom had given her his father's name, Kiri,' said Kay Rowbottom. In the long term, the distinctive name, and the heritage that went with it, would prove an incalculable asset. Kiri would come to draw on her Maori ancestry, even write a book, influenced by the magical elements of her roots. On a more practical level, she would appreciate too how it lent her a name and an image that would count for much when she left her native New Zealand.

As she herself put it years later: 'It's unique to be Maori, to sing opera, have a fantastic name; it's all rather exotic and interesting. Better than being Mary Smith with mousy hair.'

Kiri arrived at Grey Street around the time that Nell became the house's new, official owner in September 1944. The colonial style, white, weather-boarded house stood in the heart of the town, on a peninsula near the town's docks and the estuary of the Turanganui River. Nell had paid £1,400* for the property, which had been repossessed from its previous owners by its mortgagees. When Nell had first arrived in Gisborne it had been a busy guest house run by a Miss Yates. By luck or judgement she took over as its new owner as Gisborne, a shipping centre for the frozen meat industry for more than

* New Zealand's currency was the pound until October 1967, when it became the dollar.

sixty years, passed through one of the busiest periods in its history.

Gisborne, or Turanga-nui-Kiwa as it was then known, had been Captain Cook's first port of call when he had landed in New Zealand in 1769. So unpromising was the greeting he received from the local Maori, he named the sweeping stretch of coastline it overlooked Poverty Bay. The modern settlement had been founded a hundred years later in 1870 and named after Sir William Gisborne, then Secretary for the British Colonies.

By the final years of World War II, Gisborne's population had swelled to some 19,000 or so people. New Zealand's links to its former colonial masters remained strong. When Great Britain declared war on Germany it had joined the effort immediately. 'Where she goes, we go; where she stands, we stand,' its Prime Minister, Michael Savage, had pledged. The nation's navy was placed under Admiralty control and New Zealand's pilots travelled to England to form the first Commonwealth squadron in the RAF.

A battalion of volunteer Maori troops was dispatched to the front line from where it would return garlanded with honours. While Mita Te Kanawa was among them, his brother Tom stayed behind to help maintain the flow of mutton, wool and food supplies that was among the loyal Kiwis' greatest contribution to the war effort.

As New Zealand played quartermaster to the warring northern hemisphere, Gisborne's harbour was filled with cargo ships bound for Britain and other parts of Europe. As it did so, its industrial base mushroomed. As well as freezing factories, the town became a centre for dairy, ham and bacon processing, tallow and woolscouring works, brewing, canning, hosiery and general engineering. Such would be its growth over the following decade that Gisborne would be officially recognised as a city in 1955.

For the young Kiri, the bustling quays were a place of endless fascination. She would make the short walk to the docks and stand for hours watching the ships sailing in and out, flocks of sea birds attached to their masts.

Her home at Grey Street was no less a source of fascination. In the grounds at the back Tom tended a few chickens, there was a disused tennis court and apricots, peaches and strawberries grew freely. At the front a huge, old pohutakawa tree, to be rigged with a swing later, stood outside the porch. The house stood opposite one of the town's

17

main 'granaries', or general stores, Williams and Kettle. The store had donated the Te Kanawas' two cats, unimaginatively christened William and Kettle.

Given its central position, and the town's hyperactivity, the Te Kanawa guest house was never short of boarders. Recounting her earliest memories later in life, Kiri realised she could barely remember a time when there were less than twenty people in the house. The one permanent fixture was an elderly boarder, known simply as 'Uncle Dan', who inhabited an upper storey bedroom he liked to call his 'office'.

'Every available space she could find Nell put someone in it,' recalled one boarder, Myra Webster, sister of Nell's son-in-law, Tom Webster. 'Every little store shed was done up as a room. Upstairs she would have about four people crowded in each room. She wouldn't turn anyone away,' she added.

Nell's head for business extended to a detailed knowledge of each tenant's financial arrangements. 'She always knew when their paydays were. She'd stand at the bottom of the stairs when they came home and she'd make sure they were paying up to date. Most of them were young Maori people who came down from the coast to work in Gisborne. She charged the going rate, about one pound ten a week, so she had a pretty good income.'

The healthy living the boarding house provided meant Nell could move away from her earlier sideline. According to one member of the family, Tom insisted that she stop performing abortions when they married. When he discovered she had defied him on one occasion, an enraged Tom grabbed his golf bag and broke each of his hickory-shafted clubs across his knee.

For Kiri as a child, the house – and its sprawling grounds – was a wonderland in which she could run free. Bedrooms climbed all the way to the third floor attic. Downstairs was dominated by a huge, farmhouse-style kitchen and dining room. At the front of the house, a lounge, complete with comfortable sofas and an upright piano, family portraits and Nell's collection of knick-knacks, offered the only real refuge from the constant comings-and-goings. While the rest of the house was left in a 'take us as you find us' fashion, the lounge was kept spick and span for entertaining guests drawn from Nell's ever widening social circle.

Nell's social aspirations were clear to see. 'Nell used to play croquet with a group of ladies at a club in Gisborne,' remembered Myra Webster. 'I think they enjoyed afternoon tea more than the croquet, but whenever these ladies came to the house, out would come the best china and all the dainty little trinkets and cakes.'

In his own way, Tom was upwardly mobile too. Unlike many of his family and the vast majority of the Maori population, he was in favour of assimilation into New Zealand's dominant, white European culture. As he removed himself further from his family he immersed himself in the middle-class enclaves of the town, becoming a popular figure at the Poverty Bay Golf Club. 'I think he wished he had a paintbrush and could paint himself white,' one relation used to say.

His success in business only opened the doors wider. On his wedding certificate, Tom listed his profession as 'winchman'. Since leaving school early he had worked on construction projects all along the east coast, specialising in driving trucks and operating cranes. With the contacts and cash he made from the most lucrative, blasting a road link to Gisborne via the previously impenetrable gorge of Whakatane, he had set up a small contracting company.

Tom, though no more than 5ft 10in, was a muscular and powerful man and prided himself on his physical strength and his capacity for hard work. 'He had fingers like sausages, and these wonderful hands, worker's hands,' Kiri recalled once. 'He never believed that he couldn't dig a tree trunk out, lift a boat, lift anything because he was so strong.'

By the end of the 1940s he was able to build his own holiday home, a comfortable cabin, or 'bach', on the shores of Lake Taupo, a favourite New Zealand holiday destination in the heart of the North Island. Tom had always been famously industrious. In Kiri he had found a reason to work even harder. Nothing was too much trouble if it was for Kiri, the unquestioned apple of her father's eye. When she was very young Tom built an elaborate dolls' house complete with fitted windows, linoleum floors and a dressing table. 'Kiri stayed in it for about a week, and then the old lady put a tenant in it,' said Myra Webster.

In time Kiri came to value the Maori qualities bequeathed by both her natural and adoptive fathers. 'I was given two marvellous gifts. One was white and one was Maori,' she said later in life. It was not an opinion she voiced often as a young girl, however.

19

Kiri admitted later that Tom had 'basically rejected the Maori side' of his life. 'My father would not speak Maori and I would not learn Maori because it was just not fashionable to do that,' she said. 'I was brought up white.'

Yet as Kiri took her first steps into a wider world, at St Joseph's Convent School in Gisborne, her unmistakable heritage drew unwanted attention. Mixed race marriages were far from unusual in Gisborne. At St Joseph's, however, Kiri found herself in more conservative company. She recalled once how her entire class had been invited to a grand birthday party at a well-to-do home in Gisborne. 'They sent me home because I was the Maori girl.' At the time, she claimed later, she was too young to notice, but Nell's anger at the humiliation ensured the incident was burned into her memory. 'My mother kept reminding me, and I thought, "Why does she keep reminding me?"'

The treatment meted out to Kiri and the two other Maori girls at St Joseph's on another occasion left even deeper psychological scars. One day, without any warning, the three children were taken from school and forced to have a typhoid vaccination. 'At that time in New Zealand, Maori children were considered to be dirty,' Kiri wrote three decades later in *Vogue* magazine, the memory still painfully vivid. 'It made me ill. I was on my back in a darkened room for two weeks afterwards. My mother was furious that she hadn't been consulted and I never forgave the powers that be for doing that to me without bothering to find out that I came from a good clean home.'

At school, Kiri's sense that she was somehow apart from other children was confirmed on an almost daily basis. Nell never appeared at the school gates to collect her, she recalled. 'When it rained there would always be a little crowd of mothers outside the school with raincoats and umbrellas,' she said once. 'I always half expected her to be there but she never was. I don't know why. She just didn't bother, so I walked home in the wet.'

Her sense of her own uniqueness only deepened as she began to learn more about her origins. According to Kiri, Tom and Nell told her the truth about her background when she was a little over three years old. They drew short of revealing the identity of her real mother and father but made no secret of the fact that she was adopted. As a young girl, Kiri's emotions would have been no different from any other adopted child's, a tearful confusion of anger, shame, insecurity and isolation. It was only years later that she began to understand the deep and divergent impact it had on her personality. Asked once about the legacy of her adoption, Kiri admitted it had added to her sense of isolation from the world. Kiri could be a naturally solitary child. 'You grow up with this capacity to cut off,' she said. 'It's a protective device. I become alone, totally alone when something goes wrong.' At the same time the knowledge that she had been abandoned by her real parents instilled in her a tenacity and a determination she would never have known otherwise. 'It turned me into a survivor. I felt I was special and had special responsibilities. I'm quite sure if I hadn't known I was adopted I'd have stayed a nobody and would be in New Zealand breeding children now. But that turned me into a fighter.'

As her childhood progressed, she found a natural opponent in her mother. Kiri was, by her own admission, a classic example of a spoilt only child. It is easy to see how the distrust, antipathy towards competition and often naked jealousy Kiri has displayed throughout her life was born in her early years alone at Grey Street. 'I was an only child. I didn't make friends easily. I always wanted everything my way and I wasn't very happy in a great bunch of children,' she said once. While Tom doted on Kiri it was left to Nell to administer the discipline she undoubtedly required. If the young Kiri misbehaved she would be forced to sit silently in a chair. If she looked too unhappy she would be sent into the bathroom and told not to come back until she was smiling. Kiri described once how she learned to offer a sickly fixed smile even when her young heart seemed as if it was breaking. The ability to mask her mood would prove useful in later life.

If the crime was considered severe enough, her mother was not beyond dealing out physical punishment. Nell would take a large wooden spoon or a belt to the errant Kiri. Years later Kiri would recall how she had run mischievously through a patch of poppies Nell had planted in the Grey Street garden. 'As I skipped through I hit the head off each flower.' Nell's reaction was instantaneous. The blow she dealt Kiri was 'so hard it was unbelievable'.

At least once she threatened to run away. Packing a bag in a temper one afternoon she announced her departure to a disinterested Nell, who was entertaining visitors. Like so many other reluctant runaways, she made it no further than the garden gate where she sat sobbing quietly until the evening.

'Thought you were going to run away?' her mother asked as she limped back into the house.

'I was going to but it got too dark,' Kiri replied, still sulking.

It was Kiri's greatest good fortune that she grew up in a house dominated by music. Nell liked to claim that her mother Emily was a niece of the great English composer Sir Arthur Sullivan. The story, repeated by Kiri throughout her life, was a blatant piece of fiction. In fact the roots of Nell's mother Emily Sullivan's family tree extended back to Lancashire and the town of Radcliffe. It had been there that Emily's father, Jeremiah, had grown up with his father, a local school-teacher also called Jeremiah Sullivan. Sir Arthur Sullivan's only sibling, a brother, Frederic, lived in Fulham, London.

Nell's talents as a musician seem to have been genuine, nevertheless. Visitors to Grey Street invariably found its halls and corridors echoing to her fluent piano playing.

As the 1950s dawned, the television age was being born in America and, to a lesser extent, Europe. On the other side of the world, however, New Zealand would have to wait another decade before its first broadcasts, even then only one channel broadcasting three hours a day. In the meantime radio remained king, with racing and rugby forming the three Rs that were the bedrock of New Zealand life. At Grey Street the family would often sit around and listen to concerts and entertainment shows on the local Gisborne station. In the absence of decent music on the airwaves, Nell would provide the entertainment herself, conducting evening singalongs from the stool of her upright piano. 'She was a very big personality, and a lot of people loved her,' Kiri said later.

In this environment, Kiri's raw musical gifts were soon apparent. At the age of two, according to her mother, she had danced to the sound of Uncle Dan's harmonica. Nell would also sit her on her lap to show her the rudiments of the keyboard. To her mother's delight, Kiri was soon accompanying her as well as playing solo. It was her tuneful singing voice that impressed Nell most, however. As a five-year-old, Kiri regaled Nell and Tom with her versions of songs like 'Daisy, Daisy' and 'Cara Mia'. 'By the time she was eight she had a nice little voice,' her mother said.

At St Joseph's, Nell encouraged Kiri to study the piano. To her mother's frustration, however, Kiri was more interested in sport, in particular fishing and swimming, which she had learned at an early age with her father at Hatepe. 'She used to be a real tomboy,' Tom proudly proclaimed. She would not be deterred, however. Soon Nell was engineering Kiri a reputation as a new star in Gisborne's musical firmament. Nell had begun to encourage Kiri to sing solo at Grey Street gatherings. Drawing on connections in town, she had won her a place on a popular local radio show. Kiri was seven when she made her public performing debut on Radio 2XG singing 'Daisy, Daisy'. She proved such a success she was invited back at regular intervals. Victorian ballads and songs for more mature voices, like 'When I Grow Too Old To Dream', seemed to offer no difficulties. To Nell each of her daughter's successes only served to fuel her belief that she had real talent. Her mother would reward Kiri with clothes and presents she would pick up on shopping expeditions to Auckland. To the young Kiri, however, the increasing attention became a source of resentment and confrontation.

Kiri got her first indication of the future being planned for her in her bedroom one morning as Nell came in and sat on the edge of the bed. 'My mother had had a dream where she had seen me on the stage at Covent Garden,' she recalled once. To Kiri it seemed meaningless. 'I thought, "Oh, that sounds nice", and thought no more about it.' In time Kiri would come to share the same dream. 'You have to believe in dreams. I don't think I would have gone on if I hadn't believed.' In the meantime, however, she found herself becoming an often unwilling vehicle for her mother's fantasies.

Kiri's love of music was real enough. She had been fascinated by the new radiogram that had arrived in the house and had played the family's first discs, 'If I Knew You Were Coming I'd Have Baked a Cake' and 'Sweet Violets' endlessly. When she broke one of them she had run out of the room screaming in fear of what Nell might do to her. Yet she had no real interest in devoting her young life to music. Her defiance was, in part, down to a laziness she confessed stayed with her for years. 'I can see Mummy constantly kept the music going. I'd tend not to feel like it because I was a lazy child, but she'd insist that I sang,' she recalled later.

Its roots lay also in her natural need to test the parameters of her

23

relationship with her parents. Kiri knew that whatever her wishes she would find a supporter in Tom, in whose eyes she could do little wrong. In truth, Nell loved her just as much. She was a far less pliable personality, however. Kiri had yet to discover how far she could push her.

Ultimately, Kiri's dislike of the ever-strengthening spotlight now being turned on her owed most to a simpler truth. For all her high spirits around those she knew and loved, she was painfully reserved among strangers. In the house on Grey Street there were times when she was literally 'sick with shyness', she confessed once. She was intensely sensitive, too. Kiri often cried when she was taken to the cinema, the sight of violence or sometimes even a phrase threatening it could reduce her to floods of tears.

When she came to take stock of her early years later in life, a prisoner of an operatic diary planned years in advance and a fame by then extended from Gisborne to Glyndebourne, Kiri's memories of her childhood were not dominated by memories of dresses or dolls' houses, living room recitals or early radio stardom. 'If I had to name one aspect of my early life in New Zealand it would be the aloneness of life there,' she explained. 'I was able to be alone and I still seek that, I suppose.'

Nell seemed determined to knock her reticence out of her. Kiri's earliest motivation for singing in public was the sheer terror with which she viewed her mother. 'She frightened me into singing,' she said once. When she threatened rebellion Nell's words were as predictable as they were menacing. 'I'll speak to you when everyone goes,' she would promise.

Few who watched the effervescent young prodigy singing would have believed it. 'I was not an extroverted child. You have to learn to be extroverted,' she lamented later.

Gradually, however, Nell's bullying began to transform her. Soon Kiri was demonstrating the first, formative hints of self-confidence. She went on to one of her regular radio shows nursing a bad cold. When she hit a false note she heard a voice laughing. It might have been a moment of crushing importance, yet Kiri took it in her stride. 'It was my first sobering experience of somebody being jealous,' she said later.

The cold was a far from rare event. The harsh New Zealand winters brought a succession of colds and flus with them. For all the robustness of life at Gisborne and Hatepe, Kiri's health was a constant worry to Nell. 'I was very sickly,' she once confessed. Her sports-loving father had encouraged her to take up some of his favourite pastimes to improve her health. Archery had been suggested as a good exercise to strengthen her lungs. Under Tom's watchful eye, she would later learn to play golf, too.

It was around the time of her radio debut that Kiri was diagnosed as having 'a touch of TB'. With the medical establishment conducting a love affair with the relatively new science of X-rays, Kiri's young body was repeatedly 'zapped', without any real consideration of the long-term consequences.

Asked years later about her mother's past, Kiri replied that Nell had been deserted by her first husband. 'Or maybe she left him, I'm not too sure,' she added hastily. In truth Kiri knew precious little about her mother's turbulent background. As a seemingly strict Catholic there can be little doubt first that Nell's shame would have been intense and lasting and secondly that her pain remained confined to the confession box. She certainly never shared its details with her adopted daughter. 'My mother was rather secretive about that part of her life. It's something I didn't delve into,' is all Kiri has confided in the years since.

Nell's children from her first marriage provided the most positive link with the past. Stan, on whom Nell doted, had served in the army during World War II but had returned to run a poultry farm with his wife Pat in Gisborne. Nola had married Tom Webster, a local farmer, and lived at Patutahi on the outskirts of town. A one-year-old Kiri had been a flower girl at the Websters' wedding in Gisborne in 1945. Nola had been unable to have children and had adopted a daughter, Judy. By 1954, however, Nola's marital fortunes were mirroring those of her mother. Her marriage to Tom in ruins, she and Judy arrived on the guesthouse doorstep. Mother and daughter would become a permanent fixture at Grey Street.

Kiri quickly discovered she had much more in common with her five-year-old niece than she did with her grown-up half-sister. In the years that followed, Judy became the closest thing to a sister Kiri would know. Like Kiri, Judy knew she was adopted. Nola had told her she had found her in a shop window in Gisborne.

'Every time we went into Gisborne to the shops I would have her going all round the streets looking for this bloody shop so that she could get all my brothers and sisters that she left behind in the window. I wanted them all with me. And of course she had to play along with it,' recalled Judy. Inevitably the knowledge bound the two closer.

Judy recalls how at a 'do' once, Kiri had joked about the fact that they were sisters. 'No we're not,' Judy had told her.

'Yes we are, we are all adopted.'

Kiri's loneliness as an only child seems to have been a source of concern to Tom and Nell. There was frequent talk of Kiri's 'brother' joining the family, according to Judy.

'Apparently there was meant to be a brother. I always remember it being talked about that Nana wanted to adopt him as well,' she remembered. All Judy – and her 'sister' – knew of Kiri's real mother was that she was 'a blonde lady' who lived somewhere on the coast of the East Cape.

To Judy, Grey Street seemed more like a hotel than a home. Uncle Dan still lived upstairs and appeared to act as an unpaid nanny for Kiri when Nell and Tom were not around. 'Come up to my office,' he used to joke with Kiri when she was alone in the house. Kiri recalled once how 'Danny' would fill his pockets with stolen bread rolls from a bakery across the road. 'I used to have one for breakfast every morning. He used to pull out the middle and I'd eat the middle and he'd eat the outside,' she said.

'He used to give Kiri and I handfuls of peppermints,' Judy recalled. 'As long as we didn't tell Nell.'

Judy quickly discovered that her 'Nana's' authority was absolute and her temper truly volcanic. 'When she lost it, we didn't ask "How high?", we asked "Excuse me, when can we come down?",' she smiled. Yet, as far as Judy was concerned, beneath her teak-hard exterior beat a generous and genuinely loving heart. 'She was tough, but she had a soft side,' she said.

Judy loved nothing more than to hear Nell play the piano. 'Kiri and I would always be on at her after school to play. She would ask: "Have you finished what you were meant to do for school?" If we said yes, she would play.' 'Greensleeves' was a favourite which Kiri too could play well.

A less musical child, Judy had shown a talent for poetry reading

26

instead. A year or so after Judy's arrival in Grey Street, Nell persuaded the radio station to showcase the two girls as a double act. Judy's radio career was short-lived, however. 'Kiri had to sing and I had to read a poem,' recalled Judy. 'Kiri did her piece fine, no problem, but I forgot the words and said "Oh shit",' she smiled. 'Well, of course, it was a live show and it went out clear as a bell to all of Gisborne. I think Kiri started to laugh which didn't help. That was the start and finish of my broadcasting career all in one night.'

Nell waited until Judy was back at Grey Street before unleashing her anger. 'I remember getting a scolding for that,' she said.

For all her ferocity, Nell was vulnerable to bouts of ill health. She had been overweight for years and suffered from related illnesses and general tiredness. She spent much of her time confined to her bedroom where she would listen to the radio, read music magazines and summon Tom and the children to talk to her. 'She didn't move around that much,' Kiri explained once. 'She liked to lie in bed and hold court.' Kiri and Judy would lie on her bed with her listening to her read stories from the imported *American Post* magazine. 'She was a big lady. She had these big arms we used to push up and use as pillows. I can remember her lying on the bed with me and Kiri either side, tucked up on her arms while she lay there reading the story of the Incredible Journey out of this magazine,' Judy said. 'She read the whole thing, from start to finish. We weren't leaving until we found out what happened to these dogs and the cat.'

In the miniature fiefdom that was Nell's home, the kitchen was the place where she wielded her ultimate power. 'She was an absolutely brilliant cook, always cooking scones or something,' recalled Judy. 'She filled up jars and tins with all sorts of things, making her own jams and pickles.' The sublime smells that wafted out on to Grey Street seem to have made it a magnet for friends, neighbours and passers-by. 'When people bowled in, it was "Have a cup of tea." If somebody wandered in off the street she would cook for them as well.'

In the kitchen, Kiri and Judy were Nell's chief underlings. 'She was like a chef. She made the mess and Kiri and me cleared up,' recalled Judy. The two girls spent much of their time bickering over who would wash and who would dry. 'Kiri and me fought constantly over that because if you washed you had to do the benches and the stove as well.'

The most intense arguments were reserved for the nights when Nell served mashed potato. 'She used to make it in big old aluminium pots. They weren't soaked of course, so the potato stuck to the sides like concrete.' As far as the girls were concerned, the highlight of the year would be the family's annual Christmas trip to the cabin at Hatepe on the shores of Lake Taupo. The cabin allowed Tom to indulge his twin passions – tranquillity and trout fishing. For Kiri, too, Hatepe provided some of the earliest and most magical moments of her early life. She recalled once the excitement of catching her first fish with Tom.

The fact that the house had no electricity only added to its enchantment somehow. 'There was no power. We would drive up from Gisborne and my grandfather would get out the paraffin lamps from the shed,' recalls Judy. 'It was a huge big event down there. Stan and Pat stayed on the poultry farm because they had to work but there was my grandparents, mum, Kiri and all the locals would pile in too.

'Christmas in those days was like a fairy tale for us and I always remember it as a happy time. Kiri and me used to go into the woods looking for big red toadstools. Sometimes we would sit in the trees very quietly, keeping very still, and wait for the fairies to come,' she says. Kiri's love of the open spaces of Lake Taupo had been inherited from her shy, self-contained father.

'Daddy' could not have presented a quieter, kinder contrast to the gregarious Nell. When she had the house filled with guests, Tom would blend into the background, a benign, watchful influence. 'Tom was always there but he was always very quiet,' recalled Judy. 'If there was a big pile of people he would be stuck in the corner with his glass of ginger ale.'

Tom's even temper was the stuff of legend within the family. Judy recalls only seeing him lose his composure once. 'He was working on a car motor and said "bugger" when he hit his thumb with a spanner,' she laughed. His love of speed seems to have been his only rebellious outlet. While Nell slept on the drive to Taupo the girls would encourage him to put his foot down on the treacherous, twisting inland roads west of Gisborne. 'He used to drive like Stirling Moss. He was a brilliant driver, fast but not dangerous,' recalled Judy. 'My grandmother would doze off and his foot would go down and away we'd go. When she woke she'd bark: "Slow down, Tom, slow down!" It was hysterical. He'd slow right down and keep looking over at her until she nodded off again and then he'd roar off again. She'd wake up, shout at him, and on it went. Every trip was like that.'

The young Kiri lived for the mornings when Tom would wake her with a gentle kiss at 5 a.m. as he left for work. She would slip out into the dawn and spend the day sitting in the cab of his truck. At Taupo she would sit on the edge of the lake in silence as he fished for trout or simply took in the scene. Sometimes father and daughter would sleep out under the stars, 'to be there when the fish rose in the morning'.

'What was wonderful about him was you didn't have to talk,' she said later. 'We used to look at the lake and we'd say nothing. For hours. That was the best part.'

For Kiri, such serenity was in increasingly short supply back at Grey Street. By the time Judy and Nola moved in, the evening get-togethers had taken on the air of a showcase for Nell's prodigious discovery. If the gathering was confined to the immediate family, Nell would command the stage as usual. If there were visitors present, however, there was only one star. 'Kiri was the big thing,' said Judy. 'Always, whenever anybody came around, I would have to sing,' Kiri confessed later. 'I felt at the time like a performing monkey.'

For large parts of her life, Nell had known little more than disappointment and disillusionment. With Tom she had, at last, found security. In Kiri, however, she glimpsed an opportunity for something more. She would not be the first mother to find her life revitalised and ultimately taken over by the vicarious thrill of her child's success. Few stage mothers would drive their daughters from such unpromising beginnings to such unthinkable heights, however. By Kiri's twelfth birthday, Nell's ambition for her daughter had already far outgrown Grey Street and Gisborne.

Lying on her bed upstairs, Nell would listen avidly to the many musical competitions broadcast on the radio at the time. The contests had proliferated all over New Zealand and Australia. In 1956 the Mobil Petroleum Company had added to their credibility and popularity by sponsoring the most prestigious of New Zealand's domestic contests, the biennial competition from then on known as the Mobil Song Quest.

The competition had produced its share of stars within New Zealand, none greater than the Auckland nun widely regarded as the finest teacher in the country. Sister Mary Leo had been born Kathleen Agnes Niccol, the eldest child of a respectable Auckland shipping clerk and his wife Agnes. In later life, she was mysterious about her exact birthdate in April 1895, as it fell only five months after her devoutly Catholic parents' wedding. Kathleen Niccol became a schoolteacher and budding singer before, at the age of twenty-eight, she walked into the sanctuary of St Mary's Convent in Auckland and the Order of the Sisters of Mercy. She never left.

A college had first been established at the convent in 1929. Two decades later, in 1949, Sister Mary Leo persuaded the Order to allow her to establish her own independent, non-denominational music school within the St Mary's grounds. While she concentrated on voice coaching, four other nuns were enlisted to teach piano, violin, cello and organ. Each year as many as 200 aspiring musicians from all faiths and all corners of New Zealand received their education there. In the aftermath of the war, Sister Mary Leo's pupils had begun to dominate the lucrative singing competitions. It had been her success with an emotionally frail but extraordinarily gifted singer, Mina Foley, that had transformed her into a national celebrity.

An orphan, Foley had begun singing as an alto in the St Mary's Choir at the age of thirteen. At sixteen, encouraged by Sister Mary Leo, she had won the prestigious John Court Memorial Aria in Auckland. From there she went on to win almost every domestic singing competition. Her successes turned Foley and her teacher into stars. Crowds of well-wishers and pressmen followed them to their triumphs. When, in 1950, they travelled to Australia for the most lucrative of all the Antipodean prizes, the Melbourne Sun Aria competition, most of New Zealand tuned in on the radio.

Foley's freakish range allowed her voice to reach across three and a half octaves. She had already been dubbed the 'Voice of the Century' by the New Zealand media. By 1951, thanks largely to a scholarship from the British Council, the singer had been accepted as a pupil of Toti Del Monte in Italy.

When Nell discovered that Foley was due to visit Gisborne before leaving for Europe, she wasted no time in booking two tickets for the concert at the Regent Theatre. If she had hoped the trip would inspire Kiri she was soon rewarded. Kiri still recalled the impact of the moment thirty years later. She remembered how Foley had taken to the stage in a wonderful gown, 'all in green net, with off-the-shoulder puffed sleeves and sparkling jewellery everywhere. I remember it so vividly. She used to wear her hair pulled back with one ringlet trailing forward over her shoulder. It was the most awful style but at the time I thought it was marvellous.'

Kiri was transfixed by Foley's voice. 'She sang and sang and I never for one moment stopped gazing at her. I think it was then that my mother realised I was going to concentrate on music and nothing else.' In the wake of the Foley concert, Nell's dreams began to solidify. By the beginning of 1956 she was ready to swing into action.

For all its historic importance, the East Cape was far from the hub of New Zealand life. In the 1950s and sixties it was regarded as one of the least dynamic and most isolated regions of New Zealand. Nell knew that a move north to Auckland was vital if Kiri was to make any progress. Nell began by telephoning St Mary's in Auckland and asking to be put directly through to its most celebrated teacher. It was to be the first of many memorable confrontations between the irresistible force that was Nell Te Kanawa and the immovable object that was Sister Mary Leo.

'I have a daughter who sings very well,' Nell announced, matter of factly. 'Will you take her on?'

Sotto voce, Sister Mary Leo explained that, as a pupil of a school other than St Mary's, Kiri was ineligible for her classes until she was eighteen. In other words, no, she could not.

Nell was in no mind to be deterred by such a rejection, however. She began her efforts to persuade Tom that the family, including Kiri, Nola and Judy, should move to Auckland and that Kiri should be installed at St Mary's. She had clearly missed her true vocation as a saleswoman. Soon Tom had not only agreed to put the Grey Street house up for auction, but to sell his business as well.

Kiri, however, could not share her mother's enthusiasm for the move. Grey Street had provided a happy home. From Uncle Dan to the students with whom she had forged lasting friendships in the town, its cast of characters represented a loving and rather extraordinary extended family. Now she was being forced to leave them. Her protests were pointless, however. The move to Auckland was made shortly after Kiri celebrated what she later remembered as a sad and solemn twelfth birthday in March, 1956. 'It was pretty horrendous,' she came to say. 'All the books tell you that you should never change a child at that age. I had left my beautiful home, a dear old man who was my nanny, and missed my "family".'

Given the events that had led her to Grey Street a dozen years earlier, there was an added cruelty to the enforced farewells. It would only be later in life that she came to understand the significance of what had happened to her. 'I basically lost my family when I lost that house,' she would say.

'The Nun's Chorus'

With the proceeds from the sales of Grey Street and Tom's truck company, Nell was able to put a sizeable deposit down on a new home in the Auckland suburb of Blockhouse Bay, about nine miles south of the city centre. The nine-year-old house at 22 Mitchell Street stood at the bottom of a steep drive overlooking the picturesque Manukau Harbour. Only a set of nearby electricity pylons marred the splendour of the view.

At £5,500 the house was double the average house price in the area. Fortunately Nell had made a healthy profit on the Grey Street house which she had sold to a Wellington hotelier for £6,000, at a profit of £4,600 in twelve years. Tom soon averted any future financial crises when he landed a contract installing underground petrol tanks for the giant Caltex company. Judy was at first put into a boarding school by Nola. It was only after smuggling out a letter expressing her unhappiness to her father in Gisborne that she was able to join Kiri at Avondale Convent Primary school, a short bus ride away from Blockhouse Bay.

To ease her admission there, and at St Mary's where Nell intended enrolling her at the age of fourteen, Kiri had by now been confirmed. Immaculate and angelic in her white lace gown and veil, Kiri smiled sweetly for the family photographs in the spring of 1956. Yet, inside, she remained deeply unhappy at the upheaval she had been forced to undergo.

Kiri had been a poor student at St Joseph's in Gisborne and showed even less interest in her studies at Avondale, where she steadfastly refused to fit in. 'It was a child's reaction to something new,' she admitted later. 'I hated every minute of it – and they hated me.'

Kiri's unhappiness was understandable given the physical abuse she received at the hands of her new teachers. She recounted, years later, how her music teacher at Avondale repeatedly pulled at the flowing tresses she had been so proud of as a young girl in Gisborne. 'I had lovely long black hair and she used to grab it by the roots and rock me from side to side,' she said. 'I used to work really hard for her because I was so frightened, but it didn't change her behaviour.'

Eventually Kiri was driven to drastic measures. 'I got so desperate that I persuaded my mother to let me have all my hair cut off, and I mean right off, real punk rock style,' she said. 'It looked awful, but even then the teacher managed to get hold of it.'

Kiri would constantly ask her mother to 'lop off' her hair in her time at Avondale. Her peculiar look only deepened the self-consciousness that was already taking root. Even before her decision to crop her hair short, Kiri's sturdy, strong-boned features had always made her look gawky and boyish. She would never rid herself of the pubescent unhappiness she began to feel over her shape and size. 'There is nothing that I like about myself. When I look at myself I see thousands of flaws from top to bottom,' she said later in life. She particularly hated the heavy frame and legs bequeathed to her by her Maori father. 'I have a very solid body – when you look at me you'd hardly get the impression that I couldn't handle life,' she complained once. 'I hardly look delicate, do I?' As she entered her adolescence, she seemed content living up to her tomboy reputation.

Away from the tortures of Avondale, Kiri remained happiest water-skiing, swimming or sailing on the waters of Blockhouse Bay, playing golf at the nearby Titirangi Club or practising archery up on One Tree Hill with her father.

In the company of the equally boisterous Judy, she frequently ran riot. Kiri and Judy's earliest neighbourhood friends were the five Hanson boys, brothers who also lived on Mitchell Street. Their friendship blossomed from the most unpromising of beginnings.

According to Judy, she and Kiri would sometimes get involved in fights on their way home from Avondale. 'We used to scrap on the bus,' Judy recalled. As a convoy of buses dropped off their passengers on Mitchell Street one day, Judy had begun fighting with one of the younger Hansons, Mark. As the fight had spilled out on to the street, Kiri and Mark's brother Andrew had jumped off their respective buses to join in. 'It was all on. The four of us were having a full-on blue [fight],' recalled Judy. By the time the four-way contest had progressed to its climax, onlookers were left in little doubt who had emerged victorious. One of the Hansons had been carrying an umbrella. 'He ended up with the thing wrapped around his neck,' smiled Judy.

Kiri and Judy inflicted sufficient damage for the boys' mother Betty to berate Nell over the telephone. 'It was then we found out there were another three of them. From then they became life long friends,' recalled Judy.

Publicly Nell defended her headstrong daughter to the hilt. In private, however, such disappointments were only widening the distance between mother and daughter. Years later, a student of the greater psychological insight of another age, Kiri sympathised with the problems Nell must have had to contend with. 'It was tough for my mother, because at that time people were never told that kids become terrorists at twelve and stay that way until they're eighteen,' she said. 'And if you try to cover up and pretend everything's OK, the trouble you've swept away under the carpet will come back at you – twice as hard.'

On another occasion she put it even more simply. 'She didn't understand me and I didn't understand her.'

There were times when Nell's frustration at Kiri boiled over into rage. On one occasion it fell to Judy to save her from being flailed by Nell with Tom's leather belt. 'Nana didn't hit her much, and only for specific things,' she recollected. 'It wasn't unfair, but I remember defending her when she was accused of doing something wrong and she was going to get a belt on the backside.

'I grabbed uncle Tom's belt and ran off with it. Then I got his other belts from the bedroom and hid them behind the wardrobe – where they stayed for years. In fact Tom ended up with a piece of garden twine holding up his trousers.'

Such moments only served to tighten the conspiratorial bond between the two 'sisters'. Judy and Kiri spent much of their adolescent lives in defiance of Nell's tyranny. They would spend evenings running up their own rough and ready clothes on Nell's sewing machine. It was hardly *haute couture*. The cut and colour co-ordination left much to be desired. 'If you had yellow material and green cotton then too bad,' said Judy. Nell loathed seeing her girls, Kiri in particular, looking scruffy and frequently flew off the handle at the sight of their latest piece of crude needlecraft. 'She would go crazy, screaming, "What are you doing? You do that properly or not at all!" She used to pull the things apart so the job could be done properly.'

Nell's musical ambitions for her daughter provided the most frequent source of friction. Like Grey Street before it, the house at Mitchell Street quickly become a magnet for all manner of visitors. Nell had continued to coach Kiri at home and wheeled her out at every opportunity when entertaining guests. Whether or not Kiri complied or complained depended on her mood. 'There were times when she would resent it, when she would feel like a prize pig,' recalled Judy. 'But there were others when she was happy as a sandboy. Kiri herself liked to sing.'

At times Kiri and Judy seemed to be fighting a constant war on Nell's nerves. The menagerie of pets that had begun to accumulate at Mitchell Street provided another battleground. The by now aged black cat William had made the journey from Gisborne. Kettle had been replaced by another black cat called Two-Ten. 'From the cost of having it neutered by the vet,' said Judy. Tom had also bought a cocker spaniel called Whisky. Soon they were joined by a rabbit that Tom had found at work, and which Judy and Kiri named Peter.

'My grandfather absolutely adored Peter,' recalled Judy. 'Peter followed Tom everywhere.' Tom, Kiri and Judy spent much of their time protecting Peter from the predatory instincts of Two-Ten. 'Two-Ten used to want to kill this rabbit and the rabbit used to fly up and sit by my grandfather's leg.'

Nell posed almost as great a danger. 'We had this green carpet in the lounge and Peter started to eat holes in it,' said Judy. 'Kiri and I kept moving the furniture over the holes but eventually Nana found out and the rabbit was in big trouble.'

Almost half a century later, a mother of five herself, Judy cannot condemn Nell's overbearing behaviour towards Kiri. 'My grandmother was just very proud of her,' she said. The more she heard of Kiri's confident, commanding voice, the more Nell was convinced her decision to move the family to Auckland had been justified. Her conviction only deepened in the summer of 1958 as Kiri finally began making the daily bus trip across Auckland to the most celebrated music school, and the most feted singing teacher, in New Zealand.

Shortly after her fourteenth birthday, dressed in her new, navy-blue uniform, Kiri became one of the 500 or so girls entrusted to the care of the Order of the Sisters of Mercy at the Convent of St Mary. The Order's nuns liked to claim that one in every four of their pupils remained with them for life. Kiri would never be a candidate for holy orders. Yet in her own way she would keep faith with St Mary's and its principles as devotedly as any nun. 'The poetry of earth is never dead. And the music of St Mary's never really sleeps,' read a two-line verse in the 1958 St Mary's Annual, summing up the alternative gospel for which the Order were rightfully famous. Kiri would embrace it like no other pupil in the hundred-year history of the college.

The Order of the Sisters of Mercy had arrived in Auckland from Ireland around 1850. They had erected an elegant, wooden church on a hilltop overlooking the middle-class suburb of Ponsonby soon afterwards. By now the striking, Spanish-style buildings erected on the site dominated the skyline. However, it had been the achievements of Sister Mary Leo that had lifted its profile not just in Auckland but all over New Zealand.

As Kiri arrived at St Mary's the achievements of the teacher's latest crop of prodigies filled the pages of St Mary's Annual. Lengthy reports described the successes of Mary O'Brien, the soprano who had won that year's John Court Memorial Aria in Auckland, and the former pupil Betty Hellawell who had sung that year in *Boris Godunov* opposite Boris Christoff at Covent Garden. Artistic portraits of St Mary's prize-winning choirs and orchestras, star instrumentalists and singers seemed to feature on every page.

The main musical event of March 1958 had been a gala concert held inside the college chapel in aid of the Hard of Hearing League. The event would have offered the young Kiri her first glimpse of the legendary Sister Mary Leo and her stable of stars. Afterwards the Archbishop of Auckland, James Liston, addressed the audience. His words were directed particularly at St Mary's prized performers. 'Music is a wonderful gift which God has bestowed on you to give pleasure to others,' he said. As she settled into college life, however, Kiri found her own gifts overlooked.

The Sisters of Mercy lived a less rigid existence than other orders within the Catholic Church. Its nuns were among the first in New Zealand permitted to wear the looser, less stifling 'modern' habit. Yet, as she settled into the rhythms and rituals of college life, her days dictated by the muffled toll of the church's bells and their seemingly endless calls to prayer, Kiri could not help but absorb the powerful influence of her surroundings. The faith she discovered there would never desert her. Somehow her belief in God filled the void she still felt when she thought about her uncertain past. 'I was brought up a Catholic and I know there is a God,' she said once. 'You need to believe it when you've been given a pretty sticky start, being adopted – as I was – by a couple who didn't have very much. Sometimes I feel strongly that there is somebody looking after me personally. It gives me an extra strength.'

Kiri joined a third-form class led by an Irish nun, Sister Mary Leila. For the first year her timetable was dominated by English, Arithmetic, Social Studies, Art, Sport, School Singing and, naturally, Christian Doctrine.

Under St Mary's 'parental preference' system, however, Nell and Tom were soon required to chose the direction Kiri would take for the remainder of her two years there. The choice was a simple one – Kiri could take the academic path, learning languages and preparing for New Zealand's equivalent to the British O level, 'school certificate', or else opt for the 'commercial' curriculum in which girls were prepared for business college or secretarial jobs with classes in typing, shorthand and book-keeping.

Kiri, a self-confessed non-academic, remained an underwhelming performer in the classroom. If Kiri shone anywhere during her early months at St Mary's it was as a sportswoman. In 1958 Kiri made her first noteworthy appearance in the school annual not as a singer but dressed in a gymslip and plimsolls as a member of the 'Post Primary C' basketball team. The accompanying report described her as 'the mainstay of the team'.

In later life she blamed her lack of academic progress on the demands of her musical education. In a 1990 television profile, for instance, she told interviewer Melvyn Bragg, 'I think my formal education suffered because I would be trying to sort of study . . . and more often than not I was pulled out in the middle of the class to have another singing lesson or rehearse with the choir and while I was doing half these subjects I never ever got a full lesson done.'

Later she added, 'Sister Mary Leo enabled me to miss classes so that I could study music. I can now see that I might have been good at many subjects – languages, arts and crafts – which I never got the chance to study. I never received the formal education my parents sent me to school for.'

Nuns who remember Kiri are confused by these accounts, however. 'There's some misunderstanding there, maybe,' said Sister Mercienne, the college archivist. She explained that throughout Kiri's time at the school, she was not seen as exceptional and was not treated any differently from any other pupil. That meant that her English and arithmetic lessons, and of course Christian Doctrine, were sacrosanct, and that if Sister Leo had chosen to give Kiri any extra tuition it would only have been with the agreement of her class teacher. The truth seems to be that Kiri's academic ambitions were ultimately frustrated not by Sister Mary Leo's demands but by her own mother's grasp of the situation.

As decision time arrived, without much deliberation Nell told the school principal to stream her daughter in the commercial class. To Nell's frustration, Kiri had arrived at St Mary's to be told that Sister Mary Leo still refused to teach her personally. With 200 mature pupils attached to her music college and only a limited number of places available to girls from the school itself, Sister Mary Leo insisted that all fourteen- to sixteen-year-old singing pupils were also proficient at the piano. Despite Nell's early efforts to teach her, Kiri had failed to make the grade required. It took Sister Mary Leo's accompanist to spot the latent talent in the Order's midsts.

'Kiri was pestering Mary Leo for singing lessons but Sister wouldn't teach anyone who couldn't play the piano so she kept fobbing her off,' recalled one of the members of the present day Order, Sister Dora, at the time one of the youngest teachers within the music school. Kiri was forced to take lessons with the college's keyboard specialist, Sister Francis Xavier. While Sister Mary Leo revelled in the spotlight, her colleague Sister Xavier was so painfully shy she rarely revealed more than the tip of her nose from behind her wimple in photographs. She was every bit as canny a judge of musical talent as her colleague, however. 'Kiri went to Sister Francis Xavier for piano lessons but still kept on and on about singing, so she gave her some singing exercises just to keep her quiet,' recalled Sister Dora.

The college pianist was immediately struck by the beautiful clarity of

Kiri's voice and raised the subject of her joining the stable of singers with Sister Mary Leo. Sister Francis's influence was considerable. Away from the music room she and Sister Mary Leo would share feasts of sweets and ice cream and it was perhaps during one of these that the college pianist pleaded Kiri's cause. 'She noticed there was something terrific in the voice and talked to Mary Leo about her,' recalled Sister Dora.

At first Sister Mary Leo remained stubbornly disinterested. 'She kept urging her to have a listen and eventually she did. From then on Kiri never looked back.'

In the years that followed, even the most reserved member of the Order could not resist the odd gentle boast. 'Sister Francis Xavier always used to joke with us saying, "I was the one who discovered Kiri",' said Sister Dora.

To her contemporaries, Kiri seemed one of the more carefree spirits at St Mary's. 'I have fond memories of Kiri sliding down the banisters,' recalled one classmate from Commercial IV, Elsa Grubisa, now Vujnovich. Yet, for all her outward exuberance, Kiri was, with good cause, intimidated and a little awestruck as she finally underwent her first encounters with her formidable new teacher.

Sister Mary Leo taught in a light, airy, L-shaped room on the first floor of her music school, a two-storey building in the St Mary's grounds a short walk from the Convent and the main college. With its miniature brass busts of Schubert and Wagner and framed photographs of former pupils, the room was a shrine to her second religion. Sheet music was piled neatly in almost every alcove. The room was equipped with a modern, reel-to-reel tape recorder and a radiogram. The floor was dominated by a highly polished grand piano. To a fourteen-year-old, it seemed an utterly intimidating place. Sister Mary Leo's reputation for toughness only added to it. She often began work after early morning prayers at 8 a.m., hardly pausing for breakfast, and continued teaching long into the evenings. She expected the same dedication from her pupils and was intolerant of any signs of immaturity. Nervousness, for instance, had no place in her music room. 'She hadn't much time for nerves. She'd just tell us to pull ourselves together and stop that nonsense,' recalled Sister Patricia, another of Sister Mary Leo's former pupils. The greatest sin a pupil could commit was to turn up underprepared. Sister Mary Leo would expect an apology before the lesson could continue.

'With Sister Mary Leo you had to be totally committed to your singing. She would not tolerate anything but total commitment,' said another pupil of the time, Diana Stuart.

For those who did not match up to her exacting standards, the punishments were severe. For all her air of saintliness, Sister Mary Leo possessed a withering tongue. 'There wouldn't be a pupil of Sister Mary Leo's that she hasn't had in tears,' said Gillian Redstone, another contemporary of Kiri's at St Mary's. 'I always remember her telling me I had expressionless eyes, like a cow's,' recalls Elsa Grubisa. 'That was her style. You had to accept what was being said to you and either shape up or ship out.'

Having been accepted as one of her personal students, Kiri was called to sing with Sister Mary Leo twice a week. Her first impressions, she said later, were that Sister Mary Leo 'seemed enormously old to me, even then'. As she overcame her fear, the knowledge that she had relinquished all to devote herself to God only deepened the respect she demanded. 'She was first of all a nun and a very devout Catholic. When I was singing, wherever I would go I would always have to go into the church,' Kiri recalled later in life. Her knowledge and undoubted love for her music was quietly inspiring. 'I think she was sometimes torn between the two because the music sometimes took over and God had to take a small backseat. But she was a very dedicated person and that's, I think, why I liked being taught by her because she had no other interests, it was just music and God.'

As a tutor, she could not have presented a starker contrast to Kiri's mother. At home she had been showered with praise by her family and their house guests. She soon discovered Sister Mary Leo operated according to different principles. In her classes conversation was kept to a minimum. Sister Mary Leo often spent an entire lesson scribbling notes to herself. 'She never stopped writing in her notebook,' said Diana Stuart. 'She would make copious notes but she never told you what she was writing.' If a passage was sung to her liking she would say 'good' or 'fine'.

'She was not a great one for compliments,' Kiri said once. Yet as she began working with Kiri, Sister Mary Leo quickly understood why Sister Francis Xavier had recommended she take on her discovery. Her only disappointment was that Kiri's raw yet powerful voice had been trained to sing undemanding material from musicals; what Sister Leo later rather loftily referred to as 'music of an essentially trivial kind'. During her first weeks with Sister Mary Leo, Kiri sang nothing more taxing than folk songs.

In the meantime she set about preparing Kiri for more serious music. Sister Mary Leo's teaching methods bordered on the bizarre. Kiri found herself joining other girls in curious physical exercises designed to improve her physical ability to project her voice. 'She got these bees in her bonnet. She'd have this new idea or she'd hear or read something and we'd be on that for a week,' recalled another student, Hannah Tatana. 'There was singing with a pencil in your mouth which was supposed to loosen your throat but tightened your jaw. Then another time she'd read somewhere about Caruso pushing a grand piano two inches with the expansion of his diaphragm and we had to do that.'

The Caruso exercise was preferable to another recalled by Gillian Redstone. 'One method she used to teach us to control breathing involved Sister's big old reel to reel tape recorder, a very heavy machine in a case,' she said. 'We had to lie on the floor with the tape recorder stuck on top of the diaphragm and then lift it with our breathing for a few minutes. It wasn't on long enough for us to go purple, but it was certainly quite a lesson.'

Such was her pupils' faith in their teacher's near divinity, no one ever protested at the tortures they were put through. 'We didn't dare question it at the time. And we believed in her, that she was doing the right thing,' said Redstone. Like every other pupil, Redstone knew the potential cost of dissent. There was too much to lose.

Sister Mary Leo controlled her singers with an almost absolutist power. Her word, and her word alone, dictated the speed with which they progressed up the St Mary's ladder. If a girl had talent, Sister Mary would invite her first to join the St Mary's Choir. If she shone there she would be encouraged to sing the occasional solo at the choir's frequent public and charity appearances. The ultimate accolade was to be invited to represent St Mary's – and therefore Sister Mary Leo herself – in one of the highly competitive singing contests. A girl only had to look at the portraits of Mary O'Brien and Mina Foley to imagine what might lie ahead from there. Talent and success were not necessarily related. It was no different in the rarefied world of St Mary's. Sister Mary Leo alone ordained the chosen ones. It paid to stay on her side.

Kiri's late start did little to inhibit her rapid progress through the ranks. She was quickly installed as a member of the St Mary's Choir. In keeping with the traditions on which their Order was founded, the nuns visited Auckland's less privileged, performing at hospitals, mental institutions and prisons.

Kiri sang at church and charity events all over Auckland. Sister Mary Leo also added her to the list of girls recommended for engagements in and around Auckland society. The christening, wedding and funeral – 'hatches, matches and dispatches' – circuit could provide a girl with a tidy supplementary income. Booking agents invariably had to go through Sister Mary Leo, who insisted any flowers a girl was given be donated to the St Mary's altar. She was motivated less by money than control, and although she did charge her private students the going market rate of a guinea an hour, brown envelopes stuffed full of the cash fees collected from her singers would gather in small piles round her music room. Kiri's years as a 'performing monkey' at home stood her in good stead. Soon she was one of the most assured performers at the school. Tom bought her a secondhand Standard Ten as a fifteenth birthday present. The car was soon clocking up the miles as Kiri spent more and more time shuttling to and from her various engagements.

If the compliments were in short supply in Kiri's presence, Sister Mary Leo was soon leaving few in any doubt that she sensed St Mary's had an important new discovery. Elsa Grubisa recalls that she outshone Kiri in a singing exam carried out by an English examiner, a Mr Spinks. 'He actually gave me a better score than Kiri. But Sister Mary Leo made no bones about telling me that she didn't know what the examiner was thinking about and I had no business scoring better than Kiri,' she remembered. The moment confirmed two suspicions that had been forming in Grubisa's mind. Personally she no longer had any interest in subjecting herself to Sister Mary Leo's authoritarian regime. 'That was it for me. I gave up after that,' she said. She also sensed St Mary's once more had a star on its hands. 'I think Sister Mary Leo realised from the beginning that she had someone a bit special in Kiri,' she added.

Sister Mary Leo saw her role as more than a mere voice coach. She was a Mother Confessor and best friend, musical guardian and Svengali all rolled into one. 'I suppose I mother the girls to a certain extent. I don't just teach them singing, I am interested in their own lives,' she said once. 'To be able to get the best out of them one has to be a bit of a psychologist too. I don't treat them all as peas in a pod. I try to understand them and realise that, like everyone else, they too have their problems.'

One day during her second year at St Mary's, Kiri visited Sister Mary Leo's room with a gift of handkerchiefs she had bought with a group of other girls. Sister Mary had invited her new discovery to sit down for a lengthy, intimate talk. Unlike most of the St Mary's girls, Kiri had quickly overcome her fear of her mentor. 'Kiri was confident and could communicate with her,' recalled Elsa Grubisa. As she grew to understand her precocious new pupil, Sister Mary Leo had, in return, been 'completely frank' with Kiri. By now Sister Mary Leo recognised a gift as natural as anything she had encountered in her long career. She also understood how easily that talent could be squandered through indiscipline and over-confidence. 'You have got a lot of ability, dear, and you're going to have a lot of people giving you all the encouragement and praise in the world,' she explained. She went on to explain why Kiri could not expect her to be anything other than her toughest taskmistress. 'I'm going to be harder on you than anyone else, because it is better for you.'

Moments later, as she walked Kiri to the door, Leo revealed the real reason for her wanting their little tête-à-tête. 'Now tell me, Kiri,' she smiled. 'Next term, would you like to go for competitions?'

At the dawn of the 1960s, with the exception of live commentaries on the All Blacks rugby test matches and the races of the Olympic middle-distance star Peter Snell, few radio programmes drew such avid audiences as the transmissions of the singing competitions that had by now proliferated all over New Zealand. Since the Mobil Petroleum Company had begun pouring sponsorship cash into the hugely popular Song Quest, so the smaller competitions held all over New Zealand became more popular and highly publicised. During the autumn and winter months provincial outposts like Tauranga and Te Awamutu, Te Aroha and Rotorua became the focus of intense interest among New Zealand's music-loving public.

The aria contests helped many young singers develop into stars. Long player recordings of the winning competitors sold well. Recording contracts and overseas scholarships were commonplace for the feted few who made it on to the winner's podium. Financially the rewards were considerable. The Mobil Song Quest first prize was £300. The purse at the most high profile of all Australasian contests, the Melbourne and Sydney Sun Arias, was £1,500, about double the average annual wage at the time. In short, the contests offered a stairway to stardom, a tantalising route to fame and fortune, in New Zealand terms at least. Perhaps most importantly, they offered New Zealanders an opportunity to overcome the inferiority complex they felt in comparison to the mother country, the 'cultural cringe' as Kiwis called it.

'With rugby and horseracing, singing was the big thing in New Zealand at the time,' recalled Diana Stuart. As a gifted soloist and cellist, Stuart was given a deeper than average insight into this competitive world. She often played in the orchestras accompanying the singing finalists. To the New Zealand public, the competitions seemed like genteel, elegant affairs contested between neatly groomed young ladies and gentlemen. The backstage reality was rather different. 'The rivalry really was ferocious.'

Nowhere was the competition more intense than among the teachers themselves. Publicly Sister Mary Leo tut-tutted such petty jealousies. 'I hate that competitive spirit,' she told the *New Zealand Weekly News* once. 'I tell all the girls: "Do your best. Don't merely concentrate on winning, music is too beautiful, the voice is a gift they have been given, to give joy to other people."' The truth was no one hated losing more.

Sister Mary Leo's main opposition invariably came from singers attached to a small group of rival teachers, the Drake family and Mary Pratt in Dunedin and a Madame Narev in Auckland. Her representatives were left in no doubt what was expected of them. 'She would say things like: "I'm going to be very disappointed if you don't do so and so,"' recalled Diana Stuart. 'She loathed losing.'

As Sister Mary Leo began preparing Kiri for her entry into this new world she quickly realised she had unearthed a natural born winner. Like every other Sister Leo girl Kiri found herself taught how to dress, pose and behave on stage.

'She endeavoured to train them even in things like how to walk, how to look gracious, how to bow, how to accept applause,' recalled Sister Mary Leo's contemporary, Sister Mercienne, now the school's archivist. 'She would do her best to bring them to the point where

45

they could make the most of themselves and stand up there like young queens and sing their hearts out.'

Perhaps Sister Mary Leo's greatest gift, however, lay in her ability to teach girls to express their personalities in their singing. 'She was not a flamboyant person herself, but she encouraged that in her singers because it is what you need on the stage. She was very good at drawing people out and getting them to express themselves,' recalled Hannah Tatana.

Tatana had been educated at Queen Victoria's, Auckland's all Maori girls' school, where she had come to the attention of Sister Mary Leo. By 1960, she was already being talked of as the first female classical star to emerge from the Maori population.

Tatana had first heard Kiri sing at a talent competition held at Taupo in the Christmas of 1960, where, with her brother, she had been asked to act as a judge. 'Kiri sang "Ave Maria" and I was bowled over by her voice,' she remembered.

Back at St Mary's, she had taken a keen interest in her progress under Sister Mary Leo. 'There was this wonderful sound that was new and so gorgeous and luscious that it gave the impression that with judicious choice of repertoire – which was something that Sister Mary Leo was good at – there was no limit to what she might achieve,' she said.

As Kiri took her first tentative steps on to the competition circuit, her towering talent made an immediate impact. Kiri's first important competition appearance came in her home city's premier event, the Auckland Competitions, in 1960. She sang two songs, 'When the Children Say Their Prayers' and 'Road to the Isles', in the sixteen-year-old age group. She won with ease.

In March 1960, as Kiri celebrated her sixteenth birthday, her days within St Mary's College itself were drawing to a close. By now she had been accepted for a year-long ATCL course at Auckland Business College. As far as Nell was concerned, her schooling there was subsidiary to her continuing education as a member of Sister Mary Leo's 200-strong group of private, fee-paying students. Her Sisters at St Mary's regarded Sister Mary Leo in much the same way Kiri's family saw Nell Te Kanawa. 'The other nuns quivered in her shadow,' Kiri laughed later in life. To Kiri, her teacher was 'a very grand lady – a "*grande dame*"'. However, my mother was also a "*grande dame*", who liked to command and demand everything so the two characters didn't get on very well.'

Yet the two women had formed an alliance that was as formidable as it was unlikely. Nell had made no secret of her ambitions for Kiri. 'It was mainly her mother's wish and ambition on Kiri's behalf which led her to devote herself chiefly to more serious music,' Sister Mary Leo conceded later.

As Kiri continued her studies, however, she realised the financial cost of maintaining her embryonic career was considerable. The differing demands of the competitions and choir performances and her less formal wedding engagements required a well-stocked wardrobe. Resourceful as ever, Nell made a collection of full-length evening costumes, cocktail dresses and ballgowns. Her eyes were also eternally open to opportunities to acquire or borrow outfits that enhanced Kiri's image. As Kiri reached the end of her studies at business college, emerging with an honours pass, Nell made it clear that she too would have to contribute to maintaining her lavish professional lifestyle. A succession of menial jobs followed, the first at the main telephone exchange in Auckland where Kiri began working from 6 a.m. to 1 p.m. every day.

By May 1961 the Te Kanawa household was forced to find the money for the most glamorous addition yet to Kiri's wardrobe. With a handful of other girls from St Mary's, Kiri was invited to attend the highlight of the Catholic community's social calendar, New Zealand's equivalent to London's debutantes' ball.

For the girls of St Mary's the event represented the romantic zenith of their adolescent social lives. 'It was a big thing for us,' recalled Gillian Redstone, who joined Kiri in walking the length of the Town Hall to meet the Archbishop of Auckland, James Liston, that night. 'We all looked forward to reaching the age of seventeen when we could actually be presented.'

Kiri was one of the undoubted belles of the ball afterwards. The tomboy was rapidly metamorphosing into a striking young woman. Her emerging beauty shone through in the carefully posed studio portraits taken to mark the event. Kiri's dazzling white lace dress was set off by a pair of long silk gloves, an elaborate pearl necklace and floral earrings. The pictures offer a jarring contrast to the story of the girl who, in Kiri's own words, 'came from nothing'. They stand as evidence too of the skill with which Nell was now moulding her daughter's image.

Nell had become friendly with the leading Auckland couturier Colin Cole. Cole's salon on Queen Street was the domain of New Zealand's high society. The designer's exquisite garments were all one-offs. A Cole blouse cost around £250, four months' wages for the average New Zealander, while evening gowns retailed at a stratospheric £1,200 – the cost of a modest home.

Cole's client list included the Governor General's wife and her social circle. Cole was regularly asked to lend his clothes to his socialite friends but invariably refused. Few New Zealanders possessed the persuasive charm of Nell Te Kanawa, however. The designer's manageress of the time, Terry Nash, is unsure when the friendship started but saw its results.

'Her mother was one of those ladies, a big lady, who really pushed,' said Nash. 'She would come and say, "Oh, it's for Kiri, you know, so I think you should be giving it to her." She expected people to do things for Kiri.'

Cole found it impossible to resist her. Kiri, in return, sang for free at several of Cole's shows. 'I don't think Colin ever turned her down. He was a big softie,' said Nash. Terry Nash is unsure whether Kiri's debutante ballgown was a Cole creation. Regardless, it was magnificent, typical of the clothes which gave Kiri an allure her rivals could not match. As Kiri took the debutantes' ball by storm, however, only one accessory was missing – a steady boyfriend with whom to share the romance of the night.

Kiri's first experience of dating the opposite sex had been less than successful. She had begun seeing her first serious boyfriend when she was sixteen. According to her own account of the relationship, he was 'several years older but rather less wise'. The courtship had come to an abrupt ending during a telephone conversation in which Kiri invited him to watch her sing at the prizewinner's concert following the Auckland Competition of 1960. The boyfriend had been utterly disinterested in her music and had never once watched her perform publicly. 'He replied that if I went in for the concert he never wanted to see me again,' Kiri recalled. 'It had never entered my head that anyone was going to try and stop me, so I just said goodbye and slammed down the receiver.'

Of her other crushes, only one, on the most handsome of the Hanson brothers, Robert, had lasted for more than a few weeks. Gillian Redstone would travel to Taupo for summer holidays with Kiri and the Hansons. 'There was a bit of rivalry, boy-wise,' recalled Redstone. 'Kiri was keen on Robert at one stage.' Kiri's hopes may have risen when Robert Hanson agreed to accompany her to the debs' ball. His lack of interest was immediately apparent, however. She had settled on the least promising prospect of all the Hanson boys.

Her dawn shifts at the Auckland telephone exchange left Kiri exhausted and often too tired to concentrate fully on her singing with Sister Mary Leo. For a while she tried working the 'graveyard shift' instead, rising at 2 a.m. and working until breakfast time. Even after a morning 'nap', however, Kiri arrived at her weekly lessons with Sister Mary drained of all energy. 'They were terrible, terrible hours,' she later opined.

Soon Nell had found her a less taxing alternative, at a sheet music store in Mount Roskill, not far from Mitchell Street. As well as offering less demanding duties and more convenient working hours, Nell's logic argued that Kiri might also learn a little more about the great composers and the great music of the world at the same time. This did not work out either. Kiri soon clashed with the two elderly women who ran the store. She later claimed that they forced her to stand on her feet all day, eventually leaving her in need of a varicose vein operation. Six months into the job she quit.

Kiri worked briefly as a stenographer. Ever the dutiful father, it was Tom who eventually found his daughter the ideal job, however. Through his connections at Caltex he got Kiri an interview for a position as a receptionist at the company's head office in Auckland. The work was undemanding – Kiri recalled once how she would spend most of her day chatting to people and the other half 'enjoying tea and biscuits'. Monday mornings were frittered away shopping for flowers for the office. Most importantly of all the relaxed nature of the job meant she had time to travel to St Mary's for lunchtime singing lessons with Sister Mary Leo.

Sister Leo's doubts about Kiri's dedication had deepened. Like Nell she knew that Kiri's easy-going nature posed the greatest threat to her progressing as a serious singer. In addition, her fears that, freed from the cloistered peace of St Mary's, Kiri would be drawn to the more straightforward, 'trivial' music she regarded with such disdain had quickly been justified.

While at Caltex Kiri had been introduced to Auckland's 'dine and dance' circuit. For a few pounds a performance, Kiri would charm nightclubs full of inebriated couples with full-blooded renditions of hits from *West Side Story*, *My Fair Lady* or *The Sound of Music*. She would roar around Auckland in her car, accepting as many engagements as she could fit in a night. Often she would work until 1 a.m. to earn £20. At her lessons with Sister Mary Leo the legacy of her late nights in smoke-filled rooms was obvious. Eventually Nell was summoned for a council of war. Nell's relationship with Sister Mary Leo had remained a difficult one. 'I rather liked it, a certain aggravation going on there,' Kiri laughed later. 'I thought it was quite fun, rather a good floor show.' Both women realised that Kiri had reached a crossroads, however. Sister Mary Leo suggested Nell might want to look for a scholarship that would pay for Kiri's fees and allow her to concentrate more fully on her singing, Nell was in complete agreement. Back on the phone at Blockhouse Bay, she had soon identified a potential source of funds.

After generations of marginalisation the Maori were discovering their voice within New Zealand life. In the post-war years thousands of New Zealand's indigenous people had moved away from their old lifestyle in the rural heartlands. Predictably the incoming population had found assimilation into the European-dominated cities a difficult process. By the 1960s the majority of Maori lived in conditions defined by poor housing, poor sanitation, poor health, poor education and a rising crime rate. The comparative life expectancy of the two communities in 1964 illustrated the point perfectly. For Europeans it was sixty-eight years, for Maori it was a mere fifty-four.

Driven to act, the New Zealand government had introduced a raft of initiatives designed to alleviate the problems. Among the most important stemmed from the Hunn Report on Maori education which in 1961 highlighted the low achievement of Maori pupils; just one in 200 of whom reached the seventh form. At the end of that year the government established the Maori Education Foundation (MEF) to provide scholarships to enable Maori secondary school pupils to continue their studies. An initial grant of £250,000 was soon attracting applications from talented young Maori. One of the first to arrive at the MEF's Auckland offices was from Mrs T. Te Kanawa of 22 Mitchell Street, Blockhouse Bay.

Nell's awareness of the quiet revolution under way may have been provided first by Kiri's St Mary's colleague Hannah Tatana. While Anna Hato from Rotorua had won great acclaim singing the pop songs of the day during the war years, Tatana had become the first female Maori singer to follow the pioneering trail into the classical field blazed by the barrel chested bass Inia Te Wiata in the 1950s.

'The feeling then was that the Maoris were quaint, rural people,' said Tatana. 'Maori culture was looked on as being very "pop", as it was, because the real culture had been suppressed.' Tatana's breakthrough had come that year at the 1961 Mobil Song Quest where she had come second. She had already been approached to take the lead in a new production of *Carmen* in Auckland the following year. 'People were so surprised that Maori were capable of doing a little bit more than boogie woogie. It made them all the more keen to promote the traditional Maori thing,' she recalled. Nell Te Kanawa had watched Tatana's progress with interest. Kiri would go on to sing in a Maori group with her. 'She was aware of the advantages I had with my Maori background,' recalled Tatana.

Nell sensed a changing mood – and acted.

In the Gisborne of the 1940s and the Auckland of the 1950s, her daughter's Maori heritage had remained a source of unease. Tom continued to be almost completely estranged from Maori life and from his family, to the extent that his youngest sibling, Te Waamoana, only learned that he was, like her, living in Auckland, when she saw his picture in the paper with an unusually large catch of Taupo trout. When Te Waamoana attempted to rebuild the bridges with the family Nell welcomed her and her daughter Kay, now Kay Rowbottom, to the house on Mitchell Street. According to Rowbottom, however, Nell 'was very selective about the members of the family she liked to have at Kiri's events'.

Suddenly, however, the pendulum had swung in a new direction. The MEF's regional committee in the city was run by two cochairmen, Thelma Robinson, fourth wife of the city's Mayor, Sir Dove-Myer 'Robbie' Robinson and a charismatic war veteran and sportsman turned schoolteacher, thirty-five-year-old Hoani 'John' Waititi. Waititi was one of a new generation of university educated Maori academics

51

and a pioneer in the introduction of Maori lessons to secondary schools.

It was Thelma Robinson who recognised the name on Nell's application. Robinson and her husband had seen one of Kiri's first public performances at the opening of a Maori church a year or two earlier. 'We saw this young Maori girl in a white dress sing in the open air and were stunned by her voice,' said Robinson. 'We made a point of finding out who she was.' Kiri's situation didn't fall readily into the Foundation's brief. As Kiri herself later recalled, 'It was mainly for the academic rather than the musical child, and I certainly wasn't academic.' However, once Waititi and the Foundation's trustees, including Maori MP Sir Eruera Tirikatene and Maori Women's Welfare League leader Mira Petricevich, now Dame Mira Szaszy, had heard Kiri sing, the technicalities were overlooked.

The moment was one of the most significant in Kiri's young life. When Nell received the phone call from John Waititi confirming the Foundation's willingness to make a grant of £250 to fund Kiri's full-time study with Sister Mary Leo she could barely conceal her excitement.

No sooner had she put the phone down on Waititi than she had summoned Tom home and headed off to the Caltex office with him to collect Kiri from work. Kiri later recalled sitting with Tom at her side in the car. There Nell effectively issued their daughter with an ultimatum. 'Either you sing or you just keep working at Caltex,' she told her. 'It's one or the other, but whatever you do, you've got to do it totally.'

Kiri admitted years later that she had been far from certain of her response. 'I couldn't think, did I want to study music full time? I didn't know anything about what it entailed. So for peace's sake I said yes.' Peace, however, was the last thing she was granted as she settled down to the life of a full-time student.

In a television interview many years later, Kiri presented a stark picture of the demands Sister Mary Leo's regime placed on her. 'I would study from nine in the morning till five,' she said. 'She would listen to me through the wall all day and the moment I'd stop even for a breath or a drink or anything she would knock on the wall and off we'd go again.'

Nell too became even more relentless in her control. 'You have a

God-given voice which gives people pleasure. It's your duty to show them,' she would berate Kiri if ever her daughter slackened, in a phrase echoing Archbishop Liston.

Back at Mitchell Street the transformation was remarkable. Kiri would spend endless hours rehearsing single notes or scales, much to the irritation of her young niece Judy. 'One night my grandmother and grandfather were out and we were doing the washing up. She was going through the scales, just to annoy me,' she recalled. 'I remember shoving the dishcloth in her mouth, I was so angry.' When Judy ran out into the night, Kiri locked her niece outside as she continued singing.

Judy and Nola would soon leave Mitchell Street. In 1960 Nola married again. With her daughter and new husband Bill Denholm, she moved briefly to Waihi beach, near where Nell had been born, where she and Bill ran a fish and chip shop before returning to Auckland. As they readied themselves to leave, Judy and Nola could not help notice the new seriousness with which Kiri was now treating her music. One day she, Kiri and the Hanson boys had playfully lit up a discarded Peter Stuyvesant cigarette they had found in the lounge. 'We heard Nana's footsteps coming down the passage from her bedroom and we were frantically trying to get rid of the smoke,' she recalled. 'Nana came in. She never raised her voice, she just looked straight at Kiri and said, "You smoke, or you sing." That was it. Simple,' she said. 'I never saw Kiri smoke again.'

Wicked Little Witch

A year after Kiri's decision to devote herself to full-time singing, she and her mother already formed an irresistible double act. What Kiri possessed in talent, Nell had in tenacity; what Kiri had in beauty, Nell had in belligerence; what Kiri had in charm, Nell had in sheer chutzpah. For two months in 1962, conductor Neil McGough and his colleagues on a new and as yet unperformed Maori musical, *Uwane*, witnessed the partnership operating at the peak of its powers.

If McGough's memory serves him correctly, his first audition for the show was held in the less than glamorous setting of an ice rink near Auckland's city centre a few weeks into the New Year. Around seventy nerve-racked singers and dancers had turned up, each of them hopeful of a role in the musical to be staged at Auckland's premier venue, His Majesty's Theatre, that April.

More than three decades on, McGough, who went on to become one of New Zealand's most respected musical administrators, struggles to recollect the faces that filed past him during a long and at times tediously exhausting day of auditions. However, he remembers the words with which the morning's most remarkable character introduced herself as if it were yesterday.

'Excuse me, I'm Kiri Te Kanawa's mother,' she announced, interrupting him, the show's director David Rossiter and choreographer Beverley Jordan as they compared notes mid-way through the auditions.

'Every other singer and dancer came in and filled out a form and plonked it on the table. We'd ask them what they were going to sing, they'd sing it and that was that,' recalled McGough. 'I auditioned dozens and dozens of shows and it was always the same procedure.

But Kiri arrived with her mother, and it was her mother who came to the table. Instead of just putting the form on the pile we got the big sell. She just rabbited on and on.'

After what seemed like an eternity listening politely, McGough's frayed nerves got the better of him. 'I got a bit mad and said, "Look, this is all terribly interesting and I'm sure we will all entirely agree with you once you've sat down and we've actually heard your daughter sing." And on that unsubtle put-down she got the message.'

While her mother had been at the reception desk, Kiri had stood quietly in a corner. As McGough invited her to the centre of the room she handed her sheet music to the pianist and announced that she was going to sing a favourite St Mary's aria, 'Oh My Beloved Father'. They were her first – and virtually her last – words of the morning. The consensus was quick in coming. 'She got the job after about three bars,' said McGough. 'She put her hands out in front of her and sang, like all the others, except the sound that came out was unbelievable. It had style, it had diction, she'd clearly been well taught, but it had that magic extra as well. Elisabeth Schwarzkopf was going to have to walk in to beat her.'

When Rossiter and McGough offered Kiri the role of the eponymous heroine, Nell accepted immediately.

Nell had taken Kiri along to the ice rink audition after another St Mary's girl, Lynne Cantlon, had declined the leading role in the musical due to other commitments. She had sensed an ideal opportunity for Kiri to make her mark as a rising star, and a Maori star at that.

Written by an Auckland electroplater, Lindsay Gordon Rowell, *Uwane* represented the first attempt to blend Maori and European influences on the theatrical stage. Conceived as a European style light musical comedy, the three act 'musical fantasy' was set in a Maori village and revolved around the story of two warriors and their efforts to woo the beautiful but mischievous Princess Uwane, 'the wicked little witch of Whakatane'.

Nell would have known that Rowell had booked His Majesty's Theatre for a ten night run beginning early in April. What she probably did not know, however, was that behind the scenes the portents were already far from encouraging. A number of Maori singers and actors had turned down offers of leading roles in the show, claiming it affronted rather than celebrated Maori culture. Both Rowell and his sister Zella, who had mortgaged their homes to finance the production, had been warned they would find little enthusiasm for such a show within a still deeply conservative Pakeha public.

While his make-up artist wife was already working on the sticky brown dye that would be used to darken the skins of the Maoris' European replacements, Rossiter was approaching familiar faces to help him out of his crisis.

The role of the male hero, Manaia, had been given to a handsome English ex-soldier, Vincent Collins, who had been a hit as Joe Cable in *South Pacific*, Rossiter's previous show at His Majesty's. As a member of the British Army, the London-born Collins had seen his share of the world. He had been among the troops sent out to Africa to quell the Mau Mau uprising. He was something of a romantic adventurer too.

As rehearsals got under way the thirty-one-year-old Collins was instantly drawn to the eighteen-year-old with whom he would share most of his scenes in the coming weeks. Kiri had matured into a strikingly attractive young woman. Her thick-set frame and puppy fat features still lent her an air of girlish gawkiness. Her oversized personality and air of vaguely seductive self-confidence more than compensated for it. She had grown into a woman capable of inflaming passions. If she had not known it before taking up her role in *Uwane*, she certainly did by the end of the troubled production.

At the first rehearsal Collins had been as impressed as everyone else by Kiri's voice. 'I remember hearing her for the first time and realising there was a magic attached. It was not just another voice, Kiri was able to get a bird-like clarity,' Collins recalled. Her personality was, if anything, even more beguiling. 'She had a wonderful innocence and charm,' he recalled. Collins found himself smitten almost immediately. 'She was electrifying.'

Collins had recently broken off his engagement to a beautiful young ballet dancer, Beverley Jordan. The embers of their stormy relationship had yet to be fully extinguished, however. When Rossiter and McGough began searching for a choreographer, it had been Collins who had suggested his former girlfriend for the role. Over the coming weeks Jordan's primary role was to teach Kiri to dance. It would present one of the sterner tests of her career so far.

Neil McGough had spotted Kiri's lack of mobility almost immediately. He took the view that she had been hired for her voice and that it was Jordan's job to polish her stagecraft. 'It was the opposite of Fred Astaire's famous audition. With Kiri it was "can't move, can't dance, can sing a bit",' said McGough. 'But if she'd been a quadriplegic I think we'd have let her do the show in a wheelchair.'

On stage it quickly became apparent that Kiri was incapable of singing in anything other than the studied operatic pose she had struck at the rehearsal. 'There's not a lot one can do with a person who had never ever had any movement training unless they go home and work at it,' said Jordan. 'Kiri at that stage could obviously swing a golf club but she was not naturally co-ordinated.'

Director David Rossiter was soon despairing at Kiri's deficiencies. 'After the third rehearsal, David Rossiter lined them all up and said there was someone on the stage who was not up to it and they should shape up,' recalled Lindsay Rowell. 'He didn't name her, but everyone knew it was Kiri.'

By the next rehearsal the following week, Kiri had undergone a Damascene conversion. 'She went away to Sister Mary Leo and whatever she told her did the trick because the next time she came back you would not have recognised her,' said Rowell.

Rowell, McGough, Rossiter and Jordan were experiencing a pattern that would become familiar to all who knew and worked with Kiri in later years. When the chips were down her application was absolute. At other times her relaxed approach could easily be construed at best as disinterest, at worst arrogance.

'She was a little monkey for whom life was a big giggle,' said Jordan. 'She had no idea about the value of time and money. People had staked their houses on the success of this production but Kiri had no responsibilities.

'To me she was an ignorant little twerp,' she added unequivocally. 'I think if the situation were repeated today there's no doubt she would have been thrown out.'

McGough recognised the same immature tendencies. 'She was late for things and then thought it was all funny, never took it seriously at all. She would not knuckle down and it was so tragic because she clearly had all the material there. Her voice was already powerful and accurate, although I found very quickly that if she got tired she went flat.' What he came to call 'Kiri notes' could also be induced by lack of concentration. It was soon apparent that such lapses were an intrinsic part of Kiri's professional persona, a trait she would never shake off.

If Kiri was treating her big break as something of a giggle, her mother was approaching it with the utmost seriousness. Nell's Blockhouse Bay parties had become well known in musical circles. She used them as a showcase for Kiri's talent and a vehicle for introducing her daughter to potential benefactors. For many they were simply occasions to be enjoyed. 'There was a bloody good atmosphere up there, always plenty of drink and food,' said Neil McGough, a talented trombonist, who attended many of Nell's impromptu soirées with his Dixieland band, the Bridge City Jazzmen. 'It wasn't glamorous food – it was Pavlovas and Cheerios – but what there was there was always plenty of it. Nell would always carry out the biggest trays.'

To the eyes of others, like Beverley Jordan, they only served to 'give an appearance of Kiri being popular' and deepen the dislike of her bludgeoning mother. As far as many were concerned the hefty figure they saw urging her daughter on from the side of the stage was little more than a crude and at times intimidating bully. Their thoughts echoed feelings that had been widespread on the competition circuit for some time.

The bitching and backbiting which accompanied the singing contests had been apparent from Kiri's earliest experiences at the Auckland Competitions. Kiri had seen one mother attempting to stop a rival singer from entering the competition hall because she had arrived 'too late'. The girl ignored her, entered the hall and the competition on time and duly won. Kiri had quickly come to refer to the Competitions as 'a scrap'. Nell had taken to these treacherous new waters like a duck to water. In the run-up to contests, she would think nothing of spending an hour on the phone to a rival singer, relentlessly holding forth about Kiri. 'Her voice was very heavy and she spoke very slowly and deliberately,' recalled one member of the Sister Mary Leo stable at the time. 'She would talk about Kiri and how good she was. It was almost like she was trying to intimidate. It happened to us all.'

No tactic seemed too underhand, provided it ensured Kiri outshone her colleagues. 'Sometimes if three or four St Mary's girls were singing at an event together, she'd ring around asking each of them what they were going to wear that night,' recalled the same Sister Mary Leo pupil. 'She'd ask, "What are you going to wear tonight?" I'd say, "I thought I'd wear a long dress." She'd say, "Kiri's not going to wear that, she's going to wear a short dress." It might be a modest engagement, so everyone turned up in the short dresses except Kiri, who turned up in the long dress with the gloves and the whole works and looked the most attractive and glamorous. That really got up people's noses and that's why the general consensus was that she was not good for Kiri.'

Beverley Jordan was close to some of Kiri's St Mary's colleagues. 'I know there was a lot of unhappiness and dissension at Sister Mary Leo's because of the pushing and conniving that Nell did,' she said. 'Nell tried to tell Sister Mary Leo her job and she would undermine other singers, tell them they were no good, they weren't talented, that Kiri was the star and was the one that would go to London and have her name in lights.'

'Nell was very one-eyed,' Kiri's St Mary's colleague Gillian Redstone said succinctly.

During the *Uwane* rehearsals Nell's technique amounted to a form of telephone terrorism. She would sit quietly enough during rehearsals. Once the show's production team were isolated at home, however, the phone would begin to ring. 'It was always on the phone. It never stopped rehearsals and never happened publicly,' says Beverly Jordan.

Lynne Cantlon's early offer of the role of Uwane had come partly by courtesy of her mother, Una, who had been hired as the show's wardrobe mistress. Relations between Una and Nell were already difficult – Una Cantlon was no shrinking violet herself – yet they were soon strained further. 'She was always baling up poor Una,' recalled Neil McGough. 'She was saying Kiri's costumes weren't quite as nice as someone else's and couldn't she have a little more of this here and a bit less of that there.'

Beverley Jordan's mother also suffered. Like Una Cantlon, she could not curb her tongue for long. 'I remember both my mother and Lynne's mother asking her whether she had any experience or had she just come off the marae in Gisborne?' she said. 'They both told her if she didn't know anything about stage work she should keep her mouth shut.'

Even the show's writer was not beyond a little lobbying. 'She didn't want Kiri described as a wicked little witch,' recalled Lindsay Rowell.

'She asked me to make a change to the script but I wasn't changing it for anybody.'

Neil McGough had been exposed to the breed before. Nell's weakness as a stage mother lay in her inability to know when to stop. 'We didn't dislike Nell, we admired her drive,' he said. 'She came to all the rehearsals. Everywhere you went, there was Nell. But she always went a step too far.' To McGough, at least, the real worry was that Nell seemed to be the controlling influence in Kiri's career. 'Kiri never gave an impression that she cared terribly that her mother was like this,' said McGough. 'Kiri herself was very dominated by her mother.'

Inevitably Sister Mary Leo had also attempted to assert herself on the evolving drama. She had loftily insisted that the script and score were sent to her at St Mary's. She wanted 'to check whether there was anything too racy,' said Lindsay Rowell. Satisfied that her emerging star's wholesome image was not endangered, she turned her attention to the score itself. 'And then she stopped Kiri from singing any of the really high notes in case she damaged her voice.' After that, at least, she maintained a dignified distance from proceedings.

Inevitably Sister Mary Leo and Nell could not protect Kiri at all times. On the rare occasions when she was left to her own devices, however, it was clear she was perfectly capable of looking after herself.

Kiri's habit of turning up late for rehearsals had done nothing to boost her popularity within an already disgruntled production. 'Quite often she and her father would be out in the morning playing a round of golf. Everybody thought what a lovely life she led,' said Beverley Jordan. When, to general dismay, Rowell's sister Zella eased herself into a position of power within the production Kiri became the inevitable target. Even her own brother declared Zella Rowell 'a bitch, born and bred. Zella had a way of putting everyone's back up. She was greedy and selfish and everyone hated her.' Her attention soon turned to the show's youngest, least experienced performer.

'Nasty little sarcastic comments were made between them,' recalled Lindsay Rowell. 'Kiri was young and couldn't really fight back, but she was stubborn and she had quite clear ideas about how she wanted things done.' The confrontations between the two reached a climax during one of the final rehearsals. 'Kiri hid in the chorus when she was supposed to be up the front of the stage,' said Rowell. When Zella demanded she move to her proper position on stage, Kiri refused to budge. 'She turned to Zella and said, "I don't care. You can like it or lump it."'

'Kiri could be emotional if people upset her. She was pretty strong willed in her own way,' said Vincent Collins, who witnessed the scene.

If Kiri's spirits ever sagged during the increasingly fraught rehearsal sessions, comfort was always close at hand in the virile form of her leading man. Kiri and Collins had found few difficulties in conjuring up a convincing chemistry between Uwane and Manaia. Away from rehearsals they had begun seeing each other discreetly.

'It was a romance for a little while,' Collins confirmed. On stage at His Majesty's Collins and Kiri were careful not to arouse suspicions. 'In my innocence I had thought that Kiri and Vince were just acting,' remembered Lindsay Rowell's wife Madeleine who watched most of the rehearsals from the stalls. 'There was an atmosphere but I thought that was because they were playing lovers.' Others were able to put two and two together to form an educated opinion of what was unfolding.

'Kiri was a flirt, and a very pretty flirt at that,' said Neil McGough. 'Vincent was a good-looking joker and he thought it was very nice. He did respond a little further than he should have,' he added. One member of the production was more acutely attuned to developments than anyone, however. Beverley Jordan was all too familiar with the wiles of Vincent Collins.

'I broke things off with him because he was a charmer and had a lot of ladies on the go,' she recalled. 'That wasn't my cup of tea.' Jordan claims to have shrugged her shoulders at the romance. 'I couldn't have cared less. It was over and if he wanted to get involved with her that was his business,' she said.

Her mother was less philosophical when she discovered what was going on, however. Jordan returned one night to find her involved in a heated telephone conversation. It was soon apparent who was on the receiving end of the abuse. 'It turned out to be Nell Te Kanawa,' Jordan recalled. 'My mother was telling her she should keep her daughter in check and not keep waltzing off with other people's boy-friends.'

If the tirade had an effect it was the diametric opposite of that which had been intended. Soon Vincent and Kiri were making no secret of their relationship.

On the evening of Wednesday, 11 April 1962, His Majesty's Theatre was filled to capacity. For the producers of *Uwane*, however, the grim reality was that only 200 or so of the 2,000 seats had been paid for. 'They flooded all the nursing homes with free tickets. You lassoed people off the street if you had to on the night the critics were there,' said Neil McGough.

The lack of interest in the show's 'world première' could not be blamed on Nell Te Kanawa. In the run up to the opening night she had turned her attentions to drumming up support within her ever extending circle of patrons and supporters within Auckland. At another time and in another place, Nell's innate skills could have made her a mogul within the world of public relations. She wielded flattery and force with well-practised ease. 'She could charm the birds from the trees,' recalled Beverley Jordan. 'She was an absolutely brilliant PR woman.' Nell had by now begun to cultivate contacts within the Auckland media. The New Zealand press were intrigued by *Uwane*'s curiosity value if nothing else. Her mother ensured Kiri's face became a familiar one as the opening night loomed.

Kiri featured in a lengthy article on the musical in the leading magazine of the day, the *New Zealand Woman's Weekly*. On the morning before the show a photograph of Kiri in her traditional flax skirt, or piu-piu, taken at a dress rehearsal the previous Sunday, filled page three of the nation's most respected newspaper, the *New Zealand Herald*. Kiri had placed great store in the fact she had no plans to desert her teacher at St Mary's. In the official *Uwane* programme she repeated her promise that she had 'unlike so many of our talented young singers, no desire to travel abroad'. Her words would have gone down well with John Waititi who was among the many to have been given free seats that night. In a late effort to win a little support among Maori organisations, Lindsay and Zella Rowell had announced that all proceeds from the show would go to the Maori Education Foundation. It would soon be clear that the organisation would be the least of the evening's losers.

At the end of the show the audience applauded enthusiastically. Kiri and Vincent Collins held hands as they took their curtain call together. The following morning, however, Auckland's small circle of theatre critics damned *Uwane* with faint praise. '*Uwane* – a good try, but . . .' ran the headline in the *Auckland Star*. 'Brave Effort' was the best the *New Zealand Herald* could muster for the show as a whole.

While the critics couldn't warm to the Rowells' blend of the fantastical and the formulaic, they were united in their praise for Kiri. 'Whether *Uwane* is a public success or not, it has done a service in bringing forward at least two good voices, the warm mezzo of Kiri Te Kanawa and the resonant baritone of John Morgan,' wrote Desmond Mahoney in the *Star*.

'The star of the show, and a bright one at that, is Kiri Te Kanawa,' wrote the *Herald*'s L. C. M. Saunders. 'Natural and graceful in her movement, speech and singing, she reveals a real talent.'

To judge by the telegram which arrived at the stage door of His Majesty's Theatre the following morning the previous evening had been a five-star triumph. The brief message bore Nell's unmistakable imprimatur.

Congratulations, and my personal thanks. I would never have had such nice things said about me in the paper without your wonderful help and support. Thank you all and God bless you.
    Kiri Te Kanawa.

By the time the cast took the stage for the second night's performance, however, the damage caused by the reviews was all too obvious. Even fewer paying customers were dotted around the auditorium. In the absence of the adrenaline of the previous evening, Kiri understandably failed to shine as brightly. In the first half, to Neil McGough's horror, she accidentally left out a verse from one of her solos. As her conductor attempted to repair her mistake he looked up to see Kiri frozen on stage. 'She looked straight ahead stoically and carried on until the end of the song while I waved my arms like a demented grasshopper. She just didn't have the experience to know what to do, to look at me and let me fix it.'

During the interval McGough headed for her dressing room but was intercepted by the stage manager. 'He said, "She's locked herself in her room, she's in tears and mum's with her. She's never going to sing again."' McGough passed a message on to Kiri via Nell. 'I said, "Tell her not to break her heart about it and that everyone makes mistakes." Kiri had never sung with orchestras before and I think that was a contributing factor, that she thought it was our job to follow her, because that's what pianists did. She thought conductors were just for collecting tickets on the trams.'

By the third night she had corrected her mistake like the trouper she had quickly become. This time, however, there were only thirty-two there to witness her performance. Before curtain up that evening Kiri and the fifty-four other members of the cast had been called onto the stage to be told the following night's performance, the fourth, would be the last.

'Even though the reasons were obvious it came as a great shock,' recalled singer Brian O'Connor. 'Shows didn't close early in those days.'

While her brother kept a dignified silence, Zella Rowell lashed out. 'I have no faith left in New Zealanders' patriotism. I am appalled at the public's apathy,' she told the *New Zealand Herald*. 'I have lost everything.' Rowell had promised to pay every member of the cast and crew from the show's profits. Unsurprisingly few remember ever receiving any money.

In the months and years that followed, almost everyone downplayed their connection with *Uwane*. It was completely erased from Kiri's curriculum vitae almost immediately and she appears never to have spoken of her first starring role since. She did not thank McGough when he saw her a few years later and mentioned it. 'I said, "You've come a long way since *Uwane*." She said, "You rotten bugger, I've been trying to forget that for years."'

In the immediate aftermath of the show's failure, however, Kiri fared better than almost any other member of the production. Among the audience on the opening night had been a well-known talent scout Peter Claman, an expatriate Englishman who had been president of the Wembley Music Club in London. He had been sent to the show by one of the country's leading recording producers Tony Vercoe of Kiwi Records in Wellington. His written report to Vercoe ran along the lines: 'Tony, you want to get after this one.'

To Claman's eyes and ears at least, Kiri was the sole redeeming feature in the ill-fated musical. 'He told me that she stuck out a mile. She was head and shoulders above the music and anyone else in the cast,' recalled Vercoe.

Drawing on the quiet determination that had helped him survive a lengthy spell in German PoW camps during World War II, Vercoe had turned Kiwi Records into one of New Zealand's prestige recording labels. Owned by the Wellington publishers A. H. & A. W. Reed, the label had already registered successes with classical recordings of other members of Sister Mary Leo's stable of singers, including Malvina Major.

Intrigued by Claman's recommendation, Vercoe decided against approaching Kiri directly. 'She was so young,' he recalled. 'So I approached Sister Mary Leo, who I knew anyway.' Within days Vercoe was sitting in St Patrick's Cathedral, captivated by the sight and sound of Kiri singing the solo in 'The Nun's Chorus' from Johann Strauss's *Casanova* with the St Mary's Choir behind her. 'She put on a special performance just for me,' he said. As the final notes of the chorus faded into the air, Vercoe shared his first thoughts with Sister Mary Leo. 'I was so impressed I said, "Well, we'd better start off by recording that."' Tony Vercoe would transform the star of the unloved *Uwane* into the most idolised popular singer his country had ever seen.

Amid the rancour and recriminations that followed the collapse of *Uwane*, one relationship flourished. Soon after the final curtain came down the show's leading man moved in to the Blockhouse Bay home of his leading lady. Collins was given a room in the basement beneath the main house and became a familiar face to Kiri's friends. Her closest allies from St Mary's had been two fellow music school students she had met in the choir, Raewyn Blade and Sally Rush. Kiri and Blade in particular were passionate lovers of the great Broadway and Hollywood musicals. At the end of that year they joined Collins in an amateur production of *The Student Prince*. Blade and Kiri would go on the following year to perform in the chorus of a production of the musical *Annie Get Your Gun* at the King's Theatre, starring the English singer Anne Hart in the title role.

Nell and Tom seemed content to have Kiri's boyfriend living under the same roof. 'Nell was great, she had a great sense of humour, although no one dared sit in her chair,' laughed Collins. Kiri's boyfriend grew particularly close to Tom with whom he would go to rugby matches. 'He was the most gentle man I have met in my whole life,' he said.

As he got to know the family better, Vincent sensed Tom and Nell were readying themselves for the inevitable moment when Kiri would fly the nest. 'I think the parents were thinking about what the future held. Her mother worked tirelessly and Tom in his kind way was always there to support,' Collins recalled. 'But they couldn't be there for ever. They were getting older and I think Tom and Nell were anxious that Kiri should meet someone who would look after her.' For much of that year, it was clear that the witty and worldly Collins was considered a candidate for the role.

Judy and Nola, by now back in Auckland and living in a home nearby, warmed to Collins immediately. 'He was a nice guy,' recalled Judy. To Judy it was clear that Collins had been given Nell's stamp of approval. 'Boys always had to be run through the grill,' she said. 'They were always checked out by my grandmother.' The suave Englishman remained a part of the Mitchell Street fixtures and fittings for eighteen months.

Judy recalled how Nell insisted on giving Kiri and her advice on how to behave in relationships with the opposite sex. Her prim and proper pep-talks ranged from the etiquette of the first date to the ending of a romance. One particular piece of wisdom would soon prove useful to Kiri. 'I remember she told us once how you should never two-time anyone,' recalled Judy. 'You got rid of one person and got on with the next.'

A Princess in a Castle

In September 1963 Kiri made the long drive south to Hamilton and the finals of the most prestigious of all New Zealand's singing prizes, the biennial Mobil Song Quest.

From the moment she stepped on to the red carpeted entrance to the city's grandest hotel, the Hamilton, it was as if she had entered a world attuned to her every whim. Upstairs in her room maids placed bouquets of flowers in cut-glass vases and the telephone rang constantly with dinner invitations and interview requests. Downstairs in the lobby staff introduced themselves politely, complimented her on her appearance and ushered her into the chauffeur-driven car permanently at her disposal. It was, she said later, her first taste of being treated like 'a Princess in a castle'. Yet in her heart she still did not quite feel worthy of it all.

Even though her voice had matured into a glorious, rounded mezzo, Sister Mary Leo's lack of praise had done little to ease Kiri's occasional insecurity about the real depth of her talent. At the semi-finals for the Song Quest in Auckland, Kiri had been convinced her renditions of 'Come to the Fair' and 'She is Far From the Land' were disasters. Her performance was recorded for transmission on a special radio show days later when the six finalists would be chosen. She could not bear to listen as her voice filled Nell's bedroom in the early evening broadcast. She had hidden in her own room with pillows over her ears as the names of the six singers chosen to travel to Hamilton were read out. Even the pillows had been unable to drown out the sound of Nell booming 'You're in, you're in', from the top of the stairs.

Kiri and Tom had spent the day of the radio broadcast trying out a new Simca to replace the battered old Standard Ten. The Simca was more expensive than the Triumph Herald Tom had intended buying. That night, with the prospect of a £300 windfall if she won again in the final in Hamilton, the decision was made to go ahead and buy the more expensive car. After listening to a repeat of the show on the radio, Kiri later recalled, she, Tom and Nell drove the Simca up to the Waitakere Ranges overlooking Auckland. 'That night all of the streets were sprinkled with diamonds and gold dust,' Kiri said, looking back sentimentally on the moment.

Kiri was one of two St Mary's girls to be chosen for the final. Both girls knew Sister Mary Leo expected one of her singers to collect the prize for a third consecutive time, following the successes of Mary O'Brien in 1959 and Patricia Price in 1961. Malvina Major's colourful, beautifully enunciated singing style made her one of the immediate favourites, especially in her home town. Yet many saw Kiri as an equally likely winner. Despite her youth and relative inexperience, Kiri had channelled her natural personality into an irresistible stage persona. Her ability to strike an instinctive rapport with her audiences had already won her an under twenty-one aria competition in Te Awamutu that year.

It had been at the less serious engagements that her regular accompanist Susan Smith had watched Kiri's natural appeal begin to blossom. Smith, the daughter of a Blockhouse Bay butcher and another member of the St Mary's musical circle, had known the Te Kanawa family since childhood. In many ways Kiri remained the same carefree girl she had first seen running amok with her niece Judy. 'Kiri never had a confidence problem then. It was all a bit of a game,' said Smith. 'She wasn't singing at these engagements because she was thinking "One day I'm going to be a star", she was just singing because it was a fun thing to do and she did it well. If an audience wanted her to sing another six songs she would. She often told me she'd sing down a coal mine.'

Kiri enjoyed ad-libbing her repertoire. Her carefree attitude only added to the audience's enchantment. Smith recalls how at one concert Kiri had come over to her and whispered in her ear that she was going to sing 'The Laughing Song' from Strauss's *Die Fledermaus*. 'But we haven't rehearsed that. We don't know that,' a panic-stricken Smith whispered back. As the audience watched on the two girls continued their giggled conversation before pressing on with an impromptu version of the song. 'Halfway through the song, where it goes "Most amusing, ah ha ha ha", she really burst out laughing. Kiri had a really infectious, throaty laugh,' Smith recalled. 'She laughed and laughed and laughed, it was real hysterics. The whole hall just erupted. Soon everybody was laughing.'

When she eventually regained her composure Kiri explained that she was laughing at the conversation she had had with her accompanist. 'Then she said, "I'll turn around three times and we'll do it again, and we'll sing it properly this time,"' recalled Smith. The audience sat there simply entranced. 'Those sorts of things were special and the audience would never have forgotten that. They would have thought, quite rightly, "What a lovely, natural girl."'

Kiri drove to Hamilton with Tom, Nell, Judy, Nola and Vincent Collins. As they mixed with the judges and officials from Mobil, the Te Kanawas were introduced to the four male singers chosen to make up the final six competitors. Among them was Rodney Macann, a Christchurch bank clerk whose fine bass voice had been polished in the choir of the Baptist church where his parents were staunch members.

During rehearsals at Hamilton's main music venue, Founders Hall, Macann had been struck by the clarity and power of Kiri's voice. On the night of the competition itself, however, he witnessed something else. 'The initial impact in that hall was just electric,' he recalled. 'She sang a couple of songs and of course she was very beautiful, but it was this desire to communicate with people that she had which was unique. I've never seen anything like it since and I had certainly never seen anything like it at the time.'

For Kiri, however, the tragedy was that her performance was ultimately wasted. The format for the competition involved the judges listening to the performances in a radio booth at the other end of Hamilton. The thunderous applause that accompanied Kiri's bow to the audience was the only clue the panel would have had of the dazzling performance they had missed. The competition's main judge that year was James Robertson, a distinguished English musician working with the New Zealand Opera Company at the time. Back in England he was a favourite to be appointed the first director of the soon-to-be-opened adjunct of the Royal Opera House, the London Opera Centre.

Impressed as he had been by Kiri's creamy voice, Robertson had found Malvina Major the more classical singer at that stage. With the six singers on stage he announced that he had placed Major first with Kiri second. A baritone, Alistair Stokes, was placed third.

As the winners were presented with their cheques and sashes, Kiri could not resist playfully upstaging her rival. Sister Mary Leo's student Diana Stuart had been playing the cello in the orchestra pit. 'I remember Kiri taking a handkerchief from one of the male singers and dabbing her eyes,' she said.

As she watched events in Founders Hall, Stuart had not been surprised at the result. 'The difference in the two was that between a huge canvas that Kiri had and a small but highly colourful canvas which Malvina had,' she said. 'On the night I thought Kiri had wonderful performing potential but the song didn't do her much of a favour.' Crucially, unlike Kiri, Malvina had concentrated on singing to the judges. 'Malvina was not really involved with the audience.'

Even as a distant member of the Sister Mary Leo stable, Stuart knew the shock waves the surprise result would cause at St Mary's. The result was precisely what the two girls' teacher wanted. 'Sister Mary Leo did want Malvina to win because she was ready for it and Kiri wasn't,' she said. Nell Te Kanawa, however, would never accept the result. 'There was rivalry between Kiri and Malvina and I think that was precipitated by Nell. Nell would always ask "Why, why, why?" "Why did somebody beat Kiri?"'

Kiri declared herself overwhelmed with her second place. 'I don't think she was in the least bothered,' said Rodney Macann, who joined Kiri at the post competition party. 'At that stage she was new on the block and was just pleased to be there.' Macann found Kiri even more charming than she had been on the Founders Hall stage. 'She actually said to me afterwards she was disappointed that I hadn't won.'

Nell, Tom, Judy, Nola and Vincent had decided to head back to Auckland that night. In the absence of her family and her boyfriend, Kiri and Macann soon began monopolising each other's company. When the formal celebrations finished the party continued in Kiri's room. She later recalled how her suite was so full she was reduced to sitting in her wardrobe where she sipped lime cordial. For most of the young singers there was no need for anything stronger. 'We were all pretty high. Some of us were away from home for the first time,' said Macann. Eventually Kiri, Macann, Malvina and one or two others slipped away from the celebrations and walked along the moonlit bank of the Waikato River together. Kiri and Macann stayed out under the stars until the small hours.

'It was a beautiful evening, and quite a romantic sort of a thing,' smiled Macann. 'It was about that time that things sort of sprung up a wee bit between Kiri and myself.' Kiri returned to Auckland the following day to sing in another of New Zealand's premier competitions, the John Court Aria in Auckland. Close to exhaustion from the travel, the excitement of the competition and her night with Rodney Macann, she performed Sibelius's 'The Tryst' on automatic pilot and expected little in return for her efforts.

A friend, Ann Gordon, called her at Mitchell Street to tell her she had won with a remarkable mark of ninety-five per cent from the judges. The judge, Clifton Cook, could barely contain his excitement at the discovery. 'If I had had a bouquet I would have laid it at her feet. She is one of the finest New Zealand artists I have heard,' he eulogised.

Kiri's mind was already elsewhere, however. Within days of returning from Hamilton she telephoned Rodney Macann reiterating her invitation for him to come and stay in Auckland. Even in Hamilton Macann's starchy Baptist background had left him unprepared for Kiri's whirlwind openness. She had made no secret of her involvement with Vincent Collins, in whose company Macann had seen her in Hamilton. No sooner had he arrived in Auckland than Kiri matter-of-factly announced his path was now clear. For once Kiri had heeded Nell's advice to the letter. 'I supplanted Vincent Collins,' he said. 'She dropped him when we met.'

Like Collins, Macann was welcomed with open arms at Mitchell Street. However, he switched to a hotel for the rest of his stay. Macann found it difficult to warm to Nell's uninhibited blend of bluster and blind faith. 'Nell was not an easy person. She was determined that nobody would be ahead of Kiri,' he said. Macann was appalled at the manner in which Nell belittled Malvina Major. 'Nell put around all these rumours after Malvina won the Mobil that it had all been agreed beforehand. She said that Malvina came from a much poorer background and needed the money. It was part of her coping with the fact that Malvina had won, which was a huge shock to everyone to be absolutely fair.'

71

As he returned to Christchurch, however, he and Kiri pledged to keep the relationship alive. 'We got very interested in each other, although we were living a long way from each other,' he said. 'We had something quite special. We were both moving towards musical careers and there was this huge passion that we both had for singing.' Kiri's spontaneity could not have presented a starker contrast to the stolidity of Macann's life. Back at work in his bank in Christchurch Macann was amazed when Kiri called out of the blue to announce she was making the thousand-mile journey to see him.

'She just announced that she was coming down to Christchurch and she wanted to see me.' Kiri's parting words to a startled Macann were, 'I expect you to be at the airport and I want a big kiss when I arrive.'

'I was amazingly inhibited when we first met,' he said. 'It was the last thing I'd be seen doing in those days because I was terrified.' Kiri was not Macann's first girlfriend. He too had broken off a relationship in the wake of Hamilton. Yet he had not met a girl remotely like her. 'I didn't find her a terribly sexy person, it was rather an energy. She was very lovable and she had these wonderful eyes. It was energy and eyes that got me.'

After her success in the competition circuit Kiri had begun charming the malleable New Zealand media with equal ease. In one of her first in-depth interviews, with the *Auckland Star* in September 1963, she presented herself as a serious and dedicated young artist. She said she was working hard at learning Maori. 'I'm part Maori so I feel I should learn to speak it properly – it will also help me when I sing Maori songs,' she said. In May and June that year, Kiri had sat through eight lessons in Maori with her friend the mayoress, Thelma Robinson. They were members of a class being used as guinea pigs for a new Maori textbook written by Johnny Waititi. Throughout the interview Kiri did all she could to reassure the Maori trustees of the wisdom of their investment.

Despite her headline grabbing success at that year's competition, Kiri said she was determined to protect her voice. 'If a baby tries to walk too young, then its knees might go wobbly,' she smiled. 'In the same way when a voice is as young as mine it can easily be killed by wrong use.' Her instrument would remain under wraps for another two years while she studied with Sister Mary Leo, she reassured her new following. 'Until I feel I know more about technique and my voice has developed I do not feel competent enough to accept many public engagements,' she told the *Star*.

In reality her blossoming popularity left little room for such sacrifices. Kiri was still the queen of the 'hatches, matches and dispatches' circuit and the uncrowned diva of the dine and dance circuit.

Like the Standard Ten before it Kiri's blue Simca became a familiar sight flying around Auckland. 'She had this sports car and I'd see her roaring off from the church to get to the next wedding. She was a wild girl with a real lead foot in the car,' recalled John Lesnie, one of Auckland's premier society photographers in the 1960s.

Kiri accepted as many engagements as she possibly could – and was capable of cut-throat tactics to ensure her diary remained full. During her early St Mary's days she had been friendly with another of Sister Leo's star singers, Pettine-Ann Croul. 'She came to our home and I would go through songs with her. She wanted me to mark them down for her voice. We had two entirely different voices. I was a coloratura and she started off as a mezzo,' explained Croul, who went on to earn an MBE for her work in teaching singers and today runs her own performing arts college. Relations began to sour when Nell began subjecting Pettine-Ann's mother, Mercia, to her interminable telephone calls. 'She would tell her how Kiri had sung so much better than me, and everyone else. It was always how Kiri had been hard done by,' Croul said.

Nell would call Pettine-Ann too. 'I had calls from Nell asking what I was going to sing at a competition and she'd say I couldn't do such and such because Kiri was going to sing that.' Like Kiri, Pettine-Ann desperately needed extra money to support her singing education. Her father was a clerk of the works at the city council and was unable to afford the lessons she needed. She too had begun to sing at society weddings around Auckland. 'I lost engagements because they would offer to do them for a lower fee. I remember one society wedding where I had quoted £15, which was reasonable for a full day's work as it was, and later they rang back and said Kiri had undercut me by quoting £10.'

Inevitably the tensions strained friendships. 'It became difficult to have a friendship with Kiri and we moved apart.' If Kiri's combination of talent, drive, good looks and influential support was not sufficient cause for jealousy among her rivals, her popularity as a nightclub singer only added to the deepening resentment. New Zealand's stringent drinking laws meant that its pubs still closed at six o'clock in the evening, even on Saturdays. Londoner Bob Sell's Colony Club had become one of the most popular venues for couples in need of an evening's entertainment. 'Women wore little bolero jackets and tucked bottles of gin or scotch under their arms,' said Sell, the owner of a chain of restaurants who had converted an old city centre warehouse into his most successful venture.

Sell would hire three or four acts to entertain his clients from 8 p.m. until 2 a.m. in the morning. At first he had been unsure how Kiri's studied elegance would go down with his raucous regulars. 'She was a good Catholic girl and when she came on stage, the dress came up to her neck and down to her ankles. I used to say to her, "Why don't you shorten the bloody thing?" ' he recalled.

Yet Kiri's combination of talent and charisma conquered even the rowdiest of Saturday night gatherings. 'Everybody was, as I put it politely, Brahms and Liszt, yet they loved her. Absolutely. She had this magic.' Kiri's renditions of favourites from musicals like *West Side Story* and *The Sound of Music* regularly brought the audience to its feet. Soon Sell's other acts refused to follow her on the bill. 'She might have started off as an opening act but she certainly finished as a closing act,' he said. 'I couldn't get anybody to follow her because she killed the audience for everybody else.'

Such was the spell Kiri cast at the club, she could reduce the room to silence with a rendition of a favourite hymn from St Mary's. At first Sell had feared the worst when at 1.30 a.m. one morning Kiri suddenly began singing an unaccompanied version of 'Ave Maria'. 'I thought to myself, "What the hell is she doing? Is she mad or something?" And all of a sudden, you could hear a pin drop.'

From then on the aria, along with 'Oh My Beloved Father', became Kiri's signature song at the Colony. Sell remained close to Kiri long after she had graduated to rather grander establishments. 'I said to her once, "You may think it's tough when you stand up and sing at Covent Garden, but I reckon the toughest audience you ever faced was at the Colony," ' he said.

At the Colony Club Kiri learned to make every member of the audience feel as if she were singing for their personal pleasure. 'She could hold them in the palm of her hand,' Sell remembered. By the end of 1963 it was a feeling Rodney Macann understood better than most. In the months since the Song Quest Kiri's relationship with Macann had intensified. 'She made you feel at times that you were the only person in the world, and it was genuine,' said Macann. 'She gave me lovely presents, sent me endless photos and we wrote a letter a week.'

To the straight-laced Macann, Kiri could be a maddening collection of contradictions. He was in no doubt that she saw her career as her primary concern. 'The career came first from a very early stage and the boys came second. She had a huge determination to succeed, to be the best. She was absolutely single minded,' he said. Yet beneath the outgoing exterior lurked a deep and at times painfully obvious insecurity. Macann would constantly hear Kiri complain about her rivals. 'One of the things that characterised her in the early days was she needed a rival. She had to have somebody she could set her sights on.'

The placid Macann found her occasionally poisonous outbursts hard to handle. 'She would veer between very lovable and hugely frustrating. She was enormously giving as a person but she could be pretty difficult at times. She'd drive you crazy because she'd do very silly things, which I found incredibly irritating being a more sedate person. Things like saying something so bitchy and stupid about another singer that it was totally unnecessary because she was so much better than that person anyway.' Kiri was still demonstrating this thinly disguised disdain for her rivals many years later. She once described herself as blossoming 'like a petunia in an onion patch'.

It was hardly difficult to detect the influence that had produced her straight-talking manner. 'My grandmother would say exactly what she thought, and if you didn't like it, too bad. She wasn't going to back down,' said Judy Evans-Hita.

'It may have been something that was instilled by Nell,' agreed Macann. 'Kiri was not a devious person in any sense, and therefore if she was thinking something that was a bit bitchy she would say it.' Macann wondered whether Kiri had the dedication to go with her mother's overpowering ambition. 'She was lackadaisical because she had a limited intellectual ability to grasp some things and therefore she got very, very bored,' he said. 'She just had a lot of energy and found the discipline of concentrating on musical things very frustrating, I think.' As he watched her perform, however, her talent was unmistakable. 'Kiri is not someone like Elisabeth Schwarzkopf who has a very intellectual approach to music. There was something within her which was innately musical, and it's not something that you can train somebody to have. You had the voice, you had the personality which communicates itself, but then you had this amazing musical gift as well. She was also a person, at that time, really without inhibition on stage. It was just there.' Soon that gift was winning a wider audience.

In the two years since she had performed 'The Nun's Chorus' for Tony Vercoe, Kiri had begun to wonder whether she would ever be given an opportunity to become a recording star. By the winter of 1964, however, the wait was over. Vercoe contacted Nell with the news that he was finally ready to record her daughter for the first time.

Vercoe had resisted the temptation to release a choral work first. His instincts told him that the key to Kiri's success lay in her Maori heritage. 'It was just a feeling I had. I felt the time was right perhaps for someone of a Maori background to emerge,' said Vercoe. Yet the *Uwane* débâcle had reinforced Vercoe's hunch that the New Zealand public were not quite ready for musical marriages between European and Maori music. Kiri's first careful steps should be taken down the traditional path, he felt sure. Vercoe understood the Maori sensibility better than most. He had been a close friend of Inia Te Wiata while studying opera and theatre at London's Royal College of Music after World War II. He commissioned the composer Ashley Heenan to arrange five traditional Maori love songs. On 5 June 1964, in Wellington, Kiri, a rising Maori tenor Hohepa Mutu and an instrumental quartet began recording work on the songs: 'Hokihoki tonu mai', 'Hine e hine', 'Tahi nei teru kino', 'Haere re e hoa ma' and 'E rere ra te Matangi'. Mutu recalls the studio sessions as 'quite arduous' and with good reason, according to Tony Vercoe.

To the experienced and perfectionist Vercoe, Kiri was the rawest of raw recruits. It fell to him to instil the effervescent twenty-year-old with a touch of discipline. 'She had other interests and she was very outgoing,' he recalled. 'She was part of a group of young girls and wanted to be out doing things with them.

'I was a bit of a restricting influence on her. I would demand all

76

her time while she was going to be recording and that was a bit hard for her.' Punctuality was never his new protégée's strong suit. 'We would get into the studio at nine o'clock and she mightn't be on time. I would be as tough as I felt I needed to be,' he said. Vercoe also insisted on perfectionism in the studio. 'She had the voice and a fairly natural musical feeling. But she was not so wonderful note for note. Instead of a crotchet, a dot and a quaver, she might put in two crotchets and say, "Oh, that's near enough."'

Inevitably Kiri's devil-may-care attitude drew Vercoe's fire at times. 'I wouldn't say they were fights, but I insisted on it being right. Not in an unpleasant way, but for a while she kicked against it,' he added.

Vercoe would not be the first nor the last to detect a streak of laziness in Kiri. It is something she has freely admitted to herself, over and over again. 'She didn't like hard work very much. And of course it is hard work in a recording studio. You can get away with singing a song in public and people think it's marvellous, but put that on tape and all the flaws show up,' he said. 'The number of takes we would have to do irritated her slightly.'

In truth, Kiri was actually working hard to moderate her behaviour in Vercoe's presence. Don Hutchings, Vercoe's sales manager at Kiwi Records, got to know the high-spirited soloist socially as well as professionally. He saw her temper her behaviour in front of one of New Zealand's leading musical lights. 'For Kiri, Tony was a stepping stone to something very bright and he was someone to be respected,' he said. 'With others, she would use all sorts of language but she was very demure around Tony.'

Ultimately, the balance of power would shift and Vercoe would pay the price for his exacting standards. He, more than anyone, saw the likely scenario from the start. 'There was a future, and I saw that to some extent I had to prepare her, not just for the recording, but for whatever might follow. She was going to need this discipline and I was the mug who was going to have to impose it initially,' he said philosophically.

Kiri's impatience was understandable enough. By now her growing reputation had begun to draw interest from a variety of quarters. As she had taken her first tentative steps into the recording studio, she had already made her debut as a screen actress. The producer and director John O'Shea had raised the £67,000 he would need to make his film *Runaway* himself. Before she had completed her recording work with Vercoe, he contracted Kiri to play the female lead, a young girl who undertakes an illicit affair with an older man. Nell agreed on a fee of £20 for the week's work.

Kiri had been suggested for the part by O'Shea's male lead, Colin Broadley. Broadley had known her through his Auckland record store The Loft and his television show, In The Groove. Around Auckland, Broadley knew Kiri had earned herself a reputation as something of a wild, party-loving spirit. As O'Shea prepared for a three-week shoot near Opononi, towards the northernmost tip of the North Island, she remained a paragon of decorum, a good Catholic girl of whom Sister Mary Leo could be proud.

Kiri insisted on one crucial change to the original script. 'She wouldn't get into bed with the leading actor,' recalled O'Shea. Broadley had originally raised no objections to the love scene in which he and Kiri would end up in bed together. He was surprised but equally easy about removing the scene to spare Kiri's blushes. 'I don't remember the discussion, but I know we decided it wasn't appropriate for whatever reason,' he said.

Kiri was acutely conscious of her figure, and her small bust in particular. Her unsubtle nickname among the St Mary's set was 'tiny tits'. Her preference for long dresses had been instilled at St Mary's but she also had a dislike of her chunky calves. Even though she remained fully clothed, Kiri became increasingly nervous as the camera scrutinised her face and figure.

Her key scene came when Broadley proposed marriage to her character. 'When I proposed she pointed to a hedgehog and said, "No, no. I'm like a hedgehog. You can't get close to me. I'll roll up and you'll get prickled,"' recalled Broadley. When it came to shooting the scene, however, Kiri's nerves had become so severe she had broken out in a livid rash. 'Kiri was nervous about acting. It was all new to her and she did very well but the stress contributed to her getting eczema.'

O'Shea and his make-up team tried all they could to mask Kiri's problem. 'We held a willow branch in front of her to put shadows over her face to disguise the eczema, but it didn't work,' said Broadley.

When, months later, Kiri, accompanied by her niece Judy, turned up for the première at New Zealand's Civic Theatre cinema in Queen Street, she found the scene had been cut from the final film. 'It had to be left out, which was a pity because there was a later scene with me about running over a hedgehog which then made no sense,' said Broadley. It was a common enough reaction within the cinema.

'At the time it was wonderful because Kiri was in it, but looking back now it was probably the most dreadful movie I've ever seen in my life,' recalled Judy. 'At one point I turned to her and asked what she thought. She just said "Boring!"'

The film failed to set the box office alight, leaving O'Shea to spend the next fourteen years paying off the debts he had run up during its production. Once more Kiri was left ruing her journey down what, at the time at least, seemed like another creative cul-de-sac.

The disappointments of her short-lived movie career were mercifully brief. In the winter of 1964 'Maori Love Duets' was released as a 7-inch EP (extended play) record, complete with a painfully posed photograph of Kiri and Mutu dressed in traditional Maori costume. The record sold well, particularly among souvenir-hunting tourists. As his investment provided an early return, Tony Vercoe activated his original idea of recording 'The Nun's Chorus'.

Shortly before Christmas in 1964, Sister Mary Leo and the St Mary's Choral Group, with Lenora Owsley at the organ, repeated the performance that had caught his imagination two years earlier. Vercoe had asked Sister Mary Leo to suggest a B-side that Kiri could sing as well. Her suggestion, Handel's 'Let the Bright Seraphim', would become one of the more significant pieces of music in Kiri's life. The recording at St Patrick's Cathedral was overseen by Don Hutchings.

Hutchings's official title of sales manager failed to do justice to his role within Kiwi Records. In reality he was Tony Vercoe's right-hand man, a combination of record plugger, A&R man and all-round Mr Fixit. Based in Auckland rather than Wellington, Hutchings was a familiar face to many of the St Mary's Choir. As the popular, not to mention handsome host of his own television show, '21 And Out', he was one of Auckland's more eligible bachelors. He had dated most of Sister Mary Leo's starlets. Hutchings had also got to know Kiri and Nell Te Kanawa during the making of the 'Maori Love Duets'. He had formed a particularly good relationship with Nell, who had, he recalled, 'taken an instant liking to me'.

As far as Hutchings was concerned, Nell was far from the ogre he had heard described by the girls of St Mary's. 'She was a stage door mum, but an innocent,' he said. 'She knew she had a diamond in Kiri and all she wanted to do was make sure no one mucked it up for her.'

During Kiri's lengthy spells in the recording studio, Nell had begun to confide in Hutchings. She left him in no doubt as to the dominant item on her agenda. 'Because Kiri was not academically brilliant, mum felt that the greatest protection she could offer her was a marriage to someone who had managerial skills, entrepreneurial skills, all of those things,' he said.

Nell and Hutchings shared the same earthy sense of humour. 'One of the great jokes of the time was Mum's list of "10 who might be",' he recalled. Nell and Hutchings would often discuss the roster of eligible bachelors she kept scribbled in her diary. 'I think I got on to it for about a week. I disappeared off it again because I was courting a beautiful woman from Wellington.'

As he got to know Nell, Hutchings was left in no doubt that her primary target for a husband for Kiri was Peter Webb, an English television producer. 'Mum saw Peter Webb as the number one for a long time,' said Hutchings. Kiri had begun seeing Webb in Auckland while still continuing her long-distance love affair with Rodney Macann. He was only one of several difficulties slowly driving Kiri and Macann apart, however.

Macann's relationship with Kiri had always been fraught with problems. In the year or so since the Mobil Song Quest, he had come to see that he and she were polar opposites.

'At that stage the Baptists were very anti-drink, anti-gambling. I was a very inhibited Baptist and she was a much looser Catholic. That was a big barrier in those days,' he said. Macann's worries had been exacerbated by a speech he had heard by a leading churchman of the day on the subject of inter-denominational marriages. 'He said that basically it was very difficult.' To Macann, already a deeply religious young man, the speech precipitated a crisis. 'As far as I was concerned, at any rate, this was a turning point in our relationship. I was just being aware of all the prejudice you had to deal with in those days.'

Macann had seen other girls in Christchurch. 'It was pretty embarrassing one time because I was going out with someone else and Kiri just arrived and said she wanted to stay,' he recalled. At the same time Kiri had made no secret of the fact she was also close to Peter Webb. 'I was the one out of town and he was the one in town for a while.'

Matters came to a head in Wellington when Kiri travelled down to spend time with him at Macann's aunt's house. Macann's relationship with Kiri had never progressed to sex. 'There was none of that in our relationship,' he confirmed. Instead they spent the hours through till dawn discussing their chances of a life together. 'We talked right through the night and decided that, although we were pretty smitten with each other, ultimately our relationship had no future,' he said. 'Things moved on to a more Platonic footing after that.'

If somewhere in her mind Kiri had hoped this would clear the way for Webb, however, she was soon disappointed. Kiri had met Webb while making one of her, by now, regular appearances on television, on the station AKTV2. Like Vincent Collins before him, the blond producer had moved into the basement at Mitchell Street. To those who were close to Kiri, however, it was already clear that the relationship was not progressing as she wanted.

Kiri's need for affection was acute. 'I'm the kind of person who needs to be loved,' she admitted a few years later.

For those who knew her well it was not difficult to detect where the source of her vulnerability lay. 'She was very insecure, mainly because she didn't know her background,' said Hannah Tatana. 'She was very aware of the fact that she was adopted and did not know where her roots lay.'

To her friends at the time it seemed clear the men in her life were expected to fill the void. 'Her men had to prove that they loved her. The relationship itself wasn't enough,' said Susan Smith. 'It was a case of her saying, "If you really loved me, you'd do this, this and this."' For much of the time that Smith and Kiri performed together, Susan had a steady boyfriend called Ronald, an Auckland pharmacist. 'Very often he brought me presents, make-up and stuff that he could get through work, and he also loved writing poetry, so I got poems,' she recalled. 'She couldn't bear that, because Peter never did that for her.'

Susan realised the extent of Kiri's insecurity when she suddenly began showing off presents she had been supposedly bought by her boyfriend. 'She started buying things and sending the bill to Peter. She ordered anything, even a gown from Colin Cole,' she said. 'Then she could say, "Look what Peter bought me." It was extraordinary, it all sounds so petty, but that's what she did.'

The sense that Kiri's neediness was driving Webb away was inescapable. Kiri's problems were helped little by the fact that, at Mitchell Street, Webb had to contend with Nell's demanding personality too. 'He was under both of their thumbs,' said Susan Smith. Inevitably his patience ran out. 'I think in the end Peter just thought, "I can't do this any more." '

At a wedding early in 1965 Webb's eye fell on a pretty young ballet dancer turned television presenter called Nerida Nicholls, sitting in the sunshine in a rocking chair. When he approached to introduce himself she smiled coolly and said, 'I think you're supposed to fall at my feet.' He then did precisely that.

'I think we pretty much decided there and then we were going to be together,' said Nicholls. When Nicholls suggested they move on from the party together Webb had admitted his involvement with Kiri, with whom he had a date later that night.

'We were keen to go on somewhere but he told me he was supposed to take Kiri out somewhere,' said Nicholls. 'I told him to call her, and if she was in then he'd have to go, but if she was out we should carry on. We drove off in Peter's Mini, stopped at a phone box and he rang. She was out. We went to a jazz club called the Montmartre and two weeks later we were engaged.'

The first the Te Kanawas knew of the unfolding drama was when Webb suddenly announced he was moving out from Mitchell Street. 'Peter just upped and packed his bags one day,' recalled Susan Smith. 'There was no discussion, he just left, whoosh, end of scene.' For Kiri the humiliation was made even worse when she turned up at a party she knew Webb was attending soon after his sudden departure. She arrived to find him there with Nerida Nicholls and her parents.

'We had decided that afternoon to get engaged. We hadn't even told my parents and then suddenly we were up in front of everyone saying, "We've got something to tell you all . . ." ' recalled Nicholls. Amid the passion of her new romance, Nicholls had learned little about Webb's now discarded girlfriend. 'I didn't know how serious it had been with Peter and her, otherwise maybe I would have taken off. Peter didn't tell me much about it,' she said. The party offered her her first glimpse of the girl she had now replaced in Peter Webb's affections. Amid the excitement of the celebrations that followed her announcement, she can recall nothing of Kiri's reaction.

Webb and Nicholls were married in Auckland in June, three months later, with Kiri in attendance. The two girls were to meet frequently, appearing together on television. The subject of Peter Webb, however, was never mentioned.

Instead Kiri reserved her displays of anger for friends like Susan Smith. 'I don't know if she particularly wanted Peter for being Peter,' said Smith. 'But she wanted a partner and she always felt that she offered so much no one would dare let her go.'

Now is the Hour

In March 1965, around 300 people packed the Eden Roskill War Memorial Hall in suburban Auckland to celebrate Kiri's twenty-first birthday. The black tie gathering amounted to a 'Who's Who' of New Zealand's musical talent. Radiant in a shimmering, low cut dress, her hair piled high in a voguish French twist, it was a new, sophisticated Kiri who monopolised the limelight.

Nell had done all she could to make the party one of the social events of the year. Resourceful as ever, she had persuaded Cliff and Billie Trillo, owners of Auckland's premier restaurant Trillo's, to provide free catering. The mayor and mayoress of Auckland were present, as was John Waititi and a representative of the Maori King Koroki. The numbers were also swollen by people who barely knew Nell, let alone her daughter. Susan Smith recalls turning up with an aunt and uncle who had never even met Kiri.

A few formal presentations ensured the Auckland press had their photo opportunities. Kiri was presented with a greenstone pendant by the King's representative. Johnny Waititi delivered a speech and an elaborate scroll addressed to 'Dearest Kiri' on behalf of the Maori Education Foundation.

In the years since he first offered support, Kiri had become increasingly close to the quiet, dignified Waititi. In 'Uncle John', as she often called him, she saw a younger version of her father. Yet it was Tom who provided the emotional highpoint of the evening with a powerful and heartfelt speech. 'We didn't know he had it in him,' said Don Hutchings, who like everyone else in the hall had grown used to Tom's almost invisible presence.

In the time he had known the Te Kanawas, Hutchings had been

touched by the quiet devotion Tom had shown his daughter. 'He would sit there and look at her and not say a word. His eyes would twinkle and you knew what was going through his head,' he said.

For the first time he expressed those feelings publicly. 'He called her his jewel and said this was the magic part of his life because he had been gifted both the time with her and Kiri the person. Kiri was his gift from whoever was looking after him.' Kiri's tears were not the only ones shed during Tom's oration. 'It was a magnificent presentation, a very moving address,' said Hutchings.

Kiri, naturally, was asked to sing at one point in the evening. Her performance opened at least one guest's eyes to the true extent of the talents she had, as yet, barely tapped. 'Everyone was asking Kiri to sing and eventually she said "Alright.",' remembered Neil McGough, her old conductor from *Uwane*. 'Everything went quiet and she sang a lovely aria. As Kiri came to this great, glorious moment in the aria and everyone had their mouths open, Lou Clauson and Simon Mehana, the popular radio comedy duo, tiptoed in the door and stood quietly at the back. She stopped in mid-phrase and shouted "Hello Lou! Hello Simon! Be with you in a minute", and then finished the song.'

McGough was stunned by Kiri's seeming disconnection from her singing. 'It was one of the most amazing things. You'd think that to sing like that would have taken complete focus. But she could have been thinking about whether there was enough pâté in the fridge at home,' he recalled.

For McGough, at least, it was the most revelatory moment of the night. 'That really made me realise Kiri had no idea how good she was.'

Kiri ended the musical interlude by inviting Lou and Simon to join her on the stage. Her hammy performances with the duo had become hugely popular at Mitchell Street. 'The three of them would have us all in tears of laughter singing "There's a Hole in My Bucket, Dear Liza",' recalled Kiri's niece Judy Evans-Hita. That night, however, they played it straight, linking arms with Kiri for an emotional version of the Maori favourite, 'Pokarekare ana'.

It was clear that Kiri was having the time of her life. 'She had an absolute ball that night,' remembered Hutchings, who had done more than most to contribute to her high spirits. By now the best-selling success of 'The Nun's Chorus' was transforming Kiri into a new musical star.

Hutchings had begun the job of chivvying and charming 'The Nun's Chorus' on to the New Zealand airwaves early in the year. At first the record's sales had been sluggish. Over a friendly beer Hutchings had persuaded Les Andrews, an old friend of Tony Vercoe and the host of the country's most popular radio show, on the ZB station, to inject a little interest with a few, contrived early plays. Hutchings smiled at the memory. 'Obviously, we dreamed up a few requests. It was marketing ploy people are not reluctant to use today either.'

In its two-hour Sunday lunchtime slot before New Zealand's television service cranked into life at 3 p.m., Andrews's show drew an audience any Royal wedding or cup final would be proud of. It may only be a small exaggeration to say that, with the whole country listening, the gift of stardom was his to confer. 'It was the most popular programme in the country. It had the market to itself,' Hutchings recalled.

After three weeks of false solicitations Andrews suddenly began to receive genuine requests for the record. 'There was a trickle at first and then an avalanche,' recalled Hutchings. Soon 'The Nun's Chorus' became the most requested record Les Andrews ever had. It was perhaps an indication of New Zealand's curious musical taste that the only record that remotely rivalled it was Spike Milligan's quirky 'Bad Jelly the Witch'.

Kiri's popularity was soon being translated into record sales. 'It was in the hit parade for weeks,' said Hutchings's colleague Tony Vercoe. 'It was extraordinary.' As he travelled around New Zealand capitalising on the momentum now under way, Hutchings heard the same response when he asked people's opinions of her. Kiri's striking looks and simple, girl-next-door appeal were as important as the quality and clarity of her singing. 'She looked the part and that was a great help,' he said. Most significant of all, however, she was presented as a Maori. Kiwi Records had hit on a nerve.

'It was a method of marketing. If you'd said, "Here's Pettine-Ann Croul and she sings opera", they'd say, "Well, so what?",' said Don Hutchings. 'The argument then was, "Maoris can't sing opera; they don't have the discipline either with the voice or personally." Here was a Maori who could sing opera, and that was how we got the door open.'

Vercoe's colleagues at Reeds wasted no time in capitalising on the breakthrough. Their PR assault had soon put Kiri's face on the cover of magazines and newspapers across the country. As she became a favourite on television shows like '21 And Out', the bandwagon became unstoppable. Suddenly she was a star. The marketing drive focused on Kiri's Maori credentials. She was willing to play along with the image, dressing up in the piu piu and other items of ceremonial wear. The approach impressed both sections of the New Zealand community: to the Europeans she was something of an oddity, a Maori capable of singing music hitherto unheard by a mass audience; to the Maori she was a beautiful and aspirational role model, the most enviable ambassador their people had yet produced.

Yet Kiri's sudden transformation into a Maori singer seemed curious to those who had known her in her formative days. After she had won the Tauranga Aria in May 1964, Susan Smith had seen Nell's unease at a newspaper headline. 'It said something like "Maori girl wins aria" and Mrs Te Kanawa was furious,' she said. 'Kiri had no interest in Maoridom at all. She didn't even like to be called Maori.' This was, in many respects, far from surprising given Tom's distance from his roots and the racism Kiri had encountered as a child. Nell's instincts would also have been alive to the danger of Kiri being stuck with a patronising 'Maori-girl-does-good' label that might limit her future scope.

There was, however, no mistaking the realignment under way. St Mary's other Maori star, Hannah Tatana, had helped Kiri out by lending her traditional clothing for her concerts. 'I had a feathered cloak which she borrowed a couple of times because she didn't have that sort of thing,' she said. 'It's a heritage Kiri didn't have.'

If Susan Smith was surprised at Kiri's sudden embracing of the Maori cause, she was dismayed by the transformation in her personality which she witnessed in the period before and after her breakthrough into pop stardom. Smith's first glimpse of the shift in Kiri's attitude had come back at the Tauranga Aria the previous year. As well as working with Kiri, Smith had happily accompanied other St Mary's girls who approached her for her help. In the run-up to the contest Kiri had asked Smith that, in return for a generous fee, she play exclusively for her. 'She said, "I want you to play just for me." I said, "Yes, no problem."'

Days before the competition another soloist rang asking Smith to play at Tauranga. 'I said I couldn't do that, at which point she went back to Sister Mary Leo and all hell let loose,' recalled Smith. 'It had never happened before. It caused a lot of strife.'

Kiri's request merely reflected the new determination she had begun to demonstrate. In the week before Tauranga, she and Smith closeted themselves away at a boarding house. Smith duly played exclusively for Kiri, who, dressed in a shimmering white robe, won the major aria competition and its first prize. Smith remembers 'bursting into tears of sheer relief' at the result, while Kiri accepted what was her biggest triumph to date with perfect poise. Kiri gave her pianist a giant panda bear as a token of her thanks. 'She was very generous to me,' said Smith, who also received jewellery from Kiri.

For Smith, however, Tauranga marked a watershed. 'From being a very happy, natural, outgoing girl, she became a very scheming, conniving person.'

To Smith, it seemed Kiri was now willing to use whatever means necessary to succeed. Among her most enthusiastic supporters was a contact Nell had cultivated, H. J. 'Bill' Barrett, boss of the ASB bank in Auckland. At a private function attended by Barrett and his wife Shirley, Smith was taken aback when Kiri set off on a story that was clearly less than the truth. 'I was a bit shocked and horrified, and I remember sitting with her in the car afterwards and I said, "You can't do that, Kiri, that's not right." And she just said, "Look, I know I use him, but if he is too silly to see, who cares?" I thought that was an appalling attitude, really.'

In Smith's eyes, it was clear that stardom had transformed Kiri when she accompanied Kiri and the Maori tenor Michael McGifford to sing at a raffle evening. In a spirit of fun, McGifford had followed a duet with Kiri with a solo serenade of Smith at the piano. When it came to drawing the evening raffle tickets, Smith rather than Kiri had been asked to select the winning numbers. Smith was stunned at Kiri's reaction in the car on the way home. 'I was told that was not the way to behave. I wasn't to overshadow her,' she said. 'You and I would not take a bit of notice of that, but Kiri did. She was furious.'

The end of Kiri's relationship with Peter Webb represented the final turning point as far as Smith was concerned. It had been soon afterwards, in the car as they travelled from St Mary's towards Blockhouse Bay one day, that Kiri broke the news that she no longer required her services. Smith understood Kiri's need for male attention better than most. 'Afterwards, she didn't want to be seen with me,' she said. 'She felt she needed to be seen with a male accompanist-cum-escort.' Smith played her final engagements with Kiri soon after the twenty-first birthday party. At the time she was deeply wounded by the rejection. Eventually, however, Smith looked back on her relationship with Kiri with a mixture of philosophy and fondness. 'I always feel I got the best of Kiri,' she said.

Kiri's male accompanist materialised soon enough. A few weeks after her twenty-first Kiri was introduced to a talented Auckland pianist, Brooke Monks. Monks's father Raymond had built the family business, David Elman Shoes, into a thriving enterprise. Brooke's mother Berys, known as Billie, was a prominent figure in Auckland's polite society and a keen supporter of arts and music charities in particular. It had been Billie Monks who engineered the introduction. When Kiri suggested her twenty-one-year-old son become her accompanist at her non-competitive engagements he accepted immediately.

Brooke's love of the piano had been instilled in him by Billie. His playing style was flamboyant, full of florid embellishments and unashamedly romantic touches. On the dine 'n' dance circuit he soon added a new dimension to Kiri's performances, his flowing melodies combining perfectly with his partner's voice on *West Side Story* numbers like 'Maria' and 'Tonight' in particular. The looks of affection the duo were soon exchanging across the piano only added to the romantic effect.

According to Brooke it took little time for their musical partnership to develop into something more serious. 'It didn't really take very long. We were doing a lot together and it started to change certainly in the first couple of months,' he recalled.

Brooke was drawn to Kiri's down-to-earth beauty. 'She was a very attractive girl and a great personality. She had no airs and graces,' he recalled. 'We were very much alike in lots of ways. We both enjoyed life and we were both musical and there was a great opportunity to do things.' Soon Brooke and Kiri began using their performances as a way of escaping Auckland. 'We never turned things down. We did so much.' Country hotels at Rotorua and Wairaki and, in particular, near the hot pools at Waiwera, became their regular romantic hideaways. On occasions they also hid away at the Te Kanawa cabin at Hatepe.

Often they would travel with Kiri's fellow Maoris, Hannah Tatana and Michael McGifford. Kiri's career had already begun to eclipse Tatana's. To her older partner's eyes, however, her success was a success for the Maori population as a whole.

As she travelled the country with McGifford, Kiri and Brooke, Tatana was unsure of her friend's new beau. Yet there was no disguising the passion Kiri felt for her flamboyant pianist. The trio had become particular favourites of the Maori Queen, Te-Ata-i-rangi-kaahu. After singing at her home at Ngaruawahia one weekend evening, Tatana and McGifford discovered their colleagues had left before them. As they arrived at the steamed-up car the reason for their early departure was all too apparent. 'Obviously something had been going on in the back of the car while we were in the hall,' said Tatana.

Invariably Kiri and Brooke would sit in the front of the car while Hannah and Michael sat in the back. For years afterwards McGifford teased Tatana about her naivety. As Brooke drove, Kiri's head would disappear out of sight at the front of the car. 'What on earth is she doing down there?' her older, but less worldly-wise colleague would ask McGifford. He would sit in embarrassed silence. 'She was clearly besotted by him,' Tatana said.

As ever, Kiri wasted little time in introducing Brooke to Nell and Tom. After 'running him through the grill', Nell was impressed by what she saw. 'My grandmother always liked Brooke,' recalls Judy Evans-Hita. 'He always made time to chat. He was a nice guy.'

Nell's feelings for Brooke were reciprocated. 'She was a real old battleaxe but we got on very well,' recalled Brooke. 'I think she was on my side right the way through the relationship.'

Brooke's parents were less enamoured with the idea of the couple. Raymond Monks expected his son to follow his hard-working example. Instead Brooke's devotion to his university studies in German and Italian waned alarmingly as his romance with Kiri deepened. Having brokered the friendship in the first place, Billie Monks was even more horrified at the turn of events. 'I suppose my parents thought that things moved a bit fast for them,' Brooke said. Kiri eventually charmed Raymond Monks into accepting her but Billie remained cool. 'In those days my mother was looking after her son like Nell looked after Kiri, protecting their own.'

Brooke's mother certainly shared Nell's resourcefulness. When she heard talk of Kiri's involvement with Vincent Collins, she invited the English actor's former fiancée to visit her for a chat. Beverley Jordan had put the horrors of *Uwane* behind her and was now happily married. 'She asked if I would go around and have a cup of coffee because she wanted to know about Kiri and her involvement with Vincent,' she remembered. 'She wanted to know whether she could trust her son with Kiri. I can't remember what was said,' she added diplomatically.

Billie Monks's frostiness towards Kiri was almost certainly a matter of class. To members of Auckland's polite society, Kiri was the daughter of a pushy provincial *arriviste*, a crude country bumpkin with ideas above her station. Nell's reputation was, by now, beginning to embarrass even Kiri. 'She could not help be aware of her mother's background. I think she was insecure about it,' said Hannah Tatana.

In the years since her daughter's breakthrough Nell's unsubtle blend of aggression and avarice had offended many within the musical establishment. Kiri had begun singing on the radio show hosted by Ossie Cheesman, New Zealand's top musical arranger and bandleader at the time. 'Ossie kept getting Nell on the phone demanding more money. After a while he got fed up and stopped using Kiri,' said one of Cheesman's closest friends, Neil McGough.

McGough had heard a similar story repeated all over the city. 'Radio had a strict regime of set fees for singers. If it was three pounds ten, Nell would demand seven pounds for Kiri.' For a time Kiri's voice had become a rarity on radio. 'Nell simply pushed too hard. She thought the world had to be changed to suit Kiri, but there were plenty of other good singers,' McGough said.

Her granddaughter Judy has many happy memories of Nell Te Kanawa, but even she admits, 'Nana's life was spent polishing Kiri. Anyone or anything that got in the way of that goal would be removed. Perhaps I would do the same, but that's the way it was.'

Even the unerringly honest Tony Vercoe, renowned all over New Zealand as a man whose verbal contracts were watertight, found her an awkward customer. 'She was not as objective as one would have hoped,' he admitted. 'I do not want to be criticising those who are no longer with us, but it could have been difficult at times, I will say that. Nell had her likes and dislikes and they were fairly well defined. If people got across her then that was a bit unfortunate for them.'

As the winter of 1965 wore on, however, Vercoe did all he could to remain on the right side of Nell. Kiri had become the hottest property his company had come across in years. In the truest traditions of showbusiness, the success of 'The Nun's Chorus' had caught everyone by surprise. 'There was a bit of publicity, but there was no payola, no palm greasing, no big hype, nothing like that,' remembered Vercoe. 'It wasn't like the Spice Girls, although I suppose there are similarities. It was much more spontaneous. A big wave started to roll and grew and grew, naturally, somehow. The whole country got behind her. It was extraordinary.'

Kiwi Records wasted no time in putting Kiri back in the recording studio. In June 1965, Vercoe oversaw another EP, 'My Lady Greensleeves', a collection of English folk songs arranged by Dorothea Franchi. Public appearances and signings, television appearances and radio recitals were organised to coincide with its release. As the record became another hit, Kiri's popularity as a performer grew even more. 'Young girls thought she was a terrific symbol for them. They wanted to sing like her and look like her,' said Vercoe. 'Little old ladies saw her as the ideal daughter or granddaughter.'

As she mingled with her new following, Kiri's common touch only added to her appeal. Vercoe hadn't encountered a phenomenon like it. 'She spoke to all these people naturally – and they responded. She was so nice,' he said. 'I think she was our princess here in those days. Our Diana.'

By now Kiri had been invited to sing with some of the country's best-known personalities. No one was more impressed with her ability as a live performer than Les Andrews, the DJ who had done so much to make her a star. Before becoming a DJ, Andrews had studied with Inia Te Wiata and Tony Vercoe in London. He remained an accomplished singer and began performing with Kiri at the Mission Bay Club in Auckland and elsewhere around the North Island. Andrews was soon witnessing Kiri's gift for manipulating an audience at first hand. He and Kiri arrived for a concert in Rotorua to discover the audience sitting far from the stage. 'It was big barn of a place and there was a big crowd there, but they were all around the fringes or sitting up in the stands, not on the floor in front of the stage,' he said. 'That was no good.'

Andrews's attempts to move the audience failed miserably. 'Then Kiri came on she talked to them. She more or less said, "If you don't come down I won't sing for you", but in a nice way. And they did. They gathered around her and she put on a wonderful performance. She could make a simple song sound important and individual to each person who was hearing it.'

Andrews, too, had seen nothing like it. 'She could walk into a room and because she was, still is, a beautiful woman, she could command attention. She had a regal sort of bearing,' he said.

As Kiri's popularity soared, it was left to Sister Mary Leo to apply the brakes. It had been Kiri's teacher who had stymied plans for her to take on the role of Clara in the New Zealand Opera Company's production of *Porgy and Bess* that summer. The production was to star the Maori hero Inia Te Wiata.

'I tried very hard to book her. She was magic – the whole country was crazy about her,' said the company's general manager, Ulric Williams. 'But she was still with Sister Mary Leo and like all her pupils she said, "Well, you'll have to ask Sister." Sister would not release her. She said it was too much. In the end a girl called Isobel Cowan did it and when she got ill halfway through I asked Kiri again. She told me to go back to Sister and she still wouldn't let her do it.'

Around the same time Sister Mary Leo engineered one of the most significant musical collaborations of Kiri's early career.

Even by the occasionally plain-speaking standards of the musical world, Barbara Brown was not a woman to mince her words. Her opinion of her alma mater, St Mary's College, and its collection of debutante divas, for instance, was as damning and direct then as it is today. 'It wasn't a stable of singers. It was a stable of aspiring young vocal socialites, mass-produced by this terrible woman Sister Mary Leo.' As Barbara Connelly, Brown had left Auckland to complete her piano studies at London's Guildhall School of Music in the mid-1950s. She had returned married with a daughter to set up her own private piano-teaching business.

Brown's disdain for 'trivial' music ran even deeper than Sister Mary Leo's. Back in Auckland she had grown disillusioned by the number of lacklustre St Mary's pupils who approached her to act as an accompanist. 'I was a purist. I had finished my studies in Europe and come back to be faced with all these silly, young vocal twits,' she recalled. 'They were the loveliest girls, and they worked hard, but they just didn't have it, although they were pumped up to believe they did.'

Midway through 1965, however, Brown could not resist the intriguing invitation her former teacher made in a telephone call from her Ponsonby sanctum. 'I have someone I would like you to meet.'

Brown travelled to St Mary's with low expectations and at first found herself alone with Sister Mary Leo. 'I went into her room and there was someone practising in the adjacent room. She told me she wanted me to work with the voice next door and that the ultimate goal was to take her to Australia for the Sun Aria,' recalled Brown. Mystified at first, Brown was soon impressed by the glorious, rounded sounds emerging through the walls. When Kiri walked in to greet her minutes later the reasoning behind Sister Mary Leo's bizarre behaviour fell into place. 'In strolled Kiri, and Sister introduced me to this very lazy girl. I saw the Maori blood immediately,' Brown said.

As a part-Maori herself, Brown immediately understood why she had been called in. Sister Mary Leo wanted Kiri to concentrate her efforts on the year's major singing contests, the Mobil Song Quest in New Zealand and the Melbourne and Sydney Sun Aria competitions in Australia. With the most demanding year of her singing career ahead of her, Sister Mary Leo knew Kiri needed the most demanding accompanist possible.

'The shrewd old devil had the whole thing mapped out when she made the phone call,' Brown smiled. Her influence in the coming months would be crucial. Brown had heard the stories of Nell's inflated ideas and bullying manner. 'She was like Cleopatra, lying in bed with her big old telephone. She sort of ruled the world from her bed.' Brown's suspicions about Nell's more fanciful ideas were quickly confirmed. 'Nell used to tell everyone that she was related to Arthur Sullivan. It was all lies. I think Kiri might have been the one who told me that.'

In truth, few appreciated the role Nell had played better. 'Kiri needed a person like that, someone that would push her to work,' Brown said. In June and July of 1965, Brown began doing precisely that herself.

The year's first target was the Mobil Song Quest, held this time in

Dunedin on the South Island. Rodney Macann was once more among the finalists. Despite their break up he and Kiri remained Platonic pals. With the South Island in the grip of winter and her system already suffering the effects of a mild cold, Kiri this time avoided the official receptions and parties. The night before the contest itself she warded off the cold by laying in her bed fully clothed. On stage the following night she wore a pair of slacks beneath her elegant dress.

As Kiri sang the 'Habanera' from *Carmen* and 'Do not go, my love', the crowd-pleasing touches of Hamilton, two years earlier, were discarded as she concentrated on singing to the microphone and the judges, once more installed in a radio booth elsewhere in the city. This time Kiri's performance was technically close to flawless. As the judges announced the prizes in reverse order, the home audience loudly applauded their decision to place the Dunedin mezzo Patricia Payne second. The reaction was just as generous when Kiri was placed first.

In the weeks that followed, her £300 first prize was soon eaten away. Kiri had entered her name for both the Sydney and Melbourne Sun Aria competitions, the highest profile and by far the most lucrative contests in Australasia. Nell, Barbara Brown and Sister Mary Leo had already begun planning a busy itinerary in which Kiri would combine rehearsals for her main targets with entries into other categories within the Sydney and Melbourne Eisteddfodau. Like the New Zealand competitions, the Australian contests were spread out over an intense week of competition in a number of different classes.

Sister Mary Leo had insisted that Kiri and her other entry in the Australian competitions, Lynne Cantlon, also compete as a duet in one contest, in Ballarat. As she and Kiri arrived in Australia, Barbara's worst suspicions were confirmed. Distracted by Brooke and her burgeoning recording career, Kiri admitted she had not learned one of her chosen arias, the famous 'Vissi d'arte', or 'Love and Music', aria from *Tosca*. Brown had to organise having a recording sent over from New Zealand.

Kiri and Barbara stayed with friends of the Brown family in Sydney. Sister Mary Leo remained at a convent where Kiri practised. The trio, along with Lynne Cantlon, had arrived to find Sydney was in the grip of a September heat wave. As the thermometer edged towards the ninety-seven degrees mark, relations between Kiri and Cantlon frequently boiled over.

The two were due to sing a duet from *Madam Butterfly*. Kiri had incensed Cantlon by insisting that the roles were reversed so that she could sing the more prominent part. The fur flew again when Barbara Brown rang to chastise Cantlon for failing to turn up for a rehearsal. A furious Cantlon blamed Kiri for not having told her it was taking place. Eventually, Cantlon's mother Una had to send another accompanist, David Harper, across to Australia.

Relations between the two girls hit rock bottom during one of the minor competitions in the run-up to the two main Aria contests. Cantlon had travelled to Australia with a silver Arctic fox stole, given to her by her mother. Backstage with the other singers Cantlon had been overcome with nerves and had visited the ladies' room. She returned to the sight of Kiri in full flight on stage, draped in the fur herself.

Barbara Brown lets slip a sigh at the memory of the duo's confrontations. 'Sister Mary Leo should never have sent those two away together.'

Nell and Tom splashed out on tickets on board the new trans-Tasman, Air New Zealand service to Sydney and joined the audience for the first of the main competitions at the city's Town Hall. Kiri's performance of 'Senza Mamma' from Puccini's convent opera *Suor Angelica* and an aria from Weber's *Oberon* were greeted with cheers and stamping of the feet from the audience. Kiri's melodramatic delivery of the Puccini piece in which she had crouched theatrically on her knees to deliver the climactic notes provided, to most eyes, the highlight of the evening. Curt Prerauer, the critic of the sponsoring newspaper, *The Sydney Sun*, was convinced she had 'the best voice and showed by far the greatest artistry and acting ability'. Yet the judges awarded first prize to a young Russian emigré Serge Baigildin, placing Kiri joint second with baritone Tom McDonnell. The decision brought cries of 'She should have won it' from the stalls where, as well as Nell and Tom, Kiri's friends Lou and Simon had watched the contest.

While Barbara Brown slipped home, Kiri headed out on the town with Lou and Simon. 'We went to a Returned Services League club and played on the poker machines. It was a chance for Kiri to let her hair down and we had a good time. I don't remember talking about the Aria – I think we all decided to just put that behind us,' said Clauson.

The depth of Kiri's disappointment was visible in the days that followed, however.

'Kiri was absolutely devastated,' said Barbara Brown. Such was her anger at the decision she remained bitter at Baigildin for years, particularly as he was, in her words, 'never heard of again'. Baigildin did in fact have a long career in Australia.

A quarter of a century later, Kiri reflected, 'I don't think I was a very good loser that night . . . Maybe it was the first time I decided that defeat did not sit very well on my shoulders, and I think it's been like that ever since. It's rather degrading, to be second.'

Barbara Brown saw things differently, however. 'It was the best thing that could have happened to her.'

Brown and a deflated Kiri flew to Melbourne where they were to rehearse at another convent, this time in the suburb of Ballarat. Brown used their fortnight together to drive Kiri to the outer limits. 'I was terrible. I really laid the law down to her,' she said. 'We got up at dawn and every day was planned in advance.' Brown coached Kiri in the two arias they and Sister Leo had chosen for the Melbourne Sun Aria, 'Leise, leise' from Weber's *Der Freischütz* and the problematic 'Vissi d'arte'. Kiri had been so stung by her failure, however, that she responded in a manner Brown had barely thought possible.

'I put a challenge to her and she worked like a Trojan. She did everything I told her to do. It was just unbelievable. That showed me that she could really work when she wanted to.' Brown only relaxed the regime once, taking Kiri for an evening at the cinema.

The letter Kiri received one morning in Ballarat provided an even more powerful source of motivation. She had left New Zealand for Australia knowing Johnny Waititi had been admitted to hospital. For months he had complained of pains in his back. Kiri would often drive him around in her car because the vibrations eased his agony. He had telephoned her days before she left asking her to visit him, but she hadn't been able to fit in the time to do so. When she opened the letter Kiri burst into tears. On 30 September, Waititi had died of leukaemia at the age of thirty-nine. In the run up to the Melbourne contest Kiri talked constantly about Waititi.

As the competitions got under way, Kiri began to win in each class she competed in. While in Ballarat, Kiri and Lynne Cantlon had patched up their differences sufficiently to take the $100 Grand Opera

Duet prize. It was the latest addition to a growing list of prizes Kiri was collecting in Australia, among them the Nellie Melba Cup and the Star of Opera prize. Kiri confessed to Brown that her performances were all directed at her departed friend. 'She was just so sad and full of emotion,' Brown recalled. 'She would sing things for him and win them for him.'

Countless triumphs and many years later, Kiri herself said of the Sun Aria, 'The only thing I have ever really wanted in my entire life was to win that. I wanted it more than anything I have ever wanted.'

By the time of the contest itself, Tom and Nell had flown back to Auckland where they gathered around the Mitchell Street radio set in the bedroom with Judy, Nola and other friends and family. Kiri's rendition of both her arias was immaculate. 'Each contestant had a number. When they read the results they gave the number before the name,' recalled Judy. 'As soon as they gave the number I was leaping up and down and shouting "Kiri's won, Kiri's won."' She was promptly told to shut up until the name was confirmed.

Kiri's reaction was equally disbelieving. Clutching a large bouquet, she had closed her eyes as the results were read out. When the judge announced, 'The first prize goes to New Zealand – to Miss Kiri Te Kanawa,' the flowers were dropped to the floor as her hands covered her tear-soaked face. As she accepted the silver laurel leaf trophy Kiri was invited to say a few words to the audience.

'Thank you, Melbourne. Thank you, Australia, for letting the prize go to New Zealand,' she said, her voice faltering. Unprepared and unsure what to say next, she simply held her hands to her chest. With one final piece of operatic melodrama she gushed, 'My heart – it is beating.'

When Pettine-Ann Croul and Malvina Major had won the Sydney and Melbourne Sun Arias a year earlier, their wins had been greeted with a few minor headlines. In contrast, Kiri returned to New Zealand a national heroine. Such was her mass appeal that a crowd of several hundred people gathered at Whenuapai Airport to welcome her and Barbara Brown off their Air New Zealand flight. A group of Maori dancers, including a reluctant Kay Rowbottom, under orders from Nell via Nola, performed a ceremonial haka on the tarmac as they walked down the steps. Kiri and Brown posed for photographs and faced an impromptu press conference as they made their way into the terminal.

To the New Zealand press she was now 'the undisputed queen of song'. To mark the win, a special celebration concert was held at Auckland Town Hall where she sang Bach and Puccini to a packed house. 'Hers is a magnificent vocal instrument which could carry her as far as she wishes to go,' wrote the *Auckland Star*'s critic the next morning. The paper, like many others in New Zealand, now felt the time was right for Kiri to travel to Europe to further her career. Almost immediately a public campaign to raise funds for Kiri was born.

As ever, no one understood the reality of Kiri's situation better than Sister Mary Leo. According to a much-repeated anecdote, the nun brought Kiri down to earth by greeting her with the phrase, 'Well, Miss Te Kanawa, back to work again.' In reality, her wily old mentor had already begun thinking about how Kiri should now broaden her horizons. Kiri had returned to Auckland with more than £2,000 in prize money. Sister Mary Leo at least had already formed a clear opinion of how that money – and the hundreds more already being pledged – should now be spent.

For more than a decade Sister Mary Leo had been haunted by the spectre of Mina Foley, previously her most gifted pupil, who had fallen spectacularly from grace.

Foley had gone to Italy in 1951 alone, with no guardian, speaking no Italian, and boarded with a family who spoke no English and did little to help her. She wasted away, describing her physique as that of an eleven-year-old girl, before suffering a calamitous breakdown. Brought back to New Zealand, she had been intermittently hospitalised and became a long-term patient after a woman was wounded in a stabbing incident at Auckland's premier department store, Smith and Caughey.

A distraught Sister Mary Leo knew that her role had to be much more than a mere voice coach. She had herself spent long hours sitting at her fallen protégée's bedside. 'Sister Mary Leo had huge guilt about Mina Foley because she pushed her,' said Diana Stuart, who had visited Foley at her private psychiatric hospital. Attempts had been made to rehabilitate the fallen prodigy. According to Judy, Kiri stood in the wings at a small comeback concert, ready to sing over Foley's voice if she ran into difficulties. Foley survived the concert but retreated into herself again afterwards.

To those who knew Sister Mary Leo, it was clear that in Kiri she saw her opportunity to make amends. 'Mina would have been New Zealand's Callas, there's no doubt about it,' said Don Hutchings. 'She had it all – except, of course, the temperament to be able to cope with it. By Kiri's time, Sister realised that Mina was never going to make the comeback and this was the replacement. But this was the one that was going to make it.'

Three decades later, when she returned to St Mary's in 1996 to open the new music school building, Kiri was taken aback on hearing Foley's voice played through loudspeakers. 'I thought to myself, My God, I had forgotten her for a moment, and how dare I? She would have done extremely well if she had been given the opportunities that I have been given,' she said. Kiri would never publicly cite one single inspiration for her career. Foley, however, was as powerful an influence as any.

Sister Mary Leo had acted to further Kiri's career even before the Sun Aria victory, according to the version of events she herself gave later. Earlier that same year she had written a letter to James Robertson at the London Opera Centre. She concluded the letter, 'Kiri is a very attractive girl in every way. She is childlike and easily guided, she has a striking personality, good looks and figure. Her parents have left the decision to me as to where to send her. It has been a toss-up between England and America.'

It had not been the first letter Robertson had received regarding Kiri. Weeks before Sister Mary Leo's note, he had been contacted by Dobbs Franks, the Artistic and Musical Director of the New Zealand Opera Company, where Robertson had worked two years earlier. Franks had auditioned Kiri but felt she needed 'professional advice as to the proper pursuit of training for her career as a singer'. Robertson remembered Kiri from the 1963 Mobil Song Quest in Hamilton and wrote back to Sister Mary Leo within days of receiving her letter. He told her about Franks's recommendation and concluded: 'She thus has three strong recommendations – yours, his and mine – so that we shall accept her without audition.'

Kiri went through the formality of sending off an application form and was quickly informed that there would be a place available for her the next March. Money, it was soon apparent, would not be a problem. In the wake of her success in Melbourne Kiri had already attracted donations from the most unlikely quarters. In late October, only days after the Sun Aria win, a visiting Australian theatrical promoter, Harry Wren, had announced that he intended donating part of the proceeds from his latest show, featuring an African dance troupe, to Kiri. 'If I can help get this lass to the top it will be a privilege,' said Wren, whose gift eventually amounted to £900.

As the publicity surrounding Kiri continued, the country's Queen Elizabeth II Arts Council found itself fielding phone calls from irate New Zealanders angry at their lack of support for Kiri. 'We have never had an application for assistance from Miss Te Kanawa before the council,' Allan Highet, chairman of the organisation's public relations committee explained before adding, 'But if she did make an application I, for one, would give it favourable consideration.' Nell ensured the application was soon in the post.

Kiri's mother was, naturally, in the vanguard of the movement now under way. In mid-November, as the campaign to raise funds for Kiri's trip to Europe built up steam, Nell announced the formation of a new trust. 'Kiri has received a lot of gifts to help her studies, and I felt the money should be put into a trust and only paid out at the discretion of the trustees,' Nell told the press. While her old ally Bill Barrett was appointed chairman, two prominent musical figures – Charles Nalden, Professor of Music at Auckland University, and Peter Godfrey, conductor of the Symphonia of Auckland – were named as his fellow trustees.

As the storm broke around her, however, Kiri was left feeling confused. She was as excited as anyone at the prospect of travelling to London. At the same time she knew she would be leaving at a point when her life in New Zealand was just shaping up. Could she really turn her back on friends, family and her newfound stardom to gamble all in a strange and daunting new country? The greatest dilemma, however, was Brooke Monks. Brooke had remained her accompanist around Auckland. Professionally they made the perfect couple. A recording of 'You'll Never Walk Alone' provided the couple and Kiwi Records with another hit that year. Yet on a personal level there were those who wondered at the match.

Monks conformed to a male stereotype Kiri herself would recognise

101

at the time. 'The New Zealander expects – and gets – women running after him,' she said.

On her travels around New Zealand with the couple, Hannah Tatana had been dismayed by Brooke's treatment of Kiri. 'He was callous towards her, always telling her to shut up. She thought he was the best thing in the world. She really did love him,' she said.

'It was sort of raw sex appeal,' said Don Hutchings. 'He was very macho and quiet. He understood what he had and he knew how to use it. There was an aura of masculinity that I think she grabbed on to.'

Brooke's strong silent act appealed hugely to one part of Kiri's personality, but it left the other, more vulnerable part of her feeling despair. 'Brooke had a very nonchalant air about everything,' recalled Barbara Brown. 'He wouldn't ring up when he said he would or write a letter when he said he would. It was always rather casual and she would be very upset about it.'

In the vacuum, Kiri could not stop herself accepting the devotion of others. In Wellington she had secretly begun seeing a cousin of the Hanson brothers, Donald Perry, whom she had met through her old friends. During increasingly frequent visits to Wellington she had begun staying at the Perry home where she had grown close to Donald, heir to his father's engineering company. Perry's relationship with Kiri never progressed beyond a little clandestine 'kissing and cuddling'. He soon realised he would never be a serious rival to Brooke.

If Kiri was faced with a dilemma on the eve of her departure to England, so too was her boyfriend. 'I knew that Kiri was going to be something big and I always told her that,' Brooke said. 'She thought she had a very good chance because she was winning everything and she had a lot of backing from the media. But she knew she would have to work very hard.'

While Kiri's future was suddenly filled with new possibilities, Brooke's life was mapped out for him. He was committed to first finishing university and his stint of compulsory military training, then to taking over the reins of the family business. A move away from New Zealand to England was, he reasoned, unthinkable.

As people speculated over the direction their relationship would now take, Brooke found himself the subject of vitriol. As far as some were concerned, nothing nor anyone should now prevent Kiri from fulfilling her destiny. The suggestion that he was a millstone around Kiri's neck angered Brooke deeply. 'Some people felt that I was ruining things for her and that hurt me at the time because I would never have dreamed of holding her back for anything.'

As the couple talked about their future, the starkly contrasting attitudes of their parents did little to lift the confusion. Brooke still lived in his parents' large house in the affluent Mount Eden suburb, but was spending much of his time at Mitchell Street where Nell had turned a blind eye to the flexible sleeping arrangements. 'Ma was a very open person, but she didn't like Tom to know because he was much more reserved,' said Brooke. Yet his own parents were still vehemently against any headlong rush into marriage with Kiri. 'They were concerned that I should just throw everything away on a sort of romantic fling, even though they knew we were serious.'

Five days before Christmas 1965, the Queen Elizabeth II Arts Council revealed details of how it would spend its £20,000 grant fund the following year. The biggest award of all had been allocated to Kiri, who was to be given £2,500 to fund three years' study at the London Opera Centre. The award was only part of an ever-increasing flow of money now heading Kiri's way. 'Mrs Te Kanawa actually told news bulletins and reporters that Kiri could not go overseas unless people gave more. They accepted money from old age pensioners who gave them two or three dollars,' said Susan Smith.

Kiri's five per cent royalty on her record sales by now amounted to a significant income on its own. On the day after the grant was announced, she boosted her future income by returning to the recording studio. It was hard to escape the impression that Kiwi Records was making the most of its asset before she fled from its grip. As well as an EP, *Kiri Sings The Sound of Music*, featuring 'Climb Ev'ry Mountain' and 'My Favourite Things', she also laid down the music for a complete LP. The album, titled simply *Kiri*, contained the best of the EP plus songs from *West Side Story*, 'Summertime' from *Porgy and Bess*, 'Habanera' and even 'Havah Nagilah'. Both sessions were conducted by Ossie Cheesman.

The Te Kanawa coffers were swelled even further by a series of six farewell concerts organised during her final weeks in New Zealand. While Kiri's farewell in Wellington raised the most, around £2,000, each of the four others raised around £1,000 each.

Her final farewell concert in Auckland had to be shared by her fellow St Mary's pupil Pettine-Ann Croul, who was attempting to raise money for her studies in America. Relations between the former friends had become even more fraught. At one stage Pettine-Ann Croul and her father, incensed by comments they believed Kiri had made, drove to St Mary's. 'We spoke with Kiri on our own, outside the school,' remembered Croul. 'My father invited her to sit in the car and we sat and talked. He said he was upset about some things that were being said, and I carried on and said what I was fed up with.'

Their confrontation left Kiri unfazed. 'She just brushed it off, from what I remember. I don't think we were expecting her to buckle, but we were hoping to give her a bit of a jolt and it might just stop her. Dad did say that if it ever came up again there would be a lawyers' letter.'

Reluctantly the two girls shared the stage for a concert in which they raised £1,000 each. If that money seemed a small fortune to Croul, who was working as a schoolteacher, it was a fraction of Kiri's rapidly growing fund. At the time Kiri's total fund was generally agreed to have been of the order of £5,000. 'Oh, I think it was rather more than that,' said her former trustee Charles Nalden. Given that, on top of her £2,500 grant from the QEII Arts Council, Kiri's six concerts earned at least another £6,000 to £7,000 and that she already had the £2,000 she had won at the Sun Aria, her record royalties and the unspecified donations to her trust fund, it is safe to guess she was ready to leave the country having earned, or been given, as much as £12,000 in just a few months. At the time in Auckland that would have bought her two comfortably-sized family homes.

Predictably, Kiri's cash-starved contemporaries protested at the generosity. Even members of the Maori community were expressing their distaste at the money flowing in Kiri's direction. 'Mrs Te Kanawa was a manager extraordinaire. She really got her hooks into the Maori thing and used it to help Kiri get away, and also for financial funding. I wasn't happy about it,' said Hannah Tatana. 'Kiri has fulfilled all that was invested in her. But like all the others I'm sore about the opportunities she had. I could have done with some help too.'

Although Tatana continued to sing professionally her musical career was eventually overtaken by the commitments of marriage and children.

Barbara Brown also felt a sense of injustice as she watched the Maori community succumb to Nell Te Kanawa. 'They emptied their bank account for Kiri and it was most unfair. There were others who should have shared that money.'

Kiri's benefactors had no qualms about their generosity, however. 'It was the right thing to do,' said John Thompson, then artistic director of the New Zealand Opera Company, whose glowing reference attached to Kiri's application to the Arts Council helped sway any doubts. 'A lot of people complained about that, but this was the big one and they had to make sure it worked. There was a lot of mumbling about it from the have-nots, who couldn't bear it any longer, but relative to her talents the others were mediocre prospects, I thought. I felt the way the world was, you needed every cent you could get.'

By the end even Kiri was almost embarrassed by the size of her grants. She later called it 'much more than any student deserved'. She would feel much the same way about the proprietorial claims New Zealanders seemed entitled to make on 'Our Kiri' for years afterwards.

Yet, as her departure for London drew closer, Kiri remained unsure whether she really wanted to leave her home and the love of Brooke Monks. With their time together running out their relationship was at its most passionate. During the Christmas holiday Nell had innocently suggested that Donald Perry should act as a chaperone while Kiri and Brooke travelled from Taupo to Auckland for a meeting with the musical impresario Henry Rudolph, who, like a host of other stars, had agreed to perform for free at one of Kiri's final concerts. Perry and Kiri's clandestine 'kissing and cuddling' relationship had cooled. Perry recalled the six-hour round trip drive as one of the most uncomfortable of his youth.

'It was a bit awkward. I was sort of the odd man out,' he said. Kiri and Brooke made sure they engineered time alone together during the trip. Despite Nell's attempts to keep tabs on them, Kiri and Brooke were determined to make the most of their final days together.

Don Hutchings had been given the job of recording one of the farewell concerts for release in the New Year. On two or three occasions he had to cover up for Kiri's absence when Nell telephoned. 'I'd say, "I can't interrupt her at the moment, love, she's rehearsing."' I'd put the phone down and immediately ring a number that I'd been given. I'd tell Kiri, "You'd better ring your mother, dear." I don't know where they went but they had a little hidey-hole they used to go to.'

In the two years or so since he had first met her, Kiri had matured from a flighty teenager into a mature young woman. 'She was typical of young, Catholic women, once they escape the nun's habit,' he said. 'They fall in love with at least the first twelve men they meet.' As far as Hutchings was concerned, Kiri regarded Brooke as the great love of her life. 'I'd never known her to be so absolutely and completely head over heels.'

As far as many were concerned, however, Kiri's offer of a place in London was a lifeline she simply had to accept. Barbara Brown was in no doubt that Kiri needed to break away from Sister Mary Leo's benign but ultimately limited musical control. 'Sister Mary Leo churned out these coloratura type voices. Regardless of the sort of voice that the student turned up with, it was pushed higher and higher until it became a coloratura or very high soprano,' said Brown. 'If Kiri had stayed the voice would have been ruined. It was a big, heavy voice and needed a lot more training than these thin soprano voices.'

Don Hutchings, too, sensed that Kiri needed to free herself from the premature stardom with which she had been conferred. Early in 1966 the *Kiri* LP became an instant best-seller. Kirimania ensured that 10,000 copies flew out of the shops, a remarkable achievement at the time. As he accompanied Kiri at signings and public appearances, Hutchings would watch Kiri cast her eyes down at the floor and smile sheepishly. 'It was a Diana look,' he said. She lacked the poise of a Princess, however. 'She was slightly gawky, anyway. She used to bump into things.'

He saw the dilemma Kiwi Records' new star was now wrestling with. 'She didn't want it really,' he said.

'I'm sorry for people who are idolised. When it happened to me I was very young and I did not think I was worthy of it,' Kiri said a couple of years later in London.

A few days before Kiri's departure, in February 1966, Hutchings arrived at the main farewell party at Mitchell Street with his wife, Clyde Scott, another Colony Club singer, and Colin Broadley and his wife. Kiwi Records' gauche young discovery was now surrounded by the sort of media machinery the Beatles had brought with them on their chaotic visit to Auckland that year. A PR man greeted Hutchings and his party. 'Then he whispered reverently, "If we're very, very good, Kiri will sing for us." I thought, "Shit, I hope not." Not because I didn't like her voice, but because I was sure she wouldn't want to go through that at all. It was a farewell party for her mates.' Inside, Kiri duly took to the stage to sing.

Neil McGough saw the poignant reality of her situation when he found himself sharing a quiet moment with Kiri at the party. As Kiri lay on her bed with her dog Whisky alongside her, McGough talked to the young woman he had cast in *Uwane* four years earlier. He recalled the comment Kiri had made in the programme and her promise that she would not join the musical exodus from New Zealand.

When McGough asked her whether she was looking forward to her journey Kiri's reply was immediate. 'She said, "No, I'd rather stay and get married." I think she meant that quite sincerely. She would have been quite happy to marry Brooke, I think.'

For all her achievements since her unpromising stage debut, Kiri remained deeply unsure of the true magnitude of her talent. 'Kiri actually believed in her ability less than anyone else. I think she felt like some other Maori performers, "How can I, this little girl from Gisborne, be as good as all these people are trying to say?"' he said.

She and McGough knew her destiny had been placed in the hands of others, however. 'She had won competitions and been fêted. She couldn't just turn round and say, "I don't want to go." There was also pressure from the Maoris, leaning on her to represent them, and mum, towering over her. She was trapped.'

Kiri spent her final days in New Zealand with Brooke. Still on compulsory military training, he had been stationed at a camp three hours away from Auckland. When he was eventually given leave, he and Kiri headed for their favourite spot at the Waiwera hot pools. 'It was difficult,' he said with a weak smile. By the end of their time, however, they had promised to stay faithful to each other while events unfolded. By the time they were back in Auckland they were happy to let people say they were unofficially engaged. A professional portrait of Kiri taken at her farewell party clearly shows an elaborate gold band on the ring finger of her left hand. The ring had been in place in Wellington for her final concert, but had somehow escaped the attention of the press.

On 8 February, loaded down with all her household belongings, 'pots and pans and six or eight trunks full of clothes', Kiri boarded the liner *Australis* with Nell. In return for an undertaking that she would sing at a concert during the four-week voyage, the liner's owners, Chandris Lines, had given them free passages to England.

Tom and finally Brooke were the last to see them up the gangplank. A tearful Kiri had assured her boyfriend she would think of him whenever she looked at Brooke the teddy bear he had given her after the Mobil Song Quest triumph.

Afterwards the two men joined the crowd of several hundred that had gathered on the quayside to wish her a final farewell. Waving as they sang, the gathering broke into the traditional Kiwi farewell. As the haunting strains of 'Now Is The Hour' drifted towards the upper decks, the guide ropes were loosened and the liner eased itself away from its moorings. The sky was filled with streamers as Kiri looked down to see the figures of Tom, Brooke and the rest waving. The tears flowed freely as her friends and family, Auckland and finally New Zealand faded inexorably into the distance.

During the voyage Kiri's emotions were a predictable confusion of sadness and excitement. As the long journey began in earnest, there were times when she felt dreadfully alone once more. 'For the second time in my life I had been pulled from my little community,' she said later. Yet she could console herself with the knowledge that she had left New Zealand a heroine. 'I felt as if I had this sort of cocoon over me, that no one would really harm me and that I was blessed by them all.'

PART TWO

'In art, as in love, instinct is enough.'

Anatole France, *Le Jardin d'Epicure*, 1895

Apprentice Diva

On the morning of Monday, 7 March 1966, the insistent rhythm of the *Australis*'s engines began to thicken and slow. The ship's 13,000-mile journey was coming to an end. As the liner eased its way towards Southampton harbour, Kiri's first impressions of the landscape now looming into view were sorely disappointing. She had left New Zealand at the height of a glorious summer. In comparison, she later recalled, England on the cusp of spring looked 'black and dead'.

The scene was no less depressing as she and Nell disembarked. In stark contrast to Auckland, the quayside was filled with grim and unfamiliar faces. Struggling with the weight of their baggage, Kiri and Nell were too tired to face the evening's boat train to London's Waterloo Station. They booked two seats on a bus the next morning instead.

Their change of plans induced a mild panic at the New Zealand High Commission. The High Commissioner, Sir Thomas Macdonald, had dispatched his former private secretary, Jeremy Commons, to meet them at Waterloo late on Monday. Commons, a keen music follower, had recently been installed in the new post of cultural affairs officer. He had scanned the station concourse for the face he had seen countless times in the newspapers sent from home. He made two, fruitless and frustrating visits to Waterloo before learning they had caught the bus instead.

Kiri and Nell had taken up a vacant flat in well-heeled Richmond-upon-Thames in west London, which friends from New Zealand had offered them. Within days of settling in, Kiri and Nell travelled east into central London and presented themselves at New Zealand House on the Haymarket, armed with letters from their high-profile patrons back in Auckland.

'To be perfectly frank, they were a slight embarrassment,' remembered Commons. 'Her supporters back in New Zealand were suggesting that the High Commissioner should launch her in England and give her a concert at New Zealand House.' Macdonald's passions did not run far beyond rugby and cricket. Besides, as far as he was concerned, Kiri's appearance in England merited no more fanfare than that of other recent arrivals like Malvina Major and Marie Landis, both of whom had also enrolled at the London Opera Centre. 'His reaction, quite rightly I think at that stage, was that she was coming to be a student and we should let her be a student first and then he would get in behind and help launch her,' said Commons. 'He thought that it would have been premature.'

The foyer of the London Opera Centre on east London's Commercial Road was dominated by giant blow-up photographs of Wagnerian heroes and heroines, melodramatic scenes from great Covent Garden productions of *Das Rheingold* and *Götterdämmerung*, *Parsifal* and *The Flying Dutchman*. For all their grandeur, however, the images could do little to disguise the Centre's humble origins. Until the Centre had taken over the lease two years earlier, the building had been the local fleapit, the Troxy Cinema. Kiri wasted little time in forming her opinion of the building. 'I hated it then and still do to this day,' she said two decades later, shivering still at the prospect of returning there, which she still had to for Royal Opera rehearsals. 'It's a revolting place.' The Troxy would always symbolise the dour, depressing reality of the new life she faced in the spring of 1966.

Kiri could not deny that what the Troxy lacked in grace it more than made up for in gravitas. The main cinema auditorium – a stage area overlooked by stalls and a circle – had been converted into a venue fit for the Centre's regular public performances. It provided the sort of 'big space' students would need to grow used to. Elsewhere, every nook and cranny had been taken up by departments of the Opera Centre or its parent company half a dozen miles away in Covent Garden, the Royal Opera. The rear of the stage area had been taken over by the Covent Garden paint shop. In the bowels of the building, a rabbit warren of windowless rooms served as rehearsal and class-rooms. The circle foyer, overlooking the Commercial Road, served as a multi-purpose meeting and teaching area. At the very top of the building, the old projection rooms had become offices for James Robertson and the Centre's director of studies, John Kentish. To Kiri, it seemed a daunting environment.

Kiri had arrived in England midway through the first term of the new year. She took James Robertson's advice and spent a fortnight simply acclimatising herself to the place before beginning her studies in earnest after Easter, at the beginning of the summer term.

Her hopes of blending into the background for the first two weeks were quickly disappointed. The Centre's small clique of 'colonials' had provided plenty of advance publicity. At least she lived up to expectations. 'I was there on the day she arrived,' recalled Sheila Thomas, a repetiteur who taught Kiri her earliest roles at the Centre. 'She came in and she had this charisma and charm about her. All the other students said, "Who's that?". She was a star.'

Her reduction to rank and file membership of the student body was soon under way, however. The Centre's vocal students worked in small groups. Kiri was allocated to a class of half a dozen or so colleagues with whom she would be expected to study and sing excerpts from well-known operas and prepare a part for the public performance held at the end of each term, usually under the baton of James Robertson. Kiri was initially given two pieces sung by Dorabella in Mozart's *Così fan tutte* and Vera Boronel in Menotti's *The Consul*. In preparation for the term's public performance, she also began studying the 'trouser role' of the Marquis de Bluettes in Delibes's *Le Roi l'a dit* (*The King has said it*).

She soon discovered this was just the beginning of the work she would have to tackle. Students were also schooled in all elements of opera, from languages, to acting and movement, even fencing. In the months ahead lay long hours devoted to German and Italian diction and musical composition. Kiri took one look at her study schedule then put it to one side. It would be three months before she could bring herself to pick it up again. Instead Kiri concentrated on displaying her innate abilities. Here, at least, she could make an immediate impact on the Centre's starchy, serious-minded teachers, the 'warlords', as she was soon referring to them.

'Her voice was stunning,' Sheila Thomas remembered.

'She had a marvellous sense of movement and a great ability to

113

move on stage,' said John Kentish, who taught movement classes with another colleague, John Rolla.

Kiri's natural, sportswoman's eye also helped her excel in fencing classes. Her well-honed stagecraft was equally impressive from the beginning. 'Some of the students looked as if they were close to bursting into tears the first time. Kiri didn't. She had that stage animal in her,' said James Robertson's Viennese widow, Osvalda, then the Centre's librarian. 'The minute she walked on stage it was a different world, and that was it. Some have it and some never acquire it. She had it.'

It was a view quickly echoed by the man already considered New Zealand's finest musical export, the bass Donald – now Sir Donald – McIntyre. McIntyre, recognised as one of the great Wagnerians of his time, had inevitably heard of Kiri's pop star status back home. He met her soon after her arrival, as he readied himself for his move from Sadler's Wells to Covent Garden the following year. 'I already knew she was someone to be reckoned with. She looked as though she had it,' he said. 'She was a beautiful looking girl and she was a lot of fun. She had a very good sense of humour.'

Since his earliest days at the Guildhall School of Music, McIntyre's self-belief had been total. He and another student, Benjamin Luxon, had surveyed the school's canteen early on and come to the same conclusion. 'There were hundreds of singers there. We looked at each other and said, "We're the only two here who'll make it", and that's exactly what happened. We didn't really doubt it.' He quickly detected the same steely inner confidence in Kiri. 'I have a feeling that she just expected it all to happen for her.'

Kiri and McIntyre chatted regularly, yet Kiri felt no need to draw on her more experienced colleague's wisdom. 'We talked about the set up of agents and that sort of thing. She didn't seek advice and I wasn't particularly interested in giving it,' he said. 'Really you have to decide all these things yourself. People who are always seeking advice, I don't think it helps them a great deal.'

For all her natural gifts, however, it soon became apparent that Kiri was lacking in many of the fundamental requirements for a London Opera Centre student. Even to those homegrown talents nurtured in provincial music colleges and opera companies, the Opera Centre regime was an intimidating one. Students were expected to work from

10 a.m. to 5 p.m. on normal days, and until 11 p.m. or midnight on performance nights. Lateness and absenteeism were dealt with severely.

'There was an incredible work ethic. It was a hothouse,' said the English soprano Teresa Cahill, who joined a term after Kiri.

To an unnatural student like Kiri, the demands soon proved overwhelming. 'I'd been cocooned in New Zealand and taught by people who'd never really been over here and seen how it was done,' she said later. 'They tried hard to give me some sort of discipline but I was very undisciplined – I still am a slightly undisciplined person.'

Kiri's most immediate problem was purely geographical. The flat in Richmond, on the other side of London to the Centre, was impractical. A move to a spacious, basement flat in Forest Hill, south-east London, reduced the journey time a little but Kiri was still faced with an hour or more on trains, tubes and buses to get to the Commercial Road. Eventually Kiri used some of her savings to buy a large Ford Zodiac, but even that proved incapable of getting her to the Centre on time every day. In the classroom, too, she began to struggle. Languages had never come naturally to Kiri and she was soon falling behind her classmates. The technical side of her music education was also proving a problem. Even Sister Mary Leo had despaired at Kiri's sight-reading ability. Her knowledge of opera was little better. As a girl in Auckland she had been taken by Nell to *The Magic Flute* and *Don Giovanni*. Neither had made much impression on her. Her personal tastes remained rooted in Rodgers and Hammerstein rather than Rossini and Handel. She struggled to get to grips with her first singing roles.

Throughout her life Kiri has displayed an occasionally bewildering duality. 'I am a typical Piscean, an opposite sort of person,' she has often said. 'When someone wants me to do something one way I will always go the other way.' Her early days at the Opera Centre often brought out the worst in her complex and contrary nature. Singers were expected to undergo voice coaching outside the Centre. Kiri had been given the telephone number for the German teacher Margaret Krauss. Each day she would be asked whether she had called to make her first appointment. Each day she found a different excuse, usually a variation on how she had lost the number. 'They would give it to me again and almost make me ring up,' she confessed at the time. 'But the more they made me the more I didn't want to.'

Soon she was a frequent visitor to the office of the Centre's director of studies. 'She was a little bit lackadaisical about her studies. All she lived for was performance. The bits between were not altogether something she enjoyed very much,' John Kentish remembered.

Kiri would generally have an explanation for her transgressions. 'She was a very endearing character. She came to me once – I had been a little doubtful about her explanation for her non-appearance – and she said, "Mr Kentish, I have to tell you that there is no such word as 'lie' in the Maori language." It was one of the most elegant excuses I'd heard,' he smiled.

At other times, she fell on Kentish's sympathy. 'She could weep more easily than any other student we had. Tears could flow over quite minor things,' he said. 'Everybody treated her very gently. They could see she was sensitive.'

To less susceptible spirits, Kiri's behaviour merely offered proof that she possessed the subtler skills she would need if her career progressed. 'She had a habit of twisting everybody round her finger so that they did exactly what she wanted them to do,' said Osvalda Robertson. 'Which is good in this profession. You have got to be able to hypnotise people on and off stage.'

Robertson was less convinced by Kiri's tears than most. 'She had good waterworks, whenever she felt it might help. She was an actress,' she smiled.

In truth, however, the tears were all too often genuine. Like so many students before her, Kiri felt displaced, depressed and horribly homesick. Unlike all her contemporaries at the Opera Centre, however, she also felt confused and a little aggrieved at her sudden loss of celebrity status.

'I used to have people coming in from the New Zealand High Commission making sure I was looking after Kiri, presenting me with Maori spoons and stuff like that,' remembered John Kentish. 'It must have been difficult. She had had all that glamour in New Zealand.'

Kiri's loss of her star status was only a minor part of her difficulties. At the root of her unhappiness lay her lack of ability to apply herself to the academic side of her studies. Kiri had been expected to learn music at the same speed as her vastly more experienced peers, some of whom were postgraduate music students. She was being embarrassed on an almost daily basis by the Centre's German and Italian teachers. While many students ran to the library and the comforting company of Osvalda Robertson, Kiri found her most understanding ally in James Robertson's secretary, June Megennis. Megennis's tear-stained sessions with Kiri in her office provided her with an understanding of the Opera Centre's most problematic pupil. 'It was really traumatic for her. She'd come into my office in tears and say she couldn't face it again, and that she wanted to run away,' Megennis said later.

More than any other event, the breakthrough Kiri made at the end of the summer term ensured she did not resort to such drastic measures. On 24 June, the conductor Richard Bonynge arrived at the Centre to begin a three-day masterclass. The Australian's creative collaborations with his wife Joan Sutherland were already the stuff of legend to the more starry-eyed students, Kiri included. He had heard of Kiri through the singing competitions in Australia and, on the second day of his visit to the Centre, asked her to perform.

Kiri regarded the masterclasses as the closest thing the Centre had to a competition. Under Bonynge's watchful gaze her competitive streak shone through. Despite Sister Mary Leo's description of her as a 'heavy lyric soprano', Robertson and his colleagues had categorised her as a mezzo. Madame Krauss, by now finally in charge of Kiri's training, had begun coaching her accordingly. It had been Bonynge who had transformed the reserved Sutherland – as a student, a mezzo like her mother – into La Stupenda, the most expressive coloratura soprano in the world. By the end of his time with Kiri, Bonynge suggested to Robertson and his staff that Kiri should be encouraged to move in the same direction. Afterwards Bonynge took the unusual step of ringing Margaret Krauss and advising her personally to treat Kiri as a soprano. It would be some time before Kiri fully appreciated the importance of his intervention.

A few years later the Opera Centre's treatment of another natural soprano, Rosalind Plowright, became something of a scandal. Robertson and his staff's refusal to accept that she was better suited to the higher range led her to the brink of a physical and mental breakdown. 'My hair began to fall out. Alopecia was diagnosed as a result of stress,' complained the singer, who never lost her bitterness at Robertson and the Opera Centre. 'Everything in me was destroyed there; my voice, my confidence, my immediate professional prospects.'

Without Bonynge, Kiri could easily have suffered a similar fate.

On the other side of the world, Kiri's success with Bonynge soon made headlines. In her subsequent interviews with the ever attentive New Zealand media, the confidence the masterclass had instilled was clear. 'Without boasting', she said she felt she had as good a chance or a better chance than her rivals of succeeding. 'Of course, I am the only Maori girl there and there is that difference,' she said, 'and then there is no other voice like mine there. I mean, each one would say, "Ooh, I almost sound like Kiri now", or, "How do you do this, Kiri?". A lot of them can't sing softly, and that was the first thing I was taught – how to mark your voice, you see. All these are little things but they all build up into one big thing.'

Nell, of course, kept the New Zealand press supplied with regular snippets of news. At one point she told reporters Kiri was on the verge of being accepted at the Royal College of Music, at another that Dame Eva Turner had accepted her as a pupil. Neither prediction came to fruition. When Dame Eva criticised Kiri during another Opera Centre masterclass, the young Maori consoled herself with the thought, 'We used to eat people like you.' The stream of stories only stoked the appetite of Kiri's legion of fans back home.

Soon after her departure from New Zealand, her latest LP, *Kiri In Concert*, had been released – a collection of songs and arias recorded at performances, including the Dunedin Song Quest, Melbourne Sun Aria and Wellington and Auckland farewell concerts. Like its predecessors, the record flew straight to the top of the nation's charts.

So potent was Kiri's popularity by now that, midway through 1966, Kiwi Records' owners, the publishers Reed, commissioned a biography of its twenty-two-year-old star. An eminent London-based New Zealander, the journalist Norman Harris, was asked to ghost-write the book, to be called *Kiri: Music and a Maori Girl*.

Harris, author of an admired book on prominent expatriate New Zealanders, *The Flyaway People*, became a frequent caller at the Forest Hill flat where he interviewed his subject at length. A collection of saccharine-sweet stories from her childhood and awe-struck reminiscences from the song contest circuit, the book was written by Harris in a breathless prose style that mirrored his impression of Kiri's natural personality. 'She was quite a simple, direct, open personality. Not terribly mature but not a prima donna either,' he recalled. 'I just reflected that in the book.'

Time and Kiri's reluctance to commit herself to extended interview sessions proved Harris's greatest problem. 'She was a willing enough interviewee but she did not have a terribly long attention span,' he said. To compound matters, Nell, as ever, was there to cast her considerable shadow over the interview process. 'She was there to correct and prompt. It was clear that she was pushing Kiri along,' he recalled.

In her own way Kiri was no different from Harris's previous subjects – among them Donald McIntyre, the Kray brothers' QC John Platts-Mills and the Forsyte Saga actress Nyree Dawn Porter. 'There was a feeling then that if you were going to make it you had to leave New Zealand,' he recalled. Yet Harris found Kiri unsure as to whether she had made the right decision at all. 'I remember there was a sense of frustration and disillusionment. She had been a star in a small country and she was not prepared for the hard work at the Opera Centre.'

On one visit Harris recalls Kiri sitting on the double bed her mother was occupying in the flat. 'One of them, mother I think, said, "To Hell with them. You can go back and fill any hall in New Zealand whenever you want." And Kiri sat there agreeing with her.'

Such consensus was, however, increasingly rare. Nell's early attempts to impose herself on the Opera Centre had been easily rebuffed by James Robertson. She retired to the Forest Hill flat where she devoted herself to ruling Kiri's home life instead. For a while Kiri indulged her mother by heading straight home from the Opera Centre at the end of each day. There, Nell cooked her dinner then bullied her into getting on with whatever homework she had. 'She would expect me home at six o'clock and that was it – that was my life,' she explained later. 'All the other students were going out to parties.'

The arrival in London of her St Mary's friend Raewyn Blade shifted the balance of power within the flat, however. Blade, as vibrant and vivacious a character as Kiri, had arrived to study singing and acting at the Guildhall School of Music. Her first flat had been so damp, she told Kiri, 'mushrooms grew on the wall'. Kiri invited Blade to take the spare room at Forest Hill where she could 'share my mushrooms instead'. Soon the duo were defying Nell's dictats.

'I realised there was fun to be had and I was about to have it,' Kiri

119

said later. 'But my mother kept getting in the way and unfortunately she knew it.'

The process was, of course, a perfectly natural one. For Kiri it was essential that she finally establish her independence. 'I was twenty-two at the time, which is quite late to be breaking away from your parents. I had been protected in a cocoon of music, studying constantly and not very much fun company. It can really get to you, you can go under with it. But I started knocking through the top and saying "Right, that's it, I've had enough. I don't want to be suppressed any more by my parents."' Nell, however, was unwilling and perhaps even unable to let go. The rows became more frequent and more hurtful. 'She was always upset and hurt. She was constantly crying,' Kiri recalled later.

For all her outward robustness, Nell had never enjoyed the best of health. As the strains of life far from home mounted, she took to her bed complaining of severe pains. Eventually she was admitted to hospital where she underwent an operation to have gallstones removed. 'She was really ill. We were told that she very nearly died,' said her granddaughter, Judy Evans-Hita. 'Afterwards she lost a huge amount of weight.'

For Kiri, the illness marked a milestone. When Nell returned to Forest Hill Kiri summoned the strength to tell her she no longer wanted her in London. Nell's distress would leave Kiri feeling guilt-ridden for years. 'I hurt her terribly,' she said later. 'But there again, mothers of that time . . . never understood the workings of young women.'

In the autumn of 1966, Nell reluctantly booked her passage back to New Zealand. She set sail in November.

Kiri had not just freed herself from Nell's apron strings, she had freed herself from her past. The oppressive influences of New Zealand – the unholy trinity of Sister Mary Leo, her family and her fame – were, for the moment at least, forgotten. Only the London Opera Centre now remained to cage her. She had no intention of allowing it to spoil the party, however. For the first time in her life Kiri was free to indulge her immense capacity for having fun. With Blade and their friend Sally Rush, who had also arrived to study in London, she duly had a ball.

In Forest Hill, Kiri, Blade and Rush had become favourites of the local police constabulary. Officers had first come to the flat when Raewyn Blade had spotted a peeping Tom. Blade had been singing in the flat's basement bathroom and had looked up to see a pair of eyes staring through the window. Kiri had chased the man down the street brandishing a kitchen knife. For the following three months the trio had enjoyed the station's 'full-time protection'. For all their high spirits the trio remained young ladies St Mary's could feel proud of. According to Blade, the trio of girls shared a bed together when three policemen invited them away for a weekend at an Oxfordshire cottage.

The connections to the police force had been strengthened at the Opera Centre. James Robertson's secretary June Megennis had become Kiri's closest confidante. She had recently become engaged to a constable with the Port of London Police, David Hall. Through Megennis Kiri had been invited to sing at police events. Her experience at the Colony Club stood her in good stead. Soon she was a frequent guest at the West India Dock Police Club, performing for a bottle or two of whisky rather than cash.

Kiri had also made a few close friends at the Opera Centre. 'She was an extrovert, great fun to have around. She kept us all in stitches,' said one of those with whom she spent time, Osvalda Robertson. To Robertson it seemed as if Kiri was living life to the hilt. 'She always liked pop music and jazz. She was always saying, "I went to see that last night, it was fabulous." She really enjoyed life.'

London was alive with opportunities. The mop-topped features of the Fab Four stared out from every magazine cover; Mary Quant had been anointed high priestess of fashion. It was an age of mini-skirts and Mini-Mokes, the heyday of Carnaby Street and the Kings Road. 'It was the big world, an exciting time,' Kiri said later.

As far as her adoring New Zealand public were concerned, Kiri had remained devoted to Brooke Monks, to whom she wrote every week and whose teddy bear took pride of place in the flat. Asked a few months into her studies whether she had any boyfriends, she had flashed a wistful smile at the photograph of Monks she kept on a bookshelf and replied, 'There is only one, and he is 13,000 miles away back home.' That news would have come as a surprise to Rodney Macann, who had once more found himself drawn to Kiri. Macann had also travelled to London where he had joined the BBC Singers. Towards the end of 1966 he and Kiri began to spend time together, attending concerts, recitals and parties. Kiri was, if anything, an even more frustrating personality than she had been in New Zealand. 'She was this outgoing person who I couldn't really cope with in some ways,' he said. 'She was very straight from the shoulder.'

Inevitably the 'warlords' were soon pulling Kiri back into line, however. Kiri's lack of progress at the Opera Centre had continued to cause concern. The conspicuous comfort of her life only added to the resentment some of her teachers and fellow students felt. Years later Kiri presented a picture of an impoverished student, perpetually living on the breadline as she struggled for a break. 'You eat very badly when you are a young student,' she said years later. 'You are being fed by other people because you don't have enough money.'

In reality she was by far the most financially secure of the forty or so singers at the Opera Centre. Inevitably her cavalier attitude towards money offended those who did not have it. 'She spent money and gave the impression that it did not matter,' said Osvalda Robertson. 'She would buy a Christian Dior scarf for £10. In those days students had to live on less than that for a month. And then she would make matters worse by showing it off. She did not realise she made the others jealous. She had that carefree nature, and she had the demeanour of a star from the beginning.'

Jeremy Commons was also familiar with Malvina Major and Marie Landis, two other New Zealanders studying in London. Major had travelled to London with a jobless husband and a £100 donation from her local Rotary Club. 'Both Malvina and Marie had a much tougher road. They really had to scrape and work hard,' he said. 'Kiri was the one who had the silver spoon in her mouth from the word go. She was lavish and somewhat tactless. She would turn up at the Opera Centre in a taxi, whereas the others were scraping to make ends meet. I think anyone with a little more tact would have been dropped off round the corner and turned up on foot.'

Such delicacy seemed beyond the twenty-two-year-old Kiri, however. 'Clothes are so cheap,' she breezily told one reporter at the time. In another interview a journalist described how she 'fetched her fashionable fur hat from her new Zodiac car' and wore an up-to-the minute red, double-breasted trouser suit and a one-inch cube stainless steel ring she called 'gear'.

'I love fashionable clothes,' she said. 'I hope to be just a little ahead of the average when I arrive back in New Zealand.'

Her unpopularity was not aided by the fact she was regarded as something of a favourite of the Centre's principal. 'As a conductor James liked to go for pretty girls. I suspect the plainer girls, even if they had wonderful voices, didn't appeal to him so much,' suggested Tom Hawkes, a Sadler's Wells director who worked on many of Kiri's earliest Opera Centre productions. Hawkes often heard other singers complaining about the roles that went Kiri's way. 'There was a certain amount of resentment of Kiri at the beginning. She was seen so much as James's little protégé. Other students did tend to say, "Oh, Kiri's going to get this, isn't she, because James will want her."'

Within the Opera Centre, James Robertson undoubtedly remained Kiri's champion and staunchest defender. Outside, however, even he expressed his doubts about Kiri's suitability. Aware of Kiri's high profile, Robertson kept New Zealand House abreast of the worsening situation.

'The High Commissioner and I were kept informed,' said Jeremy Commons. 'I was aware of the difficulties they were having with her. James Robertson told me that she was extremely lazy, that she did not turn up for classes. She went her own way.'

For those who chose to read the signals, Kiri's problems were plain even back in New Zealand. Kiri had been engaged in an ongoing battle with John Kentish and James Robertson over her right to work outside the Opera Centre. Under the terms of her acceptance by the Centre, all performances outside the Centre needed to be approved. In August, Kiri had been allowed to travel to Carlisle to appear on a Border Television programme. She donned her piu piu to sing a traditional Maori song then headed back south to London. To her anger, however, Robertson and Kentish had vetoed her plans to travel to Toulouse for a singing contest in November. She and Malvina Major had both been forced to cancel plans to appear in the event, which offered a first prize of £400. Back in New Zealand, Nell publicly complained at the decision.

The one contest the Centre had allowed Kiri to enter, the Stella Murray competition at the Royal Commonwealth Society in London on 16 November, had been a disaster. Dame Eva Turner was among the judges at the RCS's elegant, Pall Mall headquarters. Kiri arrived suffering from what she later called 'a terrible cold'. To the surprise of the audience, many of whom had come specifically to see Kiri, the first prize went to a Dunedin singer, Beverley Bergen, who had arrived at the Opera Centre in 1962 and gone on to Sadler's Wells and Glyndebourne. Judge Joan Davis then went on to praise Kiri's 'great sense of the dramatic and beauty of person' before singling her out for criticism by adding, 'We think, however, her intonation is insecure and feel she must go away and think, listen and study and become a very great singer.'

'Something went wrong towards the end, she either went out of tune or fluffed a cadenza, so that, though she undoubtedly had the finest voice of anyone taking part, she was – correctly, on the evening's showing – pipped at the post by Beverley Bergen,' said Jeremy Commons who was present that night.

Whatever the merits of the decision, news of the result flew back to New Zealand where Davis's demolition of Kiri overshadowed Bergen's win. 'NZ Soprano Criticised By Judges' ran the headline in the *New Zealand Herald*. At least Commons and Kiri's supporters in London were able to put the mishap in its proper perspective. By now they were far more worried by the growing rumblings of discontent over Kiri's progress as a student.

Commons had attended the contest with Kiri's old patron from Auckland, Thelma Robinson. Earlier that day the pair had held a meeting to discuss Kiri's problems at the Opera Centre where James Robertson had begun to make noises about throwing New Zealand's pride and joy out. 'It got to that very awkward, difficult stage,' said Commons. In the wake of an acrimonious marital split, Robinson had arrived in London where she had become a frequent companion for Kiri. The former mayoress acted as a surrogate mother and shopping partner and regularly spoke to her on the phone. Robinson was aware of Kiri's problems at the Opera Centre.

'All the rest of the students were years ahead of her, and yet she had this beautiful voice, and they resented her. And, also, I think she felt racial discrimination,' she said.

Both she and Bill Barrett, who had also been in London, were involved in the discussions designed to avert Kiri's dismissal. Even her mentors found it hard to instil a greater discipline in their charge, however. As Kiri picturesquely put it years later, she was in a phase of her life where authority was her enemy. Her teachers in particular 'would try and hit me with a baseball bat. I played hookey all the time, but that's what youth is all about. I just went for life, it was so much fun.'

The nadir was reached at the end of the winter term. Kiri had been chosen to play the role of Eleonora in the winter term's closing public performance, a one-act excerpt from Wolf-Ferrari's little-performed comic opera, *Le donne curiose*. While James Robertson conducted himself, Tom Hawkes was called in to direct. As separate casts were chosen for the two performances scheduled to be held at the Opera Centre in mid-December, Kiri was initially chosen for the first cast. Hawkes's reputation as one of London's more sensitive directors was already established. As he worked with Kiri for the first time he saw her greatest inadequacies lay in her acting. 'At the beginning she didn't have any technique, she didn't know what she was doing,' he said. 'One really had to explain very carefully to her, take her through the process of what the characters were feeling then let her develop it.'

Hawkes found Kiri a pliant if demanding pupil. 'You had to work to pull things out of her,' he said. 'She wasn't difficult or resistant. Where some of the brighter students would come back and question things, she was more passive and would take things in.' Unlike others at the Opera Centre, Hawkes felt sympathy for Kiri's particular problems. 'She was in a new country, finding her feet around a lot of other singers for the first time. It wasn't secure. She hadn't come through the musical colleges. She didn't have all that background that the others had. She was more vulnerable really.' As rehearsals progressed, however, it was plain that Kiri did not know her part well. 'It was a prevailing fault at the beginning that Kiri didn't learn her stuff very well. She didn't know it as well as she should have. The homework hadn't been done. She just didn't know the words properly.'

Robertson's perfectionist streak was well known to his students. 'James was a very meticulous chap. He liked perfection in everything and was very thorough,' said John Kentish. Eventually Robertson's patience snapped. Kiri was taken to one side and told she had been relegated to the second cast as punishment for her lack of application.

'Kiri, naturally, was in the first cast but she was demoted because she didn't learn it properly,' remembered Tom Hawkes. Her reaction, as usual, was to burst into floods of tears. This time, however, nothing could reverse the decision. 'It brought her up with quite a shock.'

Kiri dutifully performed on the second night of the performance on 17 December, but failed to shine. 'The part of a middle-aged woman didn't really suit her,' admitted Hawkes.

Kiri spent Christmas with Blade and Rush in Forest Hill but had already made her mind up to defy Robertson by heading back to New Zealand for a three week break in February. After a full year in London, homesick and pining for Brooke, she had arranged to sing at an open air concert celebrating the annual Festival of the Pines in New Plymouth.

Despite the troubles of her first year at the Centre, James Robertson still retained his basic faith in Kiri's abilities. As a peace offering in the wake of *Le donne curiose*, he called her into his office to tell Kiri he had cast her in the role of Dido in Purcell's Carthaginian tragedy, *Dido and Aeneas*. It was to be the Centre's showpiece performance of early 1967 at the Caen Conservatoire in Normandy, as part of the city's British Week in March. As Kiri left London for Auckland, however, Robertson, like many at the Opera Centre, must secretly have wondered whether he would see her again.

In early February 1967, almost exactly a year after she had left her country, clutching a thirteen guinea pink elephant called Harold and dressed in a black felt toreador hat and a black mini-skirt, New Zealand's musical sweetheart climbed down the steps of an Air New Zealand flight on to the tarmac at Auckland airport. A crowd of around one hundred had turned out to greet her, almost as many as had cheered the arrival of American actor Robert Vaughn, star of 'The Man From U.N.C.L.E.', weeks earlier. Kiri used the occasion to announce her casting as Dido for the Caen performance. She had been given the role, 'Simply because the London Opera Centre wanted to make sure I went back after this trip,' she joked with reporters.

The press were more interested in rumours that she intended to get engaged to Brooke Monks while she was back in New Zealand. 'There's no question of that – for the present at least,' Kiri teasingly replied. This, at least, was perfectly true. Kiri arrived to discover that Brooke had broken his shoulder in Australia and was in a Sydney hospital recovering from an operation to insert a steel pin in his upper body. By the time he returned they would have just over two weeks together. Kiri arrived back at Blockhouse Bay to discover a second Christmas had been laid on for her. Nell had put the tree back up and surrounded it with a small mountain of presents. More than two dozen friends and family gathered around for a grand turkey dinner.

Kiri's niece Judy detected a new grandness in her former fighting partner. 'I've heard of people having a plum in their mouth but you, a Maori, having a whole bloody tree stuck in there – it's terrible,' the straight-talking Judy told her.

'I don't speak like that, do I?' Kiri half-smiled in reply.

Nell, however, reassured Kiri's fans that she remained the homespun Kiwi girl they had helped turn into a star. 'She hasn't changed a bit since she went away – she never will.'

For the remainder of her visit, Kiri happily lived up to her image as an apprentice diva. With Tony Vercoe and other Kiwi Records executives, she undertook a small number of public appearances and interviews. Inevitably the press followed her every move. Kiri brushed off her problems at the infamous London competition of the previous year. 'Miss Davis made more comments about me than the actual winner,' she complained. In the long run the setback had been character building, she claimed. 'I like to be criticised. You shouldn't just be able to walk away with things. You should be corrected if you're wrong.'

Kiri's drawing power in New Zealand was greater than ever. She was due to sing two concerts at the Brooklands Bowl, an open air amphitheatre overlooking a lake in a New Plymouth park. The Bowl's Hogmanays and beauty pageants, ballet and country and western nights routinely pulled in crowds of between 1,500 and 3,000. Under a flawless sky, 9,000 people poured into the arena on the first night, lapping up Kiri's repertoire of Rossini, Strauss and Puccini arias, old dine 'n' dance favourites like 'Tonight' and 'Climb Ev'ry Mountain', and Maori standards like 'Pokarekare-ana'. A further 6,000 would turn up for the second concert.

Her performance was heralded a triumph. As the New Zealand press eulogised about its Queen of Song, complaints were even made in parliament that the concert had not been broadcast live on television. Amid such idolatry, it was left to Sister Mary Leo, there as guest of honour, to sound the only critical note in public. She had been impressed by the results of Kiri's tuition in London. 'Her voice has matured since she went away,' she conceded. She knew Kiri well enough to recognise the tell-tale signs, however. 'I must be honest,' she said, 'I thought Kiri sounded tired.' Behind the scenes, Kiri's jaded performance drew more direct fire.

Tony Vercoe had arrived in New Plymouth to oversee a recording of the concerts for Kiwi Records. He regarded the project as crucial. Vercoe knew Kiri's public popularity remained as high as ever. It was exemplified by Bill Barrett in New Plymouth where he told the local paper about a letter, along with a £5 note, that he had been sent by a woman in Wellington. It said, 'Just tell her it is from an admirer and that with her singing she has the ability to lift her listeners above all earthly things and give them pure pleasure.'

'That is how people are affected by Kiri,' said Barrett. 'I get a lot of these letters.'

Like Barrett, however, Vercoe knew that the truth was that Kiri's success in London was far from assured. Vercoe and his colleague Don Hutchings had heard the rumours of troubles at the Opera Centre. They had also been worried by the reception Kiri's biography had received.

Music and a Maori Girl was published at the end of 1966 to an underwhelming welcome. The reviews of the book were as withering as the genteel New Zealand media could manage. 'This is the type of book more commonly written at a later stage of success,' suggested one leading critic, L. C. M. Saunders. His view confirmed the worries of those who thought Kiri was being exploited and over-exposed.

'It was premature,' recalled Hutchings. 'It was probably an early example of what we have today with the attempts to make instant stars of people who have not yet matured enough to be called stars. There was an attempt more to cash in rather than seriously represent Kiri and I think it could have done her a bit of damage actually if she hadn't moved on.'

Even Norman Harris realised his book was little more than an exercise to oil the wheels of Reed's marketing stratagems. The author's sixty pages of text were accompanied by sixty-four pages of photographs. 'It was a potboiler,' said Harris. 'It was put together in a great hurry and you could tell that reading it.' His view was clearly shared by Kiri herself. On the few occasions Harris has seen her over the years she has studiously avoided his gaze. 'I don't think she thought very highly of it either,' he smiled.

Vercoe travelled to New Plymouth convinced that a high quality recording of her concerts would redress the balance. He found Kiri deeply distracted, however. Kiri had arrived in New Plymouth still exhausted by jet lag. She had been waking at 5.30 a.m. and by early evenings had struggled to stay awake. Far more draining, however, was the attention she was lavishing on Brooke Monks.

Brooke had finally arrived from Australia and had driven down to New Plymouth with Kiri. Vercoe, like everyone else, had heard the rumours of an impending engagement. In the day leading up to the first concert, he had found it increasingly difficult to prise Kiri and Brooke apart. 'I had to give Kiri some very clear instructions about remembering the microphone,' he recollected. 'Brooke was there the whole time and Kiri was very distracted.' While the conductors for the two shows required rehearsal time, Vercoe remembers Kiri 'was mooning about with Brooke, difficult to track down and I was concerned not merely about the recordings but about the prospect of her acquiring a less than professional reputation.'

Eventually even the stoical Vercoe could not contain his anger any longer. 'I merely expressed an opinion about where her concentration and attention should go,' he said with a shrug. 'As a friend and sort of mentor I felt impelled to put in a timely word. This was not well received.'

News of his attack on Kiri soon reached Nell. Nell remained Brooke's number one supporter. She had done little to dampen the belief that an engagement and a marriage was in the air. 'She is very much in love,' Nell said in New Plymouth. 'All I want for her future is for her to be happy.'

It was not hard to understand her reasoning. Nell was torn between her yearning for Kiri to succeed and her hopes that she would one day return to New Zealand. In Kiri's absence she and Brooke would frequently spend time talking about the girl they both loved and missed. Friends like Don Hutchings believe Nell saw Brooke as the man who could bring Kiri home to her. Tony Vercoe's intervention posed a threat to those hopes.

'I think Nell had realised at that stage that they no longer needed Tony. He had served his usefulness,' said Hutchings. 'There were other, much bigger operators in the domestic market, like HMV. So she was saying, "If you're going to start criticising my daughter and her boyfriend you'd better be careful because this is the man who will make her pregnant and keep her here."''

Nell reacted furiously to Vercoe's criticism of Kiri. She met Vercoe and his wife Mary on the street in New Plymouth and was, Mary remembers with understatement, 'somewhat belligerent'. Relations between Vercoe and Kiri were never the same again.

'The possibilities were beginning to shape up. I could see this affecting the whole future, not just for the company but for her. I had to say my piece, but I'm afraid Mum got offended and it was never quite the same for me after that,' said Vercoe. 'I was "interfering" and "overstepping the mark".'

Vercoe recorded another album with Kiri in 1970. He was left in no doubt, however, that in the wake of New Plymouth he had been 'excised from the family thinking'.

The greatest irony of the situation was that Brooke Monks had begun to see things in much the same way as the music producer. In the year that had passed since he had seen Kiri off on the *Australis*, Brooke had remained as confused about Kiri as ever. He had spent the first hours of their separation in tears. After waving off the *Australis* and leaving Auckland harbour he had made the long drive back to his barracks at Waiouru alone. 'I was a real mess by the time I arrived. It was a fair way,' he remembered. 'It was a pretty traumatic few days.' As the days turned to weeks and months, Brooke had kept photographs of Kiri in his locker and had contacted her as often as his duties would allow. In their letters and conversations he and Kiri regularly discussed getting married. Yet in his heart he knew the practicalities remained as hopeless as they had been a year earlier.

Brooke was painfully aware of the criticism that had been made of him. 'She used to tell me about it,' he explained. 'I think I was described as a destructive influence, a phrase that galled me a bit. Some people felt I was ruining things for her and that hurt me at the time because I would never have dreamed of holding her back for anything.' In his heart he knew if he proposed marriage, Kiri might well stay in New Zealand. Nell might thank him for it, but ultimately few others would. Both he and Kiri knew she had to pursue her studies in London, despite her bad start. 'She always knew what she had to

Noeleen Rawstron, Kiri's blood mother, pictured around 1940.

Jack Wawatai, Kiri's blood father, pictured at the time of his wedding in 1937, aged twenty.

Left In the wings – Kiri prepares for an early appearance.

Below Kiri and canine friend at Hatepe on Lake Taupo.

Stepping out. Kiri models a sumptuous creation at the debutantes' ball,
Auckland, May 1961.

Left 'Wicked Little Witch.'
Kiri on stage in *Uwane*,
April 1962.

Below Leading man. Kiri
with Vincent Collins;
her *Uwane* co-star and
boyfriend.

Left The winning way. Kiri sings the 'Willow Song' at the Tauranga Aria, May 1964.

Below Divine inspiration. Lynne Cantlon (*top left*) and Kiri (*bottom right*) pose with Elisabeth Schwarzkopf (*centre*, next to Sister Mary Leo) on her visit to St Mary's.

Left Coming of age.
Kiri with Nell and Tom
at her twenty-first
birthday, March 1965.

Below Bon voyage.
Kiri with her uniformed
boyfriend Brooke Monks
(*left*), 'kissing and cuddling'
friend Donald Perry (*top
centre*) and accompanist
Barbara Brown (*top right*)
at the farewell celebrations,
February 1966.

do,' he said. His own destiny still lay in Auckland, however. 'I was still at university and I wanted to go into the family business. It would have been wrong to sort of just up and go.'

On top of all this, Monks's mother remained steadfastly opposed to him marrying Kiri. Once more, the pressure had mounted on him. Once more, however, he simply could not commit himself.

Nell had, naturally, organised a party for Kiri's departure for London at the end of February. Kiri had hinted to her friends that the party would mark the formal announcement of her engagement to Brooke. Lou and Simon had been invited to join the festivities after the final curtain had come down on a performance they were giving elsewhere in Auckland. They arrived shortly before midnight to discover a look-out waiting at the end of the Mitchell Street drive.

'Kiri thought we might come in singing so she had someone there to tell us that it wasn't happening,' said Clauson.

Clauson headed towards the house fearful he would find a devastated Kiri inside. His concerns were soon evaporating. 'Kiri came running up the drive and said, "There ain't no bloody engagement, but we're still having a party." '

Mr Ideal

On the afternoon of Saturday, 4 March 1967, Kiri drove to the Opera Centre for one of the happier events of her time there. June Megennis and David Hall had got married earlier that day and Kiri had been invited to a champagne reception in the upstairs foyer overlooking the Commercial Road.

As she mingled with familiar faces from the Centre and the Port of London Police, Kiri was soon bemoaning the fact that she would have to leave early. With Sally Rush and Raewyn Blade she had agreed to go on a blind date with three eligible bachelors 'up West' that evening. By late afternoon she had already begun to talk herself out of joining her flatmates.

'She didn't really want to go, but we all told her she had to,' recalled Osvalda Robertson. 'We said "You've made a commitment, so don't drink so much, you're driving."'

As the wedding party got into full swing, Kiri said her goodbyes to the new Mr and Mrs Hall and dutifully turned up outside the Swan & Edgar department store at Piccadilly Circus to meet Rush and Blade.

In fact the date was only partially blind. Kiri already knew one of the trio of men with them, the New Zealand photographer Bill Double for whom she had posed for publicity shots back home. He introduced her to two friends she had not met before, David Barr and Desmond Park, an Australian mining engineer Double had met on his passage over to England.

The sixsome headed off to see Peter O'Toole and Omar Shariff in *The Night of the Generals*, which Kiri didn't enjoy at all. Afterwards Kiri was at a loss to remember where she had parked her car and the group – rather conveniently – became separated. Barr and Blade vanished, not to be seen again that night. Kiri and Sally invited Double and Park back to Forest Hill where they talked and drank long into the night. Kiri found herself becoming more and more attracted to Park, whom Blade had promised her friend in advance was 'absolutely gorgeous'. He and Double eventually spent the night at the flat, but in spare beds the two girls made up for them.

In years to come, Kiri and Des's memories of their introduction would vary like a verse from *Gigi*, and Maurice Chevallier's 'Ah Yes, I Remember It Well'.

'That night was really quite terrible,' Des would reminisce. 'We saw a terrible movie and Kiri and I just didn't get on.'

Kiri, on the other hand, would describe the blind date as the pivotal moment of her life. 'It had been a good evening – and I'd found my Mr Ideal.'

Kiri had left New Zealand in late February resigned to the fact that her relationship with Brooke was heading nowhere. As she cast around for new male company, however, she was distinctly unimpressed by the locals. To Kiri Englishmen seemed 'deprived of good sunshine and good food'.

'They have had too many sweets, tinned fruit and tinned cream,' she told one New Zealand reporter at the time. Their one redeeming quality, she admitted, was their manners. 'They are such gentlemen,' she said, pointedly referring once more to New Zealand men's habit of expecting women to 'run around after them'. If Kiri had a notion of the perfect man, he probably blended the rugged masculinity of the New Zealander with the attentive and respectful manner of the quintessential Englishman. It was little wonder she took to Des Park so instantly.

Des Park had been born on 20 July 1942 in Brisbane, where his father Frank ran a successful piano tuning and French polishing business. Frank Park and his wife Doris were staunch members of the local Christadelphian movement. At their home in the Corinda suburb of the city, Des and his two younger brothers, Ray and David, had been raised according to the rigid rules of the family faith. As boys they had attended church every Sunday. As young men they were forbidden from smoking, drinking and even joining the neighbourhood corps of the army cadets because of the Christadelphians' disapproval of all military activity.

Despite the comfort of their life, the Park children were taught the penny-wise values of a hard day's work for a fair day's pay. Displays of ostentation were unthinkable. 'Frank's business did very well and the family invested in property,' recalled a boyhood friend, Adolf Lacis. 'But they were not flashy with their money.'

In his adult life Des would discard most of the principles by which his parents lived their lives. He smoked and drank with the gusto of a true Australian. 'My parents would have parties and he would often come and stay with us,' said Lacis, a member of the local Latvian community. 'Des would even come Latvian folk dancing with me. I was a good outlet away from the strict regime at home.' Des's belief in thrift and the work ethic would never leave him, however. His entrepreneurial streak revealed itself at an early age.

'He earned pocket money by growing vegetables in his back garden and selling them to neighbours in a wheelbarrow,' recalled Bob Morgan, a lifelong friend who grew up in the same neighbourhood.

'He always had a quid,' added Adolf Lacis.

Des's good looks, dapper dress sense and charming nature won him no shortage of girlfriends to ferry around town in his VW Beetle. 'I think even at primary school he had a steady girlfriend,' recalled Lacis. 'The girls loved Des because he was a natural gentleman, the type of bloke who would buy a girl a flower when they went out. That was his nature. It wasn't an act. And whereas the rest of us were Aussie slobs, he always dressed well.'

As an adolescent Des had helped himself to the pick of the female crop in Corinda, but with mixed fortunes. Among his conquests were the daughters of the Latvian minister and a prominent Jewish family. The latter relationship was far from popular with the girl's father. 'He threatened to kill Des if he carried on seeing her,' recalled Lacis.

Diligent and intelligent, Des graduated from the University of Queensland with a degree in engineering. From there he went straight into the mining industry. After a stint at a copper refining plant in Townsville, on the coast north of Brisbane, however, he decided to take one of the extended holidays so popular among Antipodeans then and now. Keen to hang on to him, his company had arranged for a stint with the Britannia Lead Company in Gravesend, Kent, but the job had done little to rid him of his restlessness. In the spring of 1967 he had lined up a new job working for an aviation company in Rockford, Illinois. He was due to leave for America at the end of the year.

Despite his family's albeit loose connections to the musical world, Des had little interest in classical music. When he met Kiri he knew nothing of her reputation or her fame in New Zealand or indeed Australia. It would be a month before he rang to ask for a second date. By then her reputation had spread even further afield, across the English Channel.

The part of the tragic Carthaginian Queen Dido had provided Kiri with a perfect opportunity to prove the case for her elevation to soprano roles. The role required a low soprano rather than a mezzo voice. At the Opera Centre, Robertson had been impressed with Kiri's performance in rehearsal, in particular her rendition of the much-loved, closing act lament, 'When I am laid in earth'.

In Caen, however, she had seemed far more interested in the local shopping. 'She would disappear for hours, then reappear laden with bags,' remembered John Kentish. As usual, Kiri was saving herself for her public. On the night of the performance, the city's Conservatoire was filled to capacity for the highlight of a week of cultural exchange. Kiri utterly stole the show. 'When I am laid in earth' brought the audience to its feet. So insistent was the applause that Kiri was persuaded to sing the aria a second time. 'She won the hearts of everyone there that night, she really did,' said Kentish. 'Performance was her life blood.'

Kiri's stunning performance left the local French newspapers floundering for words. 'What can we say . . . of the beautiful, the royal Kiri Te Kanawa, of her exceptional voice, the mastery of which should lead her to the firmament of operatic stars?' one critic wondered.

If the reviews ensured Kiri's spirits were high when she got back to London, her mood was improved further by the developments that lay in wait. First she found herself offered a rather glamorous new home. Kiri's rise in New Zealand had been followed closely by a wealthy English actress, painter and writer, Veronica Haigh. Haigh had a lifelong interest in New Zealand and Maori culture in particular. She had contacted Kiri at the Opera Centre and invited her to dinner at her home, a rambling mews house in De Vere Gardens, within a short walk of the Albert Hall in Kensington. Nell's knack for charming wealthy patrons had clearly rubbed off on Kiri. By the end of the evening, Haigh had offered the flat to Kiri at a peppercorn rent.

It had been as she moved from Forest Hill that Des Park had called asking for a second date. Kiri played coy at first. 'I said it was Desmond Park and she said, "So what?"' Des smiled later.

As the two began dating, however, things quickly took off. Rodney Macann was perhaps the first to realise precisely how quickly. For the second time, Macann had found himself falling under Kiri's siren spell. In London he had continued to see Kiri on an occasional basis. Shortly after Kiri moved into De Vere Gardens he finally summoned the courage to spell out his feelings.

'I was finding Kiri incredibly attractive and I thought, well, maybe we should be thinking about whether there is a future for us together,' he remembered.

It was soon obvious that his hesitation had been fatal. Kiri confessed that for a while she too had felt exactly the same way. 'Apparently she had sort of fallen in love with me again, watching me sing, and I hadn't known anything about it.' The moment had passed, however. 'She said, "Rodney, you've chosen the wrong time."' She went on to recall a night a few months earlier when they had been together at one of Macann's concerts. "If you had brought it up then, I would have done anything for you," she said. This was typical of Kiri.'

There were times in the days and weeks that followed when the quiet, contemplative Macann bitterly regretted his indecision. 'But really, in my saner moments, which I had particularly when I was away from her, I realised it would have been a total disaster.'

Des and Kiri's romance continued throughout the summer. Most weekends he would travel up from his flat in Gravesend and stay at De Vere Gardens. In Kiri's account, at least, relations remained 'perfectly above board'. Somewhat ambiguously, she added, 'Mummy would have been proud of me!'

Kiri had tested the depth of Des's interest early on. She had primed Raewyn Blade – by now also installed at De Vere Gardens – to tell him she was not available when he telephoned. Soon a large bunch of flowers and a note signed 'love Des' had arrived at the front door.

Des had begun introducing Kiri to his circle of friends in London. In Kiri's version of their story, a weekend boating trip on the Thames cemented their future. Des and his Australian friends had booked the boat for a long trip down the river. Kiri had been so unsure about whether to join them, the party had been kept waiting at the moorings for half of Saturday while she made up her mind. As she and Des glided along through the Thames Valley, however, Kiri saw her life finally falling into some sense of order. 'Suddenly the fresh air, jeans, T-shirts and sun changed my whole attitude and I thought "To hell with it, goodbye Brooke!"' she confessed later.

Given the dramatic speed with which events unfolded, and the rawness of the emotions they exposed, it is perhaps not surprising that Kiri, Des and Brooke Monks's memories of July and August 1967 diverge. What is in no doubt, however, is that by the end of the English summer, Kiri was a married woman.

Des had already suggested that he and Kiri should live together. Kiri, still hesitant about telling Brooke it was over, had asked that she be given a chance to sort things out in New Zealand first. Des, however, was in no mood to wait and risk losing Kiri. According to his ultra-precise version of events, he proposed at 3 a.m. precisely on the morning of Tuesday, 25 July. Kiri accepted within hours; they ran out into central London where he bought her an engagement ring of three white diamonds in a traditional setting.

At around 5 p.m. that afternoon he telephoned his parents in Brisbane. 'I didn't give a thought to the fact that it was 1 a.m. there,' he laughed later. If Des's memory serves him correctly, Kiri 'saved the surprise' until she arrived back in New Zealand in August when she flew back for her next concert. He, in the meantime, went ahead with his plans to take a holiday to Italy. He would wait to hear Nell's and Tom's response from there.

At the time Kiri supported this version of events. 'We were unofficially engaged before, but Desmond had to meet Mum and Dad. I told them about it when I arrived home,' she told reporters in New Zealand when the announcement was formally made.

By the time she came to recount the event in her authorised biography, fifteen or so years later, however, a slightly different version emerged. In this account, Des formally wrote to Tom and Nell telling them of the engagement before she flew back to New Zealand. The news that she was engaged had quickly become common knowledge among her friends. On her flight back to Auckland she had met

Raewyn Blade's parents who had 'discovered with relief' that her fiancé was someone other than Brooke Monks. According to Kiri, Brooke had made a 'furious' telephone call to Mitchell Street. Brooke himself knows little about what happened between Des and Kiri. He vividly recalls the telephone call and its aftermath, however. When Kiri had left New Zealand in February Brooke had said farewell once more assuming their relationship was still intact.

'When she went back to London everything was good between us,' he said. In his heart, however, the insecurity was gnawing away. 'I always had it at the back of my mind that it was going to be pretty much an impossibility, really. When you're apart for a long time things can happen.'

When the news of Kiri's engagement to an unknown Australian reached him he was devastated. When he finally reached Kiri by phone he quickly realised his attempts to change her mind would be pointless. 'I must admit I was shattered when she told me what was going to happen,' he said. 'She seemed pretty set on it.' Kiri seemed angry at Brooke's past indecision. 'It was a sort of "to hell with you" attitude, I suppose, because we hadn't made the commitment together.'

When Brooke eventually saw Nell, she berated him for his hesitancy. 'Nell sort of said to me "I told you so! You should have done something." I'm sure she would have wanted things to turn out differently,' he said.

Nell was undoubtedly stunned by her daughter's announcement. 'Nana always liked Brooke,' said Judy Evans-Hita. 'Like everyone, she had expected Kiri to marry Brooke. But if you expect the predictable you're always going to be in for a shock.' Nell had sat stony-faced in the car after meeting Kiri off the plane. When Kiri told her she and her mysterious Australian boyfriend wanted to marry 'straight away' she had been convinced Kiri was pregnant 'and that once again I'd destroyed her life and wrecked her dreams', as Kiri put it. Her mood brightened when she realised there was nothing more sinister to the matter than love. She was ecstatic when Kiri agreed to her suggestion that she and her fiancé marry while she was back in New Zealand.

While Nell began making arrangements, however, Kiri kept quiet about the impending nuptials. She told reporters she had come home just for 'Mum's cooking and care – and a reunion with her spaniel Whisky'.

Des had gone ahead with his Italian holiday with his friend Franco Pieri. He called Kiri from a remote phone box, as arranged, to hear how the engagement announcement had gone down. Kiri broke the news that he had a week or so to fly from Rome to Auckland via London and Brisbane. A friendly Maori priest, Father Henare Tate, had agreed to marry them. St Patrick's Cathedral had been booked for 2 p.m. on the afternoon of Wednesday, 30 August.

Des was forced to use the money his father had given him to fly to his new job in America to pay for his passage. He arrived in Brisbane in the last week of August. Des's friends there were amazed at the speed with which events had overtaken him. 'The first I heard about Kiri was when I had a telephone call saying Des wanted me to get in touch with him in England,' said his old Latvian dancing partner, Adolf Lacis. 'He wanted to know if I could go with him to New Zealand for the wedding.' Lacis and another university friend, James Love, were both able to organise time to travel. In Brisbane, Des flipped a coin to choose his best man. Lacis landed the top job and Love was relegated to the status of groomsman, a role he would share with Robert Hanson.

As eleventh-hour flight arrangements were made, Lacis learned that Des's family were deeply opposed to the wedding. At the airport, Des confirmed that neither his parents nor his brothers were willing to travel to New Zealand.

In London Bill Double, who had taken a set of soft-focus portraits of Kiri and Des to mark their engagement, had warned Des what sort of reception to expect in New Zealand. Sure enough Des walked off the plane from Brisbane straight into a phalanx of Double's old camera-wielding colleagues and became an instant celebrity. He travelled straight to Blockhouse Bay to meet Tom and Nell. For once Nell took a back seat as newspaper reporters, radio and television crews poured into the house for a hastily-arranged press conference. Pictures of Des and Kiri together had already made the evening news on television. The engagement made front page news all over New Zealand the following morning.

The in-depth interview Des gave the assembled media proved to be the first, and last, of his life to date. He admitted he had been overwhelmed by the reaction to his marrying Kiri. 'I had heard that Kiri was popular in New Zealand but I had no idea such a reception would await us,' he said. 'When we turn to settling down and raising our family, I feel sure this is the country we will choose.' He diplomatically revealed he used to be a rugby player. 'I would still be playing myself if it wasn't for a leg injury,' he smiled.

'He'll do us Kiwis', ran one headline the following day.

Over the following days, the New Zealand media ran gentle profiles of the lovebirds and their plans for their big day. Kiri told Wellington's *Dominion* that: 'We have differed over two things. I don't smoke and I don't like to see Desmond smoking. I love television and he doesn't.'

She was already aware of the stabilising influence Des had had on her. She derided her former self as 'scatty', saying, 'I don't laugh, giggle and shout as much as I used to.' Kiwi housewives would have been thrilled to know that their Maori diva had 'certainly become more domesticated'.

Double's engagement portrait of the couple was reproduced in newspapers from Gisborne to Dunedin. The *New Zealand Woman's Weekly* mobilised their forces to make Kiri their 'Bride of the Year'.

Amid the acreage of newsprint the name Brooke Monks was never mentioned once. In another country, or another more intrusive media age, Kiri's decision to drop her former boyfriend and accompanist in favour of a man she had met on a blind date only weeks earlier would have been a cause célèbre, a love triangle to be dissected and discussed in microscopic detail. What did Des have that his rival did not? How had Kiri come to such a whirlwind decision? No one in New Zealand put Des and Kiri through such inquisitions, of course, but the answers were not difficult to fathom.

In Des, Kiri had found a man with all the qualities Brooke manifestly lacked. For two years Brooke had been indecisive and inattentive, inflexible and generally uncommitted. To Kiri, at least, his relationship with his parents and his connection to his family business often seemed more important than she did. In the short time they had been together Des had made her feel like the centre of his universe. He had already pledged himself to following Kiri wherever her career took her. He had ditched his plans to work in America and was already actively looking for a place at the London School of Economics or for a new job in England. Nothing would be allowed to interfere with their happiness.

'Our professions are both pretty flexible and could take us anywhere in the world. We are prepared to accept this and go where and when we have to – but always together,' he had told the New Zealand press. As if all this was not enough Des had already shown he had no intention of allowing his own parents' feelings to come between him and Kiri. After years of confusion, Kiri saw things clearly at last. Her instincts had been sound. For her, Des Park really was Mr Ideal.

If Nell felt she had lost control of her daughter's life she was at least able to reclaim the reins temporarily. Whatever her misgivings, she was not going to miss out on the prospect of organising a wedding the likes of which New Zealand had never before witnessed. As Kiri later put it, 'Mummy wanted the full bit – and got it.'

Nell recruited the biggest names in Auckland society. One of her first calls was to her old friend, the couturier Colin Cole. After a series of fittings, he created a dress that would have cost an ordinary customer the then staggering sum of £2,000. Cole, generous as ever, says his then manageress Terry Nash, gave it to Kiri as a gift. New Zealand's most famous society photographer John Lesnie was hired to take the photographs and make one of his celebrated wedding cakes at the same time. Trillo's in Westhaven had been put on alert to expect a wedding reception for three hundred people.

Only Cliff Trillo had dented Nell's grand design for her daughter's big day. In her own, inimitable style, Nell had attempted to persuade the restaurateur to provide the reception free of charge. 'Cliff was persuaded to do the catering for Kiri's twenty first for free,' said his widow, Billie Trillo. 'When the wedding came up, dear old Nell decided that he could do the wedding for nothing as well. Cliff couldn't afford to do it, and told her so. She said, "Just think of the publicity, Mr Trillo!"' This time, however, even Nell's powers of persuasion failed her.

Back at Mitchell Street events began unfolding at a speed that had induced a sense of pure panic. 'It was just bloody bedlam, in a nutshell,' recalled Judy. In the confusion, curiously, the stiff card invitations mistakenly asked guests to RSVP to 22 Mitchell Road, rather than Street. The lion's share of the work had fallen to Kiri's sister, Nola. From dawn to dusk she was camped in the kitchen cooking, cleaning and catering to Nell's every whim. 'Picture it like a general dogsbody in an office. That would cover Mum's stature within the family,' sighed Judy.

141

If Judy expected to represent the family among her aunt's brides-maids, she was to be disappointed. Alongside Sally Rush, Kiri's friend from St Mary's and London, were another well-known St Mary's singer, Lindsay Kearns, and Nan Taylor, a beauty queen Kiri had met for the first time on her fleeting visit to New Plymouth six months before.

Amid the chaos Tom was sent away from the house. With Adolf Lacis, he set off on a miniature tour of the New Zealand interior. 'Tom took me on a trip around the North Island for a couple of days. He wasn't needed for the organising. Nell did all of that,' said Lacis. 'If she needed him she would scream and Tom would run.'

Lacis, like everyone else, had quickly grown to admire Kiri's father. 'Ma was very bombastic, but Tom was a true gentleman,' he said. Lacis sensed that in Tom's adopted daughter, his old schoolfriend had found true love. 'Kiri was a wild girl. You wouldn't consider her wild now, but she was for her day. Des really loved her, you could see they had really clicked.'

As the preparations continued, Kiri concentrated on fulfilling her two major public engagements, one at Auckland Town Hall and the other at Wellington on the Saturday night before the wedding. Neither concert did much to ease her nerves. In Auckland she attended a packed party where she met many of the patrons who had funded her move to London. 'I came out of the dressing room carrying sheets of music,' Kiri told the *New Zealand Herald* afterwards. 'I seemed to be surrounded by hundreds of people and just wanted to get home.'

Back in Blockhouse Bay, Kiri realised her bag, containing passport, driving licence, chequebook and other papers, was missing. Although Kiri felt it had not been stolen, its disappearance drove home just how close to her her fans were. Their attention and proximity was not always desirable.

The Wellington concert five nights later was another sell-out. For more than two hours Kiri held her audience, including a host of government ministers and Maori leaders, entranced. Her version of Dido's lament had, by now, become a highlight of her repertoire. She had sung it again in London in June. The reaction was equally ecstatic weeks later when she repeated the performance at the Royal Festival Hall's Purcell Room. The respected critic Alan Blyth, then with the *Daily Express*, watched the performance. 'Trying to spot the next decade's operatic star is nearly as difficult as picking a winner on the race-course – and just as intriguing,' he wrote. 'If I had to put my money on it, I would back a magnetic twenty-three-year-old soprano called Kiri Te Kanawa from New Zealand.' Of her performance in *Dido and Aeneas*, he added, 'Miss Te Kanawa sang with a full, perfectly focused tone as the ill-fated Queen . . . suggesting she is now ready for employment in any opera house you care to name.'

Perhaps tiring of the fairytale coverage given elsewhere, Wellington's critics were less generous. Owen Jensen of the *Evening Post* led the way. 'To discover the Kiri Te Kanawa of 1967, one must first discount the extravagant publicity which has spun a sort of halo of unreality around her work and person since she went overseas. One must remember – or forget, perhaps? – that, one way and another, she has been New Zealand's most pampered and favoured music student, and one should put aside the sympathies of racial sentimentality,' he wrote. While recognising her 'obvious gifts', Jensen said Kiri had 'acquired most of the frills of success and some of the substance'. He added, '. . . the spontaneity and simplicity which gave her earlier singing charm has been largely lost to a mannered platform presence and studied style.'

Russell Bond in the *Dominion* pointed the finger of blame elsewhere. He praised Kiri's 'intelligence, musicianship and . . . technical skill' but railed at the extensive programme that 'would surely have daunted the most accomplished and versatile of opera stars'. It was an 'ordeal' which 'exploited the singer unmercifully', he decided. Wherever the blame lay, the strain was soon showing.

On the night of 29 August, Lacis, Love and Des joined some of Kiri's male friends for a stag party at Lou Clauson's studio next to his house outside Auckland. The participants' memories of that hard drinking night are understandably hazy, but Lacis believes it culminated in chaining Des to some railings. Clauson had been as taken aback by developments as everyone else. 'I was surprised not at the wedding, but that she perhaps hadn't waited a few years till her career was really going well.'

Back at Mitchell Street, however, no one should have been overly surprised at the toll Kiri's hectic return home had now taken. A full dress rehearsal had been scheduled for St Patrick's on the Tuesday evening. Sister Mary Leo had arrived to lead the St Mary's Choir through a final practice of the hymns she and Nell had selected. Kiri's old touring partner, Michael McGifford, who had flown back especially from New York's Juilliard School of Music, rehearsed his contribution. Soon, however, it was obvious that Kiri was not going to make it. Nell telephoned Father Tate to break the news she would not be coming. Kiri had found herself paralysed by last minute nerves. A doctor had been called to see her.

On the morning of Wednesday, 30 August, Auckland awoke to glorious, late winter sunshine. At Mitchell Street, Nell rose early and reached straight for the telephone. News of Kiri's failure to turn up for her dress rehearsal had flown around Auckland. Nell spoke to reporters working on the early editions of the country's main evening newspapers, the *Auckland Star* and the Wellington-based *Evening Post*, to assure them there would be no last-minute hitches. She confirmed that a doctor had been called to the house but explained that he had simply pronounced Kiri over-tired. 'She has had such a busy time since she came home, and she was just exhausted last night.'

Kiri had woken up that morning full of life once more, Nell reassured the newspapers. She was 'a box of birds . . . The sun has shone on Kiri all her life and we would have been surprised if it had forsaken her today.'

If we believe Kiri's own account of her wedding day, she was probably fast asleep while Nell was making her first phone calls. She and her chief bridesmaid Sally Rush overslept after the dramas of the night before. They had begun the day by ringing a city radio station with a request for Des, Petula Clark's 'Don't Sleep in the Subway Darling'. Panic had quickly overcome them, however. No one had booked a hairdresser. A last-minute appointment was made at a salon nearby.

From the number of cards, bouquets and phone calls that had poured into Mitchell Street, Nell had already sensed a vast crowd would turn up. She and Sally Rush had rung the police and the traffic department to suggest the area surrounding St Patrick's be cordoned off and extra staff be laid on. The request had been brushed off with a laugh. Only five traffic officers had been provided to control the crowd.

Late in the morning, Donald Perry, one of the ushers, was sent down to check on the scene at the Cathedral. 'The word came through about three hours before the wedding that the mob outside the

Cathedral was getting rather large and they thought the ushers better get down there to get it organised, otherwise no one would be able to park or get in,' he said. Perry couldn't believe the scale of the crowds that greeted him. 'I think we secretly knew something was going to happen but not as bad. It was all quite scary.'

People had begun gathering outside St Patrick's since early that morning. The doors of the Cathedral were opened at 10 a.m. Within minutes all the public pews had been filled. Each hour hundreds more people spread out into St Patrick's Square and along Wyndham Street, the route Kiri would take to the ceremony. By lunchtime close to two thousand people had crammed themselves into the area surrounding the Cathedral.

Perry and his fellow ushers borrowed the St Patrick's choir members' full-length, bright red robes. As guests battled through the thickening crowds, the distinctive outfits lent the ten ushers a sense of authority. 'They also helped because it meant everyone could see us.'

In his fifty-year career, John Lesnie photographed more than ten thousand weddings, including that of Everest-conquering climber Sir Edmund Hillary in 1953. Hillary's marriage had been a national event – but even that was dwarfed by Kiri's extraordinary day. 'I'd never seen a crowd like that outside the Cathedral,' he said. Lesnie had taken photographs of Kiri in her dress at Mitchell Street and had to fight his way through the crowds to reach his position inside the church in time. 'I had to get my car between two of the bridal cars and park right outside so I could get through.'

So chaotic were the scenes that even Sister Mary Leo had difficulty getting into the church. Sally Rush's brother had not believed she was who she claimed to be when she tried to enter through a side door.

Kiri, with Tom at her side, left Mitchell Street in good time. As the crowds began to jostle her car, however, she began crying openly. It took her driver ten minutes to nudge his way the few yards from the corner of St Patrick's Square to the Cathedral entrance itself. As the crowd surged forward Kiri was guided to the door by the senior traffic officer, a Sergeant Williams. Photographs of him leading a radiant but nerve-racked bride through the throng remained the enduring image of the day for years to come.

Those who were able to see Kiri cheered their approval of her choice of dress. Colin Cole's parchment-white silk gown and peaked, pillbox hat made her look like a medieval princess. Her bouquet of five off-white roses wavered in her grip as she and Tom made their way into the Cathedral.

No arrangements had been made to relay the events to the crowds outside. The service was interrupted by the sound of people hammering on the locked doors. Already overcome with emotion, Kiri repeatedly burst into tears. She had difficulty repeating the vows read to her by Father Tate. In the end it seemed a blessing that – due to Des's religion – Father Tate could not carry out a formal nuptial mass. Within twenty minutes, the abridged ceremony had ended with Kiri and Des exchanging identical, white gold rings.

Donald Perry and the ushers were sent out to form an advance guard. The red-robed men linked arms to clear the crowds away from the steps. Cheers broke out as Des and Kiri emerged arm in arm. As the onlookers fought to get a glimpse of Kiri, three women had to be helped away by policemen. An old lady had to be put in one of the bridal cars, another collapsed and had to be carried away in an ambulance.

'We all linked arms trying to hold the crowd back but it was an almighty crush,' said Donald Perry. 'A middle-aged woman standing just behind David Hanson, another of the ushers, was being pushed so hard from behind that her blouse just ripped away from her chest.'

Even by Nell Te Kanawa's lavish standards, the wedding reception was a spectacular affair. A giant soup tureen had been filled with a vast display of Bluff oysters, flown freshly into Auckland that morning. A gargantuan cut of Great Baron Beef, baked hams and roast turkeys dominated one end of the room. Cases of Great Western champagne had been placed on ice.

Nell had filled Trillo's with more than three hundred guests, but as Des and Kiri scanned the room they saw pockets of gatecrashers. 'It was a mess,' said Kiri later. 'People who thought they should have been invited decided to come anyway.'

Many of them insisted on making lengthy speeches. There was a sizeable contingent of Tom's family, and many of the male members decided to exercise the Maori tradition of speechmaking, with varying degrees of success. In all the reception lasted for five long hours. 'Kiri looked bored with the whole thing by the end,' said Billie Trillo. As the event took on a life of its own slip-ups were inevitable. The Maori

Queen, Te-Ata-i-rangi-kaahu, was among the guests. With her husband, Te Whatu Moana, she sat with Hannah Tatana, Michael McGifford and his mother. Nell's planning had failed to take account of Maori protocol and no toast or mention of their Royal guest was made. 'The Queen was disgusted,' said Tatana. 'It showed that Mrs Te Kanawa was versed in neither Maori nor European protocol.'

At one point a drunken guest stood up and demanded a song from Kiri. As she sat shaking her head, an equally drunk Des got to his feet and intervened. 'Kiri can't sing, but I will,' he said. What he lacked in musicality – 'he had a dreadful voice,' said Billie Trillo – he more than made up for in enthusiasm. His rousing version of 'Waltzing Matilda' was cheered to the rafters. Unsurprisingly, it remains his one and only public singing performance.

Des had dealt with the dramas of the day by drinking himself into a blind stupor. Arriving at the reception he had requisitioned two bottles of champagne for his own personal use and wasted little time in emptying them.

'Des was as drunk as a skunk,' remembered Kiri's cousin, Kay Rowbottom. 'Even at the Cathedral you could see his eyeballs going round and round and he just had a stupid grin on his face. I think they tried to sober him up at one stage, with coffee and fresh air.'

Kiri herself admitted that Des had been 'very drunk' at the wedding. Given the overwhelming pressures he was enduring from all sides of his extended family it was hardly surprising.

Nell had reservations about Kiri's choice of husband. Having spent years carrying around a mental list of the 'men most likely to' and having long cherished the prospect of Kiri marrying Brooke it was inevitable that she would be unhappy at the idea of Kiri marrying a man she had not personally sanctioned. The fact that she was being introduced to her future son-in-law only days before he joined the family only worsened matters. Des's slightly detached charm failed to win her over. It would not be long before Nell's feelings became apparent. 'She never liked Des,' said Judy Evans-Hita. 'I'm not sure why, but the family knew she didn't.'

The snub the Park family had delivered Nell's daughter only deepened her distrust. Des continued to make excuses for the fact that none of his family had travelled over to New Zealand. 'I really felt sorry for Des. His parents didn't come to the wedding and I don't think he ever forgave them for it,' said Lacis. In the days before the wedding, Des, Kiri and Nell told anyone who asked that Des's father had been taken ill; Mrs Park had stayed to look after him. Adolf Lacis recalls another explanation. 'The official excuse given at the wedding was that they didn't like flying, but that was rubbish,' he said.

To his credit, Des kept his emotions bottled up throughout the service and the interminable reception. The scars would be lasting ones, however. 'I think it took ten or fifteen years before Des got over it,' said his best man.

As the reception finally drew to a close, Kiri and Des moved up to Mitchell Street where an array of lavish gifts was on show. 'There was a lot of crystal and silver,' said Kay Rowbottom. 'But many of the presents were money, because that would be easier to get back to England.' The newlyweds stayed up long into the night. If they had plans of escaping the chaos by moving to a hotel, they didn't make it and were still at Kiri's parents' home the next morning.

If Des rose with a hangover, the financial headache he woke up to was only marginally less painful. Despite the generosity of their friends, the wedding bill was always going to be beyond Nell and Tom's meagre means. Kiri and Des had agreed to foot a proportion of the costs using much of the cash given as wedding gifts. As the wedding had run out of control, all thoughts of money had been forgotten, however. Des later recalled how at one stage of the reception he had heard his best man asking for 'another scotch'. 'I thought he meant a bottle, when in fact he was talking about a case.' Kiri and Des were shellshocked by the final bill from Trillo's.

The newlyweds headed for Taupo for their honeymoon. They spent three weeks skiing in the mountains, although Kiri's comment years later that they were always last up the mountain and first down suggests their energies were spent elsewhere. In mid September a tanned Kiri and a relaxed looking Des posed for photographers one last time, this time on the steps of an Air New Zealand plane bound for London. As they waved New Zealand goodbye there was no disguising the reality. Mr and Mrs Desmond Park were beginning married life 'stony broke'.

Tamed

In September 1967, Bob Morgan was lost for words when his old Brisbane schoolfriend Des Park re-entered his life arm-in-arm with a beaming new bride. Morgan, who was working in London as an engineer, and his wife Sharon had seen or heard nothing of Des since meeting him for a swift drink as he headed off for a blind date in the West End early that spring. They had often wondered how the assignation had gone. Six months later their curiosity was satisfied when they met Mr and Mrs Des Park near their new marital home at De Vere Gardens, Kensington. Over a drink, Des recounted the chaotic events of August with a sardonic smile. 'He had come third in a poll of New Zealand's most popular personalities. He told me he had got more votes than Sir Edmund Hillary – and all he had done was turn up and marry Kiri,' said Morgan. 'He thought that was a great joke.'

Des's marriage to Kiri was a far from frivolous matter, however. 'I don't know what happened, but for a guy like Des, who always had his feet on the ground, to do that within so short a time, their relationship must have been pretty strong,' said Morgan.

There was much to test the strength of the new marriage as the newlyweds faced a grim financial landscape. Before his whirlwind romance to Kiri, Des had quit his job with Britannia Lead on the assumption he would go to America. He returned to London to begin the process of looking for a new employer. After paying the final wedding bills, Kiri's bank balance was in equally parlous shape. Her bursaries from the Arts Council and her trust fund were dedicated to the ongoing costs of her studies at the Opera Centre. At least Veronica Haigh's generosity meant they had a comfortable home in which to

149

begin married life. After a few uneasy weeks under the same roof, Raewyn Blade moved out, leaving Des and Kiri alone together in the mews.

Resourceful as ever, Des soon found freelance work drafting engineering contracts. Yet for the first time in her life Kiri found herself required to count the pennies. Each Monday Des would give her a housekeeping allowance which she was expected to make last a full week. Kiri willingly threw herself into the role of happy homemaker. Bob Morgan visited De Vere Gardens one evening to find Kiri drawing on the needlework skills she had learned with her niece Judy at Mitchell Street. 'She was making a pair of black slacks with her sewing machine,' he said. 'She had it perched on top of a flimsy cardboard box and she kept having to unpick everything, recut it and start over. They never fitted at all, but she was happy. She had that easy-going Maori attitude – that it didn't matter, that it would be OK.'

At weekends the Morgans and the Parks would spend what resources they had at pubs and clubs, like the late-night Speakeasy in South Kensington. 'It was a wonderful, carefree time. None of us had children and we burned the candle at both ends,' said Morgan.

There were times when they perhaps partied a little too hard. Kiri's Opera Centre producer Tom Hawkes met them at a celebration thrown by an Australian friend Brian Stanbrough. Des had indulged himself so much he left the party without his other half. 'He totally forgot about her. He'd picked up the car, driven off and realised he'd left something behind. It was one of those sort of parties,' smiled Hawkes. 'She was fast asleep at the foot of the stairs when he rang the bell later.'

For years afterwards, Kiri herself looked back on her early days of marriage with an abiding affection. 'I think those broke times were the best of our life,' she said once.

Rodney Macann was one of the first to invite the newlyweds to dinner back in London. Recovered from the setback of earlier that year, Macann had begun seeing someone else. Macann saw Kiri still suffered from an inability to curb her tongue. Now, however, she had Des to act as censor. 'They came over to my flat very soon after they got married and Kiri started having a go about the current rival and Des just stopped her, straight away. She came to heel, basically,' said Macann. 'I thought that was impressive. It's quite a man who can stop Kiri in her tracks.'

There were times when she bridled at his treatment of her. 'He treats me like a child,' she would complain to friends. Yet Des's domineering personality had restored her sense of security. 'Suddenly I was under a really disciplined husband,' she said later. 'He was handsome and very solid. He was the sort of person I liked.'

The new influence being brought to bear on her life was apparent as she returned to the Opera Centre for the winter term. In her final performance before leaving for New Zealand and the wedding, Kiri had been at her indisciplined worst. She had sung the minor role of the second of the Three Ladies attending the Queen of Night in a production of *The Magic Flute* being directed by one of Covent Garden's star producers, John Copley. Copley had been deeply unimpressed by Kiri's lack of application, her grandiose behaviour and her habit of constantly criticising others. At one stage he sent her home to learn her words properly. Afterwards he dismissed her as a 'silly girl'.

Kiri knew she had been indulged by James Robertson in particular. 'I suppose because I was this crazy flamboyant kid they believed in me more than they did others, and put up with it and hoped I'd calm down. And somehow, within a year, I was tamed down a bit,' she admitted. As she returned to the Centre equipped with a new, more professional approach, it was obvious who was doing the taming.

'It seemed to me and it was generally accepted at the time that Des was the best possible influence,' said Tom Hawkes. 'I recall a story that at one point he said, "You're either going to be my wife or you're going to have a career, but you're not going to mess around."'

The earliest victim of this newfound seriousness was Margaret Krauss. Kiri's enforced relationship with Krauss had ended in predictable acrimony. Kiri felt the German drained her of all self confidence. 'She said I should give up,' she claimed later. As she cast around for a new teacher, she could not help noticing the great strides being made by two other New Zealanders, Ann Gordon and, in particular, Mary Masterton.

Masterton had arrived in London in 1967 having followed an almost identical path to that taken by Kiri a year earlier. Another Sister Mary Leo student, she had shone in the competitions before deciding to chance her arm with an audition for Robertson and his colleagues in London. She too had sailed for England on board the *Australis*. She too had saved herself the £200 passage by singing in cabarets on board. She and Kiri became intimate – if slightly careful – friends. 'We were wary of each other. Maybe we were a bit alike in some ways, and sussed each other out,' Masterton said.

Masterton's mezzo voice had bloomed under a Norwegian teacher, Florence Wiese-Norberg, to whom she had been introduced by another Sister Mary Leo singer, Heather Begg. In a profession awash with charlatans, Norberg was widely regarded as among the most technically knowledgeable teachers in Europe. She was credited with having helped Laurence Olivier recover his voice after illness. The model Twiggy had turned to her for help in preparing for her forthcoming debut as a singer in *The Boyfriend*. In 1967 Norberg's clear-headed views on 'voice production' were published in the august medical journal, *General Practitioner*. Her philosophy was simple. Relaxation was the key to perfect vocal projection. Singers should not be pushed too far too fast. 'Young singers, eager to make their mark in what has become a highly competitive world, are exploited and pushed into heavy taxing roles long before they are mentally or vocally mature enough to shoulder the professional responsibilities with which they are presented,' she wrote. She demanded three years with each of her students. By the end of that time they would be equipped with a voice that was *bien eglaise*, relaxed and correctly positioned vocally. All she asked in return was that her pupils treated her with respect. 'Every teacher expects certain things to be taken on trust – integrity being one of them,' she wrote.

Norberg spoke in a gruff, aggressive voice that masked her inner warmth and fierce intelligence. She and Kiri quickly sensed they could help each other. Late in 1967, Kiri joined the pilgrimage to Norberg's third floor studio on George Street near Marylebone High Street. Masterton had a regular, hour-long lesson at 10 a.m. each Thursday. Kiri became Norberg's new 11 o'clock appointment. Norberg's first task was to restore the self-belief Krauss had eroded. In this she was aided, as ever, by her faithful dog Duffy. 'He would howl if you sang a flat note. If you were in tune he just lay there quietly,' recalled Mary Masterton.

Norberg began helping Kiri develop the upper range of her voice, providing the technical knowhow that would allow her to make the step up to soprano status. 'My voice had come on a lot with Florence, she knew exactly where to pitch it and how to strengthen it. She did the same for Kiri. She was the first person to give her a really good vocal technique,' said Masterton.

Kiri's progress was also helped by her friendship with the most prominent New Zealand conductor in London, John Matheson. Matheson had met a dispirited-looking Kiri at a New Zealand House party. She had brightened up when he introduced himself. 'I bowled up to her and said, "You're Kiri Te Kanawa, I've heard about you,' he remembered. As the two chatted, Matheson asked her whether she might be interested in working together. 'She said, "Oh, I should be delighted. It's wonderful to find somebody to take an interest." I remember specifically her saying that. It was quite sad, she'd come over from New Zealand having won prizes and was a bit on the melancholy side.'

Born in Seacliff, Dunedin, Matheson had come to London in the 1950s when he had spent an eight-year stint at Covent Garden. By now he was installed as a senior conductor at Sadler's Wells. Matheson had little regard for James Robertson and his colleagues at the London Opera Centre. They were 'amateurs and mediocrities' as far as he was concerned. Sensing Kiri needed more professional help than she was getting, he invited her for lessons at his home in Ealing, west London. 'When she first sang to me I thought "Oh Lord!"' he recalled. Yet to Matheson, at least, it was obvious Kiri was not learning anything about the meaning of the music she sang so magnificently. 'It was an exceedingly beautiful voice, but she was singing Bellini and Puccini not knowing anything about the Italian.'

Matheson was close to the main Italian coach at Covent Garden, Ubaldo Gardini, and, quite rightly, regarded himself as an expert in the field. 'I doubt if it was one hundred per cent faultless but it was certainly a good deal better than the Opera Centre,' he said. 'I gave her a good grounding in German, Italian and French and I didn't charge her anything for it because she didn't have any money, and it wasn't my job so I didn't need it. I did it for pleasure and delight because this was going to be a voice of importance.'

As 1967 wore on, more influential people began to share his view.

Kiri's first major role at the Opera Centre in the autumn term was in a four-scene excerpt from *Anna Bolena*, Donizetti's 1830 work based on the life of Henry VIII's second wife. Tom Hawkes, once more hired to direct, had again double cast the piece. Kiri would play Anne Boleyn to the Australian Joan Carden's Jane Seymour in the senior pairing; Donna Fay Carr and Teresa Cahill would play Boleyn and Seymour in the second. Cahill had by now overcome the inferiority complex she had felt when she had first encountered Kiri. 'I remember the day I first met her. It was my first term and it was her second year and she sang Dido's lament,' said Cahill. 'She looked stunning and I was very shy and nervous. I was thinking "Oh God, if they're all like this I won't be able to earn a penny." It was a wonderful sound.'

As Cahill shared rehearsals with Kiri she too discovered a singer who worked off instinct rather than intellect. 'She had these amazing natural instincts for doing it right. I think she had to learn how to learn things. She wasn't a natural musician and she didn't sight read that well.' Aside from her glorious voice, Kiri's greatest gift lay in her ability to absorb the advice of others. 'Where coaches are concerned, she's a real magpie. She can take things and turn them as if she's just thought of it.'

A year after her setback in *Le Donne Curiose*, Tom Hawkes also found a more diligent Kiri. 'I think *Le Donne Curiose* was Kiri's first shock about the realities of the opera world,' he said. She remained a demanding student, however. 'To be honest, I was more taken with Teresa. She was more dramatically compelling and she was more experienced and committed. She was easier to work with. One didn't have to feed so much in as one did with Kiri.'

Anna Bolena was staged at the Opera Centre shortly before Christmas 1967. The major reviews, including one from the influential opera critic, Arthur Jacobs, went to Cahill and Donna Fay Carr. For Kiri, the consolation came days later when she was called into James Robertson's office and told he had been approached by an agent interested in representing her.

The select group of artists Basil Horsfield managed from his elegant offices overlooking Regents Park was nothing if not colourful. It included Horsfield's former lover, the flamboyant conductor John Pritchard, the imperious Welsh bass-baritone Geraint Evans and the brilliant but tortured pianist John Ogdon. A collection of rising vocalists, Evans's compatriots Ryland Davies and Stuart Burrows and the American mezzo-soprano Shirley Verrett provided a more youthful lustre to his list. Horsfield and the new man in his life and work, an

Australian lawyer, John Davern, saw Kiri as a highly marketable prospect. Kiri was deeply flattered, if a little intimidated by the approach. It would take her months to overcome the habit of referring to her agent as Mr Horsfield rather than Basil, and still longer to pick up the courage to telephone him at home at the weekends. With Des's blessing, she wasted no time in formally signing a contract with Horsfield's agency AIM, Artists International Management. The move soon bore fruit as, with Horsfield and Davern's help, Kiri found herself profiled in the *Daily Mail*'s Charles Greville diary column. 'A dolly among opera singers' read the headline above a moody portrait of Kiri and a testimonial from James Robertson, who described his discovery's voice as 'the most beautiful we've heard for years'. That, Kiri may have been, but as the end of an eventful year loomed, however, she remained a raw and promising student rather than an embryonic star.

She and Des spent their first Christmas together limiting themselves to small presents. As the New Year began they were soon facing up to the prospect of a lengthy separation. Des was offered a permanent job at Selection Trust, a mining finance company in the City of London. The post meant their immediate financial worries were over but also promised lengthy spells of overseas travel for Des. Plans for trips to Iran and Zambia were already being drawn up. At the same time Kiri had been offered her first professional role outside the Opera Centre, as Carmen in a new production of Bizet's evergreen with the Northern Opera in Newcastle.

James Robertson had by now extended Kiri's stay at the Opera Centre for another year. But, for all his faith in Kiri, there were few signs of interest from the opera companies, many of whom had been discouraged by her reputation. Under Florence Norberg Kiri was also involved in the difficult process of developing the upper range of her voice. The results of her Thursday morning sessions at George Street were impressive but – inevitably – cracks were audible to the discerning ear. No one was more aware of the strain than Kiri herself. She needed the time to mature properly. As Basil Horsfield began the slow process of selling Kiri to England's main opera companies – Glyndebourne, the English National Opera at Sadler's Wells and Covent Garden – Robertson hoped to use *Carmen* as a showcase for the regional opera companies, Scottish Opera and the Welsh National Opera in particular.

Kiri was double cast with her New Zealand friend Mary Masterton.

Masterton found marriage had not quite rid Kiri of her scattiness. She arrived in Newcastle to discover Kiri had agreed to act as the production's unpaid lorry driver. Masterton spent a bizarre twenty-four hours accompanying Kiri and a group of male stagehands to another theatre somewhere in the north of England. 'They had to take the scenery from another town to Newcastle so Kiri offered her services to drive. This is the sort of thing she'd do,' she said. Kiri asked Masterton if she would provide a little female company. 'I thought it was a stupid idea. We'd be travelling all night and we had rehearsals and we were supposed to be the leading singers, but I felt I couldn't let her go on her own with all these men, even though Kiri doesn't need a chaperone.'

Tom had taught Kiri how to handle heavy goods vehicles. She took the wheel of the large van and set off a few nights before the opening performance. Kiri got the crew to their destination late that night. As the men dismantled the scenery, she and Masterton huddled together in sleeping bags. 'We didn't sleep a wink. We lay there chit-chatting all night while they were banging, taking down the scenery all around us.'

At daybreak the following day Kiri took to the wheel of the van once more. 'She was singing at the top of her voice, getting everyone else to sing along with her. She was in her element,' said Masterton. Back in Newcastle, however, the consequences were inevitable. 'We both got stinking colds. As soon as we got back we had to rush off and get antibiotics.'

Masterton sensed Kiri was unhappy about the fact she was sharing the role with her compatriot. The attention Masterton was getting in both the New Zealand and British press did little to ease her insecurity. 'I don't think Kiri was particularly pleased that another New Zealander was doing the role. I don't think she liked to think I was a threat to her,' said Masterton.

Newcastle's duo of Kiwi Carmens caught the eye of the *Daily Mirror*'s influential arts editor David Clemens. In the run-up to the opening night Britain's biggest-selling paper ran a lengthy feature on the two singers, both of whom went to great lengths to talk about the sex appeal they intended bringing to the role. 'She mustn't be sexless, but if she's too sexy she becomes a slut,' Masterton told the *Mirror*.

'She's a fantastically alluring woman,' Kiri chimed in.

As rehearsals got under way, Kiri agonised over how fantastically alluring she should really be. At a party at De Vere Gardens, Des told John Matheson that Kiri had struggled to give herself a cleavage to compete with Masterton. 'They had great difficulty in giving her a cleavage,' he said. 'They were working quite a while to make what she had pushed up to look like a real cleavage from the front of the house. He made me laugh and was very frank about it.'

Matheson had failed to warm to Des's cagey, slightly distant personality. 'I couldn't get anywhere with Des, despite him being an Australian and me a Kiwi,' he said. 'That was the most interesting conversation I ever had with him.'

Kiri's attempts to play up her image failed to fire the imagination of some of the critics. She took to the stage in a white, puff-sleeved dress more suitable for Hansel and Gretel. One critic described her as looking like a 'tough tavern wench'.

Musically, the effects of her all-night drive were all too obvious. Fortunately James Robertson had by now learned how to cope with her occasional lapses in concentration. At one stage Masterton watched from the wings as Kiri stopped singing. 'She'd forgotten where she was. She walked back up the stage and eventually got back into it. Robertson knew what was going on and covered it up,' she said.

Only one local critic seemed to notice. 'She was a little unsure in the first act,' said the man from the *Newcastle Chronicle*. The city's other paper, *The Journal*, had no complaints, however. 'She gave us a Carmen of fire and passion,' its critic wrote. Kiri was 'obviously going far in the opera world'. As *Carmen*'s two-week run came to a close, however, she was headed no further than back to the Commercial Road. A scout from Scottish Opera had watched Kiri carefully but had left unimpressed.

By now Kiri had formed her own court within the Opera Centre. 'She always liked to be the queen, have an audience and always be at the centre of things,' said Masterton. Courtiers were invariably drawn from the lowlier members of the Centre's staff rather than fellow students or teachers. 'I came in one day and one of the girls who worked on reception was plucking her eyebrows. She liked that, she liked people fussing over her. She took it as being natural.'

It was clear to Masterton that, when necessary, Des was also expected to fulfil a similar role. One afternoon she had discovered Kiri crying in the Centre's 'green room'. Masterton knew Kiri had been working on an excerpt from Benjamin Britten's demanding *Albert Herring* with Donna Fay Carr. Kiri had been given a dressing down by the director.

'It involved a lot of character acting. She wouldn't ever consider that she had to do anything like that,' said Masterton. Masterton went in to console her friend. To her surprise she was soon joined by Des. 'Kiri was sitting in there all alone crying. The director had given her a really hard time,' she remembered. 'The next minute who arrives but Des. James Robertson had rung him and asked him to come over. To me it was just weird. I would be embarrassed to have my father or my husband come over because I was crying.'

Masterton knew Des well enough to know he had little time for the operatic world and its tauter temperaments. 'It must have been pretty hard for him, having to mollycoddle her,' she said. 'But that was the attitude we all had. We had to look after her even though she didn't need looking after at all.'

If Kiri's demands on Des betrayed a genuine insecurity, they may have been more to do with her fears over the solidity of their relationship. Des had begun work on the first of his overseas projects in Iran. Kiri coped with her loneliness by filling the house with girlfriends. Mary Masterton became a regular visitor to De Vere Gardens, around the corner from the Kensington flat she shared with her sister Lilian. The two singers would sit, listen to music and talk the nights away. During one of Des's absences Kiri asked Masterton to move into De Vere Gardens with her for a period. 'My sister objected to this because it meant she was alone. I would have gone happily otherwise. I liked Kiri,' she said. She did not hear from Kiri for a while afterwards. 'That didn't go down well. Kiri expects people to be available when she wants.'

Kiri was all too aware of her husband's effect on the opposite sex. In musical circles, in particular, his combination of good looks and self-contained strength presented an appealing contrast to the more flamboyant male members of the profession. As she had sat alone at home in De Vere Gardens, Kiri's doubts about Des's absences soon began to fester. 'She was worried about Des just after they got married,' said Masterton. 'She was convinced he was carrying on with someone else, she was very upset about it.'

Suspicion formed itself into something firmer when Des sent back a set of photographs from Iran. 'Des did a really stupid thing. He sent this photograph back from Iran but snipped off somebody sitting next to him,' recalled Masterton. 'That got Kiri really paranoid.'

On stage, at least, her gift for wringing sympathy had become a powerful part of her dramatic persona. As she approached the end of her time at the Opera Centre, it helped Kiri win a succession of important roles. In 1968, the Opera Centre's summer term production was a version of Poulenc's *Dialogues of the Carmelites*. Kiri was given the leading role of Blanche de la Force, the young French aristocrat who seeks salvation in a Carmelite convent during the French Revolution. Tom Hawkes, once more hired to direct, was surprised at the feelings Kiri's performance evoked. 'As a character, Blanche is afraid and weak and indecisive. You don't naturally feel sympathy for her,' he explained. 'But Kiri made it tremendously sympathetic. You felt for this poor young aristocrat who is terrified by her fear of death. She was absolutely lovely because she had that vulnerability.' The production was staged at the Opera Centre and in Bristol where James Robertson conducted the city's BBC Training Orchestra. The positive reviews Kiri's performance drew confirmed the progress she was making both as an actress and a soprano. Andrew Porter in the *Financial Times* was impressed by her 'expressive face which suggested poor Blanche's terror', while the esteemed Dr Stanley Sadie in *The Times* liked Kiri's 'large, well-focused soprano voice which she knows how and when to colour – her passionate, tremulous note of fear was very telling'.

The reviews helped Basil Horsfield line up more varied – and more high-profile – work outside the Opera Centre. First Kiri was offered the part of Idamantes, son of the Cretan King Idomeneus in Mozart's relatively obscure 1780 opera *Idomeneo*. Idamantes offered one of the more unusual parts available to a soprano. The part was originally written for Mozart's favourite castrato, Del Prato. In its rare revivals, modern conductors cast male tenors or female sopranos as they saw fit. In October, Kiri joined the Chelsea Opera Group in Oxford, Cambridge and then London's Queen Elizabeth Hall. Then, early in 1969, she was given a role in a concert performance of Handel's *Alcina* with her heroine Joan Sutherland in the title role and her husband Richard Bonynge conducting. Soon afterwards Kiri travelled to Monte Carlo where Decca were recording Giordano's *Fedora*. A slightly star-struck Kiri shared the studio with Tito Gobbi, Mario del Monaco and Magda Olivera in the title role.

Her most noticeable moment came back in London, early in the summer of 1969, however. In the fifteen years since its establishment, the Camden Festival had earned a reputation as a champion of neglected composers and operas. For that year's Festival, with Gerald Gover as his conductor, Tom Hawkes had been engaged to produce *La donna del Lago*, Rossini's 1819 opera based on Sir Walter Scott's poem 'The Lady of the Lake'. Rehearsals got under way after Easter at the Finchley Road Library in north London. Hawkes had assembled a top quality cast, including the brilliant young mezzo-soprano Gillian Knight in the 'trouser' role of Malcolm, and the tenors Maurice Arthur and John Serge in the leading male roles, suitors to the eponymous heroine, Ellen. Despite Kiri's reputation for lack of preparation, Hawkes had given Kiri the role of Ellen, written specifically for the great nineteenth-century soprano Isabella Colbran and acknowledged as one of the most testing in all opera ever since.

From the earliest days of rehearsal, it was once more obvious that Kiri had failed to do her homework. 'Again she hadn't learned the music properly,' recalled Hawkes. Suddenly deprived of her support network at the Opera Centre, Kiri found herself exposed to the harsher realities of the professional world. Kiri and the Londoner Maurice Arthur had formed a particular dislike for each other. 'There was great tension between them,' said Tom Hawkes. As Kiri repeatedly struggled with her lines one day, Arthur tore into her. The row reached a crescendo, according to their producer, when Arthur called Kiri a 'half caste'.

'It was a horrible scene,' said Hawkes. Eventually Hawkes and Gillian Knight helped broker the peace. 'I was much less experienced at dealing with flare-ups amongst artists then. There was a kind of a stand off,' he said. Kiri left the rehearsal bloodied but unbowed. She was already preparing her revenge. On a warm May evening at Camden Town Hall, opposite St Pancras Station, the opening night attracted a full house and a clutch of London's leading critics. The curtain rose to reveal a heavy morning mist lingering over Loch Katrine and an invisible female voice filling the auditorium. From the moment the audience caught sight of the Lady of the Lake, Kiri retained a grip on the audience's imagination for the rest of the evening. Her performance was far from flawless. Musically Arthur and Knight turned in more polished, mature performances. Yet by the final aria of the evening Kiri had pulled off a classic theatrical coup.

'The costume designer had given her this amazing, iridescent dress, with great butterfly sleeves. It hadn't been seen until then,' recalled Hawkes. In the days since the row with Arthur, Kiri had worked long and hard on the climactic solo, acknowledged as one of the most difficult in opera. Kiri delivered it brilliantly. Watching in the wings, Tom Hawkes recalled how as she approached the aria's climax Kiri slowly raised her arms dramatically so as to allow the light to pick up on her spectacular costume. The effect was instantaneous. 'The audience stood on their feet and they cheered and cheered and cheered,' smiled Hawkes. 'She knew what she was doing. She knew how to manipulate an audience. It was the oldest trick in the book. Gillian Knight undoubtedly sang better than anyone else that night, she was marvellous,' said Hawkes with a sagacious shake of his head. 'But Kiri walked away with the show.'

The critics confirmed her act of operatic larceny. The *Daily Express* headline the next day read, 'Maori is best of Italian Scots'. 'She not only looks the kind of girl to set the clans at loggerheads, but she also has a warmly expressive voice with a good grasp of Rossini's special vocal style,' its writer drooled. More pedantic observers like the *Daily Telegraph*'s Alan Blyth expressed doubts about Kiri's acting ability. 'Her stage presence is too placid, her acting too rudimentary,' he wrote in *Opera* magazine later. Blyth did not dissent from the chorus of praise for her voice, however. Its 'warm, fresh tone, easily produced, gave much pleasure,' he said.

The reviews proved timely, particularly in New Zealand where Kiri was due to reprise her Carmen with the New Zealand Opera Company, again with James Robertson holding the baton.

Robertson's presence was no coincidence. The company were well aware of Kiri's unpredictability and had insisted he join his protégée. 'He had to look after her,' said the company's artistic director of the time, John Thompson. 'The pair of them had to come. That was part of the thinking at the time. You wouldn't have one without the other. We wouldn't do any planning on it until we had James and Kiri all signed up and ready to go. There was too much riding on it. James was there to tone her down a bit.'

Kiri, says Thompson, was paid a few hundred dollars for each performance of *Carmen*, 'nothing' in international operatic terms.

Such was the sense of excitement about Kiri's return to New Zealand in her first operatic role, a farewell reception was held at New Zealand House. Kiri and Des posed with the High Commissioner Sir Thomas Macdonald and Lady Macdonald. James Robertson and other senior Opera Centre staff joined in the eulogies. It had been Robertson who had finally persuaded Kiri to take her first tentative steps into the professional world by leaving the Opera Centre after an unusually long stay.

'She didn't want to leave,' said Osvalda Robertson, who understood Kiri's reticence. 'It was safe. She was told what to do. She didn't have to audition. It was quite a different world, but James pushed her. He told her, "You have had three years, it's time you went."'

For all the progress she had undoubtedly made, Kiri herself seemed as uncertain as she had ever been about her future in the profession. 'It was at the reception at New Zealand House that she first said that she was going to stop singing,' said Osvalda Robertson. 'She just came out with it flippantly. She said, "I'm going to stop and have lots of babies."'

Kiri headed for New Zealand via Spain where she, Des, Bob and Sharon Morgan spent a sun-soaked fortnight. She arrived in Auckland equipped with a skin tone worthy of Bizet's original seductive, southern Spanish gypsy.

At the St James's Theatre in Wellington, however, Kiri still seemed unwilling to push the brazen side of her character to its limits. As rehearsals got under way, the producer Richard Campion was greeted with the sight of Kiri emerging from the wardrobe department clutching a scanty piece of clothing. 'She came tearing into my room and held out a little bit of black fabric,' he recalled. '"This is all the costume I've got for the first act,"' she complained. Every other cast member had been given a long dress. "I'm the lead!"' she bridled.

Campion knew Kiri's limits. 'She was very attractive physically and attractive vocally, but not really a sex cat, not a throbbing woman who when she feels the need can turn it on and seduce the bastard and be seduced herself,' he said. Campion feared his young star would suffer in comparison to the last Carmen New Zealand had seen. The vampish Joyce Blackham's habit of bursting out of her bra on stage had earned her the undying devotion of stage hands and cognoscenti alike. As far as Campion was concerned the costume made the maximum use of Kiri's more limited assets. 'I said, "If you wear a long frock, where would Carmen be? If you wear this, we see your arms, we see your legs, we see other parts of you. It's a hot day in the factory. You've taken things off. You're vulnerable – and you're the only one who hasn't got a frock on,"' he said. 'There was a long pause, a deep sigh as she thought it through. And then away she went and made the most of it.'

James Robertson used his time in New Zealand to catch up with old friends. As he did so he made no secret of the troubles he had faced with Kiri in London. Over lunch with Neil McGough and Ossie Cheesman he confirmed the rumours that he had issued Kiri with a final warning in 1966. 'He told us that they had taken Kiri aside and told her, "If you don't pull your socks up, we're going to put you on a boat back home." And they would have issued a press release saying exactly why they were doing it,' said McGough.

Robertson still harboured doubts. 'James didn't give the impression that he was that happy with her, just that she had the potential, still acted the goat and needed a smack on the bum now and again.'

Kiri's high spirits at the St James's Theatre did nothing to ease Robertson's frustration. As the opening act got under way, Kiri emerged to sing the 'Habanera' with her dress slashed open revealingly. The 'tough tavern wench' of Newcastle was replaced by a ravishing young woman. 'She was provocative enough in looks, dress and manner to get any young man in trouble,' the *New Zealand Herald*'s veteran critic L. C. M. Saunders later wrote.

Freed from the straitjacket strictures of the Opera Centre, Kiri was determined to enjoy herself during her 'holiday' back in New Zealand. During the Act Three moment when José aims his rifle into the wings and shoots, Kiri, standing in the wings, threw a large lifeless swan on to the stage. Robertson and the Australian tenor Donald Smith were far from amused by the laughter that welled up in the audience. 'It was a real, dead, white swan. I've no idea where she got it,' recalled Neil McGough, a trombone player in the pit that night. 'The crowd all loved it, as they do in New Zealand. The orchestra all giggled and the company laughed and got on with the show. James stood there with a face as black as thunder. He did not approve.'

Smith, a seasoned veteran of Sadler's Wells, exacted revenge by leaving Kiri bruised as he fell on top of her in the final death scene and by taking his complaints backstage. 'He had come up the hard way and was doing his best for us and he didn't like people doing that sort of thing during his performance,' said John Thompson. 'There was a bit of a blow up over that. After the show he really told her where she got off, which may have been to her advantage eventually, I think. We just went on, we didn't take any notice of her. There was still something of a New Zealand larrikin spirit in her, wanting to have a bit of fun. It was part of a learning curve for her.'

Thompson believes Kiri and Smith were able to make their peace and get on with the job. 'When the two of them got singing, then by Jove it was some of the best singing you could have heard around at that time,' he said. Despite that, however, the show was far from a well-oiled success. In Wellington, to groans from the audience, the final curtain dropped across the prostate bodies of Kiri and Smith. At times Campion packed too many people on to the revolving set. Yet the reviews concentrated on Carmen. As far as the *Auckland Star*'s Desmond Mahoney was concerned Kiri 'captivated the audience with both the natural beauty of her voice and the visual perfection of her casting'.

In New Zealand, at least, Kiri could still do no wrong. With the possible exception of the 1965 *Porgy and Bess* in which Kiri had turned down the offer of playing Clara opposite Inia Te Wiata, the *Carmen* tour was the most successful of its era. 'It was a bit of gamble on our part,' remembered John Thompson. 'We didn't know whether people would come out to see *Carmen* or Kiri. Once the thing opened, of course, there was no problem whatsoever. People were hitting one another over the head to try and get a seat. That was the way all through the season.'

Towards the end of 1969, Kiri and her old Opera Centre colleague Teresa Cahill were chosen for one of the most high-profile recording sessions of the year, a star-studded *Marriage of Figaro* under the baton of the formidable Otto Klemperer. The duo, cast as the bridesmaids, arrived trembling at the prospect of working with the tyrannical eighty-four-year-old maestro, already suffering from the ravages of mental and physical illness. 'At one point he choked on a chocolate biscuit and had to be cleaned up. He was very frail. We were terrified of him,' remembered Cahill.

To celebrate surviving their first recording session, Kiri and Cahill treated themselves to new dresses for a one-off public performance to be held at the Royal Festival Hall. 'We decided to buy identical dresses so that we would look like bridesmaids.' It was on the bus back down the Bayswater Road towards Notting Hill and then Kensington that Kiri admitted to Cahill the problems she was experiencing outside the Opera Centre. Basil Horsfield had arranged a succession of auditions at Glyndebourne, Sadler's Wells and Covent Garden. While Glyndebourne had formally rejected her for a role in *La Calisto*, Sadler's Wells had not even bothered to call Horsfield back. Only Covent Garden seemed interested in her, and even they were vacillating. Cahill mentioned that she had been accepted at Covent Garden after only one audition. 'She said, "Oh God, I've had to do three auditions",' Cahill recalled. 'She said she wasn't sure if she was going to get in even then.'

The cold realities of life in London had been apparent long before she left the Opera Centre. While she had struggled with her studies, she could only stand and watch her rivals reaping rewards still seemingly beyond her. Glyndebourne's Jani Strasser had been sufficiently impressed by Cahill's performance at an Opera Centre masterclass to have offered her a place covering Elvira in a new production of *Don Giovanni*. She had spent two, highly successful years there before returning to the Opera Centre to finish her studies. Josephine Barstow had made her professional debut as Mimì in the Opera For All production of *La Bohème*, had gone on to the Welsh National Opera and was already preparing for her debut at Covent Garden in *Peter Grimes*. Most spectacular of all, the Canadian Donna Fay Carr had been chosen to play Donna Anna in the English National Opera's opening production of *Don Giovanni* at its splendid new home at the Coliseum. In comparison, Kiri's progress in the upper echelons had been painfully slow. 'It was very competitive. There was a sense of rivalry because we were all after the same thing. We were all trying to get into the business,' said Cahill.

Funding was still coming her way from New Zealand, where every musical move she made was still being reported in fine detail. Pride would not allow her to turn back, yet as she looked forward the prospects were bleak. Fortunately a new guardian angel, in the form of agent and musical administrator Joan Ingpen, suddenly loomed into view.

Ingpen's friendship with Basil Horsfield stretched back to her own days as an agent. Ingpen's agency, Ingpen and Williams, represented among others Joan Sutherland and the man now acknowledged as the greatest all-round musician of his generation, Georg Solti, then musical director of Covent Garden.

If there was a wilier operator working in the musical world, Solti had certainly never met her. He had insisted on having his former agent as his controller of planning at the Royal Opera. Her acumen there had proven even more impressive. Soon she would be performing the same role at the Paris Opéra and the New York Met.

Horsfield had begun tentative negotiations with Ingpen even before Kiri left the Opera Centre. Ingpen's instincts had been confirmed by another look at his client at Camden Town Hall in *Donna del Lago*. Kiri's voice betrayed the transition her voice was undergoing in Florence Norberg's classroom. 'It was pretty excruciating,' recalled Ingpen. 'She was nothing like ready for it vocally, but she looked marvellous and she had great panache on stage.' Ingpen's worries were less to do with Kiri's vocal potential than another quality she immediately recognised. 'I could see she was very ambitious.'

Covent Garden's ruling troika of Solti, Ingpen and the general administrator, David Webster, had grown weary at the number of English-language singers now being lured away from London. For all her failings, Ingpen sensed a star quality in Kiri. If she was to come to Covent Garden, Ingpen was clear on her terms. 'I was afraid she would be ruined,' said Ingpen. 'There was a big danger – it had already happened – that people were given their first principal role at the Garden, then given offers and ruined. I said, let's give this girl a five-year contract, not that we won't let her have leave, but so we can control what she does while she's maturing. Otherwise it will be another "What a pity."'

Kiri had now entered another realm in her career. For the first time opera politics raised their head. In August 1969, Kiri had given the New Zealand *Listener* a glowing tribute to her teacher, Norberg. 'She has done wonderful things for me, mentally and spiritually, as well as for my voice. She has been the strength in me, the saving grace.'

Basil Horsfield, however, viewed Florence Norberg's scientific approach and eclectic collection of clients with barely concealed disdain and had begun suggesting Kiri switch to a teacher more acceptable to the powers of Covent Garden. Vera Rosza had studied singing in Budapest, then sung as a mezzo at the Vienna State Opera in the 1950s. She arrived in England in 1953 and had moved into teaching under Frederic Cox at the Royal Northern College of Music in Manchester. Rosza was already moulding the then wife of Horsfield's client Ryland Davies, the mezzo Anne Howells. Her most powerful ally, however, was Georg Solti, whom she had known since their earliest days in Budapest. As Hungarian Jews, their bond had been tightened by the horrors of World War II.

At the time Rosza's client list was far from impressive. Her dictatorial style was too much to handle for many. 'You had to accept a lot. It was almost domination,' said Teresa Cahill, who spent a brief and unhappy time as a Rosza pupil. Kiri, however, was impressed by her *'grande dame'* demeanour and powerful connections. She also recognised that Rosza, like Des, would offer the discipline she lacked naturally. Des, too, supported a change. Apart from anything else, he disapproved of Norberg's possessiveness.

'Florence used to have these Saturday classes where she liked all her pupils to go and sing,' said Mary Masterton. 'I know Des didn't like that because he liked to spend the weekend with Kiri.'

Kiri was, of course, perfectly entitled to change her teacher. Indeed, time would prove Vera Rosza her perfect foil, musically, temperamentally and intellectually. Yet the manner in which she severed her relationship with Florence Norberg revealed much about the ruthlessness with which she now intended running her career. In her authorised biography in 1982, Kiri suggested a mutual parting of the ways. According to Kiri, Norberg had agreed that their collaboration had 'not been achieving as much as either teacher or pupil would have liked' and had mentioned Rosza as an alternative. Anne Howells had then approached Rosza on Kiri's behalf. Kiri had telephoned Norberg to let her know her colleague was willing to take her on. In Kiri's version of events, Norberg said, 'If anyone else was to take Kiri on, she would be very happy if it were Vera.'

'Absolute rubbish,' argued Mary Masterton. According to Norberg, Kiri ended their two-year relationship in a short and devastatingly succinct letter. 'It was very impersonal. It was signed "Kiri Te Kanawa", not "Love, Kiri", or "Thanks", and was very formal, like a business letter. It was just dismissing her as a teacher officially,' said Masterton. As far as Norberg was concerned, Kiri had breached the basic rules of trust and loyalty. 'She felt completely betrayed,' said Masterton, who remained a friend and pupil of Norberg's until her death.

As Kiri's success continued, and Rosza's star ascended with it, so Norberg faded from prominence. She never rid herself of the feeling that she had been poorly treated. 'After teaching Kiri for two years, to a standard where she was being offered singing contracts, to then be discarded was hard for her to bear,' said Masterton. 'It was Florence's technique that got Kiri in to Covent Garden.'

In time Norberg admitted she had, perhaps, always suspected their relationship would end the way it did. 'Florence was a highly intelligent lady and knowing Kiri so well she was not really so surprised with the way events transpired,' said Masterton. 'Kiri's got animal cunning and she has often said that she feels she has to be that way. She was determined to get on and that's why she behaved as she did. Politically Rosza was more acceptable than Florence.'

During the course of her friendship with Kiri, Masterton had seen enough to share her teacher's overview. She sensed the roots of Kiri's behaviour lay deep in her past. 'When she was young she felt alone, even with the people who adopted her,' she said. To her, at least, the legacy of Kiri's early childhood was as plain as it was poignant. 'It is very sad. You must feel it if your parents don't want you. I think that is why Kiri would not trust anyone.'

In February 1970, Kiri left London for New Zealand and a lucrative, ten-date concert tour with her old mentor Barbara Brown. To Brown, Kiri seemed a meeker personality. 'She was very quiet at that time,' she recalled. 'And humble. It was one of the few stages in her life when she's been humble!'

In her interviews with the ever-present New Zealand media, however, the inner steel shone through. Kiri was forthright in her views on how to get on in the opera world. 'Rudeness is an attribute for the artist on the way up,' she told one interviewer. 'I've discovered that the ruder you are, the better you get on.' She admitted that she saw opera as an extension of the cut-throat world of the competition circuit. 'No one is your friend: you are on your own. That does not mean I will walk over anyone. But when the chance comes my way, I am ready and waiting.'

Kiri had only spent a few weeks working with Vera Rosza before leaving for New Zealand. She was already sure she had made the right musical move, however. 'She has done so much for me and taught me fantastic interpretation,' she said of her new teacher. 'Before I studied with her I didn't have that special thing I needed. Now I feel as though I have a new lease of life.' The results of her new collaboration were apparent as she packed houses in Wellington, Auckland, Napier and Hawke's Bay. Kiri's natural gifts as a performer had only been enhanced by her experiences at the Opera Centre and beyond.

Barbara Brown remembers how Kiri would arrive on stage with a scrawl of lyrics written up her arms and on the inside of her sleeves. 'She had a very stylish way of waving her arms about to read them, almost as if she were dancing, melting the actions into the mood of the song,' smiled Brown. 'She did it beautifully.'

Kiri succeeded in melting the iciness of those critics who had carped three years earlier. Russell Bond in Wellington's *Dominion* conceded that, 'Lingering doubts of Kiri Te Kanawa's ability to reach the centre of the European operatic stage were finally dispelled last night.'

A new set of doubts had attached themselves, however. Kiri's concert programmes were a mix of classical arias, from *The Marriage of Figaro*, *Faust* and *Eugene Onegin* among others, and popular show numbers. Bond, like so many critics to come, could not bear to see the two disciplines brought together. '. . . She must decide where she stands,' he wrote. 'The warmly appreciative audience that filled most of the seats in the Town Hall last night would probably have gone to hear her regardless of what she sang. Many others, more discerning, who should have heard her must have stayed away because of the rubbish in the second half of the programme. The Maori songs have a rightful place in her programmes, but she can now make her impact without the need to descend to the sentiment of *Carousel* and *The Sound of Music*.'

169

A few days later, in another paper, Kiri gave a reply which has barely varied in the three decades since. 'I want to cater for everybody,' she said. 'They don't all want to hear opera.'

The most significant moment of the trip came on 18 March as New Zealand's Queen of Song joined around twenty other prominent members of the political, Church and Maori communities for lunch on board the Royal Yacht Britannia in Dunedin's harbour. There she was introduced to the Queen, the Duke of Edinburgh, Prince Charles and Princess Anne, who were on a lengthy tour of the farthest flung corner of the Commonwealth. Kiri struck up an instant rapport with the Royal party. When she mentioned that she was auditioning for a contract at Covent Garden, she recalled later, the Queen turned to one of her aides and smiled, 'I think she should be at Covent Garden, don't you?'

That evening Kiri performed *Carmen*'s 'Habanera' and 'The Nun's Chorus' backed by the 270 members of the Combined Dunedin Choir and the NZBC Symphony Orchestra under Walter Susskind. Kiri arrived back in London for another audition at Covent Garden. Joan Ingpen had arranged for her to sing for the duo already lined up to take over from Solti in July 1971, Colin Davis and Peter Hall. Both men were entranced, Davis later recalling how he had to ask Kiri to sing 'The Willow Song' from Verdi's *Otello* again. 'I just couldn't believe my ears the first time,' he said later. 'I had to check it was not a fluke performance, but the more I heard it the more truly remarkable it seemed.' The less musically-minded Peter Hall experienced a feeling he had last encountered as a director of the Royal Shakespeare Company when the actor David Warner walked on stage to audition for Richard II. Hall had known instantly that Warner would be his next Hamlet. In Kiri he sensed the same indefinable but undeniable star presence.

Encouraged by their reaction, Ingpen had soon thrashed out a junior principal's contract with Basil Horsfield. Kiri's starting wage would be £50 per week and would be negotiable as her career at the Garden progressed. The five-year term of the contract was non-negotiable, however. Until 1975, Kiri would need the express permission of Webster or his successor John Tooley to work anywhere outside the Company. Kiri greeted the news with a combination of joy and relief. For a moment she was convinced that Buckingham

170

Palace's influence had been brought to bear. 'I felt totally convinced that the Queen had rung up Covent Garden and told them to have me at the Royal Opera!'

A Pearl of Great Price

When the Royal Opera's new musical director took up his post in 1961, he made his mission plain. 'I have only one desire, to make Covent Garden the best opera house in the world,' Georg Solti said in his distinctive, Hungarian-flavoured English. During a turbulent baptism, the maestro survived everything from the anti-Semitic jibes of his colleagues to the physical threat of patrons hurling cabbages daubed with the slogan 'Solti must go'. Ten years later, with Vienna, La Scala and the New York Met struggling with a variety of artistic and financial crises, the colossus of his musical generation had fulfilled his promise. By 1970, Solti's Covent Garden ruled supreme.

As each morning she walked through the portals of the Palladian building on Bow Street, up the famous sweeping staircases and past the bust of its founding force, Sir Thomas Beecham, Kiri could smile in the knowledge that she had brought a more modest dream to fruition. It had been more than fifteen years since her mother had sat on her bedside in Gisborne and spoken of her dreams for Kiri. Now here she was, just as Nell had imagined, at the hub of the operatic universe. For Kiri, however, the dreaming had barely begun.

In contrast to her early days at the Opera Centre, Kiri arrived at Covent Garden to find herself among familiar and friendly faces. Her Opera Centre colleague Teresa Cahill and the repetiteur Jeffrey Tate were among the others joining a new-look company being assembled by the man set to take over as Solti's successor a year later, Colin Davis.

No one was happier to see her there than John Matheson. Colin Davis had chosen the New Zealander as his first conductor. Matheson had wasted no time in suggesting that Davis and his incoming assistants, artistic director Peter Hall and general administrator John Tooley, sign Kiri to the company.

'The first thing I said to my colleagues was, "Now there's an excellent soprano, a New Zealand girl. Everybody said she's lazy and a nuisance and so on and keeps leaving to go back to New Zealand to do charity concerts, and everybody's fed up with her." And Colin Davis said me, "Who do you mean? Come on, what's her name?" So I said, "Kiri Te Kanawa", and he said, "Well, you can stop worrying because we have engaged her."'

Nine years earlier Davis had stood on the brink of greatness. His achievement when he took over a troubled production of *Don Giovanni* at Covent Garden had led one critic to compare him with the most revered of all English conductors. 'The best we've had since Beecham,' he said. He had immediately gone on to self-destruct, ending his first marriage to the soprano April Cantelo in order to enter a nightmarish relationship with their Persian nanny, Ashraf Naini. Davis's agony deepened when Naini was held captive in Iran and he had to fight an extended battle to bring her back to London. 'I decided I didn't like anything in my life,' Davis philosophised later. 'So I stood back and smashed it all up.'

Now, at the age of forty-one, Davis had once more regained control of his extraordinary rollercoaster ride of a career. He had chosen an unashamedly glamorous collection of singers for his opening season a year down the line. Soon after Kiri arrived, late in November 1970, she joined five other new signings for a photo session on the main, front-of-house staircase. Along with Delia Wallis, Norma Burrowes, Alison Hargan, Nan Christie and Teresa Cahill her features were soon staring out from the pages of the *Daily Mail*. 'Just to show that all opera singers aren't all overweight and over thirty' ran the headline.

Like Kiri, Teresa Cahill had taken her first steps into the cocoon that was the Garden wearing an expression of barely concealed awe. 'The Opera House in those days was very supportive. You weren't thrown on without knowing what you were doing. They looked ahead and groomed you for it. They did treat people with kid gloves more than now,' she said. Nothing was too much trouble if it meant it helped a singer's potential. 'Once we got in under contract we could have a coaching session every day if we wanted it.' Cahill's first major role at the Garden would be as Barbarina in a production of *The Marriage of Figaro* under Solti that year.

As Kiri worked simultaneously for the outgoing and incoming regimes, her long-term diary was soon filled with an even more terrifying date. Davis intended opening his first season with his own, lavish production of *Figaro* to be staged at the Garden in December 1971. Davis's indecisiveness was already presenting a stark contrast to Solti's iron single-mindedness, however. His reign had begun badly as Peter Hall, the other half of the management 'dream ticket' that had drawn him to accept the job, left to take over the National Theatre. John Matheson quickly capitalised on the confusion to suggest Kiri for the most glamorous role in the opera, the lovelorn Countess Almaviva.

'Luckily for her they did not have anybody obvious. They were not sure who to cast,' Matheson said. The names of the South African Wendy Fine and the Welsh singer Gwyneth Jones had been mentioned. Matheson argued strongly that Kiri should be given a chance. Kiri was asked to audition for Davis and, among others, John Copley, who would be producing. Copley remembered Kiri from the Opera Centre and was reluctant. Ultimately, however, Davis was won over by Matheson's persistent advocacy. 'Finally they decided, "Alright, let's give her a go",' Matheson remembered.

The conductor promised Kiri's detractors they had made the right decision. 'I said, "I will make sure, I promise you, that she is one hundred per cent pinpoint accurate so far as the music is concerned."' As 1970 drew to a close, Kiri began what would be the most intensive training programme of her life.

With the opening of Davis's first season still a year away, Solti's electrifying presence still dominated the building. The end of his ten-year contract had not stemmed Covent Garden's interest in staging new productions with him. Early on, Joan Ingpen arranged for Kiri to audition for Solti as he cast a new production of *Carmen*, intended for his return to the house in the 1972/3 season. Ingpen saw Kiri as a natural for the soprano role of Micaëla rather than the eponymous heroine she had played a year earlier. Kiri, however, was overwhelmed by the prospect of singing for Solti. 'She's not a person normally to be nervous, but at that stage in her career and it being Solti she didn't sing well,' Ingpen remembered. Hard as she tried to persuade Solti of Kiri's qualities, Solti remained unimpressed. He asked Ingpen to hire one of his 'favourites', the beautiful Italian singer Mirella Freni, for the role instead. Ingpen persevered in her belief that Kiri should get the role, however. 'It was very naughty of me but I kept forgetting to ask Mirella,' she smiled. 'I very much wanted Kiri to have the chance.'

Kiri and Des had begun looking for their first home shortly after she signed her Covent Garden contract. Inner London and its apartments were quickly dismissed since Kiri hated the idea of coming home to a 'pot plant on the windowsill'. Instead they travelled out to Esher, in the Surrey gin and tonic belt, where they found a three-bedroomed mock Tudor house on the Esher Palace estate, former home of Henry VIII's Cardinal Wolsey. The house was less spacious than they would have liked but backed on to open greenbelt space filled with grazing cattle, rabbits and squirrels. The house provided a haven where they could escape from the high-octane life of London and Covent Garden in particular. Kiri had saved some money from her 1970 tour. Des swallowed his pride and asked his father for a loan of £2,000. They bought the house with a £9,000 mortgage, but quickly found their finances stretched. A young, male lodger was given the second bedroom but was soon at loggerheads with Kiri. When the lodger refused to give Kiri a lift to the station, Kiri asked Des to eject him. Apart from anything else, she now wanted the room for guests like Raewyn Blade – and even her ex-fiancé Brooke Monks when he visited London.

Kiri's hopes of inviting Nell and Tom over to stay were soon dashed as Nell was once more admitted to hospital. The matriarch's health had remained a source of worry ever since her gallstone operation and her return from England. That year she had discovered a growth in one of her breasts. At first the family had been told the lump was benign. During the operation to remove it, however, the surgeons had discovered the growth was malignant. 'They ended up having to take the breast off,' recalled her granddaughter, Judy Evans Hita.

Confined to a bed at the Green Lane Hospital, Nell had managed to maintain her spirits. The twin triumphs of Kiri's tour with Barbara Brown and a hugely popular appearance in Osaka, Japan, with Inia Te Wiata at the Expo 70 exhibition on New Zealand Day, 8 July, had earned Kiri the accolade of New Zealand's Entertainer of the Year for 1970. Tom had collected the trophy at the awards ceremony at Trillo's Westhaven Cabaret, where Kiri's phoned acceptance speech from

175

London was broadcast over the public address system. Betty Hanson then ferried the gleaming trophy to Green Lane Hospital where she placed it at her neighbour's bedside. Propped up on pillows and resplendent in her best dressing gown, a smiling if slightly drawn Nell had posed for the cameras with the trophy. 'I'm getting along fine and hope to be home in about a week,' she winked at the reporters.

Her optimism proved short-lived. 'She didn't get better and they had to re-operate,' said Judy. Her family's fears for her deepened. 'She said she was fine but she got tired very easily.'

No one had enjoyed Kiri's arrival at Covent Garden more than Nell. Yet for all her pride at her daughter's achievements, she felt increasingly depressed at their separation. 'Nana was devastated that her baby wasn't there with her,' said Judy.

As she had left New Zealand the previous year, Kiri had warned her parents that she might not be able to return home again for another two years. Since then her casting as the Countess had made it impossible for her to consider a trip. Kiri wrote only a few letters home and knew it saddened Nell deeply. As her mother recuperated, she attempted to raise her sagging spirits by exchanging long, rambling tape recordings. The tapes were filled with the sort of raucous blue jokes Kiri and Nell would never have shared with what she called their 'nice' friends. 'Why don't gypsies need contraceptives? Because they've got crystal balls and they can see it coming.' 'Young man, do you want your palm read? Yes. Well then take your hand out of me knickers.'

Kiri tried to console her mother with light-hearted jokes about her 'one boob'. Yet as she talked incessantly into her tape recorder, she hinted at the loneliness she too was feeling in London and at Covent Garden and the extent to which Des's control of her affairs was beginning to cause friction in their marriage.

Kiri had already begun work on *Figaro* and had been hired to sing in a performance of Handel's *Messiah* with the Royal Choral Society at the Royal Albert Hall on 31 March. 'At the moment, of course, I'm the little blue-eyed girl but I don't mind telling you that I don't have very many friends there,' she said. 'I suppose you would gather that anyway,' she added gloomily, knowing that Nell's bruising years in Auckland's music scene had left her with few illusions about her daughter's standing with other singers. 'It's not being big-headed or anything but when you're sort of up-and-coming and quite potentially dangerous to the other "oldies" . . . the other people who have been there say two or three years, well you know, you're not all that welcome.' She went on to describe how another, more experienced singer had done 'a bit of a dirty' by sending her to the wrong room for a rehearsal of *Parsifal*.

Such behaviour failed to hurt Kiri who, by now, was switching her focus away from rival singers. 'I really don't care about them anyway,' she said bluntly. Instead she had turned her attention to the house's senior figures, men like Colin Davis and the 'queer as a coot' John Pritchard. 'It's not really what you can do, I suppose,' she said. 'It's, say, seventy-five per cent is what you can do, but the other twenty-five per cent is good relations with administration. If you are in with them, well, you keep a necessary sort of safe distance, but as long as you are not bugging them, then it's alright.'

On the evening Kiri first sat down with the microphone, Des had been 'out boozing with the boys', she said. It was significant that in the coming days, as Kiri filled up a one-hour-long cassette, Des did not find the will to record one word of greeting for his mother-in-law. Kiri worried at the gulf that still existed between them. 'He's a wonderful man, he really is, Mummy. I know you don't like him all that much. I know you both don't get on all that well because you've both got really definite ideas about different things or certain things, I don't quite know, but really he does love you very much, Mum, and I know he thinks the world of Daddy and he's a great, great husband to me. So I just hope that one of these days you really will love him. I know he's a very difficult man, and he is a really hard, a very very difficult person to . . . love, especially when it's sort of family sort of love, you know. I know there's lots of girls who say, "Oh, isn't your husband smashing", and I say, "Yes, well, I think he is", you know. He's great for me, but he might not get on with everybody.'

Tom and Nell, as ever, had spent the Christmas holidays at Hatepe, but although he would be sixty-nine that year, Kiri's father was still working hard. He had to. After all the years of exorbitant spending to finance their daughter, the Te Kanawa coffers were empty. They had taken out a second mortgage the year before and when Kiri's old Simca, which Tom was driving, began to show its age, they asked her for help.

Nell rang her daughter looking for £850 for a new car. It was not a good time, Kiri replied. 'We are sort of pretty stumped at the moment,' she said. 'I think you better just keep on saving up your pennies.' Her unwillingness to help must have seemed harsh in the light of the way Kiri talked openly of the money she was now making. 'There's no doubt about it, this year seems to be going to be a fairly prosperous one,' she confided.

For the first time in their three-year marriage, Des allowed himself to indulge his wife with expensive gifts, including diamond earrings. 'Every other year he's been rather mean,' said Kiri, who gave her husband an electric razor and 'a nice pair of slippers'. Kiri had not lost her taste for fashion consciousness. In a recent spree, she told her mother, she had come home with three midi frocks, two ordinary dresses, one trouser suit, one midi coat and a pair of boots. Such profligacy did not please Des, who attempted to rule the family finances with an iron hand. Kiri explained how each Saturday he would make her sit at the kitchen table with him as they went through the bills, her correspondence and contracts. Kiri's spending always came under the microscope. Often Des would criticise Kiri for her lack of financial discipline. 'He's a funny guy, really. I don't know, he says to me, "Oh you bought all those clothes and you shouldn't have spent all the money", and I say to him, "Well, I contribute, you know . . . now, so if I put some money in the bank surely I can spend some." And he says, "No you can't. You can't spend it without my saying you can." And I say, "Oh, get stuffed", you know. "If I want to spend it, I spend it." And then he says, "I'll take your chequebook away from you if you don't behave yourself." He treats me like a child and Jessica [a neighbour] said to me, "You know, you're a grown woman, Kiri, and he treats you like a child. He doesn't think that you can fend for yourself." ' Kiri fell silent for a moment before adding as an afterthought. 'But I rather like being treated like a child.'

No one understood Kiri's need to be nursed better than Vera Rosza. 'A singing teacher is like a psychologist,' Kiri said later in her career. If that was true then the wily Rosza had wasted little time in unlocking Kiri's complex psyche.

'She must make up her own mind. You must help her but not force her,' said Rosza. 'I recognised in Kiri a free spirit.'

Rosza sensed that many of Kiri's problems stemmed from the non-chalant manner with which she had found her early success. 'Being so gifted and such a beautiful person, everything had been easy for her in New Zealand. She thought she just had to open her mouth and make a beautiful sound and that was it. But in England they are marvellous musicians and they knew more than her.'

Their personal simpatico quickly translated into an ideal musical partnership. Soon her colleagues at Covent Garden were detecting the benefits. Rosza saw that Norberg's work in developing Kiri's upper middle range was complete. She set about the final phase of her musical development. 'The top wasn't good until she went to Vera,' said Teresa Cahill. 'She gave her that, and it was the icing on the cake.'

In addition, Kiri's interpretation of her roles was improving enormously. Others had detected her sponge-like ability to soak up ideas. In Rosza she had plugged into a wellspring of originality. 'I think they were a very good partnership because Vera is rather a Svengali type teacher,' said Cahill. 'Kiri wasn't a natural intellectual but she had such fabulous instincts that if you put the right ideas into her it came out better than even the idea was to start with.'

Kiri's initial work on *Figaro* was done with Rosza and John Matheson, who took her through every line of the Italian libretto with Ubaldo Gardini. Vera Rosza, too, enlisted the help of friends who 'knew what Mozart wanted, inch by inch'.

Kiri dedicated herself as she had never done before. She sensed, correctly, that she was being given an education she would never get again. 'I said at the time this would be the only time I would get to learn a role so thoroughly. They were trying to put all of this into me within a year.'

As she prepared for her *Figaro* debut, however, Kiri remained a far from stellar member of the Covent Garden company. Her first public performance inside the great auditorium was made from the fringes of the opera house, as the voice of the offstage priestess in *Aida*. After that she 'covered' the role of the slave girl Liù in *Turandot*. For two months she waited in vain for one of the two senior sopranos to drop out. She was far from inactive, however. She was one of a group of soloists selected to perform excerpts of Mozart church music being recorded for Philips by Colin Davis. Her most significant moments came when she was cast as the leading Flower Maiden in Wagner's *Parsifal*, then as Xenia in Musorgsky's *Boris Godunov*.

John Matheson's faith in Kiri was rewarded in both performances.

As Xenia she had impressed everyone with the sheer vibrancy of her voice. 'It soared through the house. A theatre is an instrument which you must set in vibration, if you have the right voice to do it, and she absolutely had.' The performance reassured Davis and the doubters who had wondered at Kiri's casting. 'I said to Colin and the others, "You see, it's a voice designed absolutely for this opera house."'

In *Parsifal*, Donald McIntyre also saw the progress his compatriot had made. McIntyre was singing the role of Klingsor. He could not help but notice the quality of the music Kiri was now producing. 'From the little bits I could hear I thought, "Yes, that's a voice."'

Like many New Zealanders, McIntyre had at first drawn comparisons between Kiri and Mina Foley. By now, however, he recognised Kiri was a tougher customer altogether. 'Kiri was made of stronger stuff mentally,' he said. 'She was looked after and she wasn't pushed too much. Whereas Mina went over to Italy and was terribly lonely. She had a different mentality. I think Kiri was a greater survivor.'

McIntyre did not know it, but Kiri had proved that survival instinct during *Parsifal*. The opera was conducted by Reginald Goodall, a former member of the Mosleyite blackshirts who had been eased out of Covent Garden over alleged anti-Semitic behaviour towards Solti. Throughout rehearsals Goodall looked at the Garden's new, half-Maori soprano with what she later called 'disdain'. Kiri tightened her jaw and refused to respond to the bait.

She learned an equally valuable lesson on *Boris Godunov* where she found herself subjected to a piece of backstage ritual familiar the world over to young sopranos. Godunov was being sung by the famously philanderous Boris Christoff. Christoff's penchant for inviting pretty singers to his dressing room during the interval was well known. Predictably Kiri caught his eye and she was duly summoned to amuse him during his break. She later recalled how when Christoff refused to let her leave she had to be 'rescued' by the stage manager. She did not allow herself to fall into that situation again.

By far the most important spin-off of her *Parsifal* success, however, was its indirect impact on Georg Solti. Joan Ingpen had persisted in her view that Kiri should sing Micaëla in Solti's *Carmen*. In the interim she had been called in to help the maestro cast a major recording of *Parsifal* for Decca due to take place in Germany at the end of the year. Solti was unhappy with Decca's choice of Flower Maiden. Ingpen suggested Kiri for the part and arranged an audition on the Covent Garden stage once more. 'She had sung the part well in performance and sang beautifully for Solti. He was pleased,' she said. Ingpen seized the moment. 'I called out to Kiri to sing the Micaëla. I had not warned her but she was warmed up, hadn't been thinking about it and sang that beautifully too.'

Solti turned to Ingpen and asked about his original casting idea. 'Is Mirella not free?' he wondered.

'I forgot to ask,' Ingpen replied.

'OK,' said Solti, with a knowing smile.

Carmen and Micaëla remained a long-term consideration, however. *Figaro* and the Countess Almaviva continued to dominate every working day during Kiri's first year at Covent Garden.

In June 1971, at Colin Davis's suggestion, Kiri travelled to Santa Fe in America to make her debut in the role away from the fierce spotlight of Covent Garden. As luck would have it, Des was also in America at the time, on a contract in Atlanta, Georgia. He was unable to make it to Santa Fe itself, but at least Kiri had the consolation of knowing he was at the end of a telephone in the same continent and almost the same time zone for once.

Des's absence was compensated for by the friendship she struck up with an American mezzo Frederica von Stade, hired to sing the role of the page, Cherubino. Kiri and the high-spirited 'Flicka', as she was known, struck up an enduring friendship. She made another useful connection in Sam Niefeld, an agent with the all-powerful American agency, Columbia Artists. Niefeld had a reputation as a discoverer of new talent. No sooner had Kiri walked off the Santa Fe stage than she had been offered a contract with Niefeld for American representation.

As Kiri arrived back to continue preparing for her Covent Garden production of *Figaro* her success in Santa Fe was soon forgotten. With four months before the opening night, she found herself under the guidance of the man who had been her most vehement critic.

John Copley had never forgotten Kiri's juvenile behaviour in *The Magic Flute* at the Opera Centre. He had opposed Kiri's casting in *Figaro* all the way along. His opposition was precisely the kind of stimulus Kiri had always responded to. 'I believe very much in the principle when you're down start fighting. Especially since people in this business inevitably try to box you in,' she said later.

Copley insisted that she begin working with him six weeks before the star names began rehearsal work at Covent Garden. Copley took Kiri's acting back to first principles. 'He's changed me completely,' Kiri told the *Sunday Telegraph* at the time. 'I used to be a bit of a tomboy, but he taught me how to walk and sit properly. He made me into a lady,' she laughed. 'His attention to detail is fantastic, he even made me start growing my fingernails long.'

Copley, like John Pritchard and Basil Horsfield, was one of a coterie of gay men with whom Kiri formed strong bonds. 'The best directors are gay – and I don't mind saying so,' Kiri explained in an interview years later. 'They can sublimate their own feelings and take on another person's frustrations. The director who is gay is usually sensitive and understanding, close to the actors and singers and to the work itself.'

By the time the main cast members had joined them, even Copley was having to reassess the 'silly girl'. Kiri hit it off immediately with the production's Figaro, Basil Horsfield's friend Geraint Evans. She also formed good friendships with the Canadian baritone Victor Braun, cast as the Count, and her fellow New Zealander Heather Begg, who was playing Marcellina. Only the American soprano Reri Grist, cast as Susanna, provided the sort of tension she was, by now, becoming accustomed to handling. Kiri later remembered having one major 'fracas'; with Grist. 'That's the way the stars come in and she's just trying to show me she's a star,' she told herself. 'Some people are, of course, marvellous. Others can be perfect cows,' she philosophised. 'I've learned self-protection and get on with the job.'

As rehearsals wore on, however, it was soon clear to Kiri's colleagues that Grist might soon be facing a reversal in roles. Kiri later recounted how Victor Braun had taken her for a drink in the Covent Garden pub, the Nag's Head where he predicted she was on the verge of a major success. 'Don't talk stupid. I'm only a student,' Kiri replied. Her graduation was now imminent.

On the evening of 1 December 1971, London was experiencing the first chill of what was to be a harsh winter. Inside Covent Garden, however, an electrifying buzz warmed the air. The anticipation for any new season was huge. The air of expectation surrounding the debut of the Garden's new musical director was almost too much for some to bear. It certainly was for Des, who spent the early part of the evening downing gin and tonics in the famous Crush Bar.

He was not short of support from New Zealand, at least. Donald McIntyre had heard the growing rumours about the excellence of the production. 'I remember hearing about it from John Matheson,' recalled McIntyre, who attended with his wife Jill. 'You mustn't miss this', was the gist of the conductor's message to the magisterial bass.

Matheson himself was not due to take any part in the evening's proceedings. With Colin Davis conducting, Matheson simply did all he could to make sure Kiri was in the right frame of mind. Backstage he soon realised he had little cause for concern. 'I saw her beforehand and she was pale faced, unexcited – she had that kind of calm which covers a deadly nervousness on an occasion like that,' he remembered. 'It's a very good temperament and I remember thinking that at the time, that we had a temperament as well as everything else.'

Colin Davis's final piece of advice to Kiri had been a combination of the motivational and the highly practical. He knew from experience that Kiri's greatest test would come in the Countess's first scene, the opening aria of Act Two. 'Porgi, amor' was acknowledged as one of the most difficult singing challenges in opera. The role required the aria to be sung immediately she walked on stage without any kind of warm up. Davis's advice, which Kiri adhered to for years afterwards, was that she should sing the entire aria four or five times in her dressing room before taking the stage. Davis directed Geraint Evans and company through the first act with impeccable flair. The curtain rose on Act Two to reveal a blonde, pompadoured Kiri dressed in a billowing, low-cut, lace-trimmed gown. If she looked stunning visually, her voice was even more awesome. No sooner had the closing phrases of 'Porgi, amor' faded into the upper tiers of the auditorium than the audience delivered its verdict.

'I remember her singing the first aria and knocking the place flat,' said Donald McIntyre. 'Then she sang the second aria and knocked the place flat again.' Kiri's rendition of 'Dove sono' at the end of Act III drew, if possible, an even greater response. As the cognoscenti roared for her to take a premature curtain call, Kiri heeded John Copley's advice and waited patiently in the wings until she had safely negotiated the complex finale of Act IV.

Minutes later, as she joined the rest of the cast for her curtain call she was showered with bouquets. The scenes backstage were tearful.

Basil Horsfield, Vera Rosza, John Matheson and hordes of others crushed into her dressing room. Des, slightly tipsy, was euphoric to the point of being 'over the top', Kiri later recalled. She, however, remained ice cool in the face of her triumph. John Matheson admired Kiri's composure more than anything else. 'I was delighted with her because she was cool, calm and brought everything out. There was no sign of any nerves or jitters.'

Kiri let her emotions slip a little as she and her mentor embraced. 'At the end, she was very gay and smiling, needless to say,' Matheson said with an understated smile.

The smiles were even broader the following morning as the late editions of the newspapers heralded her triumph. London's starchy critics reached for new superlatives. *The Times'* critic William Mann, a connoisseur of Mozart operas, wrote that Kiri's Countess 'looks and moves like a teenage goddess. She sings the two difficult arias and the equally important ensembles and recitatives with real dignity and assurance, and boldly spacious phrasing.'

The *Financial Times'* critic, Andrew Porter, did not have the space to sing his full praise that day. Instead he reserved his assessment of 'a dignified and memorable young Countess' for the following day. Porter's praise would be reprinted in programmes the world over for years to come. Porter thought Colin Davis's 'new regime could not have made a better start'. His piece focused on the young discovery, however. 'The new star is Kiri Te Kanawa. For years we have been praising this young New Zealand soprano . . . yet the promise of her performances had hardly prepared us for . . . well, frankly for such a Countess Almaviva as I have never heard before, not at Covent Garden, nor in Salzburg or Vienna. At once young, full-throated, a singer of great accomplishment and a vivid character.'

The reviews continued through the following weekend. The *Sunday Times'* veteran opera-watcher, Desmond Shawe-Taylor, could not deny that Kiri had 'created a justifiable sensation'. 'She has come far indeed: I should say to the threshold of international fame.'

It was left to Peter Heyworth in the *Observer* to sum up the mood of the musical world best, however. 'Covent Garden here has a pearl of great price,' he wrote.

In the days that followed her triumph in *Figaro*, the impact was obvious to everyone at Covent Garden. As Kiri put it herself, 'If I'm asked when my career took off, I say "1 December 1971: zoom – you couldn't see me for smoke".'

Teresa Cahill bumped into Kiri in the Covent Garden corridors a day or two after the opening night. Cahill had, like everyone else, heard talk of little else but Kiri's sensational debut. She could not resist joking with her old Opera Centre colleague. 'I said, "My God, look at those reviews, I reckon Karajan will be ringing you up soon."'

Kiri smiled. 'She said, "He already has." It was amazing.' The operatic world had been in search of a new star. In Kiri it had found her.

To observers like Donald McIntyre the key to Kiri's triumph lay in her voice. 'It was a very great voice, and it was done through the voice. Not like Callas, who was a great hypnotic actress,' he said. 'She is not an artist in the same way as Callas. Kiri hasn't got a lot of nuances and variety, but all the time there is this soul that comes through the voice and her looks.'

Her old producer Tom Hawkes also recognised an outstanding sound. 'It has a creamy tone which has a sensuality to it,' he said. To his, and other minds, there was an extra dimension to Kiri's success, however. 'It was the whole package. She was not the typical diva, not the typical opera singer. She had incredible beauty and then the fact that she was a Maori added an exotic element. It was something quite new,' he said.

On top of all this, Kiri had benefited from the kind of serendipity all stars ultimately rely on. At the dawn of a new era for Covent Garden she offered a bounteous breath of new air. 'The reigning divas of the Garden were quite fusty. It was the tail end of Joan Carlyle. The only real glamour girl was Elizabeth Robson. Kiri had that freshness and when she came on stage she looked wonderful.'

Teresa Cahill had been among those who had wondered whether Kiri had been cast into such a high profile role too soon. 'I remember John Copley calling me bitchy because I actually said "I hope she's ready for it." She had done some other things, but none of us had the experience to be doing big roles,' she remembered.

Now there was no question. 'She was good enough and she proved it,' she said. 'Although I don't think any of us were expecting such a colossal thing.'

Over the coming weeks, Kiri's arrival was analysed in detail by the country's senior operatic writers. The venerable Harold Rosenthal of *Opera* magazine wrote a leading article on Kiri and Colin Davis's twin triumphs. His wisest words were reserved for the house's overnight star. 'Covent Garden must not let this great talent be seduced away by offers of this or that role, for this or that large fee on the international circuit,' he said of Kiri. 'We have seen this kind of thing happen before. It would be criminal if it happened in this case.'

Kiri's five-year contract with Covent Garden, of course, meant Rosenthal had little cause to worry. The most obvious precedent for a success of this scale, in more ways than one, was Joan Sutherland. It had been thirteen years earlier, in 1958, that she had sung Lucia in Franco Zeffirelli's lavish production of the Donizetti opera *Lucia di Lammermoor* at Covent Garden. In the space of one night Sutherland was transformed from member of the company to star. At the time she knew only two other roles in Italian. 'There I was, an international star with no repertoire to sing internationally,' she joked later.

Amid the euphoria, the truth was that Kiri was in an even weaker situation. In addition to Micaëla for Solti's *Carmen* she had begun learning the role of Desdemona in *Otello* which she was due to sing at the Scottish Opera the following year. Amelia in *Simon Boccanegra* and Elvira in *Don Giovanni* were being talked of. In performance terms, however, the Countess was her only role.

In the wake of *Figaro*, Basil Horsfield was inundated with offers for Kiri. He accepted four invitations for her to reprise her role as the Countess, at Lyons in the spring of 1972, San Francisco in the autumn of the same year, Bordeaux in December and Glyndebourne in the summer of 1973. Almost everything else was rejected. In the meantime the colleagues who had elevated her to such great heights set about bringing her back down to earth. Kiri was not required to sing again until the following Tuesday. The Covent Garden audience greeted her second performance with all the enthusiasm of the first. Neither Vera Rosza nor John Copley were fooled, however.

As she celebrated her first night triumph Kiri missed her weekly lesson with Rosza. When her teacher told Kiri she sounded tired in her subsequent performance, Kiri flew into a rage in which she said she never wanted to see her again. She limped back to her mentor the following day asking for forgiveness.

Copley visited Kiri in her dressing room after her third performance.

186

He could not agree with Kiri's view that it was 'marvellous' and warned her that she had to work hard to get back to the standard of the opening night. Stung by the criticism, Kiri responded in typical fashion. Copley later admitted that the final five performances of *Figaro* were all marvellous.

New Worlds

~~~

On the night of Sunday, 20 February 1972, Kiri took her final curtain call at the Lyons Opéra. Once more the 'bravos' and bouquets rained down on the Countess Almaviva.

Kiri intended returning to her hotel to change before joining her friend Anne Howells and others for a late dinner to celebrate the end of their five-performance series in the ancient French city. As she checked in, however, the concierge told her that an urgent phone call had come through from her sister Nola's husband Bill Denholm in Auckland. He had left a message saying he would try to call again later that night.

Kiri knew it was the early hours of Monday morning in New Zealand. Sensing something serious had happened, she immediately cancelled her dinner plans and nervously waited in her room with Howells.

Kiri later admitted that when the phone next rang her first thoughts were, 'Which one was it, praying it wouldn't be Daddy.' She had sighed with momentary relief when the reply came, 'It's your mother.' She then burst into tears as she heard the news that Nell had died in the Green Lane Hospital in Auckland at around 1 a.m. New Zealand time.

Nell had never recovered fully from her cancer operation the previous year. She had steadily lost weight and, at age the age of seventy-four, had become an emaciated shadow of her former hale and hearty self. Her spirits had been further deflated by the financial worries she and Tom had been experiencing. Tom had finally stopped work and, just one month before her death, Nell had sold 22 Mitchell Street for $27,500 and moved to a dowdy, rented bungalow in nearby Wingate Street, next to Avondale racecourse.

The strain of the move could not have helped her fragile health. Three weeks later she had been taken back in to hospital on the Friday night. At first her family had not been overly concerned. Her granddaughter Judy hadn't been told of Nell's admission for two days, until Sunday. Her stepfather had reassured her there was no rush to head to her grandmother's bedside. 'He said, "Don't worry going up tonight because everybody will be there, go up tomorrow when you can have some time with her on your own",' she recalled. 'By one o'clock or so on the Monday morning she was dead.'

Kiri made hasty arrangements to fly back to Auckland via Paris the following day. Fortunately the news had come at the end of the Lyons performances and presented few problems back at Covent Garden where she was due a little leave. The funeral was delayed until Friday of that week, awaiting Kiri's arrival. Des had been in Australia working and was at Auckland airport to greet her at the end of her journey.

'All her life, my mother wanted to see me doing what I'm doing now,' Kiri told waiting reporters. 'She had dreams people should not have, but they are coming true.'

The funeral service took place at St Patrick's Cathedral at 10 a.m. on the Friday morning. Just as five years earlier at her wedding, Kiri's appearance drew a large and ungainly gathering to St Patrick's Square. A scrum of photographers jostled for position as the mourners arrived and again when they left after the service.

'That was when it really got to me,' said Judy Evans-Hita. 'When we went to put Nana's coffin in the hearse outside St Patrick's Cathedral we had to ask the photographers to get out of the way. I've always remembered that. I thought, "You vultures".'

The chief mourners – Tom, Kiri, Des, Nola, Stan and Judy – accompanied the coffin back to the Waikumete Lawn Cemetery where Nell was buried in a plot reserved for her and Tom. Afterwards, dozens of friends crowded into the Wingate Street house and its tiny garden. Nell had made her will in August 1970. Five days after her death, her son Stan and Bill Barrett were appointed her executors. She left everything to Tom and, on his death, to Stan, Nola and Kiri in equal shares. Tom had little interest in remaining at the house on Wingate Street. His neighbour there, Colin Chapman, recalled that Nell's death hit him 'very bad'. He said he would move to the cabin at Hatepe where he would retire to his fishing, golfing and gardening. Concerned at his welfare, however, Kiri insisted he fly back to England with her for a brief break.

In the immediate aftermath of her mother's death, Kiri remained outwardly calm. Over the following months she slowly came to terms with the powerful mixture of emotions the loss had kindled. Inevitably she felt guilt at the manner in which she and Nell had drifted apart since their arrival in England. In Kiri's last conversation with her mother Nell had bemoaned the lack of communication between them. 'Darling, you never write,' she had complained.

'My mother talked a lot before she died about how I caused a lot of anguish and that sort of stuff. But if only everyone had been able to tell her this was a normal thing. It was not my plan to hurt. I never stopped loving her,' she insisted, reflecting on Nell's pain at the departure from London five years earlier. 'When it came to it, she didn't want to give me up, even to music.'

There was regret that Nell had never seen her Gisborne dream come true and witnessed her little girl perform on the stage at Covent Garden. At least Kiri could comfort herself in the knowledge that Nell had died knowing she had made, as she put it, 'the big splash' in *Figaro*. There was sorrow too at the fact she had never really known her mother. The forces that had underpinned their relationship were, of course, common to most mother–daughter relationships. Nell had utterly dominated the early part of Kiri's life. Their powerful personalities almost demanded the schism that came. The best years lay almost certainly ahead in Kiri's mature, middle age. Now she knew that friendship would never be formed. The haunting feeling never left her. 'I wish I had known my mother longer,' she lamented.

Yet a part of Kiri was left utterly unmoved by her mother's passing. The bitterness of their arguments and the deep-seated shame Kiri had occasionally felt at Nell's behaviour were still hard to erase. Back at Esher, a few weeks later, two of her old St Mary's colleagues visited for a dinner at which Kiri showed few signs of sadness let alone grief. Patricia Price and Lynne Cantlon were both in London performing. Both had known of the friction that had existed between Kiri and Nell when she was alive. Neither was quite prepared for the way Kiri openly criticised her mother during the evening, however.

Des, on this occasion, did little to stem the invective. He remained silent as the rest of the guests stared down at their plates. For Tom, however, it was too much to bear. With Kiri in full flight, he placed his cutlery on the table, pushed back his chair and left the table. According to one of the dinner guests, he headed for the window where he spent much of the evening staring solemnly out into the darkness.

As he came to terms with his loss, Tom remained under Kiri's watchful eye, however. In April he travelled with her to Scotland, where she was due to begin rehearsals for the May opening of a new production of *Otello*. Kiri had been given the chance to make her debut as Desdemona, the ill-starred wife of Otello, in Verdi's tempestuous masterpiece. Basil Horsfield had lined up the seven-performance tour of Glasgow, Edinburgh and Aberdeen as a warm-up for the inevitable moment when she would debut the role at Covent Garden. In the absence of understanding teachers like John Matheson or John Copley, Kiri found the studying hard. She did not hit it off with the Italian conductor Alberto Erede and struggled with all but the two final act pieces, the 'Willow Song' and 'Ave Maria', both of which she had known since her St Mary's days in Auckland.

Kiri later admitted that she had not been helped by the delayed shock of her mother's death. At one point during rehearsals she broke down and had to be cared for by her Otello, Charles Craig, and his wife.

Kiri's Desdemona would soon develop into one of the wonders of the operatic world. Yet her first performance of the role, at the King's Theatre on 5 May, was far from an unalloyed success. The response was summed up by the respected critic Noel Goodwin, writing later in *Opera* magazine. Goodwin praised the 'rare beauty' of Kiri's vocal tone but found her acting 'lacking variety of expressive feeling'. For one member of the audience, however, the performance was the most moving he had ever seen. As he sat next to Des in the darkened auditorium, tears rolled down Tom's face as he watched his daughter perform in an opera for the first time. Afterwards Tom told Kiri how much her mother would have loved to have been there. According to Kiri, she reassured him that, somewhere, the Boss was watching over them.

Like all serious golfers, Tom's ultimate ambition had been to play a round at St Andrew's, the home of the game. With the Canadian bass Joseph Rouleau, he travelled to the famous old course overlooking

191

the windswept east coast. Tom had reached the first green when he collapsed suddenly. He was rushed to hospital where he was diagnosed with a serious prostate problem and underwent an immediate prostatectomy. He recuperated back at Esher. Fortunately Kiri was booked to return to New Zealand in July and was able to accompany Tom on the uncomfortable flight home.

Despite the obvious signs of distress his client had displayed in Scotland, Basil Horsfield continued filling Kiri's diary with engagements. She had been contracted to sing in a punishing itinerary of five concerts and six recitals underwritten by the New Zealand Broadcasting Corporation, whose NZBC Symphony Orchestra, to be conducted by John Matheson, and the Symphonia of Auckland under Juan Matteucci, would alternate on the concert dates. Her old partner Barbara Brown had agreed to accompany her at the recitals where Kiri sang favourite arias, including Handel's 'Let the Bright Seraphim', the 'Jewel Song' from Gounod's *Faust* and 'Ach, ich fühl's', Pamina's aria from *The Magic Flute*. For all her comfort with her programme, however, the strain of eleven performances in three weeks was huge. By the time Kiri played in Dunedin, she was catching up on her sleep in the late afternoon before going on stage.

Dunedin Town Hall's capacity was so vast its upper gallery had remained locked for years. As Kiri arrived in the South Island city, however, the whole house was opened up to accommodate the record audience of 3,000. For his part of the tour, Matheson had chosen to perform Berlioz's rarely seen *Damnation of Faust*. Given that Kiri's part, Marguerite, did not feature at all in the first half, she remained in her hotel room. Matheson recalls a moment of black farce almost ruining the night. 'She stayed in her room at the Southern Cross Hotel and took a taxi at the agreed time, with fifteen or twenty minutes to go in the first half,' he recounted. 'She came down to the stage door at the Town Hall, knocked on the door and got no answer. She knocked and knocked and knocked and she told me later she was almost in despair. Finally this elderly retainer appeared, opened the door a crack and said, "Yes?" She tried to tell him who she was but he wouldn't let her in. He said, "I'm sorry love, there's a performance going on here, you can't come in just now." She got through to him in the end.'

By and large the tour was met with the normal eulogistic response in New Zealand, especially when she visited Gisborne's Regent Theatre for what has been her final performance in her home town to date. Yet as they moved around the North and South Islands it was clear Kiri's energy levels were running dangerously low. By the time Kiri came to play her recitals with Barbara Brown she was close to exhaustion. Brown knew Kiri did little to help matters. Her love of the night life had never really left her and the tour provided a perfect opportunity to catch up on old friends. Inevitably her voice was the victim. 'Kiri liked to enjoy life and would go short of sleep,' said Brown. 'The first thing to be affected was her voice and she would sing under the note.'

Eventually Brown enlisted the help of Des, who had remained in Australia and joined them on part of the tour. Brown knew how far Des was prepared to go in curbing Kiri's indiscipline. He once told Brown how he prevented his wife from leaving her hotel after 'curfew'. 'He locked Kiri in her room and sat in a chair in the corridor all night to stop her going out,' she said. Once more Des ensured Kiri started taking the rest she needed to complete the tour.

Brown's opinion has not changed in the three decades since. 'Des has been to hell and back. I think he was totally responsible for her success.'

In September 1972 Kiri took her now celebrated Countess to San Francisco for a series of five performances. As she once more accepted the acclaim at the end of the opening night her eyes cast around the auditorium for one member of the audience in particular. There, as thrilled as any teenager, was the seventy-seven-year-old Sister Mary Leo, enjoying her first glimpse of Kiri in the role that had made her a star. Thanks to an Arts Council grant and the generosity of a few wealthy patrons, Sister Mary Leo was making her first trip beyond Australasia. By then, the nun's star pupils were spread far and wide in the world's great opera houses. She spent four months touring America and Europe to meet as many of them as was possible. 'It had been a dream she had had for years,' said her travelling companion, Sister Margaret Browne.

Kiri already led the way, but in recent years Sister Mary Leo's greatest hopes had rested with another Maori girl, Donna Awatere. She had confided to friends that Awatere had a voice and intellect that could take her beyond even Kiri's limits. But like Mina Foley before her, Awatere's career had been tragically cut short. Her father Peter, commander of the Maori Battalion and a city councillor, murdered his mistress's new lover with a carving knife in a jealous rage, just three weeks before Donna was due to audition for James Robertson. Despite the tragedy, Donna won the *New Zealand Herald* Aria within a fortnight and was offered a place at Robertson's London Opera Centre. The pall cast over her family by the murder meant she never took it. Sister Mary Leo's shock and disappointment were only beginning to fade when she arrived in San Francisco.

She and Sister Margaret were given an insight into the rarefied circles in which the girl from St Mary's now moved. After the performance they joined Kiri at the *Figaro* cast's opening night party on the fifty-second floor of a skyscraper. 'It was a whole new world,' remembered Sister Margaret.

To Sister Margaret, it seemed a particularly self-obsessed world too. 'These opera people were so intent on getting the critics the next day, buying up all the newspapers and seeing how they'd been accepted,' she said. 'It was very important to know who was saying what about them, and they seemed to know the names of all the music critics.'

Despite the obvious success of the performance in the auditorium, Kiri seemed as preoccupied as anyone. 'It was quite tense because she still didn't know – she'd had the standing ovation and it looked okay from the people's point of view, but it was still very important to see what the critics had to say,' said the nun. 'A couple of days later there was a big cocktail party for Kiri hosted by the New Zealand consul. Kiri and the other singers were still discussing the reviews.'

On this occasion she had every reason to – San Francisco's *Figaro* amounted to another Te Kanawa triumph. Yet within weeks, Kiri's fascination with the critics came, by her own account, to an abrupt end.

Sister Leo, a guest at Esher, was once more in the audience as Kiri revived the *Figaro* production back in London. This time, however, three leading critics, *The Times*'s William Mann, the *Financial Times*'s Ronald Crichton and Arthur Jacobs of *Opera* all voiced doubts about the previous year's sensation. They reserved their accolades for the Romanian soprano, Ileana Cotrubas, in the role of Susanna. Years later Kiri told her official biographer, David Fingleton, the moment had been a watershed. While the book admitted to 'elements of accuracy' in their remarks, she said she decided there and then 'to have little to do with reviews'.

'Nor does she,' explained the biographer. 'Seldom troubling to read them and leaving Desmond to fill in time in front of the television during evenings at home by cutting out and filing the various notices of her performances.'

Kiri's tendency towards such haughtiness was, of course, nothing new. However, her decision in this case was an act of simple self-protection. Twelve months after her initial London triumph, she had reached a dizzying and at times truly terrifying plateau in her career. She admitted herself that she wondered whether her rise had come too quickly. 'I should have done more of the priestesses and flower maidens. The thing was, no one expected the *Figaro* to go as well as it did. Everyone in the background was saying how useless I was, how lazy, that I would never make it – an undercurrent which was absolutely true. I knew I was bad. I'm not proud of it, but I admit it.'

For all the surface self-confidence, she remained as prone to inner doubt and disbelief as ever. She preferred not to look groundward. Her bosses at the Royal Opera felt much the same. Having been handed the once-in-a-generation gift of an overnight sensation, they cast their sights on nothing but the sky.

As 1973 began, after a brief holiday in Malta, where she and Des had rented a small apartment, Kiri returned to Covent Garden to face up to the Herculean year's work that lay ahead. Her stock there had risen to such an extent that, in January, she was awarded a scholarship specifically to help her prepare for the next phase of her career. The Drogheda-Mayer Fellowship allowed her to travel to Mantua in Italy to be coached by the renowned coach, Campogalliani. In the ancient Italian city she settled down to learning the three new roles that would dominate the coming year, Micaëla in *Carmen* with Solti, Amelia in *Simon Boccanegra* with John Matheson and Donna Elvira in *Don Giovanni* with Colin Davis.

Originally Kiri had been asked to learn the first two only. *Carmen* would open in April, *Boccanegra* in September. Using the Countess as a blueprint, Vera Rosza and John Matheson had laid out careful plans to teach Kiri the two roles in as detailed a way as possible. Their plans had been disrupted by Colin Davis, who had asked Kiri in addition to learn Elvira for a recording he was due to make for

Philips in May. He also asked her to 'cover' for Wendy Fine when the production opened at Covent Garden in April, and again when the Italian soprano Margherita Rinaldi took the role in the first revival in November.

The workload was daunting. With Basil Horsfield filling her diary with other, often lucrative engagements, Kiri faced the most physically demanding period of her career so far. Rehearsals with Solti for *Carmen* got under way soon after the recording was complete. Solti's misgivings about Kiri had been forgotten. The two hit it off in spectacular fashion. 'It was a musical marriage made in heaven,' smiled Solti's closest ally at the time, Joan Ingpen.

Kiri's ability to charm her male colleagues was, by now, the subject of envy and inevitable rumour-mongering. Both Colin Davis and Solti made little secret of the fact they were quietly besotted by her. On one occasion Davis's secretary saw him rolling around on the floor of his office with Kiri. Davis recounted the occasion himself later, explaining they were having a 'wrestling match'. 'God only knows why we did it. But we did,' he said. The delicate Davis had clearly picked the wrong opponent in the former Blockhouse Bay brawler. The sight of Kiri holding Davis in an armlock 'frightened the life' out of his secretary. 'She actually rang my wife to say that I was on the floor with a prima donna and it looked as though I was losing.'

Georg Solti's fondness for the female form was even more legendary than Davis's. His twenty-year first marriage to Hedwig Oeschli had collapsed in 1964 and he was already heavily involved with a New York businesswoman when a married BBC journalist, Valerie Pitts, came to interview him at the Savoy hotel that year. What he later called 'a violent affair' began at once, resulting in marriage in 1967. At twenty-seven Valerie was almost half the fifty-two-year-old Solti's age. The formidable Valerie had since become the most powerful influence in his life. Not even she could rid him of the gleam that appeared in his eye whenever he found himself in the presence of a truly beautiful woman.

His roster of 'favourites' included the American Mary Costa, the English singer Elizabeth Robson, the Italian Mirella Freni and the Spaniard Teresa Braganza. Kiri quickly complemented this cosmopolitan coterie. 'He liked good-looking women, let's face it. And he and Kiri clicked. But I don't think there was anything like that in that case,' said Joan Ingpen.

It may not have been for the lack of trying on Solti's part. Kiri had first worked with Solti on the *Parsifal* recording in Vienna at the end of 1971. Kiri told one friend how, in the small hours of the night, Solti had knocked on her hotel room door during an overseas assignment.

'Kiri, let me in,' he had whispered. When Kiri had told the maestro to go back to his own room, Solti had persisted. 'Come on, Kiri. Let me in? No one will know.'

'Yes, they will,' Kiri replied. 'Valerie will for a start, because I'll bloody well tell her.'

Kiri saw no harm in capitalising on her beauty and she made no secret of her love of male company. She was unashamedly a man's woman. 'I like men,' she told one colleague at Covent Garden at the time. 'What's wrong with that?'

Inside London's musical world, it was clear her suggestive unattainability only added to her appeal. 'A lot of conductors had crushes on her,' said her old friend Mary Masterton, by now installed at the English National Opera at the Coliseum, in whom Kiri confided during her early days at Covent Garden. 'She would use that knowing that because Des was there it couldn't go any further. It was an ideal situation. Everything worked out beautifully for her. She worked with good people and had Des looking after her. She could get out of any situation.'

Kiri herself once admitted, albeit cryptically, that she fell in love with many of the men she worked with. 'Our work is very passionate and there is often a lot of passion between singers,' she said in 1992. 'Some people let that passion take over. Sometimes people I've worked with have fallen in love with my voice and then fancied themselves in love with me, and I love them right back. But I never get to the stage where I'm out of control.'

Whatever the status of their personal relationship, there was no questioning the musical chemistry she and Solti enjoyed from the outset. Solti, much like Vera Rosza, projected an intense and overwhelming energy. It was almost as if they compensated for Kiri's laid-back persona. 'They are both Hungarian Jews, and the sheer energy and input that goes into their mere thinking about music is quite mind-boggling,' she said once. 'They are so intense about their work that they occasionally manage to turn a lazy, lethargic person like me into a workaholic.' Kiri confessed that without Solti and Rosza's inspirational input, 'I would never have had the ability, the knowledge or the oomph to go out and do what I'm doing.'

The quality of the cast Solti had assembled only added to Kiri's enthusiasm. Shirley Verrett had been cast as Carmen, while the role of Don José was being sung by the rapidly emerging Placido Domingo. Rehearsals went on at the London Opera Centre during a sweltering early summer. Kiri admitted later that the producer Michael Geliot, brought in to replace Franco Zeffirelli, had been the only irritation. He had asked her to sing the Micaëla aria from Act III in front of the entire cast. 'I did my usual bitchy thing and sang it an octave down,' she said later. Geliot failed to see the funny side.

In June, to Kiri's amazement, her remarkable progress over the previous year was recognised with the news that she had been awarded the Order of the British Empire. As if the honour was not great enough, when she arrived at Buckingham Palace with Des to collect the award, the Queen surprised her by saying she remembered her from Dunedin three years earlier. A few weeks later, on 4 July, she met the Queen Mother at the gala opening night of Solti's *Carmen*. The warmth of the greeting underlined Kiri's steady emergence as something of a Royal favourite.

Carmen itself was a muted success. What praise there was came the way of Kiri and José Van Dam. 'Kiri Te Kanawa brought her full, sweet soprano to Micaëla's music, and made of her a more natural and positive character than usual,' wrote Desmond Shawe-Taylor in the *Sunday Times*. Kiri had little time to dwell on the reviews, even if she had chosen to read them. She headed immediately to Glyndebourne to begin rehearsals for Peter Hall's production of *The Marriage of Figaro*. After that it was back to Covent Garden and the new role of Amelia in *Simon Boccanegra* where, once more, Kiri found herself in the capable hands of John Copley and John Matheson.

To Matheson, Kiri was an even more intriguing character than she had been when he first met her at New Zealand House. He had seen her develop musically and personally. The nervous newcomer had become a confident not to mention occasionally demanding star.

Kiri remained responsive and respectful to Matheson. 'We got on fine,' he recalled. On their last trip to New Zealand, however, the sight of the tour manager being hauled over the coals over an inadequate hotel room opened Matheson's eyes to the painful prospect ahead if his friendship faded. 'He was frightened out of his mind the poor fellow, utterly speechless,' he said, recalling a spectacular dressing down Kiri issued at one point. 'It was over some service or other that hadn't been rendered, but I could see that she had some dangerous fire available.'

Kiri's insecurity remained a central element of her personality. Her prickly defensiveness could still manifest itself in seemingly needless bitchiness. Kiri had, for instance, never rid herself of her adolescent need to fixate herself on rivals, despite claims to the contrary. Matheson recalls Kiri anointing another soprano 'my enemy'. 'I said, "You're talking nonsense. She's no enemy of yours. She's not in your class. She'll fade away naturally." That's what happened, but I think Kiri assisted a bit.'

There were times, too, when she seemed to take her dictum that 'the ruder you are the further you get' a little too seriously. 'She came in and did her work, and chatted happily in the canteen but she caused too many upsets – nobody was very fond of her,' said Matheson. 'There were no close friends around the opera. For her friends she went out of the house.'

Kiri's enemies inevitably made mischief. One colleague coined a particularly unpleasant and unfair variation on Nelson's infamous description of Lady Caroline Lamb: 'Mad, bad and dangerous to know.' 'Ugly, vicious and can't sing a note', earned widespread circulation.

Kiri, however, had long since grown used to such envy. 'They just sit there waiting for someone to sing a bad note,' she said of her rivals once. 'Your laryngitis is their greatest joy.'

During her epic preparation for *Figaro*, Kiri had told herself she would never again have the luxury of having a year to learn a role. Sure enough, she was expected to absorb Verdi's complex arias at a faster pace. Her preparations for *Boccanegra* were not helped by events elsewhere at Covent Garden. Colin Davis's revival of *Don Giovanni* was due to open at the end of November. Less than two months before opening night the Italian soprano Margherita Rinaldi announced she was expecting a baby and withdrew. Kiri had to begin preparing to take the significant step from singing Elvira in a recording studio to playing it on stage.

By the time she came to the opening night of *Simon Boccanegra*,

Kiri was still hesitant about some passages. She has never made any great secret of the problems she has sometimes encountered remembering lines. 'I depend on the prompter completely, perhaps that is my major problem,' she once confessed. 'The people in charge will say they can't fit one in, that there's no budget, that there's no time, and I tell them to make room and that I can't go on stage without one.'

By now she had her own collection of remedies for her unwelcome attacks of amnesia. 'Some singers get frightened that they might forget the words, but if that happens to me I just make them up. I have no qualms about it,' Kiri admitted once. 'On such occasions, Solti always shouts, "Chinese, Chinese", by which he means that if you invent Chinese words, nobody will notice.'

As she opened in *Simon Boccanegra* it was John Matheson who saved her. 'The *Boccanegra* was very good but Colin had put in *Don Giovanni* before that because he wanted to do it on his record, and so the carefully planned sequence of premières was suddenly ruined by the insertion of no less a part than Elvira,' the conductor remembered. 'When it came to *Boccanegra* she really had not had time to prepare it properly, and it was not her fault.'

Kiri was in magnificent voice throughout most of the opening night's performance. As she approached the closing ensemble, however, Matheson saw the tell-tale signs of tiredness in her eyes. 'I saw these blank eyes looking at me from the Covent Garden stage as if to say, "What the Hell happens next?",' he recalled. 'She really couldn't quite remember, so I drew the awkward cross rhythm in the air with my left hand, and she followed! I drew the shape of the tune, up and down. We were alright,' he smiled.

The critics' reaction seemed to justify Kiri's decision to ignore them. Most were too busy drooling over her devastating looks and vocal pyrotechnics to notice her difficulties. *Opera*'s *éminence grise* Harold Rosenthal called her 'the revelation of the evening'. 'Here was Verdi singing on the highest level.' *The Times*'s Stanley Sadie echoed his thought, writing, 'She lives the role, her singing is coloured by love, anxiety, terror or whatever other emotion possesses her, and her movement on stage is supple and full of life and feeling.'

Kiri had less than three weeks to make the transition from the cool and ethereal Amelia to the tigress Elvira. She was helped by the fact that John Copley and Colin Davis were on hand to guide her through. Among familiar Covent Garden faces like Teresa Cahill, cast as Zerlina, and Ryland Davies as Ottavio, there were visitors from overseas. The Italian bass Cesare Siepi arrived unaware that the new female star of the Garden was from New Zealand rather than Japan. 'Where's Kanawa?' he had asked to mass hysterics when he arrived for rehearsal.

Bored with the picturesque productions of recent years, John Copley and designer Stefan Lazaridis had come up with a coldly modernistic set made up of heavy metal tubing. The set resembled a well-lit scaffold. Cast members regularly lost their footing through gaps in the piping. At the final curtain Copley and Lazaridis were booed.

Once more Kiri responded to the challenge. William Mann in *The Times* described her as 'a tigress in desolation' while *Opera*'s Alan Blyth thought her 'frenzied, distraught portrayal . . . the finest Elvira since Schwarzkopf and Jurinac'.

Inevitably Kiri was now weakened by her over-exertions. She was hit by a flu bug and was replaced by Teresa Cahill.

On 28 January 1974, Kiri looked out from an aircraft window to see the grey and grisly outline of the east coast of America looming into view. She disembarked at JFK airport and climbed into the waiting limousine, dispatched to meet her by the New York Met. Soon she was staring up at the concrete canyons of Manhattan. When Basil Horsfield had first approached the Royal Opera for permission to allow Kiri to appear in a new production of *Otello*, designed by Franco Zeffirelli and conducted by the Met's brilliant James Levine, both John Tooley and Colin Davis had vetoed the move. The territorial Tooley wanted Kiri to make her debut as Desdemona in London. The nerve-racked Davis feared his protégé would be eaten alive. 'The Met audience will kill you,' he had warned her.

It was Vera Rosza, her psychologist's hat firmly in place, who first recognised an essential element in Kiri's make-up. Rosza had learned to accept Kiri's habit of leaving the learning process to the last minute. She understood it was simply her pupil's means of making life more interesting. 'She rather enjoys a dangerous edge to things,' she said. Davis's warning in particular had been the most persuasive sentence she had heard in years. Even Kiri's love of danger would never be so richly indulged as it would be in New York, however.

Kiri had taken leave from Covent Garden and travelled to New York well in advance of her debut, due on 7 March. *Otello* was due to open on 9 February, with Teresa Stratas in the role of Desdemona. On Basil Horsfield's advice, Kiri had allowed herself more than a month to familiarise herself with the production.

Kiri was given a flat on West End Avenue, a short, ten-block drive from the Lincoln Center and the Met itself. In the absence of Des, who remained at home in Esher while tying up business in London, a companion cum housekeeper, called Rosanne, lived in with her. At her own expense, Kiri had also engaged a public relations company to drum up press coverage in advance of her debut. In the event it would prove one of the easier commissions the PR men had earned. Kiri spent the first week inside the Met's rehearsal rooms reacquainting herself with the role she had first sung in Glasgow two years earlier and getting to know James Levine.

The Cincinatti-born Levine had arrived at the Met from Cleveland in 1971, aged just twenty-eight. Big Jim, as he was affectionately known, was a heavyweight in reputation and physique. He had been Herbert von Karajan's protégé and was widely expected to be the German demagogue's successor at the Berlin Philharmonic. The 200lb Levine looked more like a gridiron linebacker than a conductor. He would take to the podium with a brightly coloured towel around his neck. By the end of each performance the towel would be soaked in sweat. Yet his energy and drive had already worked wonders at the Met. He was credited with having revived a lacklustre, ageing orchestra and having developed a nursery of excellent new singers. Kiri responded to him instantly.

On the afternoon of Friday, 8 February news filtered through that Teresa Stratas had been taken ill. The Met phoned Kiri to alert her that she was on standby for the following afternoon. A panic-stricken Kiri was unable to raise Des or Basil Horsfield in London. As Kiri paced the apartment like a caged tiger, Niefeld insisted that a decision was taken one way or the other by nine o'clock that night. When the call came through to let Kiri know Stratas was fit and well after all, she slept what she later called her best night's sleep since arriving in New York. When the phone rang at ten o'clock the following morning Kiri told Rosanne, 'If it's the Met tell them I'm out.' When Rosanne relayed the message that Stratas had pulled out once more and Kiri would definitely be singing that afternoon Kiri felt 'like the loneliest person in the world . . . There was nobody, no coach, no accompanist, no one,' she said later.

Kiri rushed out of her apartment and climbed into a yellow cab. The snow was falling as the driver took an eternity to find the Met. 'My taxi driver was from the Bronx and didn't know where the Met was, even though I was on West End Avenue, ten blocks away.'

Kiri arrived to discover that Levine and her Otello, Jon Vickers, had arranged a steak lunch and a rehearsal for her. 'We did conspire a bit before Kiri came in,' Vickers admitted later. 'The Met debut is a very frightening experience. I tried to make a bit of a fuss of her to let her know she was among friends.'

Kiri had not set foot on Franco Zeffirelli's complex, multi-levelled set. She spent the little time available working out her entrances, exits and stage positions.

At 2.30 p.m. the house lights dimmed and Levine set his orchestra in motion. From her opening duet with Otello – 'Dark is the night and silent' – to the twin arias of the fourth act – the 'Willow Song' and 'Ave Maria' – Kiri lived off the adrenal charge of the moment. 'I have never been so nervous,' she confessed afterwards. 'I trembled until the end of the fourth act. I survived by pure concentration. The relief at the end of it!' No sooner had Vickers's Otello stabbed himself, gently kissed Kiri's dying Desdemona and fallen to the floor, than the vast auditorium had erupted into applause.

Vickers astutely read the audience's mood and nudged Kiri into making one curtain call on her own. The roars grew even louder as she did so. Backstage, Vickers observed Kiri was 'as high as a kite'. Kiri spent much of the evening celebrating. By the time she got back to the flat Des had arrived home from his lunch with Kiri's friend and English accompanist, the pianist Jean Mallandaine. Mallandaine later recalled how Des had rung her with the succinct message: 'She's been on.'

The wait for the first reviews on Monday morning was worth the anxiety. The *New York Times*'s critic Allen Hughes led the eulogies. 'Miss Te Kanawa won the audience from the very beginning and did not lose it,' he wrote. Harriet Johnson in the *New York Post* thought Kiri's voice 'a large, full, easily produced soprano that opens up on the top like a luscious rose'. Unlike three years ago and the opening night of *Figaro* there was no dissent. No critic surpassed Alan Rich writing in *New York Magazine*. 'This is a singer with a voice as beautiful as any I have heard in the house since the time of the young Tebaldi,' he said. 'Do not miss this glorious artist – in this season's *Otello*, next season's *Don Giovanni*, or any time she comes your way.'

Kiri had arrived in New York concerned at her lack of a profile in America. In the aftermath of her debut, her public relations consultants were deluged with requests from all over America. With Teresa Stratas recovered, Kiri was left with the best part of a month before her official debut.

Kiri celebrated her thirtieth birthday in New York where she had by now been joined by Des, Tom, Basil Horsfield, Vera Rosza and Jean Mallandaine. The Mayor of New York, Abe Beame, had joined in the celebrations, awarding Kiri a civic scroll. There was even a telegram from the Prime Minister of New Zealand, Norman Kirk. With her official debut in *Otello* the following evening it was, for Kiri at least, a restrained affair. The real celebration began the following evening after Kiri took a deafening, fifteen-minute ovation. Kiri made the trip more lucrative with a recital, accompanied by Mallandaine, in Long Island arranged by Sam Niefeld.

Once more Kiri was elevated to the top of every conductor's wish list – regardless of her suitability for the role. John Matheson recalls Basil Horsfield describing how Leonard Bernstein deluged him with phone calls demanding Kiri sing in his London Symphony Orchestra production of Verdi's *Requiem*. 'Apparently Bernstein, having not heard her sing but only having heard her reputation, was going crazy. Basil said, "Bernstein is round the bend! He's on the phone all the time, saying, 'I must have that girl! I must have that girl for the Verdi *Requiem*".' Basil had told him, "She can't sing the Verdi *Requiem*, it's far too big for her at this stage." He persisted and persisted and finally gave it up only when it was obvious that she was unable to do it.'

She returned to discover her triumph had been news in London, too. When a colleague at Covent Garden complimented her on the wealth of publicity she had received, she grimaced. 'You know we had to pay for it?' she said. When the colleague suggested it must have cost the bulk of her fee, Kiri nodded silently. At least she could console herself with the knowledge that she had never spent money so wisely. 'It was very well judged, because from that moment she was a sensation.'

Fallen Angel

On the night of 26 September 1974, New Zealand was a nation united in grief. Four weeks earlier, only two years after his election to the job, the country's popular Labour Prime Minister, Norman Kirk, had died of a heart attack after a short stay in hospital at the age of fifty-one. Now, countless thousands tuned their radios in for a live broadcast of the memorial service from London's Westminster Abbey.

In hushed tones, the BBC's Godfrey Talbot described the scene as 2,000 mourners, including three former Governors General, the Earl of Westmoreland representing the Queen, and diplomatic staff of sixty-four countries, filed into the Abbey to take their seats behind Kirk's widow Ruth and his two daughters.

Lessons were read by Lord Ballantrae and the New Zealand High Commissioner before the emotional high point of the service, a rendition of 'I Know that My Redeemer Liveth' from the *Messiah*, to be sung by Kiri, accompanied by a string section conducted by John Matheson.

As Matheson raised his baton, however, Talbot broke in to make a surprise announcement to his listeners. 'Miss Te Kanawa says she does not wish her voice to be broadcast outside the confines of Westminster Abbey.' Almost immediately radios all over New Zealand fell completely silent. Many of the audience spent the enforced interval of several minutes that followed shaking their heads in disbelief. Kiri's extraordinary decision had been taken after heated arguments the night before involving New Zealand's High Commissioner Terence McCombs and a phalanx of his bemused staff. The following day, as criticism mounted, she tried to justify her actions to the *Auckland Star*. Kiri admitted she was tired from rehearsing for a forthcoming tour of Australia and that she might not have been at her peak for the service, but said that had not been a factor.

'I do regret it if my motives were misunderstood in New Zealand, but perhaps the people were too far away to appreciate that I was singing solely for the immediate service,' she explained. 'It was my wish – in fact it was my insistence – that I was making a personal contribution to the memory of a great man and that I wanted it to be a private gesture and confined just to the Abbey. I felt that I could only do my very best if it were done my way.'

Back in New Zealand most understood and accepted the sincerity of her explanation. In London, however, Kiri's insistence on doing things her way was about to precipitate the first major personal and professional crisis of her career.

In the autumn of 1974, Kiri began work on a new challenge, the role of Marguerite in Charles Gounod's *Faust*. For all its popularity, the operatic version of Goethe's Mephistophelean drama had not been staged at Covent Garden since 1938. The new *Faust* was a curate's egg. An American philanthropist had offered Covent Garden £500,000 to stage his favourite work. The money came with one casting condition attached: the role of Mephistopheles must also be sung by his favourite singer, the American bass Norman Treigle. The portents were ominous from the moment John Tooley agreed to the deal. As far as many were concerned, if Covent Garden had not quite sold its soul to the devil it had committed an artistic compromise that came perilously close.

While Kiri was cast in the leading female role of Marguerite, Stuart Burrows was engaged to play the eponymous Dr Faust. John Matheson, frustrated in his plans to stage a version of Rossini's *William Tell*, reluctantly agreed to take the baton. The difficulties began almost immediately. Treigle arrived late in London looking an alarmingly undernourished shadow of his former self. Before even attending a rehearsal he had called in sick, having damaged his foot climbing out of his hotel bed one morning. As the cast assembled, Matheson himself was forced to spend time away from production rehearsals as he amended the score. Kiri's mood was not helped by the fact that rehearsals were taking place once more at the Opera Centre. Each morning she was faced with the nerve-jangling drive across London from Esher to the East End. To make matters worse, she returned to an empty house each evening. Des had been posted on a six-month assignment to Perth, Western Australia. Kiri, never happy being given new music to learn at short notice, quickly grew frustrated by the flurry of notes explaining the changes Matheson was introducing.

Matheson's main concern was Treigle, however. He had been horrified at his first sight of the American. 'If he stood sideways you could barely see him,' he said. 'There was hardly any voice there.' When he turned up for rehearsals he repeatedly challenged Matheson's authority. 'Oh, come on, maestro, I've done this 200 times,' he would protest.

Matheson discovered via Treigle's girlfriend that the singer was not eating at all. Instead he was surviving on a diet of whisky and water. Along with Basil Horsfield and others, he asked John Tooley to drop Treigle and replace him with Richard Van Allan, who had understudied Mephistopheles admirably in his absence. Eventually Tooley was forced to tell Treigle that if he did not turn up for the general dress rehearsal he would not be allowed to perform on the opening night. Treigle duly appeared in full costume – and on crutches. Earlier in his career he had been famous for his high-intensity acting style. 'His great claim to fame had been that he fizzed and flitted his way around the stage, popping up behind chairs and so forth. And here he was on crutches,' said Matheson. 'It was ludicrous, but no one could resist this millionaire who thought he was terrific and that Covent Garden should see him. It was a shambles. He was crazy.'

Matheson and the cast arrived for the opening night grim-faced. Kiri sang the famous 'Jewel Song' and its chorus, 'Oh joy', beautifully. 'The opening night was no joy for anybody, I can assure you,' said John Matheson. The critics damned *Faust* with faint praise. After the heady excitement of the Met, Kiri found herself attached to what threatened to be her first bona fide failure. Lonely and depressed, she spent the weekend afterwards in London with Basil Horsfield and John Davern.

As the run continued Kiri called on her support network of girlfriends. When Anne Howells came over to Rushmere for a curry Kiri persuaded her to spend the night in Esher. Howells found her friend's behaviour increasingly eccentric. The house's heating had been turned up to resemble 'Rangoon in the rainy season'. When Howells took a bath Kiri insisted on bringing a television and glasses of wine in to her. In the middle of the night Howells woke up to find Kiri plucking her eyebrows in a mirror. Howells later admitted she sensed a deep unhappiness in her friend.

Kiri admitted years later that the relentless schedule she worked as she aimed to capitalise on her *Figaro* sensation had left her drained.

'You just do not get noticed as someone who is steadily getting better in mediocre things. Everything I did seemed to be in the first league. It was frightening, but I was so busy doing the next thing that I never had time to look back and see if the dust had settled,' she said on one occasion. 'When I got to Marguerite I went to pieces simply because I had learned so many roles between *Figaro* and *Faust* that I had got to the stage of saturation,' she added on another.

The production's problems created even greater tensions within an already divided company. Matheson's relationship with Colin Davis had become strained. The conductor had announced that he intended leaving at the end of the following season. Soon he felt as if he was being made the scapegoat for the entire *Faust* fiasco. Smelling blood, the critics had returned to the troubled production and turned their guns on the conductor. Matheson makes no excuses for the failure of his orchestra. 'William Mann in *The Times* gave me a very decent notice but most of the others just said that the orchestra sounded dull and disparate, and quite right – so we were,' he said. 'Then Mann's boss, John Higgins, decided to come down himself to the second or third performance and proceeded to pick me out as the thing that was wrong. He gave me a devastating battery. By this time everything was focusing on me.' Soon Matheson's political antennae were aroused. 'There was a cabal against me.' Matheson's greatest sadness was that Kiri seemed to be a member of it.

In his heart Matheson was not surprised at his protégé's behaviour. 'There's not much of a gentle side to Kiri. She's so ambitious – and always has been so ambitious and quite willing to tread on people,' he said sadly. 'There's no trace of the Tebaldi, even the Callas, or Maggie Smith or Dame Peggy Ashcroft – who were all gentle people with some steel underneath but who knew how to behave.' Kiri's status at Covent Garden now demanded that she be taken seriously. 'For Kiri, I think it was an exercise of power. She could see there was room at Covent Garden for more strong personalities and she could show her power.'

At the time, however, he was deeply wounded by what he saw as an act of betrayal. 'I remember thinking, "Good God, she's turned against me, after all the work I did for her."' His fury slowly gave way to a painful sadness, however. 'I loved her. I thought she was a wonderful creature through all those early years,' he said. 'But we all recognised that she could be terribly bitchy.'

Eventually Matheson fell on his sword. He met John Tooley one day in a lift at Covent Garden. 'I went down in the lift with him and said, "Look, if it will help, John, I will step down."' Within days an announcement had been made that Matheson was leaving the production on health grounds and Charles Mackerras, then at the Coliseum, was stepping in.

As agent to each of the quartet of combatants, Basil Horsfield was caught in a hopeless position. He called Matheson after hearing rumours he had quit.

'I said, "Look, Basil, it's such a stupid mess, I've offered to withdraw from the show." He was really shocked and unhappy that all his clients were getting in strife with one another. But he was too gentle a character. Solti would have dealt with it in ten minutes. All it needed was a couple of heads knocking together. It was a foolish, feeble, stupid business.'

His treatment was greeted with widespread sympathy; Kiri's part in the drama with barely concealed disgust. In the eyes of many, Matheson had been the key to Kiri's early success at Covent Garden. 'John is not always given as much credit as he deserved,' said Kiri's old director Tom Hawkes. 'He did understand her when she first went to the Garden and worked incredibly hard with her and understood all that background. He made sure she knew things, that she did understand it. Because she was slow in understanding and taking things in, her languages were not terribly good so she had to be spoon-fed at times.'

No one was more distressed for the conductor than Donald McIntyre. McIntyre had always felt *Faust* was wrong for both his compatriots. 'I've never felt that Kiri's was the right voice for Marguerite. She's got a gorgeous, golden sort of voice. For Marguerite you need a diamond sparkling voice, and Kiri's has a beautiful roundness which is absolutely marvellous,' he said. 'Whether John was right conducting it either, I don't know. He wanted to do *William Tell*, but it was changed because the management wouldn't let him do it. They were scared. It's very long and hardly ever done.'

According to one Covent Garden singer, McIntyre later upbraided Kiri publicly for what he saw as her betrayal. In full view of the house canteen McIntyre accused Kiri of being responsible for Matheson's removal. 'You should be ashamed of yourself,' he told her. 'It's all your fault.'

McIntyre maintains a diplomatic silence on the incident. 'It was rather sad when they fell out,' is all he will say. 'John was a great admirer of Kiri's.'

Kiri later looked back on the entire *Faust* experience as a mistake, 'an awful time'. Her relationship with John Matheson was never properly healed. In her authorised biography she mentioned him briefly, acknowledging that he had been 'one of her most helpful coaches during her early years'. The duo never worked together again and didn't even meet for another sixteen years. Kiri, perhaps unsurprisingly, has never again taken on the role of Marguerite.

Charles Mackerras fared little better when he arrived to conduct the remainder of the run. The new conductor's first move was to summon his principal voices to the Commercial Road. His call to Esher came as Kiri was in the middle of a documentary interview with the journalist Bernard Levin. In the mid–1970s, Levin's column in *The Times* stood almost unchallenged as the best written and best read in British journalism. His highly-opinionated musings on matters as diverse as homosexual rights and East German Communism, cheese-making and cruelty to prawns had earned him comparisons with G. K. Chesterton. His colleague Christopher Booker best summed up his status within British society when he called him 'a national institution'.

An avid opera-goer, Levin had begun singing Kiri's praises soon after her breakthrough as the Countess. By now, barely a month went by without him purring about the soprano he, rather embarrassingly, referred to as 'the Kanawissima'. His devotion had earned him the opportunity to interview Kiri for a BBC documentary profile being produced by Patricia Foy.

To Mackerras's fury, Levin refused to break off from his filming. At a difficult time in her life, the row between the two men put a momentary smile on Kiri's face.

The tragic epilogue to the drama of *Faust* was written six weeks after the final performance at Covent Garden. Norman Treigle had continued living off his whisky and water diet. He was found dead in his hotel room.

Bernard Levin's reluctance to let Kiri out of his sight was understandable given the frankness his subject was displaying under the arc lights he and Patricia Foy had erected in the living room at Rushmere. After years of avoiding the issue, Kiri had finally decided to reveal the truth about her background.

Ever since she first aroused the interest of the media at the Mobil Song Quest in Hamilton in 1963, Kiri had shuffled uncomfortably in her seat whenever the subject of her parents arose. Interviewers would become confused at her references to her half-sister Nola. As follow-up questions flowed, Kiri would cut off leaving the journalist no wiser. Until now Kiri had been protected by the general meekness of the media in New Zealand. Times were changing, however. Kiri's deep-seated insecurity about herself had not been helped by the stories about her origins circulating New Zealand. One of the wildest yet most persistent, given credence among members of the St Mary's circle for years, was that Kiri had been the daughter of one of Tom Te Kanawa's sisters. She, the story went, had enjoyed a brief, passionate affair with a visiting Italian opera singer who had fled the country on hearing the news of her pregnancy. The sister had headed back to the Te Kanawa marae heartbroken. Tom had supposedly protected her honour by dutifully stepping in to raise the child as his own. According to a darker variation on this unpleasant fiction, repeated by some of Kiri's old colleagues and friends even now, Tom had taken his sister to Nell Te Kanawa for an abortion. When Nell somehow bungled the operation, Tom offered her an ultimatum. Either she agreed to marry him and raise the child as if they had adopted it, or he would publicly expose her negligence. With such murky and malevolent stories in circulation – and with precious little of the truth available to her at that stage in her life – it is little wonder that Kiri had concentrated on the happier elements of her story.

In her heart, Kiri knew Tom and Nell were her parents and always would be. In her head, however, she knew she was adopted. It was time to put the record straight. Kiri's decision was made easier by Tom, who had travelled over for another holiday. Kiri asked his permission to go public with the story of her arrival at Grey Street. Tom nodded quietly in agreement.

'I do not know who my parents were, and I do not want to know,' she told Levin in the interview which was aired on British television shortly before Christmas in 1975. 'I cannot understand adopted children who make a big deal out of trying to find out who their real parents were.' Kiri recounted the story, presumably passed on to her by Nell, of how a social worker had walked the streets of Gisborne in search of a home for her. She went on to recount Tom and Nell's initial rejection and subsequent change of heart. 'Obviously they were meant to have me,' she told Levin. Kiri used the interview as a platform once more to pay tribute to her parents, Tom in particular. 'The finest man in the world,' she called him.

The news was, of course, seized on in New Zealand where Kiri's honesty was greeted with almost universal admiration and sympathy when the programme was broadcast in December 1975. The emotions the interview stirred up within Noeleen Rawstron would have been far more complex, however.

Kiri's blood mother seems to have spent the thirty years following her daughter's birth trying to forget her ill-starred affair with Jack Wawatai and its unhappy conclusion. Tragically for her, Kiri's inexorable rise to fame had made the task all but impossible.

In the immediate aftermath of Kiri's adoption, Noeleen had remained in Tokomaru Bay where she had raised her first son Jimmy and made no mention of the events of early 1944. 'It was much later that we heard anything about a baby, and it wasn't from Noeleen,' said her sister Donny.

The truth only emerged when Donny and another sister, Kate, found a letter stuffed inside a mattress at the house. The note was from Noeleen to their mother, Thelma, and explained how she had handed her second child over for adoption in Gisborne.

The note confirmed that Thelma had almost certainly shared her daughter's secret. Yet in the years that followed, none of her siblings could bring themselves to discuss the matter with Noeleen. Her brother Ken had been serving in the New Zealand military when the drama unfolded. 'I was away in the war when it happened and only heard from my sister Kate when I got back,' he recalled. 'But I felt it was none of my business and never asked Noeleen about it.'

Within a couple of years of baby Claire's birth, Noeleen had married a local taxi driver, Rex 'Tubby' Williams. By 1948 she had given birth to her third child, a girl, christened Sharon. Eventually Noeleen, Rex, Jimmy and Sharon moved to New Plymouth, on the west coast of the country. It had been in New Plymouth in 1967 that Noeleen and Kiri had almost crossed paths. Days before Kiri's record-breaking shows there, Noeleen had sat proudly in the audience at the Brooklands Bowl as eighteen-year-old Sharon competed in the Miss Brooklands beauty pageant. Had Noeleen known one of the winning contestant's first duties was to present Kiri with a bouquet of chrysanthemums on her movie-star like arrival at New Plymouth airport, she may not have supported her daughter so wholeheartedly. In a strange twist of fate, it was the eventual winner of the Miss Brooklands title, Nan Taylor, who went on to become a friend of Kiri's and even acted as a bridesmaid at her wedding later that year. In retrospect, Sharon now understands the strangeness of her mother's attitude towards New Zealand's Queen of Song both then and in subsequent years. While New Plymouth was alive with Kirimania, Noeleen, to her younger daughter's bemusement, repeatedly heaped scorn on the young Maori heroine.

'She acted as if she couldn't stand Kiri,' said Sharon. 'Whenever she was on TV or the radio, or she saw an article in the magazines about her, she would say, "She's just a nobody. I can't bear that shrieking voice."'

Despite her closeness to Sharon, Noeleen never revealed the real reason for her unusual behaviour. 'She was my mother, my sister, my best friend,' said Sharon. 'It's very hard for me to know that she kept it from me.'

She can, at least, take comfort in the knowledge that Noeleen treated her no differently from anyone else in her family. Her brother Ken only came to understand his sister's relationship with Kiri much later in life. He too sensed that Noeleen was engaged in a form of denial, blocking Kiri – and the feelings of guilt, anger and loss she must always have associated with her – from her mind altogether. 'She was the one person I never heard talk about Kiri, even though she's such a heroine in New Zealand,' he said.

In the months and years that followed Kiri's revelation of her adoption, the memories of Noeleen's unplanned pregnancy and her affair with Jack Wawatai were frequently rekindled in the tight-knit community of Tokomaru Bay. Many remembered her previous, equally unhappy liaison with Jimmy Collier. Some sought to blacken Noeleen's character. Her sister Donny, in particular, had to endure many variations on the truth. She was, for many years, deeply confused by the conflicting rumours she heard. Of two things she is now certain. 'There are people who have tried to say that my sister was loose, but that's wrong,' she said. 'I always knew that if Noeleen was Kiri's mother, then only one man could be her father, and that was Jack Wawatai.'

Sadly, Donny was never able to share her certainty with her sister, however. Noeleen Williams died of a heart attack, visiting her oldest child, Jim Rawstron, in Sydney on 26 July 1979. She and Kiri never met.

As 1974 drew to a close, Kiri travelled to New York where she would give the Met its first sight of her Elvira in *Don Giovanni*. Kiri's sexually-charged performance aroused the critics once more. 'Donna Electra, almost, would seem a better name. For upon first entrance, eyes glaring, chestnut hair tousled and her pace like that of a caged tigress, it was plain that this was no standard shrinking violent impersonation,' wrote William Zakariasen for the *New York Daily News*. Kiri's version of 'Mi tradì' was greeted with what Zakariasen called 'volcanic applause'. 'No wonder – a better rendition of it today seems inconceivable.' In the days that followed her debut, only Kiri knew the damage her high-voltage performance had done.

After eight years together, Des and Kiri had finally decided to attempt to have a child. The triumph of *Otello* had given Kiri the confidence she needed to face a break from performing. Shortly before heading to New York, her doctors had confirmed that she was pregnant. In the days after her debut as Donna Elvira, however, Kiri felt unwell. As she put it later, she 'hung in there' and saw through all her performances. By the end of the run, however, her New York doctor had confirmed the worst – she had suffered a miscarriage.

By now Kiri was a slave to a schedule mapped out five years ahead of her. Rather than heading home for an extended rest, she flew from New York to Paris where she was due to make her debut in *Don Giovanni*. 'I'd reached the stage where I wasn't thinking,' she admitted soon afterwards. 'People would put me in a car and I'd get out and sing and somebody else would put me back in the car.'

Kiri arrived in Paris to be re-united with the double act who had done so much to help her career, Georg Solti and Joan Ingpen, now installed as the Paris Opéra's controller of opera planning. With Kiri still technically contracted to Covent Garden, Ingpen had to seek the permission of John Tooley before Kiri could join L'Opéra. 'She still needed leave but I think Tooley would have found it difficult to say no to me,' said Ingpen. Ingpen could not resist a wry smile as Kiri complained about the manner in which she remained handcuffed to Covent Garden. 'She said, "You put me into the Garden and they haven't been letting me go." Then I owned up and told her that was my idea because I was sure she'd be ruined – and I think she would have been,' said Ingpen. 'She said she'd been jolly annoyed at the time, but she appreciated it then. Kiri owes me a lot for those five years.'

The joy of the reunion was soon fading, however. The after-effects of her miscarriage, combined with the over-indulgent Parisian lifestyle, finally pushed Kiri over the precipice. She had picked up another throat infection and had almost completely lost her voice. In mid-February a doctor was called to her hotel in Paris. He diagnosed a relapse of a dose of hepatitis she had suffered when she first arrived at Covent Garden.

Kiri headed back to London where she saw her Harley Street doctor, Dr Briggs. As well as the hepatitis, he diagnosed that Kiri was suffering from what he described as 'anxiety depression'. He delivered Kiri an ultimatum. If she did not take a lengthy rest from work she would soon face a complete nervous and physical breakdown.

Kiri arrived back in London with two major new roles booked in her diary, Mimì at the Scottish Opera in May and Fiordiligi in *Così fan tutte* at Covent Garden a month later. With Des still in Perth, she once more felt isolated. Eventually she accepted the inevitable.

At the end of March 1975, Covent Garden made an official announcement: 'Miss Kiri Te Kanawa is suffering from anxiety depression aggravated by symptoms of abnormal liver function which became evident while rehearsing in Paris earlier this month. After medical advice there and from her London advisers, it has reluctantly been decided that the only course open is for her to cancel all engagements for April, May and June so that a complete cure can be effected.'

Kiri travelled incognito to Perth where Des was based. They rented an apartment within a motel. Kiri spent much of her time on the golf course, where she took her first professional lessons, but was also laid low with flu and lost her voice. In reality, her marriage was as sickly as she was. The demands of their disparate careers had turned Des and Kiri into a part-time partnership. Kiri had never rid herself of her anxiety over his behaviour while they were separated. Over the following weeks they painstakingly put the pieces of their relationship together again. It was clear to both of them that their careers were on the verge of destroying their marriage. Something had to give. Des realised Kiri could never give up her music. Yet as her career developed she needed his support more rather than less. He made the sacrifice himself.

Des informed his bosses at Selection Trust that he was leaving to spend more time with Kiri. He explained that he would now operate as a freelance, taking contracts as and when Kiri's schedule allowed it. 'I turfed that life in,' he said later.

Des found a local pianist with whom Kiri slowly began to rebuild her confidence in her voice. When they returned to London at the beginning of July, Vera Rosza picked up the reins of her recovery. 'They just wouldn't let me give up,' Kiri said three years later. 'I went right back to my first singing lessons and I started again where I'd begun as a child. I had to. My confidence had gone.'

Kiri only remained in London briefly. Instead she provided herself with a much-needed confidence boost by returning to New Zealand for her first concerts there in three years. The tour, sponsored by Benson and Hedges, had been sold out nearly a year previously. 'Our beloved Kiri has come home' wrote the headline writers at the *New Zealand Woman's Weekly*, unaware quite how soothing those words were.

Kiri's illness had given her and Des time to take stock of her life and career. 'I have set myself a limit for retiring from singing but I'm not willing to say what it is,' she told a local reporter. 'I want to make sure I give up while I'm still giving my best.'

Sadly for the audience, Kiri's last concerts in her homeland until 1983 did not see her give her best. Each of the packed halls were told before her appearance of the throat infection, which continued to plague her, and had to content themselves with a restricted programme.

Kiri spent time with Tom out on Lake Taupo. In the family cabin at Hatepe, Tom had settled into life of blissful simplicity since Nell's death. Tom lived alone but filled his days fishing, gardening and playing golf. The highlights of his existence were the phone calls he would receive from Kiri. 'He'd always tell me when Kiri rang,' said Terry Valentine, an old friend from Gisborne who arrived to run the tranquil community's only shop in the mid-1970s. 'He kept that place absolutely spotless, living on his own and cooking for himself. He loved his garden. He had a lot of pictures of Kiri and at the drop of a hat he'd bring out the album and go through Kiri's life from Gisborne onwards.'

Valentine would invariably drive Tom to the airport when he flew to London to see Kiri. 'If he was going over to see Kiri we used to go out at night and we would only catch the very best red-fleshed trout, and then we would smoke them and he would smuggle them over in his golf bag,' said Valentine. Tom's golf bag was one of the two most important items he always carried with him. 'The main part of his luggage was his chainsaw,' smiled Valentine.

Kiri also spent time at Rawhiti near the town of Russell, in the beautiful Bay of Islands on the east coast of the North Island. There she relaxed on the private estate of the wealthy socialite Kura Beale, a friend who had come to mean much to her since Nell's death.

In the wake of Kiri's public admission of her adoption, her relationship with Beale had become the subject of intrigue and intense speculation within both women's inner circles. Many had become convinced Kura was Kiri's real mother. Fairy godmother might have been a more accurate description. Kura Beale cut one of the more remarkable and colourful figures in New Zealand life. She had been born Iritekura Butler Beale in March, 1908 to a half-Maori mother, Rere Kahutia, and an English father, Arthur Merritt Beale, a wealthy accountant who had been born on board a ship bringing his parents to New Zealand. Arthur Beale had met his wife in Waipiro Bay, a tiny coastal settlement south of Tokomaru Bay where he had worked for the region's richest landowners, the Williams family. The Williams's heir, Arnold Beetham or A.B., had been forbidden from marrying Rere himself and, according to family legend, struck a deal with his accountant. 'A.B. persuaded

Beale to marry her instead, but he kept what you might call visiting rights,' said a member of the family. 'It's a funny world up the east coast.'

A grateful A.B. built the Beales a lavish colonial home at Waipiro Bay, a short distance from the Williamses' own grand family home, Puketiti, at Te Puia Springs.

Rere Kahutia's eight children were raised in privilege. Kura was educated at European-style private schools in Gisborne, Wellington and Havelock North. At the age of twenty-three, she travelled to England with her father when he fulfilled a childhood dream to watch the New Zealand cricket team on tour. Arthur Beale died a year later.

Within a year or so Rere married her first love, A.B. Williams, who had now inherited the family estate. A.B. brought the family to his home, Puketiti, where Kura remained until 1965.

Kura's wealth meant she never needed to work for a living. Yet she devoted herself to the Te Puia Springs hospital, serving on its board and involving herself in the day to day running of the maternity wing. At the same time she mixed in the loftiest social circles available on the east coast. She was captain of the Tokomaru Bay Tennis Club, president of the Ruatoria Gun Club, headed the East Coast Golf Club, and played a leading role in the Maori Women's Welfare League.

Yet despite her wealth and striking good looks, she never married. Her family and friends, however, believe she made at least one trip to the southernmost region of New Zealand to have a child in secrecy. In the years after the War, Kura spent more and more time in the beautiful Bay of Islands area, a haven for wealthy fishermen from around the globe. Each season she would hunt giant marlin, shark and other game fish. She became the first female champion the country had produced.

In 1965, she moved north for good, taking over a ten-acre property at Parekura Bay, near Rawhiti, bought for her by her stepfather. A.B. had wanted to buy a single acre of land on a former fortified Maori village, or 'pa', but the county council refused permission for a separate land title of less than ten acres. Instead, Kura, to use her own words, 'got the whole damned lot!' She transformed the stunning headland on the edge of the ocean, building a garden that attracted many hundreds of visitors each summer.

It had been in the early seventies that Kiri had begun making unheralded visits to Rawhiti. On occasions she would come with Des, at other times she would travel alone. Often she would fly in and out by sea plane so as to remain undetected even by the locals.

At first, Kura's neighbours saw the friendship as a meeting of two prominent women in New Zealand life. 'Kura got on with everybody. She had a natural dignity. If she entered a room people deferred to her. She was regal in a way. She gave a sort of glamour to places,' said Eva Brown, for many years the editor of the local magazine, the *Russell Review*.

Some suspected Kura simply saw Kiri as a means of advancing her own reputation. 'If there was any way she could get recognition she would, and of course money was no object to her or her family,' said Mabel Kewene, matron at the Te Puia hospital and a lifelong friend of Kura.

Author Madge Malcolm, who knew of Kura through the Women's Institute, added, 'Kura liked to cultivate friendships with important people and play the grand lady. We were just farmers' wives and accepted it if that was the way she wanted it, but I think with Kiri she just hitched her wagon to a big star.'

As Kiri's fame grew and word of her visits to Rawhiti spread, however, the rumour mill clicked into gear. 'I spoke to a niece of Kura's and she told me about her aunt having gone south to have a baby boy, who died, but if she had one she could have had two. The niece told me the family believed Kura was Kiri's mother, but they had no evidence of course,' said Madge Malcolm. Kiri's virtual silence about her mystery benefactor only added to the intrigue among both Kura's family and Kiri's own inner circle of New Zealand friends, many of whom were convinced there were blood ties. In reality, the relationship was more complex than anyone had guessed. Kura Beale's interest in Kiri had as much to do with the misfortunes of the singer's past as it did with her status as New Zealand's present-day heroine. Long before Kura came to know Kiri well, she had formed a lasting friendship with Noeleen Rawstron, who had worked as a cleaner at Puketiti in her teens.

On the face of it, the wealthy socialite and the impoverished cleaner made an unlikely pair. Yet they appear to have formed a close bond. When Noeleen fell pregnant with baby Jimmy, and later with Kiri, she may well have turned to Kura for advice in face of the hostile reaction from her mother. Kura's experience at the Te Puia hospital and her own supposed experiences with unwanted children made her a natural mother confessor. She remained a presence in Noeleen's life for many years. Noeleen and Rex Williams's daughter Sharon remembers meeting Kura often. Her mother and father would spend time fishing on the rocks at Tokomaru Bay with their well-to-do friend. Their closeness may explain the interest Kura took in Noeleen's baby better than her own later explanation that she had met Kiri as a three year old by pure chance running around the gardens of Gisborne. She claimed to have been drawn by a child with 'the most gorgeous big eyes' and to have taken an interest in Kiri from then onwards.

Could Kura have been the go-between who attempted to broker the adoption of Jimmy Junior by Nell and Tom Te Kanawa? Was it she who confirmed to Noeleen baby Claire's new identity? Did she, in return, provide Nell with the name of Kiri's real mother? It seems that Kura all but disappeared from Kiri's life until after Nell's death in 1972. Afterwards she played an increasingly prominent role in it.

Kiri returned to London in the autumn of 1975 ready to pick up the threads of her career. Her closest allies had already begun to provide the sort of supportiveness she would now need. In July, she had been due to sing Micaëla with Solti in a *Carmen* recording for Decca at the Henry Wood Hall in London. She had not fully recovered her strength and had been further weakened by another throat virus. Solti pressed ahead with the recording on his own. He waited five months to add Kiri's Micaëla to the tapes. Her operatic 'comeback' began in Paris with three performances as Elvira. From there she headed for San Francisco to sing Amelia in *Simon Boccanegra* and a new role, Pamina in *The Magic Flute*, and Vienna for a recording of her Countess, conducted by Karl Bohm, to accompany a film of *Figaro* being shot by Jean-Pierre Ponnelle at Shepperton Studios the following year.

In Europe and America her colleagues found themselves confronted by a more circumspect and secure Kiri. The source of her new strength was not hard to find. Cast into a new role, Des had quickly become a formidable barrier between his wife and the world.

His influence was noticeable almost immediately in San Francisco. In the early years of her career, Kiri had been an all too willing socialite. In California, however, she was a notable absentee from the Opera Guild's annual Fol de Rol, then one of the high points of the city's social calendar. Her non-appearance was soon the subject of a tart

221

column in the *San Francisco Chronicle*. 'I'm sure that not one among the thousands in the Civic Auditorium missed her or her aria from *La Rondine*,' bitched the paper. 'But Kiri Te Kanawa, who has gained a reputation for standing up people with no explanation given, missed one of the best parties of the year.'

Des could not have cared less about such ruffled feathers. He – and Kiri – knew that if she was to avoid the problems of the past, she had to rely on his isolationist instincts. 'He protected me from people who could have got into our lives. There are always a lot of hangers-on and he managed to get rid of all of them,' she said later. 'He has such a fierce attitude that they soon back off.'

Theirs was not the first husband-and-wife partnership to have taken on the classical world. The great Czech soprano Lucia Popp was married to a conductor, Gyorgy Fischer, as was Ileana Cotrubas, wife of Manfred Cotrubas. Elisabeth Schwarzkopf was guided by her husband Walter Legge. One rival, Rita Streich, was so envious of Legge's influence she travelled with a tape recorder she dubbed 'My little Walter'. Kiri and Des both admired the way Richard Bonynge had guided Joan Sutherland's career. Des could not provide the second pair of ears each of these husbands provided their partners. Instead he gave Kiri the benefit of a rotweiller personality and an acute business brain. In the aftermath of her breakdown, he became the rock on whom Kiri relied. 'The best contract I ever signed,' Kiri was soon saying of their born-again marriage.

It was not until 1976 that she was faced with the first major new role since her breakdown. Back, this time as a free agent, at Covent Garden, she had been contracted to debut as the tragic, tubercular Mimì in *La Bohème*. The production was notable mainly for its headline star. By now, the forty-year-old Luciano Pavarotti's position as the pre-eminent tenor of his generation was secure. So too was his right to work on his own terms. Pavarotti delivered a masterclass in taking it easy, turning up for his one and only run-out of Rodolfo with Kiri at the full dress rehearsal. The critics were unsure about Kiri's suitability for the role of the impoverished Parisian seamstress. 'Such style and beauty would not, I fancy, have been allowed to languish in the Quartier Latin,' wrote Christopher Grier in the *Evening Standard*, summing up the general feeling that Kiri was simply miscast.

The conclusion was much the same three months later in April when Kiri made her debut as the romantic Russian country girl Tatyana in *Eugene Onegin*. As if to underline the obvious truth that her following simply preferred her in the grander, aristocratic roles, her brief run as the Countess in a Günther Rennert production of *Figaro* at the New York Met had produced headlines of almost embarrassing praise. 'Kiri Te Kanawa; A Countess of Beauty, a Joy Forever' ran the banner in the *New York Post*. At least by the late spring Kiri had returned to Paris and territory in which she could feel utterly at home – her debut in the role of Mozart's elegant young lady of Ferrara, Fiordiligi in the eternally popular *Così fan tutte* at L'Opéra. Sure enough, the production was a massive success, winning what Kiri later called 'raves' from the Paris critics. Her collaboration with the producer Jean-Pierre Ponnelle continued through the sweltering summer as she filmed the action to accompany the music in his lavish movie version of *Figaro*.

Her commitments complete, Kiri joined Des for three weeks' golfing in the Portuguese Algarve. She then headed for her father's house in Hatepe, then onwards to Australia and a season of performances in *Simon Boccanegra* and *La Bohème* at the Sydney Opera House.

Kiri took over a flat in the Paddington district of the city where Des joined her two weeks later. Kiri's arrival for her first season at the magnificent Sydney Opera House aroused the curiosity of the Australian press.

By now used to the deference of Bernard Levin and the deeply serious English music writers, Kiri was irritated by the less sycophantic style of their Australian counterparts. As in 1974, on her first professional visit to Australia, her straight-talking nature won her some less than reverential headlines. 'Beautiful voice, tart tongue' ran one, above an interview in which Kiri began by taking a potentially disastrous potshot at Australia's opera audiences.

'They are not enlightened. I would not exactly call them ignorant, but not enlightened,' she told the Sydney interviewer, John Yeomans. 'They do not do their homework before they come to a performance. In Paris, the people in the audience know the opera so well that they live right through every note of it.'

From then on Kiri's conversation with Yeomans was little more than a procession of *faux pas*. She was even less diplomatic on the subject of living in Australia. 'I love it,' she said. 'But I get to feeling pretty

223

isolated from the rest of the world in Sydney. I keep longing to see an English newspaper!'

In case anyone was in any doubt of her view that Des's homeland was a cultural backwater, she added, 'Life out here is pretty protective. Life can be much rougher in the big world overseas.'

'It's good fun talking to Kiri Te Kanawa,' wrote Yeomans. 'But you want to keep your elbow over your solar plexus.'

Yeomans got the last word. His impression of the haughty young opera diva was that of a 'well-to-do young wife who plays a lot of golf'. But Kiri won the last laugh. Her performances in both operas were a sell-out success. Airliners full of her New Zealand fans crossed the Tasman sea to swell the audience. In all, 1,000 'Kiri Package Tours' were sold back in her homeland.

Kiri returned to London to make her debut as a recital artist at Covent Garden. In front of a glittering audience, even by the Garden's standard, she sang a collection of arias, from 'Porgi, amor' and the 'Jewel Song' to 'Come in quest'ora bruna' from *Simon Boccanegra* to 'Mi chiamano Mimì' from *La Bohème*. Prince Michael of Kent and Lord Mountbatten of Burma were the evening's guests of honour, joining Kiri afterwards at a lavish party at New Zealand House. Proceeds from the evening were distributed between the United World Colleges and the New Zealand Scholarship Fund. When some of London's senior critics cast doubt on the quality of Kiri's performance, Bernard Levin launched an apoplectic defence.

Levin was, by now, a regular house guest at Rushmere. His panegyrics in praise of her had become increasingly curious. Such was his devotion to Kiri, he bizarrely admitted, he had named his pillow after her. Levin could not contain his rage at Philip Hope-Wallace who wrote that her performance of the 'Jewel Song' 'failed to excite' or his paper's own John Higgins, who thought the whole evening 'a shade unsatisfying'.

'Failed to excite? A shade unsatisfying? I tell you if this pair had been present at the miracle of the loaves and the fishes, one of them would have complained that there was no lemon to go with the fish and the other would have demanded more butter with the bread,' Kiri's number one fan fulminated.

In his defence of Kiri, Levin had sung the praises of her delivery of 'Per pietà' from *Così fan tutte*. Levin, like the rest of London's opera audience, was on tenterhooks to see Kiri's Fiordiligi at Covent Garden a month later. 'Though the grave should gape for me the morning after, I would still wish next month here,' he wrote.

In November, Kiri put him out of his misery. Her London debut proved as great a success as Paris months earlier. As Kiri took her curtain call at Covent Garden she was showered with red carnations and white chrysanthemums. 'It was a captivating performance of such style, sensitivity, charm and intelligence that one almost wept with pleasure,' wrote Christopher Grier in the London *Evening Standard* the following day.

Lost Souls

Early in November 1976, Des arrived in Auckland alone on an Air New Zealand flight from London. The following days were among the most anxiety-laden of his life. As he emerged through customs, Des was met by an old Te Kanawa family friend, Shirley Barrett, who whisked him away from the airport as discreetly as possible. Barrett, the wife of Nell's old trust fund ally Bill, and a leading figure on the board of the Auckland Hospital, then took Des to a private location where he was introduced to the reason for his clandestine journey to the other side of the world: a blonde-haired, blue-eyed baby girl.

Des was told very little about the child other than that she had been born two months earlier and that her mother was a New Zealander. By the time the necessary paperwork was completed by staff from the city's adoption service, however, the past seemed immaterial. Kiri and Des were now the baby's legal parents.

Kiri and Des had completed the complex preparations for the adoption with Shirley Barrett on an equally low-profile, two-day visit to New Zealand at the beginning of October. The adoption needed high-level government clearance because of Des and Kiri's unorthodox plans to take the child to live somewhere other than New Zealand.

Afterwards a small, celebratory party was held at Barbara Brown's home. Des joined a select group of friends, including the Barretts, Sally Rush (now Sloman) and Max Cryer, a former Colony Club stalwart, in toasting the new arrival. 'Everything was kept very quiet,' remembered Brown. Soon Des was back on board a plane to London along with a twenty-four-hour 'Karitane' nurse for the baby, Lynne Newman. At the end of a hectic, highly-charged few days, his car pulled up outside the door at Rushmere. Inside, a tearful Kiri held her new daughter in her arms for the first time.

A few weeks later Basil Horsfield's brother, the Right Reverend Monsignor Frank Horsfield, conducted a christening ceremony at the Catholic Actors' Church, Corpus Christi, in Maiden Lane, around the corner from the Opera House in Covent Garden. Basil and John Davern stood as godfathers. The Monsignor christened the baby Antonia Aroha Park. Her parents' choice of middle name could not have been more fitting: Aroha was the Maori word for happiness.

The christening brought a fraught and often frustrating few months to a conclusion. The traumatic events of the past two years had convinced Kiri and Des that they wanted to start a family at whatever cost. In material terms they were already secure for life. They had already begun looking for a larger home in England. In addition, they had recently bought a large house in Des's native Brisbane. With Kiri due back in Australia the following year they had already talked of 'semi-settling' there for a time. Yet as they criss-crossed the globe fulfilling Kiri's diary of engagements their life together had come to seem horribly hollow. They felt, as Kiri later put it, as if they were 'drifting around the world like a couple of lost souls'. In the wake of her miscarriage, Kiri had undergone a frustrating series of medical examinations to discover whether she was actually capable of bearing children of her own. It had only deepened the dilemma she faced. As the specialists pieced together her medical history Kiri, at least, blamed her problems in bearing children on the constant X-ray treatment she had been given as a child. 'I had many, many X-rays and now I believe that's why I could never have children,' she confessed later. 'We didn't know anything about X-rays in those days. You just got zapped.'

Kiri's frustration lay mainly in the grim unpredictability of it all. With complete rest and hormone treatment, she may still have had a chance of bearing children normally. 'I was never actually told that I couldn't have children,' she said later. 'I just got sick of doctors quoting my temperature at me and saying, "Thou shalt make love four days after the cusp."'

The sole certainty was that her career would have to be placed on hold if she was to have any chance of seeing a pregnancy through its full term. As far as Kiri was concerned it was an unacceptable risk. 'I wasn't prepared to do it,' she told the music journalist Paul Valelly.

'I have seen the awful, heartbreaking disappointment of so many other women who have tried and tried to have children only to miscarry. I could not have faced having to give up my singing to find I could still not have a baby.'

Des later claimed the idea to adopt a child instead had been originally his. As far as he was concerned there was 'certainly no difference' in having a child of their own and adopting one. Given her own background, of course, Kiri understood the pros and cons better than anyone.

Throughout the adoption process, Kiri had drawn on her innate ability to mask her inner feelings. She had certainly given no hint of the excitement and anxiety she was experiencing in interviews during her run in *Così fan tutte* in November 1976. 'Oh, one day,' she answered breezily when asked whether she intended having children. Hidden between the lines of her explanation, there were clues at the course of action already under way. 'I don't want to spoil the once-in-a-lifetime chance I have at present to go really to the limits of my body and talent.' The mask remained in place even as she adapted her life to that of opera star and mother.

As Toni settled in to life at Esher, full-time motherhood was clearly out of the question. Toni's nurse, Lynne Newman, took on the full-time responsibilities of feeding and caring for the baby. Without having gone through pregnancy and birth, Kiri at first found her new role awkward. 'I think she realised there was someone professional looking after her and she didn't like to interfere,' remembered Newman. 'But I just thought, "No, this is her child, not mine." I made her get involved.' As Kiri completed the run of *Così* performances at Covent Garden, Newman deliberately arranged for the baby to expect a night feed. Kiri arrived home in time to give Toni her bottle.

The family spent the first five months of their life in private together at home in Esher. By March 1977, however, the inevitable rumours had reached the New Zealand press. Des confirmed the adoption through the London office of the New Zealand Press Association. 'Toni's a lovely baby and we are both very happy,' he told the agency. Photographs of the new, expanded Te Kanawa clan were ruled out immediately, however. From the outset, Kiri and Des were adamant that Toni should be kept from the public gaze.

By the time the news broke Kiri was already experiencing her first separation from Toni. That month she began a three-month stint at the Paris Opéra, first in another series of *Don Giovanni* performances then a new production of *The Magic Flute*, in which she would sing Pamina for the first time in German. Lynne Newman flew across the English Channel as often as she could, providing Antonia with a taste of the life to which she would soon grow accustomed. 'She's quite at home in hotels and she loves flying,' Kiri was soon telling an Australian magazine. 'She's been brought up to our sort of life so, like us, she's become a bit of a gypsy.'

Baby and nanny soon became a familiar sight backstage and would spend many evenings sitting as quietly as possible in Kiri's dressing room, waiting for her to complete her performances.

By now Paris and its imperious old opera house had superseded even Covent Garden in Kiri's affections. Since 1973 the House had been run by the team of Joan Ingpen and the former composer Rolf Liebermann. 'The best operatic administration I have ever witnessed,' Kiri later called them. The manner in which the city and its elites had welcomed her into its arms had only added to its intoxicating glamour. Kiri had sung privately for the aristocrats of the Paris couture houses, Pierre Cardin, Yves St Laurent and his partner Pierre Berge. Her friendships opened the doors to the city's ultimate salons, where Kiri indulged herself frequently.

Kiri still lived in mild fear of Des's penny-pinching lectures. 'She used to feel guilty because she'd been out and bought a ring,' remembered Ingpen. 'When you're at the top like that and you're young it usually never occurs to you that it might not last. It shows what a good foundation she had.' There were times, however, when a diva had to do what a diva had to do, whatever the consequences at home. Kiri's greatest indulgence was a £13,000 lynx fur coat in which she was soon sashaying in and out of the ritzy Café de la Paix and the other musical haunts around the Place de L'Opéra.

Kiri's five figure a night earnings were now the subject of conjecture in the press, causing a new rush of envy she seemed keen to defuse in an interview in London in early 1977. 'It was a vast exaggeration, and a bad thing, as it makes colleagues whom one has known and loved for years unhappy.' She was not about to apologise for her success, however. 'One needs big fees as one's professional life is short and the expenses are very high. But quite honestly I never really have time to benefit from the money and it all seems to go to the tax man.' A little less coyly, she added, 'But I do like my fur coats and, anyway, they keep me warm.'

As far as Kiri was concerned she had worked hard for her money. It was a message she was preparing to pass on to her daughter, too. She saw no inconsistency at all in the fact that Toni was dressed in hand-me-downs from friends, including her nurse, Lynne. 'I want Toni to have a normal upbringing,' she told an interviewer. 'When she starts being aware of having nice clothes we will go to Marks & Spencer.'

Kiri once more found her time in Paris clouded with unhappiness, professionally and personally. While her Elvira once more thrilled public and critics alike, her Pamina suffered through its association with a disastrous production of *The Magic Flute*.

The Viennese director–designer partnership of Horst Zankl and Arik Bauer had imbued the ancient Egyptian setting with a bizarre, anatomical theme. The pair's ambition over-reached itself during the opening night when the three 'Genii', or Boys, found themselves stuck in their elaborate chariot suspended high above the stage. The performance was halted while they were brought down. The final curtain was greeted by a crescendo of booing. Kiri's hard work in learning the German version of Schikaneder's libretto was overshadowed by what was generally recognised as a débâcle. At least one English critic, *The Times*'s Stanley Sadie, was there to record the excellence of Kiri's personal contribution. Sadie found the final notes of Kiri's opening aria overwhelmingly beautiful. 'She had sung that soaring phrase in a way that sends thrills through the spine and turns grown men's knees (not only Mr Bernard Levin's) to jelly,' he wrote. 'It was a performance in thousands, because it remained simple while being beautifully and deeply felt.'

The disappointments of *The Magic Flute* were quickly put in perspective, however. Midway through her time in Paris, Kiri was shaken to discover that she had fallen pregnant again. Once more, she fulfilled all her contractual responsibilities – singing an unusually long series of eleven performances of *The Magic Flute*. Once more, however, she was unable to hold the baby and miscarried during the early weeks of the pregnancy.

At least this time Toni could help ease the anguish. 'I was lucky,'

Kiri said later. 'In those moments of despair and loneliness which come after a spontaneous abortion they brought Toni to me. I had a baby to hold.' In the months and years that followed Kiri talked of her failure to bear children of her own with stoic resignation. At one point she claimed she was relieved to lose the second child, such was the love she and Des had formed for Toni. At another time she ascribed her situation to simple fate.

'Look, I was given everything else; a perfectly wonderful life, talent and I'm married to a marvellous man,' she said. 'It was just one of those things. Just deserts.'

Once more music provided the perfect panacea for her pain. She returned to Covent Garden to begin work on the most testing new role she had taken on since her return from the breakdown, the eponymous role of Arabella in Strauss's glorious opera under the baton of Wolfgang Rennert. Kiri had looked forward to playing Arabella, the noble daughter of a dissolute Viennese Count determined to marry her off to pay his gambling debts. The role had strong emotional resonances. 'There is a lot of me in her,' she admitted once. 'I, too, can detach myself from emotional situations and crises and look at things fairly coolly.'

Strauss allowed Kiri to demonstrate the sheer technical brilliance she had now added to her innate vocal gifts. 'The secret of singing Strauss boils down to whether you can sing all those millions of notes and feel comfortable doing it,' she said. Kiri eventually achieved both – but dangerously close to the eleventh hour, as usual.

Colin Davis, on hand to oversee the production, knew his star would need close care. With Basil Horsfield, he arranged to have an apartment near the Opera House prepared for Kiri to use during breaks in rehearsals. Kiri's demands were simple enough. 'I'd like some eggs and milk and beer,' she told Horsfield.

Kiri's tendency to leave everything to the last minute reduced her Covent Garden pianist Richard Amner to a state of hopeless exasperation. With only ten days to go before the opening curtain, he reached the end of his tether and told Kiri she would have to cancel. As ever, she treated the ultimatum as a challenge rather than an insult.

The cavalry arrived in the forms of Vera Rosza and Jean Mallandaine. For five intense days Kiri was drilled in the intricacies of the part. Mallandaine had, by now, become as crucial a part of Kiri's musical life as Rosza. The pianist had learned to accommodate Kiri's lack of sight-reading ability and individualistic learning habits and had built up a method of teaching her new roles. Mallandaine would make up tapes featuring Kiri's vocal passages and a simple piano backing. Once this had been memorised, the duo would join Vera Rosza who would then oversee the addition of the words and the interpretation of the part. By the opening night on 16 July, Kiri had once more crammed herself out of a crisis. Her performance was another five star triumph. 'As radiant and lovingly detailed as I can remember among all Arabellas in a decade of devotion to the work,' wrote William Mann in *The Times*. Only her blonde wig and heavy make-up offended the critics' taste.

Arabella proved a significant success in several ways. The affinity Kiri had now formed with Strauss's music would add a thrilling new dimension to her career. So too would the higher level of discipline she had been forced to acquire in the tense final days before her triumph. Even before her debut Kiri was talking of 'the new me'. In the aftermath of her success she confessed that it was only after singing *Arabella* that she felt her career 'was really getting somewhere'.

Kiri's love affair with Richard Strauss continued during the autumn. She toured Europe with Claudio Abbado and the Vienna Philharmonic Orchestra performing his moving *Four Last Songs*, a speciality of hers since she sang them with John Pritchard and the BBC Symphony Orchestra in 1972. Kiri later sang the songs in a television masterclass documentary with Georg Solti.

'He coached her, and the difference from the start to the end of the class was amazing because she did do and absorb everything he asked,' said Joan Ingpen. 'She hasn't got any intellect, Kiri. She has an instinct, and if she's learning from someone she respects she responds very well.' Solti's influence shone through in another recording of the work, with Andrew Davis, which later won Kiri her first American 'Grammy'.

Towards the end of 1977, after weeks of trailing around the Surrey suburbs, Kiri and Des drove through the gates of Pachesham Park, a secluded estate on the edge of a golf course and the well-heeled, Surrey market town of Leatherhead. There they were shown a seven-bedroomed, Tudor-style home, complete with its own minstrel gallery, stables, lake and seven acres of land. They knew immediately that they had found their ideal home. Fairways, as the house was known, would remain so for the next twenty years.

They had outgrown Rushmere in Esher, not least because their daughter was developing fast. 'Toni is walking, talking and being a monster, but we love her very much,' Kiri wrote in a letter to her niece Judy that Christmas. Kiri and Des had also engaged a Spanish maid to look after the cooking and cleaning. With a nanny living in as well, friends to accommodate and Tom often camped in the extension, conditions had simply become too cramped. Kiri's earning power now enabled them to consider a much larger property. But there were other, more sinister considerations.

Basil Horsfield and Des had, for years, protected Kiri from the darker side of her fame. Kiri's fan base was dominated by men, she admitted. She laughed at the psychology that lay behind the infatuation. 'It's not hard for certain people to fall in love with these figures on stage, these images of ideal mothers,' she said. 'They like to be caressed by all that, they like to fancy all that warmth. I suppose that's why we get so many young fellows who want it, but aren't threatened by it. Innocent passion.'

Amused, flattered and gratified as she was by this support, she was terrified by the idea of meeting these fans in the flesh, however. Kiri's worst nightmare, she confessed once, was being trapped in a room with a party of over-zealous admirers. 'Once, in Paris, fans crowded into my dressing room like a swarm of buzzing bees and my back was against the wall. I could see the exit but I could not reach it. This sort of situation makes me feel very afraid and out of control and I try and avoid it. I have genuine fears of claustrophobia.' So acute was her anxiety at times that Kiri had begun travelling in disguise, usually a lurid blonde wig that drew rather than deflected attention. Kiri also received a hefty postbag from her fans. Des had begun screening the mail, weeding out the unwelcome – and occasionally unhinged – correspondence.

Some of the letters Des approved left Kiri deeply moved. 'I get a lot of letters saying that if it hadn't been for you and those songs I would have taken the plunge,' she explained. 'One young man was in absolute desperation, such a gentle boy, weeping and crying, obviously loved his mother very much and he had lost her, and he said that some songs I had recorded had gotten him through her death; had allowed him to cope.'

Some, however, took their devotion too far. 'It got to the stage where some people were becoming a nuisance. One person, for example, wrote several lengthy letters about all his personal problems – and then landed on the doorstep,' she revealed at the time. Years of conducting interviews at Rushmere had made life simple for the more resourceful members of her fan club. 'We were too easy to track down where we were.'.

By the first week of February 1978, Rushmere had been sold. With Fairways unready for their arrival, Des, Kiri, Toni and Lynne, the nurse, spent a cramped month living at 4 Albert Terrace, Basil Horsfield and John Davern's London home adjoining the AIM offices near Regents Park. They moved into their new home on 8 March. Over the following weeks workmen set about remodelling the house. Soon Tom Te Kanawa and his chainsaw had joined them and was tidying up the surrounding woods.

Kiri was soon missing her new idyll, however. The highlight of the year was an extended trip to Australia, with Antonia and Lynne in tow, where she was to make her debut as Violetta in *La Traviata* at the Sydney Opera House. Once more John Copley was on hand to guide her through the performance. Her old ally Richard Bonynge was there to conduct.

Away from the Opera House and separated once more from Des, who had taken on a freelance contract in Iran, Kiri occasionally lived up to her old, tart-tongued reputation.

'She was extraordinary in *Traviata*,' said Moffatt Oxenbould, artistic director of what was then the Australian Opera Company. 'She was in great voice and she looked wonderful, but she seemed to enjoy the season less, personally, than she had in 1976.'

Like others, Oxenbould wondered whether her unease had anything to do with the fact that Kiri's arrival in Sydney coincided with Dame Joan Sutherland's appearance in a new production of *Norma* and a tour by another high-profile female voice, Marilyn Horne. 'One was in pretty strong company,' he recalled.

Relations between Kiri and John Copley had been unusually poor in the run up to the opening night. Word that Copley had complained that Kiri had been 'nasty' to him and rude to a pianist leaked out. 'It is just that I come straight to the point. I have no time to waste in small talk,' Kiri told the *Sydney Morning Herald*.

This time Kiri reserved her most outspoken language for her own homeland. After dismissing Australia as a cultural backwater earlier in her career, she now turned her guns on New Zealand. After the strains of her last tour in 1975, Kiri had resisted all offers to return there. Towards the end of 1977, as she gave a lukewarm response to an invitation from the Auckland Festival Society, she explained her reasoning. Kiri said while she was, in any case, booked until 1981, 'There are just no facilities for international opera in New Zealand. There's lots of support and good opera singers and orchestras, but no opera house. If only the New York Met, for instance, was in New Zealand. I would be there all the time.'

As she warmed up for *La Traviata*, Kiri again shot straight from the hip when asked to explain her absence. 'New Zealanders deserve to see me in an opera now,' she allowed. 'But there's nowhere to do it. It's a shame, but I think the authorities have decided – perhaps rightly – that there are more immediate priorities after art,' she told Australia's top-selling magazine, *Woman's Day*. 'But I believe that when things are bad that's when the people need entertainment most.'

'I'm only looking for an opera house,' Kiri told another reporter. 'The house would have to be as acoustically perfect as possible.' Her comments predictably precipitated a huge public debate back in New Zealand.

As so often in the past, however, Kiri arrived at her opening night utterly concentrated on the job in hand. Kiri's 1976 visit to Sydney had been a commercial if not a critical success. This time her triumph was universal, wringing emotional tributes from the hard-nosed Australian press as well as a standing ovation from her sell-out audiences.

Maria Prerauer, the influential critic of *The Australian*, had interviewed Kiri a day or so before the opening night. Prerauer's piece began with her repeating the indiscretion made by a rival singer in Sydney days earlier. 'It's unfair. She's got everything. I hate her for it. All she has to do is walk on stage in London and New York and open her mouth for everyone to fall under her spell.'

Days later the rival could add Sydney to the list. Prerauer herself called Kiri's voice: 'one of the most incredible instruments I have ever heard' and her acting so good she 'could go straight any day'.

'Here is a heroine that the composer can only have dreamed of,' she wrote. 'If Te Kanawa had been around to sing the opening in 1853 in place of the fat slob who kept the audience in giggles instead of tears as she faded away of tuberculosis, *Traviata* would have surely been an instant hit instead of a temporary failure at its world premiére!'

The rest of Australia's critics sang similar hymns of praise.

'I think to get a high profile throughout the world you have to do it country by country,' Kiri said once. With Australia at her feet, Kiri devoted the final months of 1978 to conquering new territories on the musical map. Her efforts would meet with mixed success.

At the end of September 1978, Kiri travelled to Vicenza for shooting on a lavish new film version of *Don Giovanni*. She had been attracted to the role by the Paris Opéra's Rolf Liebermann, who had nurtured the idea of a Mozart for the masses for a decade. His intentions were as familiar as they were honourable. 'Opera in Europe is largely subsidised by taxpayers – all the taxpayers – yet only a small fraction of society draws the benefits,' he said. 'A way must be found to democratise Opera.' Liebermann had persuaded the veteran Joseph Losey, maker of such subtle masterpieces as *The Go-Between* and *The Servant*, to direct.

The production was plagued with problems. The recording of the music had been done in Paris the previous year under the aloof, intellectual leadership of Lorin Maazel. The process had been a fraught and often fractious one. Tempers ran equally high as filming got under way at La Rotonda, the famous Palladian villa on the outskirts of Vicenza that had been the model for Thomas Jefferson's celebrated home in Virginia, Monticello.

Kiri found the film-making world, and its shoot-round-the-clock mentality, exhausting. 'As a stage performer I couldn't really get used to performing at all sorts of crazy hours. They would wake you at midnight for a four o'clock start, that was weird and I couldn't cope with it very well,' she said later. 'It was a lot of hard work and it shows up in people's red eyes on the screen.'

Kiri eventually took advantage of the situation by bringing over an accompanist and rehearsing for a recital concert later in the autumn. 'We would go into the room at 1 a.m. or 3 a.m. and pound away.' As the month-long shoot progressed, however, the production problems mounted. Shortly after hiring a machine to manufacture false rain,

Losey was forced to watch the heavens open, ruining five days of filming. Kiri's fuses finally blew one Friday afternoon late in October when she was told by Liebermann that she could not leave the set and return to London for the weekend as planned to celebrate Toni's second birthday with Des.

A visiting journalist from *Musical America* magazine preserved the scene for posterity. Dorle J. Soria described how the peace of La Rotonda was disturbed by the sight and sound of 'the beautiful, white gowned' Kiri chasing after her producer, Liebermann. 'She might have been the avenging Donna Elvira in pursuit of her betrayer,' Soria wrote. Soria went on to describe how Kiri eventually caught Liebermann, who had just informed her she would have to cancel her trip home. 'She was in a fury. She pleaded, she stormed, she threatened, she defied. She couldn't. She wouldn't. It was an awe-inspiring scene, worthy of Mozart,' the writer went on. Liebermann eventually calmed the storm. 'He turned on all his famous charm and persuasion. Finally he took her arm and they walked off together. Liebermann came back, his face relaxed. All he said was, "She's divine."' As it turned out, her mood only added to the divinity of her performance.

Kiri's love of the role of Elvira had continued to grow. She admitted the pleasure lay in pushing her to the extremes of her personality. 'It brings me to the brink of madness. I try to put her across as nearly insane.' Amid the cold and confusion of Vicenza, Losey extracted perhaps the most electrifying screen performance of Elvira ever seen. When his film opened in six cinemas in Paris, the queues stretched around the block from each of them. Kiri's performance was nothing less than a tour de force, full of neurotic and hypnotic energy. As the film became a critical and commercial success around the world both she and Liebermann fulfilled their goals.

Kiri's conquest of Italy remained in the balance, however. She completed the year in Milan, at La Scala where she sang Amelia in *Simon Boccanegra*, her first role at the great bastion of the Italian musical establishment. If she understood the role, she was unnerved by the eccentricities of Milan's operatic Mecca. In the run-up to the opening night, Kiri had been approached by one of the shadowy 'claques' attached to the great opera house. The centuries-old claque system empowered these strategically placed aficionados to orchestrate the audience's reaction. 'I had this man coming to my dressing room, saying he was Signor So-and-So and asking what I was going pay him, and I thought, "I don't think I can deal with this,"' she remembered later. 'I had heard of some dreadful occasions when performers had refused to pay and were left standing at the curtain call without applause or – worse still – being booed. Naturally, I paid up.'

Kiri's idea of a fair rate of pay for the claque to lead the applause at four separate performances was the lira equivalent of £12. When she told the tenor Piero Cappuccilli what she had paid he burst out laughing. It seems no coincidence that Kiri later described her reception at La Scala as 'a trifle cool', even less that she has barely appeared in Italy again since.

In early March 1979 Kiri, Des and Toni arrived at Auckland airport where they were greeted by Graeme Lindsay, owner with his wife Lurene of Auckland's most prestigious limousine company. Lindsay had headed to the airport unaware of the identity of the 'Mr and Mrs Park' he had been asked to collect. In his time Lindsay had driven some of the world's most famous celebrities. He saw the measure of Kiri's importance to her homeland as he sailed in and out of New Zealand Customs with Kiri and her family. 'If you'd said you were bringing Rod Stewart in or even Muhammed Ali, New Zealand Customs couldn't care less, they were going to search for drugs or whatever,' he said. 'Kiri Te Kanawa came straight through.'

Lindsay took Kiri and Des to their favourite location in Auckland, the White Heron Hotel, in the secluded Parnell suburb of the city, where they rented several small villas. There he undertook a ritual that was re-enacted every time Kiri visited.

'As soon as we got to the White Heron I'd ring up the seafood wholesalers and I'd say, "Dame Kiri would like to speak to you", or Kiri Te Kanawa as it was then, and I'd ask to be put through to the manager,' he remembered. 'She'd give him an order for green prawns, crayfish and mussels and oysters. I'd go down and get them or sometimes she'd come with me and give them a few autographs. There was never a bill.' Lindsay would remain Kiri's personal chauffeur and bodyguard in New Zealand for years to come. It was during those early days with her that he came to realise the curious predicament she faced in her home country. He accompanied Kiri as she attempted to live an ordinary life among the people with whom she had grown up. Invariably the crowds would swarm around her. 'She would often get me to step back and allow people to get an autograph. Other times she'd say, "No, I'm too busy", and I'd step in between them,' he said.

Kiri was caught in a trap. 'In England, if the public love you, they tend to leave you alone,' she said once. 'I really do have to hide myself away in New Zealand.'

'The trouble is that overseas Kiri is a superstar, but when she comes to New Zealand everyone thinks she's ours,' agreed Lindsay.

Once more, Kiri arrived in New Zealand with no intention of singing publicly. Her position on the need for a proper opera house had hardened further. 'People deserve to hear the best and you cannot give the best if the facilities aren't up to scratch,' she said bluntly. Already her words had been the catalyst for embryonic plans for a new arts complex in Auckland. Kiri attended a series of cocktail parties and press conferences to launch an appeal for the project. 'If New Zealanders want to hear me sing opera, they'll have to come to Sydney,' she said. 'You've got to have somewhere really good to sing opera, otherwise it's like dressing a pretty girl in rags.'

Kiri spent time too at Hatepe with Tom, flying in by helicopter and landing on the little beach outside her father's house. Even there she would face problems with unwanted advances, however. The cabin fronted on to the lake and was easily accessible. 'Kiri did come to Hatepe but it was very difficult,' remembered her father's friend, Terry Valentine. 'She came twice, to my knowledge. She was very informal, but if she walked up the street everybody knew.'

It was only at Rawhiti, at Kura Beale's idyllic estate, that Kiri could find true peace. She, Des, Toni and the nanny headed for the Sea-Bee Air charter company in Auckland and flew north to Russell where they landed on the beach. Kiri spent hours sitting on the edge of the ocean watching the porpoises, sipping beer. Kura Beale provided Kiri with the kind of protection and patronage she now needed. 'For Kiri I think it was like touching down at home again with somebody who remembered her as a child, who knew her and accepted her,' said Eva Brown of the local *Russell Review*.

'My haven,' Kiri was soon calling the place.

Kiri returned to Europe ready once more to conquer a new territory. She travelled, for the first time – as a star at least – to Salzburg to sing a series of four *Figaro*s in the annual festival. One of the performances was conducted by Herbert von Karajan. The praise she received from the legendary conductor was among the most cherished tributes she had yet received.

Yet the most important event of 1979 occurred, once more, away from the glare of the public eye. In August Des repeated the process of three years earlier and slipped quietly in and out of New Zealand. With the help of Shirley Barrett he and Kiri had been successful in finding a second child suitable for adoption.

With Antonia growing fast Kiri and Des had decided the time was right to provide a little brother or sister. 'We didn't want . . . Antonia to be an only child,' Kiri said. This time they adopted a little boy. Once the boy was safely back at Pachesham Park, Kiri and Des engaged a second Karitane nurse, Barbara. Kiri's trust in New Zealand's famously well-trained children's nurses was absolute. 'To know they are in such capable hands makes an enormous difference,' she said ten months later in June 1980, when she broke the news of her second adoption to the readers of *New Zealand Woman's Weekly*.

By then Kiri, Des and Toni had held a small christening for the little brother Toni already referred to as 'my best friend'. Again, Monsignor Frank Horsfield conducted the ceremony at the Corpus Christi Church in Covent Garden, with his brother Basil and his partner John Davern on hand to act as godfathers. Des and Kiri named the boy Thomas, after his grandfather.

PART THREE

'Ich kann nichts anders werden, nimm mich wie ich bin.'
'I cannot change. Take me as I am.'

from *Arabella*, Richard Strauss

'250,000 Covent Gardens'

At the dawn of the 1980s, Sir John Tooley, for one, was in no doubt about who now reigned as the undisputed queen of Covent Garden. As a new season got under way with a lacklustre production of *Simon Boccanegra*, produced by Filippo Sanjust, Tooley had feared a summer of half-full houses. He admitted that it was the production's Amelia who averted financial failure.

'If Kiri had not been in *Boccanegra* it very probably would not have sold out,' he confessed. 'When Kiri's name is on the boards, the public will buy the tickets. They worship her.'

In the ten years since their lives were first linked, the reputations of the Royal Opera and its star soprano had suffered starkly contrasting fortunes. Under Colin Davis's directorship Covent Garden had lost the lustre of Solti's gilded age. With five years of his contract still to run, Davis had become an irritable, occasionally paranoid figure. He would sit at press conferences with his back half turned on journalists, snapping, 'Why don't you take this job for six months and see if you can criticise afterwards?' at even the gentlest questioners. After reading one critical newspaper profile of his reign, he had rung the author up and begun sobbing loudly down the phone.

His weakness had only strengthened the hand of the House's star performers. None benefited more than the two singers now widely regarded as the jewels in the Garden's crown: Placido Domingo and Kiri. While Domingo's popularity had been built on his suave intelligence, good looks and peerless professionalism, Kiri's appeal was, by now, more multi-faceted. Her exotic looks could still reduce men like Bernard Levin to emotional rubble. Yet she also seemed a new type of opera star, a resolutely down-to-earth diva.

In March 1980, she was invited on to Desert Island Discs, Roy Plomley's radio institution on the BBC. Kiri's choice of ten recordings to be marooned with included only one classical piece, Mozart's Flute Concerto No. 1. The work would allow her to 'do my Isadora Duncan', she teased Plomley. It was no PR pose on her part. Kiri admitted that at home she loved nothing more than messing around in the kitchen with Anne Murray and Neil Diamond blaring away in the background. Her earthy humour and love of the outdoors only underlined the image of a far-from-*grande-dame*.

That summer she and Domingo were invited to play a televised round of golf against each other. The duo squared up with John Tooley as Domingo's caddie and Bernard Levin as Kiri's. The ever-competitive Kiri, who had slipped in some clandestine practice with Des, won comfortably. 'Domingo should be better,' she laughed after the show had been broadcast to popular acclaim. She appeared, to the public at least, utterly unencumbered by prima donna tendencies. When Mirella Freni pulled out of a performance of the Garden's other major production of the season, *La Bohème*, Kiri stepped in at only a few hours' notice. Her only stipulation was that a car was sent to collect her from home and that a favourite prompter was hired for the night in case she forgot Mimì's words. The house shook to its rafters as she took her curtain call. The noise was almost as great two nights later as she returned to Amelia, seemingly unfazed by her hectic week's work.

Such crises notwithstanding, Kiri was, by now, doing all she could to avoid such high-intensity workloads. In the wake of her breakdown, she had insisted on writing longer rest periods into her contracts. More importantly, she had reduced her commitments altogether. In twelve months during 1972 Basil Horsfield had booked Kiri for a punishing 101 engagements. Eight years on, that figure had been effectively halved to between forty-five and sixty-five performances a year – at no financial loss to Kiri whatsoever.

With her nightly rate set at around $10,000 in London and $12,000 in New York, occasionally even higher in Paris, Kiri was now among the best-paid sopranos in the world. In the latter half of the 1970s her annual income had, for the first time, exceeded £500,000. Her earning-power had only been boosted by the new business opportunities her fame had now brought with it. Kiri's had, for instance, become the public face of Rolex. She had been approached by the watchmakers in the wake of her triumph in *Così fan tutte* in Paris in 1976. Their research confirmed that Kiri connected directly with its affluent, aspirational and label-conscious target audience. 'For a pearl among opera singers, an oyster,' ran the copy line accompanying a dazzling photograph of her in Jean-Pierre Ponnelle's silk and lace dress and the distinctive, wide-brimmed hat. The advert had been a huge success in countries like the UK, France, Australia and, of course, New Zealand where she was best known.

Kiri's ongoing relationship with Rolex was overseen by Des, by now firmly established as the most powerful and persuasive influence in her business life. The ageing, patrician Basil Horsfield, had begun winding down AIM in readiness for a move to Monte Carlo and semi-retirement. He intended keeping Kiri and one or two of his other high-profile clients. Inevitably, however, he had already loosened the reins of his control. Des had willingly picked them up.

Kiri was bristling with pride at the acumen Des had shown since he had taken a more central role in her career in the mid-1970s. Publicly she played down his role, still dutifully referring to Horsfield as her manager. 'Desmond is a great comfort and help when the going is rough,' she told one interviewer at the time. Privately, however, she was already talking of him in almost superhuman terms.

'Even in the mid-seventies she had ideas of Des taking over the Royal Opera House, suggesting that he should be the administrator and God knows what,' recalled one Covent Garden colleague of the time. 'She was quite dotty about that.'

The strength of the professional alliance Kiri and Des now forged was plain to see when they spent a short holiday with their old friends Bob and Sharon Morgan in Brisbane towards the end of that year. The demands of careers and families had separated the couples for much of the 1970s. Over dinner at the Morgans' home they caught up on a decade of developments.

As Morgan, an engineer, talked business with Des, he discovered that his old schoolfriend had taken on a new role. 'I asked him that night what he was doing,' said Morgan. 'He told me Kiri had made £800,000 the previous year, that he could get more from running her affairs than working as an engineer.'

Des had already begun displaying an interest in property development. In addition to a villa on a golf course in Portugal, he had bought an apartment in San Francisco, Des's and Kiri's favourite American city. They had spent two months there before heading to Australia as Kiri performed *Arabella* at the San Francisco Opera in November 1980.

At first glimpse, Kiri and Des seemed little different from the newlyweds of fifteen years earlier. 'She still called him Parky,' said Morgan. Yet as he spent time with his old friends Morgan could not help concluding that a little of the magic had left Kiri and Des's marriage. 'They said the right things, but you could tell more by the body language there was not much intimacy. I said to Sharon even then that they were more of a business team than they were a married couple.' The remarkable events of 1981 would transform Kiri into a business even more worth managing.

When Kiri first picked up the phone to John Davern on the morning of 1 April 1981, she assumed her agent was playing a practical joke. Davern called her in her Paris hotel as she prepared for the twin challenges of her debut as Arabella and a prestige recording of Berlioz's *Les nuits d'Été* with Daniel Barenboim and the l'Orchestre de Paris for Deutsche Grammophon.

'Charles wants you to sing at his wedding,' Davern said excitedly.

'Charles who?' Kiri replied.

'When John told me, I thought "What a lousy joke for April Fools' Day."' Eventually, however, Kiri sensed the seriousness in Davern's voice. 'When I realised it was true, I was just amazed,' she said later. Prince Charles's engagement to the nineteen-year-old Lady Diana Spencer had seized the public imagination in Britain and beyond. Their wedding, to be beamed around the world from St Paul's Cathedral on 29 July, was anticipated to be the most widely-watched event of the television age. An estimated audience of 700 million was expected to tune in.

The aesthetic heir to the throne of England was determined his wedding would be remembered as much for its music as its pomp and ceremony. Sir John Tooley and Sir David Willcocks, conductor of the Bach Choir, had been recruited to assemble a fitting programme.

Charles's love of opera had deepened in the years since he first saw Kiri's Countess at Glyndebourne in 1974 and then her Fiordiligi at Covent Garden in 1976. With his advisors at Buckingham Palace keen to involve the Commonwealth in the event, Kiri quickly emerged as everyone's choice to sing Handel's 'Let the Bright Seraphim' during the signing of the register that followed the formal exchange of wedding vows.

The timing suited Kiri's schedule perfectly. The wedding day fell at the end of the Royal Opera's Mozart Festival, where she was due to sing seven performances of Elvira in *Don Giovanni* as well as four Fiordiligis in *Così fan tutte* in a frantic two and a half week period between 6 and 25 July. Her final performance on the Saturday night would give her four days to prepare fully for the wedding.

After a series of meetings with Tooley, Willcocks and Charles, Kiri set to work. In London, she roused Vera Rosza to help her reacquaint herself with the aria she had recorded as the B-side of her 'Nun's Chorus' in Auckland seventeen years earlier. She also spent time rehearsing with John Wallace, principal trumpet of the London Philharmonia and a contemporary of Charles's from Cambridge.

In Paris Kiri asked her favourite Parisian designer, Leonard, to come up with three options for a suitably eye-catching outfit. Her only brief was that the design be 'summery'. The London milliner Philip Somerville was commissioned to come up with a hat to set the ensemble off.

Kiri arrived back in Leatherhead at the end of June to discover England in the grip of a heat wave. With thousands pouring into London for the wedding, Kiri was prepared to take no risks travelling up from Surrey every day and booked into a suite at the Savoy on the Strand, within a five-minute taxi ride of St Paul's.

Kiri was quickly engulfed in the wedding frenzy. With the world's media now camped outside Buckingham Palace, she was called on to give a press conference in the Crush Bar at Covent Garden. If she was not already nervous enough, the American anchorman Tom Brokaw put the prospect ahead in perspective on his NBC news show. Kiri's television audience would be the equivalent of '250,000 Covent Garden audiences at the same time', Brokaw told her.

Charles came to Covent Garden to see one of Kiri's final performances in *Don Giovanni*. Afterwards Kiri and Des were invited to a vast ball at Buckingham Palace on the Monday night before the wedding. She later remembered how she spent most of her time talking to Charles and his family rather than his bride-to-be. Kiri had struck up an instant rapport with Charles's father, the Duke of Edinburgh, in particular. Diana, whom she saw at one point slumped in a chair with her feet up, seemed part of another 'camp'.

'I was more of a Prince Charles person because he was the one I was in contact with all the time,' Kiri said.

Kiri woke up on the morning of 29 July on a 'terrific high'.

'If you had stuck needles in me I would have felt no pain,' she said later.

Des was on hand to go through the long checklist of instructions she had received from a Palace equerry on the Monday night. She took his advice and limited herself to a single cup of tea. St Paul's, the equerry had ascertained, suffered from a chronic lack of toilet facilities. Kiri then slipped into the extraordinary, rainbow-hued dress Leonard had created for her, popped the thermos flask of iced water and bag of boiled sweets she carried to keep her throat clear into a handbag and headed for the car waiting to whisk her to St Paul's. It was only in the car that she realised she was heading for the society event of the century having overlooked one rather fundamental detail. She had been in such a rush to dress she had forgotten to put on a pair of knickers. 'There was no time,' she giggled to a friend years later.

Kiri's nerves were not helped by the sight that greeted her through the windows of her limousine. Thousands upon thousands of Union Jack waving onlookers had packed the Strand, Fleet Street, Ludgate Circus and the roads leading up to St Paul's. She arrived a full hour before the main Royal party began making its way through central London in the Queen's ornate, open-topped carriages.

At around 11 a.m., as Diana entered St Paul's to the sound of Purcell's Trumpet Voluntary, Kiri, like everyone else in the Cathedral, arched her neck for a view of the fairytale bride. 'I saw Lady Diana as she went past,' she recalled. 'She was under this beautiful veil which just glistened a bit and it was stunning. From then on I just shook until I had to sing.'

As Diana and Charles exchanged vows, Kiri prepared herself for her moment. At 11.44 a.m. precisely, the newlyweds disappeared to finalise the formalities in the Dean's Aisle and Kiri took centre stage. 'I was peeing myself nervous. It was very nerve-racking. You have got one chance. The music starts, you've got to start. You can't falter,' she said. A lifetime's experience was concentrated into the next few minutes. 'When I'd finished it all went a blur.'

Kiri and Des joined the visiting dignitaries for lunch at the Palace. Once more, however, she missed her chance to talk to Diana. The bride had circulated the rooms in which the sea of guests were seated. 'It was so hot and stuffy that when they opened some side doors, we went out to get some air and I missed her,' Kiri lamented afterwards.

Kiri did the rounds of television interviews in the evening. Afterwards she joined Des at Basil Horsfield's flat overlooking Regents Park. They sat up talking and drinking champagne until midnight. Kiri arrived home to find Tom sitting quietly in a corner. As ever, her father provided the reality check necessary at the end of an extraordinary day. His response to the high glamour he had witnessed was typical.

'What did you think?' Kiri asked.

'Good,' he replied with a gentle smile.

'A huge occasion and my dad says "good",' Kiri laughed.

Hyperbole was not hard to find, however. Caught in the headlights of the most glamorous event of the decade, Kiri found herself subjected to a new kind of scrutiny. Her performance of 'Let the Bright Seraphim' was greeted with universal acclaim.

'Thoughtfully, HRH had left Kiri Te Kanawa behind to thrill us,' ran a *Guardian* leader column on the occasion.

'The only sounds as brilliant as the Trumpet Voluntary were the bell-like notes of New Zealand's Kiri Te Kanawa,' added the *Daily Mail*.

Leonard's dress failed to find so many fans, however. The acerbic Clive James, then writing in the *Observer*, could not resist an aside at 'the last living example of the Maori national dress'. Kiri's dress sense even provided ammunition for Britain's arch-satirical magazine *Private Eye* and John Wells's merciless spoof of Denis Thatcher, the Dear Bill column. As he ran through his diary of the day's events at St Paul's, the gin-and-tonic loving Denis's greatest grouse revolved around the way 'this dusky songstress from Down Under in a multi-coloured tablecloth and air hostess's hat warbles on for hours'. Even her normally quiet sister Nola commented on the dress. Kiri joked later that she must have had something wrong with her television set.

Kiri met the newly married Charles again weeks later at Covent

Garden. 'Prince Charles later asked me if it had made things a bit hectic,' Kiri said. 'And I replied that I couldn't go shopping for bargains quite so quickly nowadays.'

The transformation had been obvious within moments of the wedding itself. Amid all the excitement following the ceremony, Kiri had been unable to find her official limousine. A day earlier and she would have been another face in the crowd. By now, however, her profile was familiar even to the City of London police. A duo of new admirers dispatched her to Buckingham Palace in a squad car. Later in the day, as Kiri and Des had walked through Green Park in central London, she had been approached time and time again for an autograph or a photograph. Kiri could only shake her head in wonder. 'The profile I gained from it was the highest of my career,' she said.

In the days and weeks that followed, Kiri was deluged with offers from television companies and charities, music festival organisers and even star-struck new admirers. 'I had a lot of proposals,' she laughed afterwards. 'One said he was an able-bodied nineteen-year-old, but I thought that was a bit young for me.'

For the immediate future, however, opera remained her world. Her commitments were as testing as they had ever been. At the end of the autumn, Kiri headed back to Paris and her much anticipated debut as the field marshal's wife, the Marschallin, in Strauss's *Der Rosenkavalier*. Kiri's affinity with Strauss had made the role a natural for her voice. The complexity of the role once more stretched her to the limit, however. 'A puzzle that had to be put together bit by bit,' she called it.

Much of the hard work began during an extended holiday with Des and the children at the villa in Portugal, where they were joined by another golfing New Zealand singer, Chris Doig. 'It was fantastic. We played golf every day and drank plenty of bourbon,' remembered Doig, now chairman of his country's governing body for cricket. 'I found her the most delightful person, totally unpretentious. She has the veneer of the *grande dame* but in a bikini in a pool she is just the sweetest, most charming person. I loved her.'

For all the fun, Kiri's new-found discipline was obvious. 'Kiri was learning the Marschallin for Paris at that stage and would get up religiously every morning to practise,' said Doig. 'We could have been out late the night before but, hell, we would just lie in the swimming pool and listen to this ethereal sound coming out of the bedroom where she was working. It was exquisite. She would wander around with the tape going and earphones on.'

Doig was too intimidated to spend any time polishing up his own repertoire. 'I had a big concert to sing in Vienna within days of the end of this holiday but I was too scared to open my mouth in front of her,' he said.

Kiri knew of the challenge he had ahead and passed on some hard-won wisdom.

'She was chastising me for not working, but I said, "Oh, no, I'll be fine." She said, "You're going to rue this, you know. I used to be like you but now I know you can never let your voice go for even three weeks."'

In Vienna Doig was for a while dismissive of her advice. 'I was in fantastic voice on the first day back and thought, "Bugger Kiri, she's completely wrong." But the next day, having sung for four hours the day before, I had nothing. I was a wreck. So that taught me a huge lesson,' he said. 'She was right.'

Kiri's dedication to the Marschallin paid dividends as she debuted in *Der Rosenkavalier* at the beginning of December. Her Parisian fans lapped up her controlled performance. The role would become one of her trademarks over the coming years.

Her hopes of a quiet Christmas back at Fairways were disrupted by the final shock of a surprising year, however.

A few days before the holiday season began, Kiri climbed into a chauffeur-driven car bound for the central London studios of Thames Television. Kiri had been under the illusion she was heading for a documentary interview for a new music-based television series. The driver had seemed clueless about where he was heading. Kiri had started remonstrating as he drove around in ever-decreasing circles. He apologised, claiming he was a barman rather than a driver and knew nothing of London's geography. In fact the driver had spent fifteen years perfecting his act. He pulled up at the steps of St Paul's with split-second timing. As Kiri climbed out of the car she was greeted by the television presenter Eamonn Andrews and the famous red book from his hit show 'This Is Your Life'. Kiri arrived at the studios to find Des with a fixed, Cheshire cat grin on his face. Coincidentally, Kiri and Des had watched on TV as Andrews claimed another unsuspecting victim the night before. Kiri had said to Des, 'Don't you ever do that to me.' He had replied, 'It's going to happen some day', and then walked out of the room. 'The louse,' Kiri later snarled.

The show had been carefully choreographed, with filmed contributions from Georg Solti, Joan Sutherland and a still sprightly Sister Mary Leo. Tom had been flown over from New Zealand, as had a small group of others. To those who thought themselves familiar with Kiri's story, the most surprising guest was Kura Beale, who had travelled over with Sally Sloman at the last minute. Kura told how she had known Kiri since she was three. Her appearance on the programme only fuelled further the conviction of many that she was Kiri's real mother.

The evening climaxed with Andrews reading the personal tribute Prince Charles had written to the woman he called his 'favourite soprano'. 'PS: I hope this isn't too much of a shock for you', it concluded. A year earlier Kiri may not even have been considered a candidate for the accolade of a 'This Is Your Life' devoted to her. It was a measure of Kiri's status now that the programme was broadcast at prime time on Christmas Eve.

Kiri began 1982 on familiar territory, in a new production of *Così fan tutte* at the New York Met. Fiordiligi had, by now become among her most successful and best-loved roles. An RCA recording released in 1978, with the Strasbourg Philharmonic under Alain Lombard, with Teresa Stratas, Frederica Von Stade and David Rendall, had won comparisons with the classic recordings by Karajan and Bohm. On stage her Fiordiligi was an even more alluring prospect.

Her compatriot Donald McIntyre was in New York at the time and had been invited to a dress rehearsal. He felt sympathy for the colleagues she now utterly overshadowed in the eyes of the Met's regular audiences. 'Kiri was in sensational voice that day. It was a nuisance in a way,' he said. 'The audience could hardly let her sing two phrases without bursting into rapturous applause, more or less interrupting the flow. The audience couldn't contain themselves.'

The critics felt much the same way. A special concert on the evening of 14 February left one leading New York writer, John Rockwell, rhapsodising that 'Miss Te Kanawa counts as the foremost Mozart soprano of our time'. The combination of her voice, 'framed by a lovely costume, wig and make-up' added up, as far as he was concerned at least, to 'a Valentine's Day image to cherish'.

Puccini was another matter, however. In March Kiri returned to Paris to première a new production of the Italian's *Tosca* with Seiji Ozawa conducting. Kiri had always struggled with Puccini, his rapid-fire librettos in particular. 'Bloody words,' she burst out in a recording session of *La Rondine* with Lorin Maazel that year. 'Bloody, bloody words.'

The part was traditionally sung by a lirico-spinto soprano. Kiri had problems projecting her voice in the lower register. She also had problems with the sheer physical difficulty of the role, injuring her back during the climactic scene. 'For the death scene, when I jump off the battlements, they had provided two mattresses which I asked them to lay sideways on,' she recalled later. 'When I looked down they were spread lengthwise.' Kiri jumped and realised immediately she had inflicted damage. 'I did the fall, landed between the two and did my back in.'

The role left her nursing other injuries too. At the final curtain, Ozawa was drowned in boos. While Kiri received polite applause, she received some withering notices both in Paris and London. *Le Monde*'s critic said Kiri, while highly attractive, 'seemed somehow too timid in the role. We waited in vain for the terrifying revenge of an Italian Tosca.' Tom Sutcliffe, writing in the *Guardian*, was equally unimpressed. 'On the basis of Paris, her Tosca is circumscribed by the same bland limitations in acting ability that I recognised but did not mind in her Fiordiligi,' he thought. 'In *Tosca*, she expresses tragic emotion by covering her lovely face in her hands. The voice is as beautifully produced as ever, though it lacks ballast at the bottom, but it is not informed with much perception.' *Tosca* has remained outside Kiri's repertoire ever since.

The year or so since the Royal Wedding had been an almost endless adrenal high. If her fall and the lukewarm reviews she received for *Tosca* had begun to bring Kiri back down to earth, the phone call she received from New Zealand in May 1982 completed the process.

Terry Valentine had rushed over to his friend Tom Te Kanawa's home on the edge of Lake Taupo after a phone call in which he complained of feeling unwell. 'He had chest pains and he told me he wanted to go to Auckland Hospital,' Valentine remembered. As

253

Valentine drove north, however, Tom's condition worsened. 'He collapsed in my car on the way,' he said. A terrified Valentine did all he could to make Tom comfortable, then pressed on towards the hospital. In the intensive care unit at Green Lane doctors diagnosed a serious stroke. At first Nola had not wanted to disturb Kiri. It had taken the intervention of her daughter Judy to alert her to the crisis.

'Mum and me had a hell of an argument over that,' said Judy. 'Mum never wanted to trouble Kiri, but I said, "Get her home. You have twenty-four hours to notify her or I will do it."'

Judy's instincts were justified as Kiri immediately dropped everything and caught the first available flight to New Zealand.

The stroke had left Tom's speech severely impaired. He had grown increasingly irritated at his inability to make people understand him and retreated into his shell. The moment Kiri walked in, however, he lit up. 'Hello, darling,' he beamed.

'Tom lived and breathed for Kiri,' smiled Judy.

Kiri wasted no time in laying down the law to her father. 'The nurses hadn't been able to make him drink anything for a while. He just didn't want it. Kiri hit the roof,' said Judy. Kiri immediately forced him to drink the lemon barley water his granddaughter had brought for him. 'Kiri said, "Judy hasn't brought this just to sit there. You will drink it." He did. Then it was "Have another one." And he did again.

As she sat at Tom's bedside, Kiri's warrior instinct revived her father's flagging spirits. 'Kiri asked Tom whether he wanted to come back to England with her,' said Judy. 'When he nodded, she said, "Well, you better get back on your feet and hurry up about it." That gave him the incentive.'

Kiri had arrived in New Zealand with a small suitcase and little else. Her presence had remained undetected by the press. As the doctors monitored Tom's progress from intensive care into an ordinary ward, she stayed out of the limelight at the White Heron in Parnell. She spent much of her time at the hospital, sitting patiently with Nola. Friends and relatives found it hard to imagine Nola was the daughter of Nell Te Kanawa. The family matriarch's only natural daughter was a quiet, withdrawn woman with a nervous smile. Not even Nell could have been prouder of Nola's achievements, however.

'Every time Kiri was on the telly Mum would be glued to it,' remembered her daughter Judy. 'She absolutely idolised Kiri. She just lived for her. I don't know whether it was because Kiri was a younger sister.'

Four years earlier, Nola had dipped into her meagre savings to cross the Tasman to see Kiri's *Traviata* in Sydney. When he got back to London, John Davern, Kiri's agent, had sent Nola copies of the reviews and some photographs of her sister which she treasured. In 1980, she splashed out again, this time going with Tom as far as San Francisco to see Kiri in *Arabella* as the highlight of a special tour organised by the *New Zealand Woman's Weekly*. A photograph of Nola posing proudly with Tom, Des and her sister at a cocktail party for the *Woman's Weekly* guests, printed in the magazine, took pride of place on the Nikau Street mantelpiece.

Judy, by contrast, remained the rebel she had been even back at Grey Street. As Kiri's lifestyle removed her further and further from her roots, an inevitable distance had developed between her and her old partner in crime. Over a bottle of wine in Judy's living room in the rundown Mangere suburb of the city, the two rolled back the years.

Kiri and Nola visited Judy at the home she shared with the four sons she had raised in two marriages; Tony, then fifteen, Kelvyn twelve, Klynton, eleven, and Ricky, three.

'I'd bought Kiri a bottle of wine. She said, "Why take it home?. We'll have it now,"' recalled Judy. 'We allowed Mum half a glass because she wasn't well and Kiri and me finished off the bottle.'

Judy and Kiri's relationship had passed through its stormy periods, in the early 1970s in particular. Judy's first marriage, to a forklift truck driver, Richard Alp, had lasted for five violent years before reaching the divorce courts in 1973. When Judy had Alp arrested for his physical abuse, Kiri had delivered a telephone sermon. 'Kiri got on the phone and had a word with me. She told me that I had lowered the tone of the family. She had tried to put it very nicely. It was because I had gone to the police,' smiled Judy. Nell had been horrified when she found out. 'She hit the bloody roof. I remember her bellowing at Kiri while I was still on the phone. "How dare you say that to Judy!" That was the first time I really heard her give Kiri what for.'

In the intervening years the two had managed to forget the incident. Judy wrote to keep her aunt in touch with family developments. Judy proudly kept Kiri's occasional, chatty replies, even when one came with apologies for having been typed by her secretary. Her children, whose claims of a connection to Kiri had often been mocked at school, made presents that were dispatched to England at Christmas or on birthdays. When her niece remarried Kiri sent her a tape of her recordings to be played during the ceremony.

Face to face again for the first time in a decade, Kiri and Judy quickly resorted to the playful banter of the Grey Street kitchen. 'She said to me, "I suppose I've got to make my own tea now." I said, "Yeah. Just 'cos you're an opera singer don't think you're getting waited on here. You know where the kitchen is." So off she toddled and made herself a cup of tea. This is what it was always like with me and Kiri. It was a very easy atmosphere. I didn't see Kiri a lot but we always got on well,' she said. 'I miss Kiri not being Kiri as she was.'

Kiri remained in New Zealand for four days. Even in such a short time, her simple presence was instrumental in drawing Tom out of his torpor. 'Mum ran around my grandfather like a blue-arsed fly, but she molly-coddled him,' said Judy. 'Kiri was the exact opposite. Although she really cared, she wasn't going to sit there and allow him to become an invalid.' By the time Kiri gave Tom a final kiss he was able to reciprocate her good wishes. 'Not long after Kiri came back he started talking and by the time she left he was speaking really well.'

Tom stayed with his closest friend, Norman Hagan and his wife Bernice, in Auckland. He built up his strength for a flight to England later that summer on a diet of mandarin oranges. Kiri, meanwhile, returned to London and an increasingly diverse working life.

That autumn she was invited to record her own television special for the BBC. The hour-long variety programme was a showcase for Kiri's lesser known talents. As well as singing a duet with Placido Domingo, a version of 'Tonight' from *West Side Story*, she slipped into Chaplinesque rags for a hammed-up, vaudevillian version of 'We're a Couple of Swells' with Sir Harry Secombe, and sang a selection of traditional rugby songs with a visiting team of Maori rugby players.

The BBC liked the finished product so much it was scheduled for airing at the end of the year. For the second Christmas in succession, Kiri provided one of the highlights of the television schedules.

Kiri's ever-widening British fan base had been treated to an even more intimate portrait of the soprano supreme. Kiri had capitalised further on her post-Royal Wedding popularity by collaborating on a fly-on-the-wall documentary in which she was followed around Europe for months and, more importantly, a new biography, written by the journalist David Fingleton. Sixteen years after *Music and a Maori Girl*, Kiri was not short of experiences worthy of recall. She and Des ensured, however, that it was a carefully controlled version of the events that had taken her from the North Island of New Zealand to the north transept of St Paul's Cathedral.

To Kiri's horror, in the wake of the wedding as many as half a dozen writers had mooted the idea of a biography. 'This biography has an ulterior motive behind it,' she admitted. 'It's intended to stop other people from writing books about me.' Work on the pre-emptive strike had begun three years before eventual publication. Unfortunately, the original author, the arts editor of the *London Evening Standard*, Sidney Edwards, had died in 1979 with the book little more than a draft outline. With Basil Horsfield's help, Kiri and Des set about finding a 'tame' writer to finish the job.

The chosen man's brief would be clear. 'The writer has his rights, but the subject of a biography has rights, too,' said Kiri. 'You want the writer to get the stories correct, the facts straight, and you want the opportunity to say a few controversial things.' She left no one in any doubt that she held the editorial reins. 'I had so many approaches and I feared someone would just write a book full of errors anyway,' she said.

It was a worry she had felt her during the filming of 'This Is Your Life.' 'I was genuinely frightened by it,' she admitted later. 'The fear of not knowing what might come next. Control is a huge thing in this type of life and I do have a fear of getting out of control – that I won't be quick enough to get my finger on the stop button. Still,' she added, 'confidence comes from being honest about yourself and your history. I know what I am, what I've made myself.'

Fingleton's reputation for honesty was underlined by his status as a former member of the Bar and a stipendiary magistrate. Kiri had met and liked Fingleton, husband of another arts journalist, Clare Colvin, and gave him her approval. Des kept Fingleton supplied with material from the bulging archive of cuttings, programmes and photographs he had methodically maintained over the years. His subject's husband, said Fingleton tellingly, 'worked so hard that there were times when I felt that he was doing everything for this book except actually writing it'.

At the same time Kiri cleared the way for Fingleton to be given access to a select few members of her inner circle. Contributions came from Sister Mary Leo and Vera Rosza, John Copley and Jean Mallandaine, John Tooley and Raewyn Blade, now Sprinz. The newly knighted Sir Colin Davis was recruited to write a foreword for the British edition, while James Levine composed an encomium for the American. Even Prince Charles entered into brief, if unrevealing, correspondence for the purposes of the book.

What errors there were in the published book had little to do with Fingleton. Unlike Norman Harris's book, Fingleton's *Kiri: A biography of Kiri Te Kanawa* began with an explanation of her origins in Gisborne. His minimalist account of Kiri's early life was built around his subject's still sketchy grasp of the events of 1944 and handicapped by the author not travelling to Kiri's homeland. Fingleton wrote that Kiri's real mother was the European daughter of a non-conformist minister who had become involved with a Maori man. The affair was given a rather romantic spin. 'Though her mother remained faithful to him throughout her life, they never married and were extremely poor,' Fingleton wrote. He then retold the by now familiar stories of the persistent social worker, Nell's bogus connections to Sir Arthur Sullivan and Tom's less mythic links to Maori aristocracy.

Predictably, the book concentrated on enhancing Kiri's growing reputation as, what its jacket copy described as, 'The great operatic discovery of our time.' Despite its safe, surface gloss, the book proved a notable success when it was released in Britain in October. There was, for now at least, gold in everything music's Queen Midas touched.

A No-win Situation

In the second week of December 1982, the Park family emerged through customs at Auckland Airport to be met by two waiting limousines. Despite Des's attempts to keep Kiri's arrival a low-key affair, a photographer from the *New Zealand Herald* was there to capture the moment. He snatched a photograph of Kiri carrying a thumb-sucking Tom in her arms.

When the picture was printed the following morning, it was difficult to detect which member of the family was most annoyed. In a well-rehearsed tactic, Des had hired the second car specifically to carry the children and their nanny in anonymity. He was furious that the newspaper had broken the unwritten rule that the Te Kanawa children were never photographed without his permission. Toni, on the other hand, was put out because the cameraman hadn't taken a shot of her as well. 'Why wasn't it me that was in the paper?' she had demanded to know.

For the following three weeks, at least, the family were able to disappear from the public gaze. With Kiri's father, Tom, they retreated to Kura Beale's hideaway in the Bay of Islands and a happy Christmas break. In the years since her breakdown Kiri had insisted such family holidays were cast in stone in her diary. Earlier that year, she had talked proudly of how her more carefully regimented lifestyle had protected her voice from permanent damage. 'I like to think it's because I'm sensible and don't abuse myself,' she said. As a rule she now insisted on an average break of three days between performances. After long-haul travel, she took as many days off as there were jet-lagged hours. 'For instance, if I go the States, I'll take five days to recuperate,' she explained to a London-based interviewer.

In the wake of the Royal Wedding, however, Kiri had begun to have serious doubts that she could meet the new demands being placed on her. 'I was just thinking, "How can I do all of this? How can I please all of these people? How am I going to get through all the jobs?",' she said later. The answer to each of those questions would soon be painfully apparent – she couldn't.

Kiri had returned to sing at two concerts at Auckland Town Hall on 5 and 7 January. The appearances were among the most significant of her career. Not only were they her first in her homeland in eight years, they were also being staged in aid of Auckland's long-awaited new arts complex. Kiri's long-running and bluntly worded offensive on New Zealand's lack of facilities had continued unabated. Announcing the concerts in 1982 she had referred to the Town Hall as 'smelling like a boxing ring'.

'I will close my eyes and sing for the empire,' she joked. Her words were music to the ears of the arts lobbyists leading efforts to build the new $60 million, multi-purpose arts centre.

'She got quite a lot of criticism over her comments, that she was snobbish and high and mighty but it was a perfectly logical, sensible thing to say,' said Dame Catherine Tizard, who was then about to start a lengthy term as Mayor of Auckland and later became New Zealand's first woman Governor General. 'The Town Hall is not a theatre. The Town Hall is a concert room, and when she said it smelt like a boxing ring it was absolutely literally true.'

Tizard and a committee under the businessman Sir Lewis Ross had persuaded a consortium of corporate and wealthy private benefactors to invest in plans for the modernistic project. According to the project manager, the city council's director of works David Stubbs, if it had not been for Kiri's work as an *agent provocateur*, the gleaming models already taking shape in the offices of the city architect would never have left the drawing board. Such was her influence that there were even moves to have the centre named after her. By early 1983, however, the project had been christened the Aotea Centre instead. 'Kiri shamed Auckland into getting on with the Aotea Centre,' Stubbs said.

As in the 1960s, when she herself needed money to travel to England, there was no shortage of wealthy individuals eager to associate themselves with Kiri's cause. Even though the top priced $100 seats were a record in New Zealand, the concerts were an almost instant sell-out. The sense of public duty was heightened by the fact that Kiri had agreed to perform for no fee. Eventually the two concerts would raise NZ$300,000 for the new trust fund set up by the management of Kiri's new sponsors, Air New Zealand, to help build the centre.

Kiri arrived back from her holiday having seemingly broken the laws of practice she had laid down to singer friends like Chris Doig during their breaks together. The concerts were to feature the Auckland Regional Orchestra under the baton of the Yorkshire-born John Hopkins, a familiar figure on podiums across Australasia for well over a decade and the recipient of an OBE for his services to music in New Zealand. No sooner had the conductor joined his orchestra in applauding Kiri into the first rehearsal than it was obvious something was amiss.

Kiri had chosen a concert programme as demanding as any she has sung before or since – three Handel arias, three Mozart, three Puccini, three of Canteloube's *Songs of the Auvergne* and two other songs besides. Hopkins instantly detected vocal problems. 'I could just hear a bit of edge on the voice coming and I thought that she might be overdoing it,' Hopkins said. No one was more finely attuned to the performance of her voice than Kiri. 'We rehearsed with the orchestra in the afternoon and then she wanted to come back in the evening. She had come off a holiday and she wanted to get her voice going. She said, "I must sing because I've been on holiday,"' remembered Hopkins. 'I persuaded her not to do that but to rest.'

By now, however, Kiri had resumed a working schedule that eliminated any possibility of rest. The trip had been timed to coincide with the New Zealand publication of David Fingleton's biography of her. When she could and probably should have been resting, Kiri sat in bookstores asking long lines of fans who they would like their inscriptions made out to. She was also guest of honour at the annual graduation ceremony at Auckland University, where she became the first person to be given an honorary doctorate. As a favour to Cath Tizard she had also agreed to do more promotional work on behalf of the Aotea Centre. Kiri posed with models of the futuristic honeycomb of inter-connected polygons designed by the city architect Ewan Wainscott, then took part in a lengthy press conference.

Kiri knew the conference would move on to subjects beyond the Aotea Centre to other, more sensitive areas. The links she had recently formed with American Express, for whom she had agreed to do promotional work, had raised eyebrows in her homeland. When, as expected, the subject was raised Kiri admitted that she had thought long and hard about associating with the company. 'I had to work out if I was prostituting my art,' she said. In an admirable piece of theatre, she then defused the issue by producing a $5,000 gold bar which the credit card firm had donated to the Aotea Centre fund.

The gesture brought a thin smile to Des's face. Throughout the conference, as ever, he had hovered in the background, arms folded, head bowed forward, his eyes and ears alive to every question and questioner. 'I'm just here to drink the beer,' he teased one reporter. There was no disguising the importance of his role, however.

'Des was always in charge as far as I was concerned,' said chauffeur Graeme Lindsay.

Des had changed much in his wife's life. His one abject failure had been in curbing Kiri's occasional spending sprees. Friends claim his own annual clothes budget scarcely topped $300. Kiri, however, loved heading off on what she jokingly referred to as one of her 'American Express splurges'.

During that year's visit Lindsay took Kiri to one of New Zealand's top dress designers, Kevin Berkahn. 'She spent a lot of money there and when Des found out he got very upset,' said Lindsay. 'It was thousands of dollars.'

As the first of the Town Hall concerts approached, even her retail therapy could not calm Kiri's rapidly disintegrating confidence, however. Her problems were clear as John Hopkins took her through a rehearsal on the morning of the first concert. 'She was not in the same form that she'd been in when she started the piano rehearsal,' he remembered. 'There was a bit of a problem. She didn't know what it was and was very worried about it.'

By now every member of Kiri's entourage had sensed the tension in her. Graeme Lindsay had helped Kiri, Des and the family settle into the White Heron Hotel where they had booked a group of adjoining villas. Kiri was far from her normal self and kept conversation to a minimum. She seemed uneasy and distracted, sometimes pacing her room nervously. Despite the fact that Auckland was in the grip of a heatwave she refused to use the hotel's air conditioning. To soften the arid air, a pair of powerful humidifiers had been installed to belch out vapour around the clock. Lindsay understood Des and Kiri well enough by now. 'You knew when to keep out of the way,' he said. He left the villas that day quietly concerned by his star client's behaviour nevertheless. 'If it had been anyone else I would have said it was down to nerves, but you couldn't say that with her because she was so experienced.'

That evening Kiri climbed into Lindsay's limousine and headed for her 8.15 p.m. appointment on the Town Hall stage. High in the circle, Toni and Tom sat with Lurene Lindsay. The heat was so stifling that they, like many in the audience, were using their programmes as makeshift fans. Elsewhere in the hall, some had been overcome by the heat and fainted. Under the heavy arc lights, Kiri was soon perspiring and sipping regularly from a glass of her favourite iced water. As she picked her way through 'Let the Bright Seraphim' and 'Ah, ich fühl's' from *The Magic Flute*, it was clear her voice was struggling. By the time she completed her performance with Mozart's 'Alleluia' the strain was unmistakable. At one point her voice could be heard breaking in mid-aria.

Such signs of wear and tear were, of course, far from unusual in a major artist. The cracks in Maria Callas's voice were part of her melodramatic mystique, battle scars to be worn with pride. Kiri's reputation on the other hand had been built on the seamless, creamy clarity of her voice. The Auckland Town Hall audience cared little about her technical problems. At the end all 1,700 of them stood as one, roaring their approval and submerging the stage with flowers.

Elsewhere her performance would probably have drawn more damning reviews. Yet even the kindest of her New Zealand critics could not help but record Kiri's problems. 'Kiri found the lower register of her voice often responded with a series of croaks,' wrote Terry Snow in the *Auckland Star*.

L. C. M. Saunders of the *New Zealand Herald* politely suggested the concert 'did not reveal the full glories of her voice'.

On this occasion, no one was a harsher critic than Kiri herself. Back in her dressing room, she slumped into her chair, devastated. In the car on the way back to the White Heron Hotel Des did all he could to console her. His words were of little use, however. 'She was very distressed,' said Graeme Lindsay. 'She was so mad with herself. She was blaming herself for it.'

Kiri should have spent the morning after her first Town Hall concert resting. Instead she, Des, Toni and Tom climbed into a limousine for the most high-profile day of their visit.

Kiri had been approached about the latest honour to come her way at No. 10 Downing Street in London early the previous summer. Over dinner with Denis and Margaret Thatcher, the New Zealand High Commissioner had broken the news that, largely as a thank you for her work at the Royal Wedding, the Queen wanted to make her a Dame Commander of the Most Excellent Order of the British Empire in her forthcoming Birthday Honours List. 'I sat through the dinner grinning,' Kiri later recalled.

Kiri had elected to hold the investiture in New Zealand. The eighty or so guests included Dame Sister Mary Leo, who had been given her title in 1973, in the same list that saw Kiri receive her OBE. The aged nun watched Governor General Sir David Beattie pin the silver and blue cross on the lapel of Kiri's floral dress.

Beattie read the citation, describing Kiri as, 'An opera singer of world acclaim who throughout her excellent career has retained a deep affection for and a close association with New Zealand.' Kiri cried openly as her father and other Maori dignitaries, including the two last surviving colonels of the Maori Battalion, Sir James Henare and Sir Charles Bennett, broke into an impromptu version of 'Poka-rekare-ana'.

The occasion provided the one and only officially sanctioned opportunity the New Zealand media had been given to photograph Toni and Tom, now six and four respectively. In the gardens of Government House, Toni made up for the lost opportunity at Auckland Airport and smiled sweetly.

During the three hours of speech-making that followed the most apposite comment came from Ben Couch, the Minister of Maori Affairs. 'Your talent is one to be shared with the world,' he told Kiri. The world was demanding its slice of the diva Dame again the following night.

After the trauma of the first concert, Kiri whittled her demanding programme down for the second. 'On the second night, she was cancelling one or two things as we went through,' said John Hopkins. 'She was literally deciding on the spot, in the wings, not to sing certain things.'

To Hopkins, Kiri seemed genuinely bemused by the problem. 'She was quite puzzled as to what it was. I think it was a combination of things. There was a lack of confidence, particularly in things which leap across the passaggio, as they call it, or the break in the voice.'

At her earlier press conference Kiri had admitted, somewhat prophetically, 'Sometimes you wonder if you'll get through a performance – but you do.' She survived the second concert without major incident but, by now, Kiri was seriously concerned about the condition of her voice.

The day after the second concert she boarded a plane for Los Angeles and sat with Des and John Hopkins. 'It was only really when we were on the plane that I realised that her confidence was somewhat shattered,' said Hopkins. 'Des was very good, of course. He was very calm and was saying, "We'll talk to Vera Rosza about it."'

In this case, not even Kiri's 'bloody Hungarian' would be able to alleviate her problems.

Kiri was heading for New York and a new production of *Arabella* under the baton of Erich Leinsdorf. 'They are putting it on specially for me, which is so nice,' she said in Auckland before she left. 'Nice' was hardly an apt description of the fraught few weeks that followed.

Joan Ingpen had left the Paris Opera and arrived in New York with a new title, director of artistic administration, but a familiar role. Even Ingpen's peerless gifts for managing the more temperamental of opera's stars was being stretched to the limit. Ingpen had watched Kiri mature through the 1970s and early 1980s. 'She was now the assured star, the assured figure that one always guessed and hoped she would be and one accepted her on that level,' she said. 'I didn't find that Kiri had changed. She could be a little bit crazy at times, but then they all are.' As far as many at the Met were concerned, if there was a touch of madness within the cast of *Arabella*, it lay with Kathleen Battle, the singer chosen to sing Zdenka, Arabella's flighty young sister.

The seventh child of a black steelworker from Ohio, Battle was to her nation's racial underclass what Kiri was to New Zealand's Maori. Her climb to the top in a white-dominated world was the stuff of which the American dream was made. Having become James Levine's most favoured performer, however, Battle had also become, as one music writer put it, 'a backstage by-word for diva-like excesses'. Battle could not bring herself to share limousines with other singers, once refused to sing at the Lincoln Center unless her dressing room was equipped with a bigger bar of soap, and physically removed conductor Trevor Pinnock from his podium during a Handel rehearsal. At the end of a troubled run in San Francisco, orchestra members wore T-shirts emblazoned with the slogan 'I Survived the Battle'. Battle would later send away the limousine dispatched to deliver her to President Clinton's inauguration because it was 'not long enough'. A decade later her behaviour would eventually lead to her dismissal from the Met for 'unprofessional actions ... profoundly detrimental to artistic collaborations'. In 1983, however, she was barely getting into her stride.

The problems began even before rehearsals. Battle, like Kiri, had been given Leinsdorf's version of the cuts months in advance of the rehearsal period. 'Everything was fixed and scored,' said Joan Ingpen. 'Suddenly, a short time before rehearsal was beginning, Kathy said she didn't agree with it. Something in her part had been cut that she didn't agree with. We said, "Look, you've had that for about four months." There was bad feeling from then on.'

Kiri and Battle were always going to see each other as rivals. 'Both of them traded a lot on their glamorous appearance. They did not look like opera stars. They both had good figures and dressed beautifully,' recalled Johanna Fiedler, then a member of the Met's public relations department. The eruption came during rehearsals one day. 'Kathy told Kiri not to look at her while they were rehearsing. It took off after that.'

Battle would reduce many to emotional rubble. Kiri, however, gave as good as she got. Given the fragile state of her voice and her confidence, Kiri was determined she would not relearn the opera. When Ingpen called her into her office, Kiri had her excuses ready. 'I said, "Can't you two sit down?",' said Ingpen. 'She said, "You know how slow I am learning and I've learned it like this. I'm not going to start again." It was clear to me that Kiri had no intention of changing.'

Ingpen had banged her share of operatic heads together over the years. This time she retreated to the wings. 'One knew there was this friction and that it was Kathy's fault to have responded so late. I thought if I could solve it, fine, but if not I wasn't going to press Kiri,' said Joan Ingpen. 'I thought, I'm not going to mix it.'

As the opening night neared, Kiri and Battle barely spoke to each other. Publicly, Kiri sailed imperiously through the conflict. Privately, however, the tensions only exacerbated Kiri's insecurity about the condition of her voice. She had become locked in a dangerous, downward spiral. As she worried more about her voice, so she slept less. Always prone to insomnia, she would wake up at 3.30 a.m. every morning regardless of where she was in the world. As a result she began relying on sleeping pills to knock her out for the night. When she began waking up the following morning feeling as if she had been drugged, she switched to other treatments. 'At one time I was so bad I had to have myself hypnotised in order to get some sleep.'

Even when she performed well in rehearsal there was no escape. 'My brain doesn't actually stop just because I close my eyes. The music continues like an echo,' she said once.

Superstitious by nature, Kiri also began weaving a collection of curious rituals into her routine. She had begun buying knives for purely practical reasons when she first stayed in hotels in the 1970s. The purchase of a new knife had become a requirement each time she arrived at a new hotel. Her collection ran into hundreds. 'I believe in knives. I have to buy one,' she explained. She had also begun carrying a pink crystal given to her by a woman who told her it would protect her voice. 'When I feel vulnerable and insecure I start touching my throat with it.'

Her mental state was not helped by her disconnection from the children. During Toni's childhood Kiri had promised that she would ease down in her schedule when she grew up. 'It's all right while she's small but when it's time for her to go to school I will have to stop flying around the world. You don't have children to send them to boarding school,' she said when Toni was still a one-year-old baby in 1978. Five years on Kiri's fine intentions had been over-ridden by the demands of her career. 'All I want to do now is get home to my babies. They are growing so much I will miss them if I am not careful,' she confessed to her niece Judy in a letter written on board a plane to Chicago that March.

As sickness and self-doubt threatened to consume her, she was referred by a friend to an endocrinologist, an expert in hormone-related illness. The specialist discovered that Kiri's difficulties stemmed from a physical lack of lubrication in her voice. 'I had a lack of mucous

267

juice, body juice, and it affected my throat,' she said. 'I was totally dry in my throat. I would sing for ten days in a month and the rest of it I couldn't sing at all. I was completely hoarse.' To Kiri's delight, the endocrinologist prescribed a treatment that was soon alleviating the physical problem. The specialist attributed the dryness to a hormone deficiency and from then on, Kiri would take a vitamin B injection two days before each performance.

The psychological problems remained, however. 'I wasn't really ill,' Kiri later explained. 'But it affected me mentally, because every time I came to sing I'd look forward to being absolutely wonderful and suddenly there was nothing, no voice.'

Kiri's conviction that her voice had to remain active remained absolute, however. She determined to fight her way through the crisis – regardless of the consequences. 'I sang through. I kept on going,' she said. 'I said, "If I stop now, I'll never go back on stage again. I'll just never get on there." I knew I couldn't because I could hardly face it even then. Just getting out the dress to iron it was painful.'

As ever, it was Des who provided the support that Kiri needed. On the opening night of *Arabella* in March, as he had done at Auckland Town Hall in January, Des stood in the wings, visible at all times to Kiri. On this occasion, however, he was only one source of inspiration. Ironically, Kiri and Kathleen Battle pushed each other into performing sublimely. Of all her roles, none brought Kiri quite the thrill of Arabella. By now she imbued the climactic scene, in which Arabella descends a staircase holding a glass of pure water, singing of her love for Mandryka, 'the right one', with a blend of pathos and poetry that few critics could resist. 'I tingle all over,' she said once.

The American critics tingled along with her. 'Sentimental, yes, but transcendently so: not even Garbo, one suspects, could have managed this bit of stage magic better,' the *Newsweek* critic wrote. 'Her voice, a royal blend of shining high notes and creamy low ones, soars effortlessly over the orchestra. No wonder Prince Charles asked her to sing at his wedding. She's a born aristocrat onstage.'

As Kiri returned to London, however, it was clear to those who knew her best that she should once more take an extended break from singing. However, Kiri had joined an all-star cast for a Covent Garden production of Puccini's *Manon Lescaut*, including Placido Domingo in the role of Des Grieux and Thomas Allen as Lescaut. The brilliant but aloof Italian Giuseppe Sinopoli had been engaged to conduct. Such was the anticipation surrounding their collaboration, and the new production being designed by Piero Faggioni, that the run sold out immediately. Yet there was an air of chaos surrounding the production. Problems had begun when Faggioni withdrew after his audacious designs were rejected. John Tooley had been forced to replace it with a revival of a successful production from Hamburg, produced there by Götz Friedrich, with Domingo in the role of Des Grieux, in 1979.

Sinopoli's reputation as 'the latest comet out of Italy' had just won him a job as principal conductor of the Philharmonia Orchestra. He had made it clear that he only wanted to work on new productions, but agreed, reluctantly, to stay on when Faggioni left.

Kiri went into intensive rehearsals at the new Covent Garden extension a month before opening. Domingo, who knew his part as Des Grieux backwards, started a week later. With Friedrich absent, Kiri started in good humour putting smiles on the faces of the company with her imitations of the producer's assistant, Wolfgang Bucker. As the intense and serious-minded Sinopoli worked everyone hard, however, her spirits sagged.

Kiri's old problems with learning new work soon resurfaced. Her progress was not helped by a bad case of flu. Kiri still had her supporters at the Garden. Sir Colin Davis, approaching the end of his fifteen-year tenure as musical director, was among those who sympathised. 'Everyone wants you to sing, forgetting that it takes three months' hard work to learn the thing,' he said later. 'And so you feel the world closing in on you and you haven't a hope in hell of keeping up with it.'

Sinopoli had little interest in indulging his star soprano, however. Relations between the two deteriorated badly. 'It was like a snake pit,' Kiri said.

Kiri once more relied on her visits to Vera Rosza in Willesden. This time, however, even her mentor sensed Kiri must face reality and give her voice and her body another break. 'It was the only time I have ever advised Kiri to cancel an entire operatic performance,' she said later.

Vera Rosza's Svengali influence remained the bedrock of Kiri's musical life. Her teacher's gifts even extended to an ability to lift the clouds during the 'bad days'. 'Come to the piano,' Rosza would soothe when Kiri arrived out of sorts. 'I will make you feel wonderful in two minutes.'

'Some days I turn up at Vera's feeling ghastly,' Kiri once explained. 'She manages to cheer and invigorate me in no time.' Kiri's faith in Rosza's abilities was absolute. 'The only way to survive in this business is to believe in yourself and follow your convictions. My rule is never to listen to anybody except for myself and my teacher Vera Rosza.'

On this occasion, however, Kiri found herself ruled by an even more powerful force. Kiri had recognised she was facing her own Catch 22. 'You cannot imagine how many people are always telling me I shouldn't cancel even when I know I should,' she explained. 'And the result is that you sing feeling unwell and the world judges you unfit for a certain role for ever. And if you do cancel, as you are sometimes forced to, all those people who don't care – like management, the recording industry, etc. – go about saying you cancel all the time and you get a reputation for being unreliable. You are in a no-win situation.'

The pressure to remain within the production was immense and, for once, Kiri ignored Rosza's advice and sang on. The results were predictable. *Manon Lescaut* opened with a Royal Gala performance that spring. By now, Kiri's cover-ups were fooling fewer and fewer critics. 'To put it politely, she had a less than comprehensive grasp,' wrote the *Time Out* critic, Martin Hoyle.

As the production pulled in equally poor reviews, Sinopoli let it be known that he was 'infuriated' by Kiri's lack of preparation. Kiri fought back, accusing him of conspiring behind her back. 'I'm sure that he tried to get me fired,' she said later. Unsurprisingly, when Deutsche Grammophon reunited Sinopoli and Domingo for a prestige recording of the opera later, Kiri was replaced by Mirella Freni. She did not sing *Manon Lescaut* on stage again.

In July 1983, a relieved Kiri headed for Portugal and five weeks of golf, swimming and relaxation. As she soaked up the sun on the Algarve, however, she was preoccupied with one pastime more than any other. As she left London, she told the New Zealand press she would spend the holiday – and another five weeks afterwards – trying to 'reassess where I am going and what I am doing'.

If she was a diva in distress, she soon found a knight in shining armour looming into view. The American sports agent Mark Hume McCormack arrived in her life clutching the wheel of an electric golf buggy rather than the reins of a white charger, however. It was with some pride that McCormack admitted he had never been to a classical recital let alone an opera. His musical taste ran no deeper than the Beatles. As he partnered Kiri for a round of golf back in Surrey that year, however, he became fascinated by her and the mysterious, elitist world she moved within. Soon afterwards he accepted her invitation to a night at Covent Garden.

History has not recorded the details of the performance the odd couple went to, only that Kiri had to explain to McCormack that the midway break in the evening was 'the intermission, not half time'. What is clear, however, is that by the end of the evening McCormack's fearsome business brain had begun to see an opportunity. Soon he would be transforming the modern opera industry. No one would benefit more than Kiri.

In the two decades since he had given up his ambitions to be a star of the American professional golf tour, Mark McCormack had become the most influential and controversial figure in world sport. His visionary business mind had turned his first client, Arnold Palmer, into the richest sportsman in the world. McCormack's ten per cent of Palmer's million dollar pay cheques had formed the foundation for the creation of McCormack's multi-national company, IMG, the International Management Group. The key to McCormack's thinking lay in his recognition of the overwhelming power wielded by the talented few. To McCormack, at least, golf was little more than Mark Twain's 'a good walk spoiled' without the genius of Palmer and Jack Nicklaus; tennis was a sideshow without its Borgs and McEnroes. He elevated the sportsman to the pinnacle of a new commercial pyramid and anointed himself Pharaoh of the new sporting empire he created. McCormack's IMG organised its own tournaments, held the television companies to ransom for coverage of the major events and drew in vast multi-national corporate sponsorship. The genius of McCormack's alchemy was that by doing business his way, everyone – the sportsmen, the ruling bodies, the television companies and the advertising agencies – became richer.

McCormack was quietly awe-struck by Kiri. 'McCormack, like so many people of his kind, wanted to be touched by an angel. He felt that she elevated him in some way, that she made him a better person; that just by coming into contact with this spiritual arena improved him,' said the music writer and historian Norman Lebrecht, who interviewed McCormack at length for his bestselling book on the modern classical music industry, *When the Music Stops*. 'It certainly changed his life and his business. Without Kiri it would never have crossed his mind to move into the classical music business. He had never been to an opera, never been to a classical concert.'

To McCormack, Kiri's similarity to modern day golf heroes like the Australian Greg Norman extended far beyond her ability to wield a mightily impressive five iron. 'I decided that there was a tremendous parallel between sports and classical music,' he told Lebrecht. 'Sports personalities and classical artists perform their profession without consideration of language. Both face identical tax and other financial considerations as they travel from country to country.'

By late 1983 McCormack had begun testing the new waters. One of his most trusted acolytes, Shirley Bassey's agent John Webber, had been deputed to set up a new division of his empire, IMG Artists. The agency took over the old Hamlen-Landau agency and its clients in New York. Soon they had claimed their first major defection in the violinist Itzhak Perlman, who left his old agents at ICM to join the new force.

For Kiri, McCormack's arrival in classical music was serendipitous in several respects. After the problems of the last two years, she knew she had to be even more protective of her voice. Somewhere in her mind too, she must have sensed, for the first time, that time was turning against her. McCormack's combination of creativity and commercial clout could open the doors to new, highly lucrative but, if necessary, less physically demanding opportunities. McCormack had already worked out that one showpiece concert could generate the income of an entire season at Covent Garden or the Met.

Kiri was as intrigued by McCormack as he was by her. 'I think she went to dinner with him at his house and said to him, "You do all these things for sports but you never do anything for music,"' said John Hopkins. Soon the conductor was one of the first beneficiaries of the agreement Kiri reached to work with McCormack's organisation on a series of 'special projects'.

There was no question, of course, of giving up on the opera performances that remained her lifeblood. As she had rested on the beach in the Algarve, however, Kiri realised that here too it was time to ring the changes. Kiri and Des had become increasingly irritated by the difficulties they now faced in dealing with Basil Horsfield. As far as they were concerned, at least, Horsfield had failed to deliver on his promise that he could provide the same service from Monte Carlo. Health problems exacerbated by his heavy drinking had done little to help affairs.

It had been in New York that Joan Ingpen had first become aware of the schism that now existed between her old friend and the star he had brought to Covent Garden more than a decade earlier.

'She said, "Just deal with me direct now. It's hopeless dealing with Basil in Monte Carlo." So I did,' said Ingpen.

Soon Ingpen was being confronted by Horsfield in person. 'He came over to New York and said, "I'm still looking after her."' Ingpen's advice to her old friend was simple. 'I said, "Sort it out between you."'

In January 1984, Horsfield bumped into another old colleague of Kiri's at the annual MIDEM music conference in Cannes. Tony Vercoe had had little direct contact with Kiri since their 1970 recording, *Rainbow in the Sky*. Because of Kiwi Records' continuing ownership of rights to her sixties releases, however, he had dealt regularly with the agent. Soon after sharing a drink in Cannes, Vercoe received a letter from Horsfield. He explained that Kiri and Des had severed their fifteen-year relationship. 'He was not happy,' said Vercoe.

Unpalatable as it may have been to both men, however, the reality was simple. As she moved inexorably onwards, Kiri had outgrown each of them. She signed up with a specialist musical agency, Harrison Parrott. She had met and liked Jasper Parrott, a Cambridge educated linguist who had formed the agency with Terry Harrison in 1969. As she began handing over her classical diary to him, however, her instructions were clear. Parrott's area was purely classical: her engagements at the opera house, recording and recitals. Des would now handle the bulk of her managerial role. The third, and potentially most lucrative area of all, 'special projects', would be handled by IMG.

The first fruits of Kiri's new relationship with IMG were apparent in late 1983 as she announced a four-concert tour of New Zealand to be handled by the agency the following April.

McCormack had asked the head of his Australian office, James Erskine, to organise the tour along with his New Zealand counterpart, Paul Gleeson. The dapper Erskine, born in the north of England, was more used to arranging tennis and golf tournaments. With sponsorship from American Express to support the tour already in place, however, he gave his new property – and her associates – the kind of five-star treatment and impeccable attention to detail that was his company's hallmark.

John Hopkins, rewarded for his loyalty during the troubles of the past year with a contract to conduct the four concerts, was certainly impressed by the manner in which IMG organised everything from air travel to flowers in the hotel suites. 'It was an organised tour the like of which I'd never seen before,' he said. 'Every detail was looked after.'

Hopkins nursed Kiri through the nerves that resurfaced in the run up to their first performance, in Christchurch. 'I felt that she needed quite a lot of support, mentally,' he said. 'I remember when we did the first concert she was quite tense because she knew that the New Zealand critics would be on the attack.'

His fears had some foundation. When Kiri had arrived for the concerts in New Zealand, she was immediately asked about the American Express involvement and the exorbitant ticket prices being charged by IMG. 'Don't talk about money. Let's talk about art,' she said, clearly rattled. When journalists persisted, Erskine intervened, claiming prices were 'very much in line' with the cost of concert-going around the world.

'They'd never seen prices like that in New Zealand before, but I think businessmen were prepared to pay that because it was probably tax deductible,' Hopkins said.

Kiri ensured the bad publicity was soon forgotten as she donated $10,000 to the winner of that year's Dame Sister Mary Leo Scholarship, a local soprano, Rhona Fraser.

Kiri chose a less demanding programme than the previous year. If it pleased the paying public, it left critics like the *Auckland Star*'s Terry Snow less impressed. 'Reaching deep into Rotary Club, middle management and fur coat territory, this American Express concert – and we were not spared advertising on the night – aimed consciously to present a generally easy-listening programme, and an adoring audi-

'Mr Ideal.' Kiri and Des's official engagement photograph, 1967.

'An almighty crush.' Kiri fights her way into St Patrick's Cathedral, August 1967.

'With this ring.' Des and Kiri, flanked by best man Adolf Lacis and bridesmaid Sally Rush, take their vows.

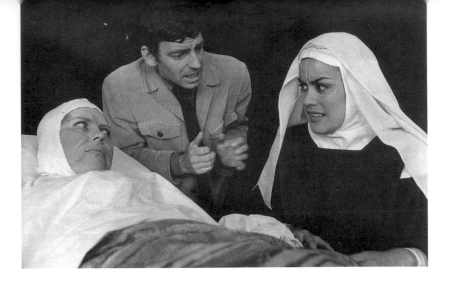

Above 'Poor Blanche.'
Tom Hawkes directs Kiri
in the *Dialogue of the
Carmelites* at the
London Opera Centre,
1968.

Right 'A fantastically
alluring woman.' Kiri as
Carmen, Wellington,
1969.

Left 'A tigress in desolation.' Kiri as Donna Elvira in *Don Giovanni*, Covent Garden, 1973.

Below left Kura Beale – Kiri's friend and benefactress – with a prize marlin caught in the Bay of Islands.

Below 'One chance.' Kiri in the midst of the performance that made her an international star – St Paul's Cathedral, 29 July 1981.

Opposite above Reunited. Kiri shares some rare time with her niece, Judy Evans-Hita (*left*) and sister Nola, 1982.

Below A couple of swells. Kiri and Sir Harry Secombe in her BBC TV special, 1982.

Right A family affair. The new Dame Kiri and Des introduce six-year-old Toni and four-year-old Tom to the press, Auckland, January 1983.

Below A whole new world. Kiri's Long Island mansion, mid-1980s.

Above Conductor of choice.
Kiri shares a happy moment
with Stephen Barlow.

Right 'A lovely pampered
creature.' Kiri radiant in
Versace's *Capriccio* chic,
1991.

Overleaf Real anxiety. The pain
of her divorce is etched on
Kiri's face as she sings Amelia
in *Simon Boccanegra*, Covent
Garden, June 1997.

ence was well prepared to cheer anything from Dame Kiri,' Snow carped after hearing her back at Auckland Town Hall.

For IMG and James Erskine, however, the sell-out shows were an unqualified success. Erskine celebrated the birth of a new and already highly lucrative marriage with a gesture that left Kiri speechless. 'James came to the first concert in Christchurch and took Kiri and Des off to an art gallery to an exhibition of a certain painter's work,' remembers John Hopkins. 'She fell in love with two of the works but couldn't decide which of them she would buy. She eventually decided on a particular one and reluctantly left the other. When we went back to Wellington, after the last concert, we were having some supper in Kiri's suite at the hotel and James suddenly said, "Oh, Kiri, I've got something for you. Just a little memento of a successful tour", and he produced a brown paper parcel. The look on her face when she saw the other painting which she loved so much was one I shall never forget. It was totally unexpected. I just thought it was a fantastic touch.'

Erskine and IMG were already planning to follow the blueprint of the New Zealand tour with similar forays into the Far East, America and Europe. At the same time, in anticipation of the vast projected earnings Kiri could now expect, the organisation's accountants had begun to work with Des on an intricate financial structure capable of maximising their income. Kiri's earlier complaints about the tax man taking all her money would be alleviated by the creation of two companies, Thor-Air Establishment in the tiny European principality of Liechtenstein, and later Mitani (Europe) AG, based in Lucerne, Switzerland.

The most dramatic impact of the IMG connection came later that year, however. Kiri's popularity at the Met had been cemented once more by her triumph in *Arabella*. IMG's power-base remained in North America. It was suggested to Kiri that she and Des would benefit from being based in New York rather than London. Kiri and Des took a long hard look at their situation. Soon the list of pros was far outstripping the cons. Kiri had grown irritated by the snobbishness of London's critics, many of whom seemed to have fallen out of love with her over the years. She had re-taken her vows never again to read reviews after learning that a London critic had based his negative review of a performance of Tatyana in *Eugene Onegin* on a dress

275

rehearsal. 'I have never been so angry in all my life as when I read that review,' she said haughtily. 'I know that most of the things which I do, I do well. If all critics can find fault with is the way I pronounce the words then I am only sorry that they can't find anything better to write about.'

As far as Kiri was concerned, the sniping was little more than another manifestation of the elitism she had suffered as a little girl in Gisborne. 'The sooner the snob factor leaves the musical profession, the sooner we'll be able to get on with entertaining people rather than boring them,' she said later. 'We are dictated to by people who say "You can't do that." Well, who says?'

America, on the surface at least, seemed a more egalitarian environment. With Christmas 1984 looming, Des and Kiri put Fairways up for lease, packed their belongings and boarded a flight for JFK airport. At first they acquired an apartment in Manhattan, a few blocks from the Met. Soon, however, they had also taken on a large home an hour's drive from Manhattan on Long Island. The huge, white, weatherboard mansion at 80 Twinponds Lane was set in three acres of land in Oyster Bay Cove. Kiri and Des chose a name for the house harking back to their first, in Esher. Fourteen years on, however, plain Rushmere had become the Rushmere Estate.

As Toni and Tom were enrolled at a nearby school, a new Karitane nurse from New Zealand, Catherine Ansett, was hired to attend to them. Des acquired a small office in the city from where he could handle his – and Kiri's – business. Soon the New World was offering a new life.

Kiri's diary quickly showed the benefits of being based in New York. Towards the end of 1984, she was booked to sing the vast Constitution Hall in Washington. Kiri had first sung in the capital in 1982 at the smaller, 1,000-seater Kennedy Center. Few singers had ever been invited to sing at the city's larger venue. It was a measure of her already increased profile that the concert quickly became a sell-out.

By the end of 1984 she had begun to rediscover her confidence. More than ever, Des was the key to her recovery. Whenever she took to the stage he stood in the wings watching and supporting her. 'Des basically didn't leave me for a year. He would always be doing his other work, at home, but every performance he was there right beside the stage,' she said. He was there again in November as Kiri returned to Covent Garden for her London debut as the Marschallin in *Der Rosenkavalier*, this time under the leadership of her old mentor Georg Solti. In times of crisis, no one was better equipped than Solti to steer Kiri through.

Kiri's understanding of the Marschallin had deepened. 'She is a real woman and a contemplative, rather introspective character,' she said of the role. 'Therefore I feel it helps if one has seen one's own first white hairs before one sings her.' Since first singing the part in Paris more than three years earlier, Kiri had survived 'quite a few bumps in life . . . Not serious bumps, not tragedies like some people in this world have to endure, but enough, I think, for me to understand the Marschallin a little better.' The critics could not argue with her. Inspired once more by Solti, her well-received performance helped recover some of the ground lost during the débâcle of *Manon Lescaut*.

As 1984 drew to a close, Kiri sensed she had turned the corner in her battle to rebuild her self-confidence. She, Des and the children spent the holiday season in New York. The energising atmosphere of Manhattan made it a Christmas to remember. Life was soon throwing up new bumps, however. 'I thought I'd got through,' she explained. 'Then my father died and it was back to square one.'

On 13 January 1985, Terry Valentine and a friend Bill Gordon had set off along the shore of Lake Taupo in search of Tom Te Kanawa. They had seen their eighty-three-year-old fishing partner the day before. Typically he had been digging a hole in the earth and was prising the stump of a tree out with a crowbar. Unusually, however, there had been no sign of him that morning.

Valentine and Gordon found the door to Tom's cabin open. When they entered the kitchen they found him lying motionless on the floor. 'He had just prepared his meal. He'd peeled the potatoes and we found him lying beside the kitchen bench. He'd just gone straight down,' recalled Valentine. A doctor soon arrived to pronounce him dead.

Valentine was too upset to call Kiri. Instead it was Bill Gordon who rang the new number in Long Island. Kiri's grief was overwhelming. Yet she dealt with the loss as she dealt with that of her mother – by withdrawing into herself.

Tom was to be buried at Waikumete Cemetery that Friday morning. Kiri knew her appearance would draw the kind of attention that had

277

marred Nell's funeral thirteen years earlier. She knew too of the controversy that Tom's wish to be buried away from the family marae was already causing within the Te Kanawa clan. All she wanted was to grieve for her father in peace.

Des offered to travel to New Zealand on her behalf. An announcement was made to the New Zealand press, explaining that Kiri was 'torn' between travelling to the funeral and settling Tom and Toni into their new schools. The fact that the funeral clashed with the first of her Washington concerts at Constitution Hall complicated matters even further, the statement said.

Kiri's absence drew predictable fire. 'I was absolutely shattered that she didn't come, to be frank, and Tom would have been shattered had he known,' said Terry Valentine. 'I never really have come to terms with that, because Kiri was Tom's life and their relationship appeared to be marvellous.'

Yet Kiri's decision seemed vindicated as the event became a platform for old family bitterness. Tom's estrangement from the Te Kanawa clan had continued even after Nell's death. He had been adamant that he wanted to be buried with his late wife in the twin plot they had bought for the purpose rather than at the family marae in Te Kuiti. Many of the family had boycotted the service. 'They thought he should have gone down country and been buried at the marae. But Tom and Nell had made their arrangements and had bought a double plot at Waikumete cemetery,' said Kay Rowbottom, Tom's niece, who with her husband Bruce drove the few members of the Te Kanawa family who did attend to Auckland for the day.

It seemed as if Tom's brother Mita had come to make his feelings plain. As Tom's coffin was lowered into the ground he produced a stream of invective in Maori. 'I asked Des what he was saying and then we asked the priest, who told us he was berating him for not having gone back to the marae to be buried, for deserting his Maori people,' said one of the mourners.

The tension was still tangible when friends and family went back to Nola and Bill Denholm's house in Nikau Streeet. Kiri's absence was, of course, commented on. It was left to her niece Judy to mount the most strident defence. 'I can remember someone saying, "Kiri should have come to her father's funeral." I remember turning on them and saying, "For God's sake, he's dead. What can she do for him now?"'

As far as Judy was concerned, Kiri's work had been done. Her priorities now lay elsewhere. 'Kiri and Des had not long been in America and the kids had just started school,' she said. 'When she was wanted she was here. When he had his stroke Kiri was here. What was going to happen? She was going to be surrounded by people asking her questions about her dead father.'

Des had been named a co-executor of Tom's will with Norman Hagan. Before leaving Auckland he was formally read the document in which Tom bequeathed the property at Hatepe and everything else he owned to Kiri, or in the event of her death, Antonia and Tom once they reached their twentieth birthdays. He then headed straight back to Kiri in New York.

To no one's great surprise, Kiri cancelled the opening concert in Washington, blaming 'bronchitis' for her withdrawal. With Des back at her side, she recovered in time to sing the postponed concert on the 28th. Washington cheered her to the echo despite the once more all too evident problems with her throat.

It was not until the New Zealand spring that Kiri was able to say her final goodbye to her father. In September she conducted a whirlwind, nineteen-venue tour of Australia. During the trip she slipped quietly and unobtrusively into Auckland and spent time at Waikumete Cemetery on her own. 'She went up to the grave and spent some time with him alone, which is how it should be,' said Judy.

Those who thought her absence from the funeral uncaring could not have been farther from the truth. In the years that followed her affection for Tom never faded. He remained in death what he had been when he was alive, the single, greatest love of her life. Publicly and privately she talked frequently of the void he had left behind. In the wake of Tom's death, Kiri continued to sing her old St Mary's favourite, 'Oh My Beloved Father'. She told one friend how every time she sang it she imagined Tom's proud, gently smiling face. In interviews, she rarely missed an opportunity to pay tribute to his extraordinary memory.

'He was a lovely man with so much simplicity. He just adored me,' she said, seven years after his death in 1992. 'If you have had a father like that you never really find anyone who adores you in quite the same way.'

*   *   *

279

It could have been a scene from the Colony Club, two decades earlier. In October 1985, in the dark recesses of the Ballroom restaurant off Manhattan's Broadway, a group of well-lubricated diners sat back and cast their eyes towards the spotlit stage. There, an immaculately dressed Kiri picked up a microphone and slipped into her 'bottom of the boots' voice for a selection of Cole Porter classics. As ever the audience were entranced. A year or so after arriving in New York, Kiri took her first tentative step into a new marketplace in front of an invited audience of influential American music writers. Kiri gave a sneak preview of *Blue Skies*, an album of songs she had recorded the previous year with the American composer Nelson Riddle.

It had been during a tour of Australia in the middle of 1984 that she had first been introduced to the most influential music arranger of his generation. Riddle's achievements ranged from a sublime period working with Nat King Cole to successful movie scores, such as *Paint Your Wagon* with Lee Marvin. His greatest achievement, however, had been to revive the flagging career of Frank Sinatra in the 1950s with their classic swing collaborations on Capitol Records. Kiri turned to Riddle hoping he could spread a little of his musical magic her way.

It took two more meetings, one in Monte Carlo and another in Chicago, to persuade him to work with her on an album of non-classical music. Kiri and Riddle went into the studio later that year where they recorded such standards as 'It Might as Well Be Spring', 'Here's That Rainy Day' and 'How High the Moon'. It turned out to be one of the last projects Riddle completed before he died of a heart attack in October 1985, aged sixty-four.

When it was released a year later, their collaboration provoked predictable sneers among the purists. Regardless, *Blue Skies* flew out of the record stores in America and around the world.

The picture was much the same later that year when she teamed up with the Philharmonia Concert under Carl Davis and the Tallis Chamber Choir for a seasonal television special for the BBC. Kiri sang a varied repertoire from 'The Twelve Days of Christmas' and 'Have Yourself a Merry Little Christmas' to the traditional Spanish carol 'The Virgin Washes the Swaddling'. The performance was released subsequently on video, the forerunner of a succession of Christmas-flavoured offerings she would produce over the following decade.

Kiri was making little secret of her intention of easing more and more into the world of what she called 'the light stuff'. 'My purpose in life is not to bore people to death or just sing for the opera purists,' she told the *London Evening Standard* early in the New Year in 1986. As if to underline the point, Kiri told the *Standard* her next project was a throwback to her old days in Auckland, a version of Rodgers and Hammerstein's *South Pacific*. 'I had a boyfriend once in a stage production of it in New Zealand,' she told the *Standard*, referring to her old flame Vincent Collins. 'I know the thing backwards.'

Kiri began the classical year back at Covent Garden. A combination of financial problems and Placido Domingo's departure for Mexico, where his family had been caught in a devastating earthquake, had meant the cancellation of a new *Otello* with the acclaimed young director Elijah Moshinsky. The production was put back to the following year, Covent Garden's centennial. Instead she fell back on Amelia in *Simon Boccanegra*. Afterwards she headed back to New York and her first outing in Handel's *Samson*, a showcase for 'Let the Bright Seraphim', the aria for which she was known the world over.

Samson opened on 15 February and ran to 6 March. Nine days after the final performance Kiri, under the baton of Myung-Whun Chung, introduced her Amelia to New York. Both performances enhanced her reputation as a darling of the Met. No group of opera lovers spoiled its stars quite like the patrons of America's self-appointed cathedral of high culture. Its Croesus-rich cognoscenti loved decorating the dining tables of Manhattan's smartest restaurants with the diva du jour. Met figures like Cissy Strauss held famously opulent soirées at their Central Park West apartments. Kiri was nobody's bauble, however. She and Des attended the occasional first-night party but generally avoided such affairs. As Kiri was tired of explaining, her all-night-party days were long gone.

'Why do they always ask me out to dinner after the show?' she laughed once. 'You're exhausted. Your hair is a soggy mass after being crammed under a wig for hours. You haven't had time for a manicure or a hairdo. You're stiff with greasepaint and powder and wrung out with tension. And they want you to mingle with women who've had all day to put themselves together.' Kiri still regarded a room full of strangers as something akin to hell on earth. 'Instead of saying, "Oh, hullo Kiri, would you like a drink?", they blow smoke in your face, they spit in your face when they are eating a sandwich and they are

281

too busy trying to find out what I'm doing, where I'm going and what I'm doing next . . . rattling off the schedule forgetting that I might be a bit thirsty.'

In Paris her idea of a perfect end to an evening's work was retiring to her hotel room for a convivial meal with one or two colleagues. In New York, as in London, she jumped straight into a car and headed home to Des and the children. 'I don't want to sleep in next day and lose three precious hours.'

The routine she described out on Long Island was as militaristic as it was reassuring in its precision. Whether she had been performing or not, Kiri set her alarm for 6.45 a.m. She would wake the children ten minutes later, with their breakfast ready. While Kiri packed Thomas's lunch and Antonia's satchel, Antonia would practise the piano. Kiri would then drive the two down to the bus stop in her jeep. On non-performing days, after a morning at the piano and on the phone, Kiri might head into Manhattan for lunch or shopping then head back to pick up the children at the end of the school day. On performing days she would take an early lunch, then arrive early at the opera house to be dressed, made up and fitted with her wig. Kiri's routine before taking the stage was set in stone. She applied her make-up herself as often as possible so as to give herself 'something to do with my hands'. She then slipped into her gown and waited for the finishing touches to be applied. 'My hair is then rolled up, the wig is put on and, because I've already warmed up, I go on stage and sing. There's no mystique about it,' she explained that spring.

As she immersed herself deeper into America, Kiri again worked hard to cultivate her image as a new breed of diva, far removed from the traditional, pampered prima donna. In the summer of 1986 she livened up an issue of Andy Warhol's radically chic magazine, *Interview*, with her earthy views on subjects as diverse as opera snobbery and her own self-image. Kiri confessed that at times her head had been turned by the adoration of her male following. 'I fancy myself as someone absolutely extraordinary, who looks like Marilyn Monroe and has all that equipment,' she said. 'Then I come down to earth and think "Come on Kiri, you old bag."'

As the interview became more and more playful, Kiri couldn't help agreeing with her interrogator Gregory Speck's view that the sniffy propriety of the traditional opera-goer sat uneasily with his interest in an art form devoted to 'lust, passion, madness and the seven deadly sins'.

'As is often said, every man wants to be married to a tart. In actual fact, most of them marry good women who won't disgrace the family, when in fact their fantasy is to have a swinger who's got everything in abundance. It's the same double standard with opera audiences, for we're all two-faced,' she teased.

Home Truths

Three decades after she had left her childhood home, Kiri returned to Gisborne for her first extended visit at the end of August 1987. On a rain-lashed afternoon she stood in the middle of a muddied car park on Grey Street. The more she surveyed the grim landscape the less she wanted to believe the evidence before her eyes. The sight of the stump of an old pohutakawa tree forced to her accept the unpalatable truth. 'It's terrible. It's gone,' she said, close to tears.

Kiri had begun the walk up from the quayside expecting the old boarding house would still be standing. A passer-by eventually broke the news that the dilapidated building had been demolished five years earlier to provide parking space for the Cosmopolitan Club, the modern building that now dominated the still bustling street. 'Maybe if we'd known . . .' Kiri said, shaking her head, her voice trailing off in the wind as she turned to Des, sheltering under an umbrella with Toni and Tom nearby.

Kiri had come to the East Coast as part of a project being made jointly by the BBC, TVNZ and an independent Canadian company. 'Return Journeys' charted the progress of international celebrities as they revisited their roots. Other films under way traced Omar Sharif's trip back to his boyhood home in Egypt and the racing driver Jackie Stewart's journey to Scotland. Kiri had arrived in Gisborne earlier that day in a light aircraft with Des, Toni and Tom. A television crew, in tow to record her every movement for a documentary film, followed in a second plane close behind.

At first Kiri found the sights and sounds of Poverty Bay as predictable as they were poignant. 'The waves are the same, the trees are the

284

same; I've changed, but my country really hasn't changed,' she said wistfully to the cameras as she walked along the beach. After the shock of Grey Street, however, there were surprises aplenty. A stone's throw from the old house she found a favourite old church had been demolished and replaced by an air-conditioning retailer. Across the road from the house, a disc jockey at a local radio station produced a recording of her singing 'Cara Mia' as a seven year old. 'Oh, God,' she said as she listened to the raw, unschooled voice. 'Not bad though,' she winked at her camera.

Filming had begun two days earlier in Te Kuiti, at the Te Kanawa family marae. Kiri, Des and the children had joined in a traditional hangi, a feast, with Tom's brother Mita and dozens of other distant relatives, in which three pigs, three sheep and forty chickens were baked in the earth. As the cameras rolled, Kiri talked of her affinity to the Te Kanawa tribe, the Maniapoto. 'This is the land of my people, the Ngati Maniapoto,' she told the camera crew. 'To we Maori people, without land, there is no soul, no mana. Here, in the Maniapoto, are my ancestors, my whakapapa.' Kiri admitted she had only visited the marae once before, on the eve of her journey to England in 1966. Yet she felt a strange connection to the place. Her family – and Uncle Mita in particular – reminded her of Tom. 'I miss my father terribly and my uncle reminds me so much of him. The Te Kanawas have strange eyes, a sort of yellowy look,' she said later. 'I keep looking into their eyes and I see my father. That's the bit that gets me.'

Kiri's emotion was apparent when her uncle showed her the family graveyard. 'I can't say I'm comfortable at the thought of death, but at least I've found a place where I want to lie,' she said. 'If you're buried here, you'll never be forgotten.' Her words struck an odd note with her host, considering his battle over Tom's burial site. But despite the awkwardness and unfamiliarity with her father's culture, Kiri's two-day visit appeared to have patched over the decades-old rift between Tom and his family.

Following Maori protocol, it was Des rather than Kiri who gave a farewell speech. 'Kiri has looked forward to this for many a long year and really it's a great sadness that both of us are unable to spend much time here at all,' he said. 'But I think this is going to be an annual trip back and one of the main reasons we'd like to do it is really for

285

our two children, Thomas and Antonia, because we do think it's very, very important for them to know where they come from and for them to know where their real friends are.'

Only men were allowed to make formal speeches at Te Korapatu. Yet Kiri was clearly emotional as she ushered her family towards the waiting helicopter.

The filming schedule was tight. After Te Korapatu and a poignant stop at Tom's Hatepe house, Kiri was due to head from Gisborne to Auckland where she would film sequences at St Mary's and at the Aotea Centre, now under construction. The film's producer, David Baldock, had hoped to slip in and out of Gisborne for two days' filming without creating a major fuss. 'If you think you can do it, David,' Kiri had teased, knowing the impossibility he faced.

Predictably, news of Kiri's visit leaked out and was seized on by the city's elders. A reception was held at the Town Hall where Kiri became the first person to be conferred with the freedom of the city. Kiri pleased the 150 or so gathered dignitaries with a brief speech. 'It's so good to be back,' she smiled. 'I have been asking myself why I ever left. In the future we will be back every year and for longer periods until I never have to go back again,' she said. The comment drew a bemused smile from Des.

The city's Maori community had insisted that Kiri also attend a formal ceremony at the Te Poho-o-Rawiri marae, belonging to the Ngati Porou tribe. Aware that protocol dictated that Kiri be represented by a Maori male, Baldock had flown Uncle Mita down from Te Kuiti to accompany her. Baldock's camera crew were forbidden from accompanying the party on to the marae, however. As they arrived at the meeting ground, Mita sensed what was about to unfold and insisted Kiri and Des break with tradition and keep their shoes on. He sat stony-faced as the ceremony began, as was customary, with a member of the marae outlining the ancestry or whakapapa of its visitor.

Kiri did not recognise the dignified figure of Pahoe Mahuika as he took the stage next to her. As his Maori speech was translated back to her by another elder, Maori broadcaster Bill Kerekere, she was visibly shaken by the story he was telling. At the age of forty-three, Kiri heard for the first time the name of her true father.

Pahoe Mahuika was a cousin of Jack Wawatai. Tired of years of rumour and counter rumour, the elder statesman of the Wawatais' tribe felt the time had come to lift the veil of secrecy surrounding the events of 1944. 'I got her to know who she is, that she's a Ngati Porou, and who her relations are, and we are her relations,' he remembered. 'That's why I spoke out loud and clear. She didn't know Jack was her father.'

Mahuika explained that Kiri's grandfather was a cousin of his own father, a member of Ngati Porou who had lived near Tokomaru Bay. He told the gathering how he had watched Kiri grow up in Grey Street always knowing her origins. He praised the job Tom and Nell had done in raising her, calling them 'lovely people'.

The gathering listened to Mahuika's speech in respectful silence. A shellshocked Kiri looked around her for evidence that the story was true. 'She didn't know what to say, mainly because she wasn't sure. Those around her were claiming kinship, but she didn't quite know whether to confirm it or deny it, because she did not know,' said Bill Kerekere. 'She asked me what I thought. I said, "I can't even say what I think, because I might sway you one way or the other." So I didn't confirm or deny what they were saying.'

The veracity of Mahuika's words was soon strengthened by the reaction of Uncle Mita. During Kiri's early years Mita had been happy to believe that Kiri was Tom's child. 'Uncle Mita always believed she was Tom's true daughter, because he had given her his father's name, Kiri. So did my mother. They really believed that,' said Kay Rowbottom. The younger members of the family were far from convinced, however. 'We didn't know if it was true or not.'

After Kiri's public admission that she was adopted, however, Mita had become increasingly agitated. According to Kay Rowbottom, Mita and his niece Winnie visited Tom in Hatepe shortly before his death in a final attempt to find out the truth. 'They told us they were going down there but they never told us what was said when they got there,' said Kay's husband Bruce. 'As far as I know, they never told anybody.' By 1987, however, Mita seems to have accepted that Kiri was not – by his own exacting standards, at least – a true Te Kanawa.

By nature, Mita was ordinarily as quiet as his brother Tom. Neither his pride nor his sense of justice would allow the claims on Kiri to be left unanswered, however. He rose to his feet, his face flushed with anger and began to speak. 'This old man well into his seventies instantly became a young warrior again,' said David Baldock, who, despite his camera's banishment, had been invited in to witness the ceremony. 'He said, "You say you are the family of Kiri. You say you are the ones who are responsible for Kiri. I say to you, where were you when she was a baby? Where were you when she needed looking after? Was it Ngati Porou who looked after Kiri? No, it was Maniapoto that took in the baby and raised Kiri, and that's why we come into your marae now wearing our shoes.'

The speech, translated for her by Kerekere, brought tears rolling down Kiri's cheeks. Intense as they were, the exchanges cleared the air. 'After that the meeting was fine. It calmed down, because it had been laid out in the open, it had been spoken about,' said Bill Kerekere.

For most of her life Kiri's past had remained fraught with secrets. In public at least she had been steadfast in arguing that she was not interested. 'Why go over that old tragedy,' she would say. She had taken the decision, in large part, to protect Tom from any distress. 'I loved my adoptive parents so much I thought it would be unfair to them.' With Tom no longer alive, however, she seemed ready at last to explore her beginnings in the world.

She would never meet her real father, however. In the wake of his affair with Noeleen Rawstron, Jack Wawatai had broken his pledge to his wife Apo that he would 'never do it again'. After six more children with Apo he had run off with another Pakeha woman, Shirley Blake, with whom he had two more children, Jason and Lynne, his twelfth and thirteenth offspring in all. By the early 1960s Jack was working in a meat factory in the south of Auckland. His time in the city coincided with Kiri's reign as its fastest rising star. He may well have been a member of the late-night audiences at the city's clubs where she sang 'Oh My Beloved Father'. There is, however, no evidence to suggest his and Kiri's paths ever crossed. He certainly never saw Kiri's rise to fame in New Zealand and beyond. On 1 February 1963, he died in hospital after complications set in following an accident at work. He was forty-five years old.

In the years that followed, Kiri's fascination with the man – and the ancestry – she had found late in life would deepen. 'In a way I think those speeches brought Kiri back into Ngati Porou,' said Bill Kerekere.

At the same time, however, Kiri's relations with her adopted family began to break down almost irretrievably. In the two years since Tom's death, Kiri had been embroiled in an increasingly bitter legal row with Nola over Tom's will. The dispute had soured relations with her adoptive sister and her extended family. Tom had made his will shortly after his stroke at Green Lane Hospital on 21 May 1982. The document bequeathed the cabin at Hatepe and everything else he owned to Kiri. No other member of his family was mentioned directly.

The will had devastated Nola, who had spent much of her life looking after both Nell and Tom. She also felt aggrieved at its violation of a verbal agreement she believed she had reached with Tom and Kiri. As far as Nola was concerned it had been accepted that, in return for relinquishing her rights to receiving anything from Tom, she would inherit Kiri's share of Nell's remaining estate. Under the terms of Nell's will, the benefits of her estate would be shared equally between her three children on Tom's death. Kiri, Nola and her brother Stan were now due to inherit the remainder of the $27,500 proceeds from the sale of Mitchell Street that had financed Tom's life during his thirteen years as a widower. 'Everyone knew that Taupo was Kiri's. That was just the way it was. But it was suggested by my grandfather that Kiri give her share of my grandmother's estate to Mum and in return Kiri would end up with all of uncle Tom's estate,' explained Nola's daughter Judy. 'It was something that was always discussed. But the only thing was, Tom made the mistake that he never ever put it into writing. My grandfather really believed he had done the right thing but he had never put it in writing and that was what caused the problem.'

Judy sympathised with her mother's feelings. Nola had spent her life in Kiri's shadow, even though she was Nell's natural daughter. 'She had run round behind my grandmother when everything was going on with Kiri. Heaven and Earth had to be moved if Kiri was coming home and Mum was the one who had to arrange it. If she didn't, well, my grandmother wasn't a happy chappy. When she found out what was in Tom's will that was the final insult, the final kick in the guts for her, because she did not deserve that. She hadn't been left so much as a pot plant or a fishing rod.'

Kiri and Des had steadfastly stuck to the terms of the written will. 'I remember Mum saying that it had been discussed before Tom died and Kiri was there and Kiri knew what was going on. Mum insisted that Kiri knew – Kiri insisted she didn't,' said Judy. When an emotional

Nola had asked her daughter whether she should hire a solicitor, her advice had been typically straightforward. 'I told her it was okay, but only to go for what she was entitled to,' Judy remembered. 'I said that Mum would be a greedy bitch if she went for any more.'

Nola's lawyers' hopes were raised when two tiny pinholes were found in the original copy of the will. They faded again when Tom's solicitor in Auckland, Stuart Comber, swore an affidavit to the effect that – despite the pinholes – there had been no notes or memoranda expanding on his client's final wishes attached to the will.

By 1987, the row had rumbled on for two years. Judy believes attempts to find a resolution had not been helped by the persistence of her mother's solicitor. 'I think he tried to push it too far,' she said.

An increasingly distraught Nola told Kiri she was prepared to go public, regardless of its consequences for the Te Kanawa family's name. Eventually Kiri agreed to visit Nola in Nikau Street in a final attempt to resolve the issue. The atmosphere was glacial. Nola reiterated her position. An infuriated but vulnerable Kiri relented.

When Kiri later called Judy at her home in Mangere she left her niece in no doubt what she felt about her treatment and the threat Nola had made. 'I nearly fell off my chair because I didn't think that Mum had it in her,' Judy said. 'She made it quite clear on the phone that the only reason she had paid it over was that Mum had threatened to go public. I don't think she ever agreed with the principle.'

Judy was distressed at the effect the row had had on both participants. Nola had suffered heart problems at the end of the 1970s and had never fully recovered. 'It wasn't a huge amount. It was a bloody pittance – about nine or ten thousand dollars – just something that Mum could have done with very well and in my opinion Kiri did not need,' said Judy. 'To be fair to her, it wasn't her fault that Tom had failed to make himself understood, but at the end of the day it was such a small amount.'

The row and the manner in which it was settled left relations between Nola and Kiri permanently damaged. Nola's husband Bill never forgave Kiri for the hurt she had caused his wife.

Kiri's feelings were clear when she spent time with Kay Rowbottom, her cousin, after the argument was settled. Kay had heard both sides of the story. She knew Nola had lived a dull, downtrodden life under Nell and needed financial help. Equally, she knew Kiri felt genuine anger at having had a gun put to her head. When her sister's name came up in conversation, she saw Kiri's jaw tightening. 'She didn't swear, but if she had I think she would have called her a bitch,' said Rowbottom. It was soon obvious that Kiri would be happier if the subject moved on to other matters. 'She didn't elaborate, she just sighed.'

Typically Kiri offered no public glimpse of her private pain. She completed 'Return Journeys' in Auckland with a visit to the ailing, ninety-two-year-old Sister Mary Leo at Mount Eden's Mater Hospital. She also joined the judging panel at that year's Mobil Song Quest, held in the city. Her advice to the singers who dreamed of emulating her famous success of twenty-two years earlier was simple. 'The person who goes overseas now has to have something no one else has,' she said. 'You cannot be ordinary over there anymore. You have to be everything.'

Kiri certainly lived by her words. Her career was as varied as it was busy. The frantic half year before her trip to New Zealand had begun with Elijah Moshinsky's postponed *Otello* at Covent Garden. The centennial performance won only muted praise, probably because her onstage relationship with Placido Domingo seemed strained. Four years after the troubled *Manon Lescaut* Kiri could barely bring herself to look Domingo in the eye. 'Kiri Te Kanawa . . . plunges through the love duet almost without glancing in Domingo's direction. (No wonder Otello harbors suspicions of Desdemona's sincerity!),' noted James M. Keller of *Opera News*.

Her own underwhelming reviews confirmed the suspicion that Kiri's operatic career remained in the doldrums. That spring she had sung another of her acknowledged fortes, the Marschallin, in Vienna. Once more, however, she had failed to reach the standards of years gone by.

Backstage she was greeted by two familiar faces, Osvalda and James Robertson. The couple had booked tickets in advance, unaware that Kiri would be singing the role. Kiri was pleased to see them, but while they waited for her to get changed Vera Rosza revealed her concerns for her protégée, however. 'She accepted the role without a stage rehearsal, she did not sing out enough and she got rather bad crits. Vera kept saying that she didn't need to accept it,' recalled Osvalda Robertson. Concerned at her return to the bad old ways of the past,

Rosza asked Robertson whether he could help. 'James had to have a talk with Kiri.'

The reality was that Kiri's career was becoming increasingly dominated by her attempts to find her niche in the rapidly evolving crossover market. Opera was being given a back seat.

The phenomenal success of the operatic version of Leonard Bernstein's *West Side Story*, which Kiri had recorded in New York in 1984 with José Carreras, had sparked a succession of similar projects. That year Kiri had played Eliza Doolittle to Jeremy Irons's Henry Higgins and Warren Mitchell's Alfred Doolittle in a live performance of *My Fair Lady* at the Albert Hall. The recording had gone on to become another popular success. Some ventures were better judged than others, of course. In June she had joined an army of other celebrities for the ill-fated 'It's A Royal Knock-out', a medieval-themed gameshow featuring Prince Edward, the ebullient Sarah Ferguson, Duchess of York and other members of the young Windsors filmed at Alton Towers. The show was a notable landmark for all the wrong reasons and marked the nadir of the young Royals' public image.

There was no question that Kiri's diverse activities were broadening her audience, however. Before arriving in New Zealand she had played a concert tour with the Tokyo Philharmonic in Japan. As the concerts sold out, Kiri's experience at the Takanawa Hotel provided a reservoir of amusing anecdotes for future interviews. 'Very few of my phone calls got through to me. The hotel receptionist thought people were just saying the name of the hotel,' she laughed.

There was little confusion among the expatriate community in Hong Kong weeks later where she was even more rapturously received. For the first time in its history, the colony's City Hall had sold all available tickets without even opening a box office. All 1,480 seats had been sold by post. 'Not even Maria Callas got a full house when she performed here,' said the promoter, John Duffus.

Kiri and Des returned to New York in the autumn of that year. Although America remained the hub of her musical life, here, too, the bloom was leaving the rose. In the three years since arriving in North America, Kiri had criss-crossed the continent, performing recitals in cities from Durham, North Carolina to Clearwater, Florida, Vancouver to Quebec in Canada. She was a familiar face in magazines and on television. She had, at her own admission, made a great deal of money. Yet acceptance within the elitist hierarchy of American musical life had eluded her. The frustrating manner in which she had been denied a *Time* magazine cover summed up the glass ceiling she found herself up against.

Kiri's connections at the Met had provided a powerful entrée into the city's social life. Among those she had impressed during her early years in New York was the formidable, opera-loving managing editor of *Time* magazine, Ray Cave. Kiri had met Cave at a tennis match. Already an admirer, the publisher left convinced she was a phenomenon worthy of a cover in his world-famous magazine. The accolade was a considerable one. In the decade since a cover story on the actress Ali McGraw had revived the fortunes of the previously imperilled movie *Love Story*, Hollywood agents had regarded a *Time* cover as the publicity equivalent of a papal blessing. Its effect on Kiri's profile would be incalculable.

As Cave made preparations, however, he found himself embroiled in a battle with the magazine's powerful music critic, Michael Walsh. The patrician Walsh later recounted the imbroglio in his book, *Who's Afraid of Opera*. Summoned into Cave's office to discuss his boss's latest enthusiasm, the recently appointed Walsh decided to chance his arm. 'I explained politely that while Ms Te Kanawa was certainly a leading soprano of her time, I felt there were other musical personalities more worthy of the honor of being on the cover of *Time*,' he wrote.

His managing editor's journalistic instincts smelled a rattling good story. For all the reviews and profiles written, America had not read a full and frank account of Kiri's adoption, her half-Maori parentage and her remarkable progress from New Zealand to London.

Walsh's objections were musical. 'I countered by observing that I personally was not terribly fond of her singing. That, in my opinion, her lack of a strong musical foundation was a crippling interpretative handicap, and that experience showed that, unable to fall back on the score for sustenance and inspiration, she generally got worse in a role instead of better,' remembered Walsh.

Cave eventually bowed to his critic's judgement. As Walsh left his office, he made his feelings plain nevertheless. 'You'd better be goddamn sure that we're not missing a good story here.' The *Time* cover was never discussed again.

Kiri spent Christmas in Mexico with Des and the children. As 1988 began, she slipped back into the, by now, comfortable corsetry of Fiordiligi in an opulent new production of *Così fan tutte*, being conducted by James Levine at the Met.

Levine's domination of the Met was so absolute that its unofficial motto had become 'What Jimmy wants, Jimmy gets'. He shared Solti's eye for beauty and had assembled a pool of attractive young singers who worshipped him, as his agent put it, 'As if the sun came up with him in the morning.'

Kiri's relationship with Levine was cooler, however. 'Kiri and James have never been soul mates. Kiri saw flaws in him,' said one member of the house's administration.

The part of Despina had been given to one of Levine's acknowledged favourites, a devastatingly beautiful young Korean soprano, Hei-Kyung Hong. Hong was exceptional in many ways, not least because she seemed happy to sacrifice a potentially great international career for the greater good of Levine and the Met.

Rehearsals progressed with no sign of difficulty. On the eve of the opening night, however, Kiri let it be known to Levine that she had a problem. 'Kiri did not believe Hong was up to it. She told Levine "She's not ready",' said one member of the Met company at the time. Despite Levine's protestations, Kiri was insistent. Hours before the curtain went up Hong was replaced.

Kiri had given hints of her willingness to throw her weight around in the past. 'Of course, now and again there are hiccups – particularly when I feel that someone in a cast or in the production team is wasting time,' she said cryptically once. Older, wiser – and, if need be – grander, she knew how to wield her power.

For the first time details of her prima donna tendencies seeped into the public domain. The *New York Times*'s well-connected music writer and aspiring conductor, Will Crutchfield, had soon latched on to the story. A wounded Hong told Crutchfield that she was bewildered by Kiri's actions. 'I don't understand. She's at the top, she sings so beautifully. Why did she do this to me?' she cried.

The stage director, Graziella Sciutti, chimed in saying she was 'disgusted' by the incident.

Hong took the stage for the following performance to a predictably effusive reception. When Kiri returned to the stage on 15 March, however, there was a rather different reaction. Fourteen years after New York had first risen to its feet to acclaim her, Kiri experienced the most humiliating moment of her career. Boos and catcalls filled the vast auditorium.

The scandal naturally became a source of endless gossip within the Lincoln Center where the theories abounded. Some thought Kiri had taken it out on the younger singer after suffering a series of sub-standard notices at the Met that season. Others saw it as her asserting her independence from the Levine circle of singers. There were those, too, who wondered whether Kiri, at forty-four, had seen green rather than red. Hong's combination of beauty and brilliance had already won her comparisons with one of Kiri's heroines, Renata Tebaldi. 'Perhaps in Hong, Kiri saw the singer and the woman she used to be,' said Johanna Fiedler. 'That was something people were saying at the time.'

Kiri herself admitted later that she should have handled the matter more diplomatically. 'I deserved it,' she said. She remained defiant in her criticism of Hong, however. 'In the end I was proved right. The girl was not ready to play the role.'

Most within the Met put the incident down to a more fundamental insecurity. 'The impression was that Kiri had attacked a younger singer without reason. Nobody could understand it. I remember being totally bewildered,' said Johanna Fiedler. 'It made me suspect something else was going on in her life.'

That something may well have been the unhappiness both Kiri and Des were experiencing in America. While her move to New York had been a commercial success, it had been, in many respects, a domestic disaster. Their friends Bob and Sharon Morgan were invited to stay in the late 1980s. To them it was obvious Des and Kiri had been drawn there by the money on offer under the aegis of IMG. 'Going to live in America was a strategic business move,' said Bob Morgan. 'Her advisors told her that she would be easily accepted there and her potential earnings would far outstrip anything she could earn in the UK.' Kiri made no secret of the trade off that had taken place. 'Kiri said she hated living there but that financially they were the best years of her career.'

To Kiri, New York could not have presented a starker contrast to New Zealand and its open spaces. She picked up cold and flu bugs within its overcrowded atmosphere, disliked its aggression, speed – even its traffic. For all its claims to libertarianism, America was also the most conservative country she had lived in yet. Kiri's disillusion-ment with the country reached new depths when she and Des began looking for somewhere to play tennis and golf. 'They wanted to join a country club on Long Island,' recalled Bob Morgan. 'Des was told he could join but Kiri would not be allowed because she was coloured.'

If anything, Des felt even more alienated. He had become accus-tomed to subsuming himself to Kiri's career. 'He never needed any personal attention. He was perfectly happy to be called Mr Te Kanawa,' said Morgan. London and its connections to Australia, its cricket and its rugby, its beer and its broadly similar sense of humour, felt like a rainier extension of home. He also had access to a clique of colonial friends. In New York he had grown to loathe the opera set he found himself socialising with in the absence of real friends. 'He doesn't like to be surrounded by all those poofs and over-the-top people. Her New York friends were all the arty-farty, lesbian type; "Absolutely Fabulous" sort of women that Des would run a mile from.'

The children, and Des, in particular, had always provided Kiri with an anchor to reality. 'Sometimes I come back . . . acting a little grand. He takes it for a couple of days, then knocks me back into shape,' Kiri once said of Des. In this environment, however, Kiri's behaviour could lapse into that of the larger-than-life diva.

Sharon Morgan recalled how, while staying with Kiri in New York, she had been particularly keen to visit an exhibition at the Guggenheim Museum. She kept suggesting the idea but with no response. When her friend finally pressed her, Kiri dismissed the idea with an imperious wave of her hand.

'I give culture,' she told her. 'I don't need to take it in.'

By the time Kiri and Des headed for an extended stay in Australia in August, their minds were all but made up. With the lease on Fairways due for renewal and Antonia and Tom between school terms, they made the decision to relocate their main base back to Surrey.

In August, it was with a sense of relief that they headed for a holiday at Port Douglas, in tropical north Queensland. Kiri returned to Brisbane at the end of the month to sing at the finale of New Zealand Week at the World Expo event. Under Des and IMG's guar-

296

dianship the show had all the makings of an instant success, selling out before tickets were even put up for public sale. The eighteen months of negotiations that had preceded the concert left few in his home town in any doubt that Des had learned a commercial trick or two since his days selling home-grown vegetables to neighbours.

The original plan for Kiri to sing at the New Zealand Expo site had been abandoned amid concerns about crowd safety. As the venue was switched to Brisbane's Performing Arts Centre, however, Kiri's countrymen still entertained hopes of mounting the show themselves and offering some tickets at reduced prices. Their minds soon changed when Des demanded a package approaching $200,000 for his wife. In charge of the New Zealand effort was the distinguished broadcaster and arts administrator Ian Fraser. He remembered, 'Early on it was our intention to take charge of the whole thing but in the end we baulked at Kiri's fee. It was a very high fee and that's not a comment on the appropriateness of it but it is a comment on our ability to swing it.'

Anxious to ensure a commercial success, IMG eventually staged the concert themselves, a move that left some of Fraser's colleagues feeling hijacked. The promoters then sold a large block booking to the New Zealand Expo committee, who were forced to allocate them to foreign diplomats, dignitaries and sponsors.

'We had obligations as a participant that we had to meet,' said another senior member of the New Zealand team. 'We did suggest that they might like to bring young people, and at least some did, so that gave us some satisfaction.'

The rest of the tickets were offered in advance to subscribers to the city's Lyric Opera company at up to $75 each and were oversubscribed by more than 500. Frustrated locals complained they had been left in the cold. On top of everything, Kiri turned in a day's work that left her old New Zealand Opera Company sponsor John Thompson unimpressed. Thompson had been on the board of the Lyric Opera as it negotiated Kiri's appearance. 'She gave a very cool performance and I felt to myself, "Oh, you're not very involved." She gave us a sort of No. 2 treatment.'

Kiri's diary was becoming increasingly dominated by such events, however. The most lucrative were invariably organised by IMG. Mark McCormack was only one of a pack of marketing men re-inventing the modern music industry. The Hungarian Tibor Rudas, in particular, was earning Luciano Pavarotti untold millions by steering him away from the traditional opera houses towards megabuck appearances in venues as diverse as supermarket car parks and tennis courts. Rudas's marketing masterpiece, a concert teaming up the three finest tenors in the world – Pavarotti, Domingo and Carreras – was already forming in his mind.

McCormack, like Rudas, saw that the economics of the opera house were fatally flawed. An elite group of singers were commanding salaries that were simply out of most houses' price range. Without state subsidies and/or the patronage of multi-national sponsors, Covent Garden and the Met, Sydney and L'Opéra simply could not afford to fill its auditoria with $15,000 a night sopranos like Kiri, Jessye Norman and Kathleen Battle, let alone $25,000 a night tenors like Pavarotti and Domingo. IMG's access to the world's corporate coffers had on occasion helped staunch the flow of red ink each of the great houses was now experiencing. At the same time, however, the agency had steered its clients towards the new, infinitely more profitable opportunities now available to them.

To McCormack's mind, at least, customised concerts and crossover recordings did for the world's opera stars what pro-celebrity tournaments and golf ball sponsorship did for members of his sporting elite. Kiri's unique friendship with McCormack left her placed better than most. She and Des would sit in the IMG box at Wimbledon and played golf on many famous fairways with the likes of Greg Norman, another IMG asset. Kiri had also joined McCormack at a celebrity clay pigeon shooting event with the Royal Family. The novice Kiri, typically, had outshot even those Royals who had been wielding twelve-bores while still in short trousers.

The relationship was mutually beneficial. 'The people McCormack is trying to get money out of are precisely the people who would like to meet Kiri in a box at Wimbledon,' said Norman Lebrecht. McCormack repaid Kiri by encouraging his executives to reach creative heights of their own.

IMG's ideas – and the price they demanded for them – were not always met with enthusiasm, of course. Soon after IMG's arrival in Kiri's affairs in the early 1980s, Moffatt Oxenbould, Australian Opera's veteran artistic director, spoke with James Erskine about a one-off concert appearance by Kiri at the Sydney Opera House. 'She wanted to do almost a cabaret-style concert. That was an IMG thing, but what they wanted and what she wanted of the profits, well, there wasn't actually any point in doing it. The ticket price would be prohibitive,' he said. The concert did not come to fruition. Instead Oxenbould walked away from the negotiating table, resigned to the harsh new realities of life at his end of the music business. 'If you have Pavarotti or you have Kiri, then it's not necessarily a great bonanza.'

Even though the discussions remained amicable, the episode led Kiri to say of Australian Opera, 'They have an attitude problem.' Elsewhere, however, there was no shortage of people willing to play according to the rapidly evolving rules of the new era. In 1988, Kiri concluded her Australian trip with what turned out to be the most extraordinary concert of her life.

The idea for a classical concert in the middle of the Australian outback had apparently been dreamt up by two electric company executives on an Adelaide golf course. By now their idea had electrified the imagination of IMG and the whole country. Underwritten by a $1 million sponsorship deal with the executives' two companies, Australian National and Electricity Trust of South Australia and the airline Qantas, Opera in the Outback formed one of the centrepieces of Australia's bicentennial celebrations. Its profits would go to the Royal Flying Doctor Service. Its ambition would have daunted even Beltana's former missionary, the Reverend John Flynn, who founded the forerunner of the famous service, the Australian Inland Mission, at the local church.

A vast 9,000-seater venue and stage had been built on the outskirts of the tiny outpost of Beltana, a virtual ghost town 540kms from Adelaide. The auditorium was set in the Yalkarinha Gorge, a natural amphitheatre surrounded by the steep, ochre-coloured cliffs of the Flinders Ranges.

Kiri arrived by helicopter on the Saturday afternoon before the concert, on 8 September, to a scene straight out of Aborigine dreamtime. Beltana's normal population of seven had been swollen by 10,000 newcomers, most of whom had made the five-hour journey by train overnight from Adelaide. The train linked together all the available sleeping carriages in the country and stretched for a staggering 3.8 kilometres. At the concert site, 100,000 cans of commemorative beer and thousands more bottles of wine and champagne lay in wait. So too did a one thousand strong body of army cooks and doctors, journalists and technicians who had based themselves in a tented village in the wilderness. The technicians were there to broadcast the concert live on Australia's national ABC FM radio station.

'I am more excited than I have been for any other job I have ever done,' Kiri had said in advance. Well-heeled executives from the cities mixed with dust-spattered bushwhackers wearing 'I walked 100kms to hear Kiri' T-shirts.

Only the New Zealand media were understandably peeved. If she was willing to sing in the middle of nowhere, why not sing in the New Zealand Outback? 'They're not making any effort to do things like this in New Zealand,' she said. 'This is inspiring.' Des, as ever, shepherded Kiri through the inquisition. He had soon intervened. 'She's got a big job to do tonight,' he told reporters as he ushered her away.

Kiri had chosen John Hopkins to conduct the Adelaide Symphony Orchestra. At around 5.30 p.m., as the sun sank below the Flinders Ranges, Hopkins warmed his musicians up with an overture from *Die Fledermaus*. A few minutes later, Kiri took centre stage in an eye-catching black gown, with spectacular magenta puffball sleeves and matching sash. The opening aria, 'Mi Tradi' from *Don Giovanni*, betrayed her day in the red dust. As the temperature dropped and she warmed up, however, her voice was at its best, soaring through staples from Puccini to Bernstein, Verdi to Rogers and Hammerstein. Even IMG's financial muscle could not control Mother Nature, however. 'It was wonderfully realised, apart from the moths. We were inundated with them,' recalled John Hopkins with a smile. 'They only come out on one day a year and they chose that day, a very hot day, to do it.'

Hopkins spent much of the concert squashing insects between the sheets of his score. 'The air was full of them and they were quite big. With the lights on stage and the white pages of the score they were attracted to us,' he said. 'I was really quite anxious that one of them didn't fly into Kiri's mouth.'

Moths and all, it was the sort of challenge Kiri loved. She drew on all the skills she had learned over the years to draw the audience out of itself. At one stage she asked the 9,000 to applaud the spectacular

Outback. She joked as she introduced songs and members of the orchestra. Kiri was rewarded with three encores and three standing ovations.

At the end, fireworks filled the night sky. Australia had not seen anything like it since the days of Nellie Melba herself. The Australian media hailed the event as the musical highlight of their bicentennial party.

The rapidly changing world of classical music would not witness a moment like it until Tibor Rudas put Pavarotti, Carreras and Domingo on a stage at the Roman Baths of Caracalla a year and a half later in 1990.

Three decades into her professional career, it was rare for a performance to live up to expectations. Afterwards, Kiri called the concert 'probably the single most exciting experience of my life . . . I loved it for its daring. No one thought it would work, but it did.'

A Gift to the Nation

~~~~~

Their American adventure over, Kiri, Des and the children began the process of settling back into life at Pachesham Park. Tom was enrolled at a local school while Toni was accepted at a private boarding school an hour's drive away. With Fairways bearing the scars of four years' worth of tenants' wear and tear, Des began overseeing a major refurbishment of the house and the grounds. He called in an architect and builder to convert the old coach house above the stables into additional accommodation for guests. The small gardener's cottage on the edge of the estate also received a fresh lick of paint.

By April 1989, as Bob and Sharon Morgan arrived to spend a month in the Surrey countryside, the new look stables were ready to receive their first guests. To his old schoolfriend, at least, Des's relief at being free from New York was palpable. He had found himself isolated and often at a loose end in Oyster Bay Cove. 'Des was happy because he was refurbishing the house, so he had a project, which I think he needs.' The Morgans' holiday provided them with a taste of a lifestyle with which their old friends were all too familiar. There was an almost celebratory atmosphere at Pachesham Park as Kiri and Des hosted a series of high-spirited dinner parties. 'Kiri is a great cook and loves to cook Japanese,' said Morgan. Her drinking habits had been toned down from the Speakeasy days in London. 'She is a very astute drinker, she doesn't get carried away.'

The Morgans briefly became part of Kiri's entourage as she gave a series of one night concerts. They travelled to Scotland and even flitted over to Hong Kong for an appearance. No one appreciated their presence more than Des. As Kiri's manager, he remained committed to joining her for big opening nights and special IMG concerts. Yet it was clear that, for him, the appeal of life on the road had long since disappeared. 'He had got to the stage where he never wanted to travel with Kiri any more,' said Bob Morgan.

With the health and confidence crises of the mid–1980s now behind Kiri, the children had increasingly become Des's priority. 'Des took the job of being a father very seriously. He was always there at weekends for the children. Every Friday night he would drive an hour each way to collect Toni from school. He was the consummate father,' said Morgan.

After eighteen months away from any London stage, Kiri's first step toward re-establishing herself in her adopted homeland came that spring with a three-concert residency at the Barbican, organised by Jasper Parrott. Each night had offered a different element of Kiri's now diverse repertoire – one night Mozart and Strauss, a second a 'Lieder' recital and the third what one writer witheringly described as 'a Boston Pops-style romp through arias and songs from the shows'.

Such sneering was commonplace as, slowly but inexorably, Kiri began to cut down on her commitment to full-blown operatic performances. A year or so earlier she had spoken of attempting Janáček's challenging *Jenůfa*. 'I don't think I'll get round to that now,' she said that year. For the first time she openly admitted that her love affair with opera was waning. 'I don't get the pure satisfaction I used to get out of it.'

Des had by now set up an office at Pachesham Park from where he ran much of Kiri's business interests. He had also increased his personal interest in property development, buying and selling condominiums with partners in America. 'They had a good income and he always wanted to maximise that,' said Morgan.

Yet there was no escaping the fact that it was Kiri who maintained their luxurious lifestyle. She took her responsibilities seriously. 'Kiri has changed a lot. Now she is much more regimented,' said Bob Morgan, who was quietly impressed by her dedication. Kiri's love of sports had now been expanded to tennis and regular gym work. She kept work-out equipment in each of her homes around the world. 'She would jump up and announce, "I am going on to the rebounder now to do my exercises." Kiri is, and has to be, like a finely tuned sportswoman.'

Thanks largely to Des's influence, she had also acquired a more disciplined approach to her financial affairs. 'Financially, Kiri is very switched on and has a very good understanding of where money is coming from,' said Morgan. 'Kiri knew that for she and Des and the kids to live the lifestyle they wanted she would have to gross a certain amount a year and she was prepared to do that. With IMG managing her they were, of course, going to maximise her earnings.'

The price she was paying was high, however. Now well into middle age, Kiri fought a frequent battle with overweight. On a typical day she would avoid breakfast altogether then eat nothing more than a Bath Oliver biscuit before dinner. 'I'm permanently hungry,' she said. 'But I'm sure that if I put on weight now I'm never going to lose it.'

The psychological pain inflicted by her prolonged absences from Thomas and Toni cut even deeper. No matter how much praise friends like Vera Rosza heaped on the job she was doing with the children – 'I'm not sure whether she's better as a mother or a singer,' Rosza said once – Kiri was riddled with the guilt that afflicts so many absentee parents.

In New York, where she was a guest, Barbara Brown could not help feel pity when she accompanied Kiri to the city's toy superstores. Kiri would, almost absent-mindedly, pile hundreds of dollars worth of presents into a shopping trolley. 'They were peace offerings. I was shocked,' Brown said.

Toni and Tom's attitude towards her work only added to her anguish. 'The children hate music, because they know if I'm singing it means separation,' she said at the time. 'Music is a monster that comes into their lives and takes me away.'

The overcompensation was obvious when Kiri was at home. 'Des did everything, but when Kiri was there he and the kids gave her the run of it because they knew she would not be there for very long,' said Bob Morgan.

At times Kiri despaired at the sacrifices she had to make. 'Sometimes I think, "Let me out of this prison!"' she said in an interview at the time.

In the autumn of 1989, the girl who had shown little sign of literary talent at St Joseph's, Avondale or St Mary's proudly displayed the first book bearing her name as author.

The Land of the Long White Cloud, a collection of children's stories based on Maori legends that Kiri had completed earlier that year, was published amid a flurry of publicity. Kiri claimed the idea for the book had been born on the marae at Te Kuiti in 1987. She described how she had spent 'three days at a great gathering of the Te Kanawas . . . While we were there the chiefs told me more myths and legends and now I've put them in the book.' She claimed too that some of the material had been inspired by the Maori folk tales Nell had told her as a child. She could be forgiven for indulging in a little myth-making of her own.

Kiri's relationship with the Maori side of the family remained fraught with difficulties. The Te Kanawas, Uncle Mita in particular, remained deeply sensitive about her connections to his family. It was little wonder Kiri confined her involvement to innocuous fairytales instead.

'She was not close to her family, and we never saw much of her,' said her cousin Kay Rowbottom, who helped administer the Te Kanawas' marae at Te Kuiti with her husband Bruce.

'I don't think that was by design, it was more by circumstance,' Bruce said in Kiri's defence.

Even when she did visit, the circumstances generally made it impossible for her to enjoy the peace of the place. Kiri, unsurprisingly, had been unable to fulfil Des's rather ambitious pledge of annual visits. It was three years after the visit of 1987 before she returned to Te Korapatu. Once more a camera crew was in tow, this time from Britain's leading arts programme, the South Bank Show, who were compiling a major profile of her life and work.

Kiri had hoped to spend some time alone with her uncle Mita. 'I remember Des saying to me when we landed, "Let's go outside and let Kiri just have time with her uncle",' recalled John Hopkins, who accompanied them. Within moments, however, the private meeting was being interrupted by the demands of the camera crew and the ever thickening crowd of locals who had been drawn by the sound of Kiri's helicopter. 'It was rather difficult,' said Hopkins sadly, 'because it was all being organised for the television.'

Kiri's awkwardness around her extended family was plain at times. On one occasion, Kay and Bruce Rowbottom were invited to visit Kiri at a motel in central Auckland where she was staying with Des, Toni and Tom. Bruce made the mistake of bringing along other members of the extended Te Kanawa clan. 'She made it very clear they weren't welcome,' said Bruce. 'Apart from saying hello she pretty much ignored them. It was all a little embarrassing.' He, at least, was willing to give Kiri the benefit of the doubt. 'You get used to your relations when you're a kid and then it's fine because you know what to expect. Kiri didn't have those early years with everyone so she's not familiar with all their ways.'

The fact was that, in her sensibilities at least, Kiri was as European and English as she was Maori and Maniapoto. After half a lifetime in middle-class middle England, she had become attuned to its customs and culture. In comparison, she didn't mind admitting, New Zealand seemed a ruder, cruder society. 'I suppose I am Anglicised,' she said that year. 'I prefer England above all places because there's a decorum, a restraint, a dignity. No animal-type arguing.'

Towards the end of 1989, Des had received a phone call from a lawyer representing the estate of Kura Beale. Kiri's friend and loyal patron had died of pneumonia at a nursing home near the Bay of Islands in August that year. Her death was the second sad loss for Kiri in four months. In May Sister Mary Leo had passed away at the Mount Eden Hospital at the age of ninety-three.

Beale's solicitor confirmed to Kiri that, in return for the friendship she had extended Kura during her life, she had been bequeathed her property at Rawhiti.

Beale's health had deteriorated badly in her final years. She had written the will in 1975, at the time when Kiri first began spending time at Rawhiti, but had kept its contents secret from all but a few confidantes. Among them were two of her most intimate friends, Mabel Kewene and Ngaire Owen, both nurses at the Te Puia Springs Hospital. 'We were very surprised,' remembered Kewene. 'She just said it would be somewhere for Kiri to come back to.'

The loss of the jewel in the family's crown to an outsider was a particular blow to Kura's brother Des. After A.B. Williams's death, Des had taken over the running of the Puketiti estate. He may have expected to take up the reins of Rawhiti as well. 'Kura's family didn't know Kiri and couldn't understand it. Des told me he was devastated,' said Mabel Kewene. 'He used to go up to Rawhiti a lot, but he didn't go near it after he found out about the will.'.

Amid the anger, there was – inevitably – more speculation about Kura and Kiri's real relationship. Kura's frail, confused state during her final days only fanned the rumours further. 'We heard she had told a nurse she was Kiri's mother and had left her not just the house but $2 million as well,' said author Madge Malcolm, an old acquaintance in Russell, repeating a popular, if totally false, rumour that did the rounds at the time.

Kura's godson, Christopher DeLautour, the son of Te Puia Springs's senior doctor, had made frequent trips to his godmother's Bay of Islands home and often heard her talk about her famous friend. 'She just spoke of her as a very good friend,' he remembered. He, like many of the two women's friends, had heard endless speculation about Kiri and Kura's relationship. 'I knew Kura had been a wonderful singer and when I saw a photo of her as a girl of nineteen it looked to me like a replica of Kiri. My godmother even called one of her boxer dogs Kiri, so to me the link was so firm that I wasn't surprised when she gave the house to her.'

Kiri once more maintained a stoic silence. In the years that followed, she claimed to be no wiser than anyone else as to why Kura Beale had bequeathed her her personal slice of paradise. 'She passed it on from one woman to another,' was her best guess. 'It is a woman's place.'

The importance of Rawhiti was in no doubt, however. Kiri arrived back in New Zealand towards the end of 1989 to deal with the formalities of transferring the property to her name. By July of 1990, 'Kura's Place', as she had always referred to it, was legally Kiri's place.

Her acquisition of Rawhiti dealt a blow to the thousands of amateur gardeners who had been allowed to visit and admire the estate's spectacular grounds during Kura's life. While Kiri retained Kura's faithful caretaker and housekeeper, Ron and Rangi Higginson, it was soon plain she intended making wholesale changes. Almost immediately she and Des submitted the first of a series of planning applications to develop the estate. Kiri had plans for a new swimming pool and a boathouse from where she could indulge her love of watersports. Even when Kura Beale was alive Kiri had said Rawhiti was the place where she wanted to die. As its new owner, she began indulging in a little living there first.

On the evening of Sunday, 14 January 1990, Graeme Lindsay helped Kiri, Des and a small group of friends out through a side door at Auckland's Sheraton Hotel and into the most luxurious and spacious car in his fleet, an American Buick stretch limousine. Des had asked for the car specifically because of its blacked-out windows. It was one of his more astute requests. Kiri had arrived in Auckland for a series of three 'Homecoming' concerts to coincide with the one hundred and fiftieth anniversary of the Treaty of Waitangi, the pact between the Maori and the British which marked the formation of modern New Zealand.

Kiri had sung the first concert the previous Tuesday at Hagley Park in Christchurch, where she had encountered another surprise from her past. Two of Jack Wawatai's daughters, 'Bubba' and Mihi, had been placed in a line-up of people introduced to Kiri backstage. A friend of the two women, aware of the connection, led Kiri along the line. 'And this is Bubba and Mihi – your sisters!' she said.

Kiri simply blanched. 'It's so nice to meet one's relations,' she said before moving rapidly on.

In Auckland she was to sing at the Domain, a huge area of parkland on an extinct volcano in the centre of the city. The concerts were free. The Bank of New Zealand, who were rumoured to have paid Kiri around $200,000 for each performance, described the event as 'a gift to the nation in 1990'. As they drove along a pre-arranged route towards the natural amphitheatre, Kiri noticed the long stream of people walking in the same direction along the road. 'As we came over a bridge, still a long way from the park, we started to come across parked cars and crowds of people walking. Kiri asked me, "Where are they going?" I said, "They're going to your concert." She shouted out, "Shit!" It was the first time I had heard her swear. As we got further up the road the language got bluer.'

By the time Kiri and Des arrived at the backstage compound the crowds stretched as far as the eye could see. The first fans had started arriving at 3.30 a.m. that morning. Even the conqueror of Everest, Sir Edmund Hillary, had planted his deckchair four hours before show time. The crowd was clearly far larger than anything Kiri – or indeed New Zealand – had witnessed before. The assembly easily exceeded the 60,000 or so audiences attracted by rock acts like U2, the Rolling Stones and David Bowie. It would be many hours before Auckland police reached their definitive estimate of the crowd. In the end it stood at a staggering 140,000 people – just over one in every twenty members of the entire population of New Zealand.

A few of the crowd almost saw much more of Kiri than they had bargained for. Kiri was due to sing in the evening. As the sun dipped down the floodlights came on and she made her way to the tent where she was changing. 'They had set up a white tent for her as a dressing room behind the stage,' recalled Lindsay. 'When she went in there to get changed they turned on big spotlights and half the crowd could see her silhouetted clear as a bell. Someone had to tear in there and tell her to turn the lights off. She was horrified.'

'Thank you for sparing the time to come,' Kiri teased as she took the stage. Over the following three hours she held the biggest live audience of her life in the palm of her hand.

The concert was conducted once more by John Hopkins. In all his collaborations with Kiri, he had never sensed her so happy on stage. 'It was special, it was a marvellous feeling,' he said. 'Kiri reached out to them and knew she was among people who loved her.'

Kiri left the Domain still on a high. Unable to sleep, she stayed up much of the night listening to radio phone-in programmes, most of which were discussing the concert.

Predictably the praise was far from universal. The deference of the 1960s and 1970s had given way to the scepticism of a new age. Some in New Zealand detected a coolness in their national diva. 'You don't get the feeling she's ever going to clasp us to her bosom and declare us the best thing since computerised tuning forks. It's unlikely the country will ever be speckled with Te Kanawa homes for elderly choir masters,' wrote one leading Auckland journalist Helen Brown in the run-up to the Domain concert.

There were also brickbats for the 'condescension' of the programme at the Domain. 'Dame Kiri is far too much the consummate artist and performer ever to play down to an audience,' wrote the critic Peter Shaw. 'It was a pity that those associated with her Auckland concert did not share her professionalism.'

Kiri, as ever, found the criticism hard to swallow. 'Whenever I visit New Zealand and people want to be critical, well, they can be critical, I accept that. It is part of life. But they really might as well be nice to me while I'm alive as when I'm dead,' she said at the time. 'Don't give me the accolades when I'm either dead or finished. I might as well enjoy them now.'

Ultimately, however, she basked in what she saw as the simple mathematical truth. By the time she had performed the final Home-coming concert to a crowd of 65,000 in Wellington, her tour had attracted a staggering 300,000 people. 'If you count the purists and the audience, the purists lose,' she smiled.

Kiri's affiliations with New Zealand seemed stronger than they had been in years. As she proclaimed in Chicago at the time, 'I feel that by advancing my own personal glory, I have also got New Zealand on my shoulders, which is no bad thing.'

Back in London she had been invited to join a committee overseeing the celebrations to mark the Treaty of Waitangi anniversary. She had become the figurehead for a special New Zealand evening organised at Covent Garden that July.

Kiri arrived at rehearsals for the concert to discover a familiar face waiting for her on stage. In the years since their first Mobil Song Quests, Rodney Macann's life had taken as many turns as Kiri's. He was soon due to be ordained a Baptist minister. As the two old friends settled down to rehearsing a sextet from *Don Giovanni*, Macann discovered that Kiri had not changed at all. She remained, essentially, two people. There were still glimpses of the beguiling young girl with whom he had walked the banks of the Waikato. 'She had a huge amount of nostalgia that night. She turned up wearing the red gown she had worn in that 1963 Mobil Song Quest,' he recalled. 'She was very warm and very generous.' Yet there were glimpses too of the novice prima donna he had first met almost thirty years earlier. 'She veered between being very warm and then suddenly remembering she was this great singer,' said Macann. 'She would start to order me about. It was quite odd. She would forget that I too had had a career and I was a pretty experienced opera singer.' At times she sounded like an echo of Kathleen Battle in *Arabella*. 'We were doing the sextet from *Don Giovanni*, and she told me, "Rodney don't look at me, don't look at me while we're singing!"'

It was as if the carefree Kiri had been trapped inside the body of the insecure, image-conscious Kiri. It was too late to hope she might still escape. 'You have somebody who is basically a very simple person, who is very strong willed, very determined, who, because of this wonderful gift, has the ability to demand almost anything she wants,' said Macann. 'But she hasn't actually got the ability to cope with being a diva.'

Kiri's commitment to New Zealand continued in September as she returned to fulfil her promise to Cath Tizard and declare the Aotea Centre open. She also performed in a special, one-off concert there. Tizard, who had that year left her job as Mayoress of Auckland to become Governor General of New Zealand, had seen her hopes of opening the venue with an opera starring Kiri dashed by construction delays. She had dreaded the ramifications of a cancellation. 'I had to go to them and say, "Look, it isn't going to be ready by then." I knew this would have quite an impact on Kiri's programme and that she had made quite a lot of adjustments to be in Auckland at that time,' she said. 'Des could be tough and he would have been quite justified in being quite put out about that, but in fact he made a special trip to New Zealand to try and look at what was happening and reschedule it so Kiri could be involved,' said Tizard.

Kiri agreed to open the centre in September that year with a gala concert. Tickets for the occasion set a new price record at NZ$115. Yet as far as many connected with the Aotea Centre were concerned, Kiri's appearance was a form of benediction. 'There had always been a feeling that the place couldn't really be regarded as open until Kiri performed in it, and she really did have her name on it to that extent,' said David Stubbs, the project director.

The main event would come in September the following year, when Kiri had agreed to sing Mimì in a revival of the John Copley production of *La Bohème* which she had enjoyed so much in Melbourne in 1989. Kiri and Des's flexibility won her the gratitude of the new Governor General. 'I have nothing but the warmest feelings for them both over the way they understood our difficulties,' said Tizard. Tizard made sure Auckland showed its appreciation. A specially commissioned sculpture of Kiri by the Auckland artist Terry Stringer was unveiled. It was as Kiri stood over the newly revealed sculpture that she was ambushed by Bob Parker, presenter of the New Zealand version of 'This Is Your Life'.

'Thank you, Desmond,' she grimaced as the cameras closed in on her.

Nine years after the British version of the show, Parker had approached Des and her IMG representative in New Zealand, Paul Gleeson, with a view to having Kiri on an updated version of the event. The complex politics of making the programme in New Zealand were soon apparent, however. As a veil of secrecy was thrown over the proceedings, Parker worked closely with two of Kiri's long-terms confidantes, Sally Sloman, and the television personality and occasional journalist Max Cryer. Cryer's friendship with Kiri stretched back to the earliest days. 'Max was always there, at the foot of Nell's bed, feeding her chocolates,' recalled Barbara Brown. 'He was Kiri's friend, and that was important to him and a lot of people.'

With Des pulling the strings back in England, Cryer and Sloman made sure Parker avoided the myriad rivalries and unresolved disputes that surrounded Kiri. 'With some programmes I have made I knew I had turned over every stone and made a couple of decisions that were more for our benefit than for the subject's,' said Parker. 'It wasn't like that with Kiri. I felt I had been led very carefully through a minefield.' It was clear that Kiri's family were the most problematic area. Parker's suggestion that Nola and Stan – Kiri's sister and brother – be invited on, was soon stymied. 'I did ask about Nola and Stan, but I was steered away from them.' In fact Cryer had called Nola Denholm to discover that she was once more seriously ill. Nola advised Cryer not to approach Judy because 'she would not be interested'.

'I think they were worried what I might do,' said Judy.

The delicacy of Kiri's relationships with other members of the musical establishment was equally obvious. 'As for people such as Heather Begg and Malvina Major, I was told it would not be a "positive experience" for Kiri to have them on the show,' said Parker with a mildly bemused smile. There was a telegram from Prince Charles and filmed contributions from Sir Colin Davis and Vera Rosza, a tribute from Sir Harry Secombe to the woman he called Tin Knickers and, at great expense, her ever faithful admirer Bernard Levin, who had flown over from London specially. 'The wonderful thing about you is you demonstrate with every word and every smile that it is not necessary for greatness to be accompanied by vanity and pomposity and selfishness . . . and that's only one of the reasons I love you,' Levin told Kiri, unblushing.

Kiri's Maori connection provided the final – and most challenging – hurdle of all. 'I wanted it to end on a Maori note because that's very much a part of her life, but it was an area in which we once again had to tread carefully because of the different families involved,' he said. 'More people perhaps than Kiri herself would realise would like to claim some sort of ownership of her. Her friends could see that this was going to be a problem.'

Ultimately, however, the dignified figure of Uncle Mita led a procession of fifty members of the extended Te Kanawa clan on to the stage for an emotional choral finale.

If Parker discovered much that he did not know about New Zealand's most famous citizen, nothing was more surprising than the sensitive status of her marriage. Parker had, like most New Zealanders, imagined Kiri and Des to be the perfect pairing. 'During the research it became apparent that it was a marriage which had obviously had its tensions,' said Parker.

To those who knew them well, the signs of disillusionment had been obvious for years. Barbara Brown was among the 'This Is Your Life' contributors to pass the extensive vetting process. 'She was a tough teacher, this one,' Kiri said as she saw her friend appear on stage.

Brown had cause to be grateful to Kiri and Des in the years she had known and worked with them. Her musician daughter had spent several summer holidays at Fairways during her studies in Europe. Kiri had regularly drawn on her professional help and advice. For all her capricious complexities, Kiri remained someone Brown felt intensely proud and protective of. At the same time, few had seen so many shades of Kiri's character. Brown had detected fissures in Kiri's and Des's marriage even in New York when she had visited them in the late 1980s. Kiri had suggested that their current nanny show Brown around the city. The nanny soon revealed that she was on the point of leaving because of the 'high volume rows' between Kiri and Des.

'She had had an absolute gutful. She couldn't get out of there quick enough,' said Brown. Brown had watched Kiri's mood swings for twenty-five years by now. Des's willingness to accommodate them seemed to be on the wane, however.

The previous October, at the time of the Auckland Domain concert, Des had bought a luxurious new apartment in the exclusive waterfront suburb of St Heliers, six miles outside the centre of Auckland. With his usual eye for a bargain, he had snapped up the property on the top floor of a small, modern block overlooking a tennis club and the sea, at the knockdown price of NZ$600,000. Brown, who had been with Des and Kiri on the night of the concert, remembers vividly the moment when Kiri arrived at the apartment. 'When Kiri arrived neighbours were hanging off the balconies peering at her. To her it was disgusting, like Coronation Street, all these common people staring at her,' said Brown.

As Kiri walked in grim-faced, she spun on her heels to face her husband. 'She said, "I will not stay here! Get rid of it, Desmond!"' remembered Brown.

Her old accompanist was taken aback, but Des simply shrugged. 'Des took no notice,' Brown said. 'He was used to that kind of thing.' Nine months later, however, he seemed careworn. 'I noticed a change in Des. He became a bit morose, not nearly as charming as he had been. He wasn't happy.'

Des's frustration could only have been deepened by the grim progress of a new project he had been working on with Kiri. Des had learned much from watching and working with Kiri's IMG representatives. McCormack's methodology, allied to his own business experience, had created a formidable negotiator. Des had become accustomed to demanding – and getting – superstar fees for Kiri in America and Japan. The volumes of money involved created resentment among those who still regarded Kiri as their own property in particular. 'Des is known throughout New Zealand as Mr Greed,' said one senior entertainment industry figure who was involved in negotiating directly with him. 'He never helped her relationship with New Zealand and New Zealanders.' There were signs that it was now he, rather than Kiri, who was overstretching himself.

Inspired by the success other musical stars were enjoying with glossy, self-produced music videos, he had taken on the role of executive producer on a film accompanying Kiri's new crossover album, *Heart to Heart*. The album would be released on Kiwi Pacific Records International, the heir of Reed's old Kiwi label in which Des had bought a forty per cent shareholding in 1989. If her husband's acquisition of an interest in her old label prompted some to imagine that Kiri was looking for young New Zealanders to follow in her footsteps, she quickly made it clear she would be no easy touch. 'If there are New Zealanders of sufficient quality I would use them,' she told one interviewer shortly after the deal was completed. 'I don't know any. There will be no compromise on quality. That should be our new motto.'

For their own project, Des had hired David Baldock, maker of 'Return Journeys', as writer and producer of the documentary, and had flown in a team of top recording producers and engineers from EMI in London. His hopes of condensing recording of the album and the accompanying film into a single week of intense activity around the opening of the Aotea Centre were soon being frustrated, however.

Kiri was recording the album with a New Zealand jazz singer, Malcolm McNeill. Together they were due to sing such standards as the Beatles' 'Long and Winding Road' and Bette Midler's 'The Rose'. While Kiri preferred singing in the morning, McNeill, more used to late night performances, didn't warm up until the afternoon. Any hope of them creating the kind of chemistry essential for crooning loving ballads to each other rapidly evaporated, and they ended up singing their parts alone.

As delay followed delay, Baldock's cameraman was soon capturing images of a browbeaten Des walking around the studio no doubt ruing the title he had chosen for the documentary: 'The Magic of Two'. As the project fell further and further behind schedule, EMI's executive Simon Woods was soon expressing his opinion to camera. 'I've said all along that it was a mistake to try and rush this album. Again we've been trying to make something that it's not really possible to make on this sort of time scale.'

Kiri tried to put a brave face on proceedings, dismissing the problems as creative tension. 'Maybe this is not the ideal situation to work, but it certainly puts everyone on their mettle. A few tempers flying and a few aggravated people, but that's the way it is and that's the buzz that's necessary, and I think we've done a pretty good job,' she reassured the cameras.

Eventually even Des had to concede a costly defeat. 'Maybe we were a little bit optimistic in thinking we could achieve as much as we hoped to achieve,' he said, riding the lift up to the Royal Suite he shared with Kiri at the Pan Pacific Hotel. Eventually EMI insisted that the album's proposed release date of Christmas 1990 be put back a year. Recording of the final backing tracks was delayed until January in London at the Abbey Road studios.

The unhappiness of the experience was symbolised in the photo shoot for the album's cover. With the cameras watching once more,

McNeill and Kiri had posed playfully. When the photographer suggested McNeill move behind Kiri for a more intimate embrace, the warmth disappeared. 'Don't hold me across my breasts,' she grimaced.

Kiri's edginess was perfectly understandable given the intensity of her schedule and the additional work she was doing to learn perhaps her most demanding operatic role to date. For what she called 'a year of hell' she had been preparing to sing the role of the Countess in Richard Strauss's *Capriccio*, which was being produced jointly by the Royal Opera in London and the San Francisco Opera. Days after recording on the *Heart to Heart* album came to a close, she was expected at rehearsals in San Francisco.

Kiri's plaintive comments to Jane Phare of the *New Zealand Herald* on the eve of her departure for America showed that, just a couple of years after conquering her most serious health crisis, she was dangerously close to the edge yet again. 'I have just had five weeks' holiday in France, Africa and on safari in Kenya and I feel as though I haven't. It's been non-stop. I start work tomorrow in rehearsals but my brain is not prepared because I don't have any space. I haven't got any time.'

Even Des's rigid control of life appeared to be faltering. 'There are a lot of people around who tend to think their presence is far more important than anything else and it really is not,' said Kiri. 'A lot of people feel like they own a part of me.'

Kiri had, by now, begun to intimate strongly that her career was heading towards its twilight and that she was weighing up when to retire. Asked what she would do if she lost her voice, Kiri just laughed. 'It would be a Godsend, it really would. I wouldn't have to sing anymore. I wouldn't have to make that decision.'

She conceded she was probably at the peak of her vocal powers. 'It won't get any better. It's like a flower and a flower grows and dies. In ten years' time I could be voiceless – in fact I'm sure I will be,' she told the current affairs magazine *North & South* in an interview to coincide with her 'Homecoming' concerts. 'My time is running out. I'm looking at the back end of my career rather than the front.'

Kiri knew the judgement she would soon be faced with was a fine one. 'I don't want to get to the stage where people say, "She used to be great, she used to be wonderful. What a shame she's still singing. Why doesn't she give up?",' she said during her visit to New Zealand that year. It was clear that she regarded *Capriccio* as, perhaps, her operatic swansong.

For some time Kiri had been telling friends within the opera world that she wanted to take on one final new role. On the face of it, Strauss's opera seemed an unlikely choice. Based around an intellectual debate between a Parisian poet and a musician over the relative merits of their respective arts, even the composer himself called it 'a delicacy for cultural epicures'. He did not recommend its performance to 'the general public'.

The London version, to be staged in January of the following year, was being conducted by her old Covent Garden friend Jeffrey Tate; the San Francisco version by the dashing young English conductor Stephen Barlow. Kiri's decision to take on the role of the Countess Madeleine was heavily influenced by Tate, who was convinced that it represented the logical conclusion of her love affair with Strauss.

'This is the last of the three great roles that are written for her voice. The first one being the Marschallin, then Arabella and Madeleine,' he told Melvyn Bragg for the 'South Bank Show'. 'He wrote it at the end of his life which meant it was a sort of summation of all that he knew about voices and particularly the female voice, so you have to come with a lot of background knowledge. I think that's why she found it important. It was going to be a great test for her, because she was going to have to bring all her experience to bear. You can't sing it as a beginner.'

A beginner Kiri became once more, however. She started the painful process of learning the role in London, once more working with Vera Rosza and Jean Mallandaine as she built the foundation stones of the piece. As the 'South Bank Show' cameras filmed her in the Pan Pacific Hotel in Auckland, she had been pacing the Royal Suite, frantically hitting play, stop and rewind on her personal stereo as she flicked backwards and forwards through the tapes Rosza and Mallandaine had prepared for her. Yet as she flew to San Francisco, Kiri knew the role was far from fixed in her mind. In California, Stephen Barlow was soon encountering the eleventh hour anxiety familiar to many of Kiri's conductors.

A child prodigy, Barlow had been a Cambridge organ scholar before studying conducting at London's Guildhall School of Music. His reputation was made within Britain's regional opera houses, Scottish Opera and Opera North, before he progressed to ENO and Glyndebourne. It had been at Glyndebourne that Barlow had begun a whirlwind love affair with the multi-talented actress, writer and presenter Joanna Lumley. After divorcing his first wife, Barlow married Lumley in 1986. At forty, she was eight years his senior. The Byronic Barlow, all flowing locks and stubble, and Lumley, blonde, leggy and lissom, cut one of the more glamorous couples in the musical world.

Once more, Kiri cut the learning process painfully fine, only conquering the part in the final forty-eight hours before opening. 'For two days I just swamped myself and finally it went in,' she admitted. 'There's a point when you have either to commit suicide or decide to face the world again. I thought I was going to go crazy because part of my head was so sore.'

Barlow's calming influence smoothed over the troubled waters and paved the way for a well-received opening night, which Des, now innured to the drama around him and still no opera fan at heart, spent drinking tea in his wife's dressing room. Out in the auditorium, Kiri knew she had found a conductor who understood her better than any she had encountered in recent years. For both it would mark the beginning of a fruitful if, at times, emotionally-charged working relationship.

Pop Goes the Diva

As if Kiri's swansong in a new role was not intriguing enough, *Capriccio*'s high profile on both sides of the Atlantic had been lifted even more by the involvement of the Italian designer Gianni Versace. Fashion's greatest showman had created a collection of forty flamboyant outfits for the opera's principal players, four of which had been made specifically for Kiri. Versace's gift for self-publicity had taken him from the poverty of Calabria to an Imperial Roman-style villa in Milan. In the days leading up to the performance, he milked every column inch, with Kiri playing along willingly. 'Do you realise how much those dresses cost?' she smiled as she posed for photographs.

On the night of 8 January 1991, she stood alone on the stage of Covent Garden, resplendent in the most extravagant of the Italian's pieces. As a thousand laser-fine spotlights reflected off the figure-enhancing dress and its whirls of translucent beading, Kiri's Countess Madeleine glowed with an unearthly beauty. The reviews were less dazzling, however. The following morning's notices once more made Kiri wonder whether her operatic career really was worth the effort. As a result of all the pre-performance posturing the London media had treated *Capriccio* as much as a catwalk event as a night of grand opera. The sheer gaudiness of Versace's creations induced migraines among many observers. 'Gruesomely overdressed,' wrote Max Loppert in the *Financial Times*.

Jeffrey Tate's leadership and Kiri's performance found few friends in the critics' circle either. *The Times*'s Richard Morrison thought her 'a lovely pampered creature'. Yet her London debut was damned by almost everyone else. The *Daily Telegraph*'s Robert Henderson thought she lacked 'the regal hauteur to carry off the opulent dress designed for her in the closing scene'. In addition, Loppert delivered the most painful truth. 'She has learned the words and makes some lovely sounds at the top of the stave, as well as some worryingly wispy ones lower down, while leaving a complete hole at the centre of the production,' he wrote. His conclusion summed up the disappointment many felt. 'It seems years since Dame Kiri strode the stage with any real theatrical animation.'

It was, perhaps, symbolic then that, as Covent Garden pored over the press clippings, Kiri herself spent the following morning at the Abbey Road studios in north London. Des had booked the studios immortalised by the Beatles to finish off work on the problematic *Heart to Heart* album with Malcolm McNeill. Kiri clamped the headphones on, slipped into her 'down in the boots' voice, and expunged all memory of *Capriccio*. Since her relationship with opera was becoming an increasingly loveless one, she would look for affection elsewhere.

Kiri's move away from the traditional role of the diva was, by now, obvious even to those with only the remotest interest in opera. That Easter, as the two-hour 'South Bank Show' film was finally aired, she fantasised over the sort of career she might have had. 'I would love to be Tina Turner. I envy her totally with all that crazy hair and that voice,' she told Melvyn Bragg. 'I find the opera world staid and boring. Pop music is just so liberating. All I would need to do is lose thirty pounds, then dress up in those mesh stockings and leather. That would be nice.'

Kiri's confession drew a predictable response from the establishment. 'I am absolutely staggered,' sniffed Margaret Rand, editor of *Opera Now* magazine. Away from the operatic world, however, Kiri's confessions were seized on with glee. One London magazine persuaded Kiri to take part in a daring photo session in which she posed *à la* Turner in leathers and a bustier while sitting astride a Harley Davidson motorbike. Meanwhile, London television executives began sounding out Turner for a possible joint concert. While neither it, nor Kiri's other fantasy – a collaboration with Mick Jagger and the Rolling Stones – came to pass, she spent the following year forming a succession of no less likely partnerships.

Kiri's career was being guided by a diverse – and at times divergent – group of advisors. While Harrison Parrott continued to handle her classical career and IMG oversaw her special projects, Des seemed willing to consider approaches from the most unlikely sources. Through his friend Carl Davis, Kiri was approached to work with Paul McCartney on his debut as a classical composer, the *Liverpool Oratorio*. She was also invited to appear alongside Elton John and the rap singer MC Hammer in a concert in aid of Kurdish refugees. She also provided a singing voice for actress Glenn Close as she played the part of a Swedish diva in David Puttnam's movie *Meeting Venus*.

In the summer she once more entered the recording studio, this time to record the theme music for that year's Rugby World Cup. By now the New Zealand All Blacks' most visible supporter, Kiri recorded 'World In Union', a lyricised version of Holst's 'Jupiter' movement from his suite *The Planets*.

Her activities were no longer confined to mere music-making. With Des, she also joined a Time Warner-led consortium bidding to launch Britain's first radio station devoted to classical music, Classic FM.

Kiri, naturally, defended her right to diversify. 'Before, I had to do it because it was the done thing,' she said of her music that summer. 'Now I'm doing it for myself. I'm more relaxed. I don't really care what people think.'

Opera still remained an important part of her life, of course, but in the aftermath of *Capriccio*, she stuck to the tried and tested. After a series of concerts in Spain, then Amsterdam and Brussels, she returned to America and two old favourites: the Countess in *Figaro* at the Met, and Desdemona in *Otello* with Pavarotti and the Chicago Symphony Orchestra in Chicago. She played safe too as, in August, she returned to New Zealand for her first full opera since *Carmen* in 1969. After a six-week holiday, she headed for St Heliers Bay in Auckland, and rehearsals for a new Mimì in *La Bohème*.

Kiri had been determined that her return to the New Zealand operatic stage be a memorable one. She had insisted on a revival of the Victoria State Opera production of *La Bohème*, in which she had enjoyed herself in Melbourne in 1989. While John Hopkins had been engaged to conduct the Auckland Philharmonia, Kiri had hand-picked a cast that included the New Zealanders Wendy Dixon, Patrick Power, Mark Pedrotti and Roger Wilson. She also insisted on bringing over the youthful VSO producer Stephen Dee from Australia.

Kiri's participation did not come cheap, of course. Des had negotiated a fee of $20,000 a night – an astronomical sum in a country where Opera New Zealand's highest previous paycheque had been $6,000. He had also masterminded a complex deal splitting the profits four ways between the VSO, IMG, the Aotea Centre and Kiri. With car makers Honda injecting hefty sponsorship and a profitable television deal,the season was an unprecedented money spinner in New Zealand terms.

This time, at least, no one begrudged Kiri her superstar salary. She seemed happy to be home. She also seemed willing to work herself into the ground for her fee.

The Aotea Centre's opening year had not been without its problems, with its acoustics in particular. As a multi-purpose venue where four out of five shows would use amplification, the acoustics were designed to deaden the reverberation that 'unplugged' singers, like Kiri in opera, rely upon for projection. An expensive electronic reverberation system, installed at massive expense to help opera singers, had encountered teething problems and had never been used. As a result, without amplification, it required an almost superhuman voice to reach all the 2,200 people in the audience. Given her high profile identification with the Centre, Kiri was as keen as anyone for it to be seen as a success.

'I can remember after one performance where it had been fairly hard work even for her because it was a little on the dead side without the electronics, she said, "Well, it's not hopeless." The tone that she used was important, because rather than damning with faint praise she was actually supporting the theatre,' said David Stubbs.

Acoustics aside, as she reacquainted herself with Mimì and the production, she seemed more relaxed and happy than anyone had seen her for years. She and Des held a soirée for principal cast and production members in their suite at the Pan Pacific Hotel. 'We were told to treat Kiri like everybody else, that she would leave her title at the door, which is exactly what she did,' said Keith Foote, the Aotea Centre's stage manager at the time.

Patrick Power, who played Kiri's lover Rodolfo, was equally charmed. 'I once worked with a Mimì who was so awful the whole cast called her Moomoo, she was such a cow,' he said. 'Some of the Eastern European sopranos are so grand and cold that you feel too overawed by their presence to even tentatively put your hand on their arm – and this at the most passionate of moments. It's just not like

322

this with Kiri. She is such a warm and friendly person that you are never overawed by her grandness. She is a lot of fun.'

Kiri's most divaesque moment was reserved for a hapless photographer who had begun taking shots of her during a rehearsal. 'You will not take any pictures of me singing – do you understand?' she exploded from the stage. 'I mean it!'

'Photographers always want to get me singing at full stretch,' she explained later. 'It just doesn't look good.'

Throughout the rest of the production, however, she left Des to play the bad cop. 'Des was the single most important person around. She absolutely relied on him,' said John McKay, the opera's production director. To McKay, at least, it seemed the perfect working partnership. While Kiri concentrated on her music, Des attended production meetings, worried about everything from the colour of Kiri's shoes to the brand of camomile tea laid on in her dressing room. 'Des could be the demanding person. He could go round saying, "I want this and I want that", and Kiri could be the pleasant diva doing her role.'

Des acted in the knowledge that, after twenty-five years together, he knew Kiri's needs better than anyone. 'He was very opinionated. He never hesitated to say what he thought. He was also apt to storm people's offices insisting on this or that,' said McKay.

Producer Stephen Dee remembers his first glimpse of Des in action more bluntly. 'He was an arsehole.'

Tickets for Kiri's performances had sold out in two hours in June. Her Mimì was greeted with almost universal praise.

In July Kiri headed back to Liverpool for McCartney's *Oratorio*. The concert took place at the city's famous Anglican Cathedral. It won few friends. 'Embarrassing,' the *Guardian* called its blend of sentimentality and seriousness.

At least the successes she was achieving elsewhere helped ease the disappointment. That autumn in London Kiri and Des heard the news that their consortium had won their radio franchise. Soon, Classic FM was being launched to almost immediate profitability. Even better, her 'World In Union' single was released to coincide with the beginning of the Rugby World Cup at Twickenham that October. It provided Kiri with her biggest-selling recording ever and, in New Zealand, her first No. 1 in the pop singles charts.

*　　*　　*

Around lunchtime on Saturday, 18 July 1992, the first of 200 or so guests began arriving at the gates of Pachesham Park. Each of them was dressed in fancy dress, clutching a cuddly toy and an invitation reading:

KIRI'S KANGAROO CLUB
AUSSIE RULES
50TH BIRTHDAY BASH
FOR
DESSIE
THE BUTCH KANGAROO

The arrivals were following the carefully laid out instructions Kiri had sent them weeks earlier. The invitations, along with a request that they 'don't tell Des', had explained that cars should be left in a specially ringed off car park from where guests would be ferried up to the house by a mini-bus also laid on specially for the occasion.

Friends from Des's and Kiri's deep and distant past had made the journey to Surrey. They included Bob Sell, Kiri's old employer from her Colony Club days. He had bumped into her and Des at the Maestranza Theatre in Seville a week or so earlier as Kiri sang at the Expo '92 festival with Franz Paul Decker and the New Zealand Symphony Orchestra. Sell had been there with Kiri's old New Zealand acolyte Max Cryer.

Sell, like everyone else, was amazed at the effort Kiri had put into springing her surprise on Des. She had transformed Fairways into an Australian themed village fête for the day.

'She said she had sent Des away to play golf in Scotland while she got the place ready,' said Sell. 'She had spent thousands on green and yellow balloons and a tent outside. There were bales of hay everywhere and plastic crocodiles in the lake.'

Kiri's old Covent Garden and Opera Centre friend Teresa Cahill was equally bowled over. 'She spent a fortune on a didgeridoo player, a band and a stripper who was dressed as a policewoman. She really went to town. At the time, I wondered, "Gosh, Des, if Kiri's done this for you, what the hell are you going to do for her?",' she said.

Guests were asked to come in Australian-themed fancy dress outfits.

In lieu of presents, they were also asked to bring cuddly toys in aid of a local cancer charity. A mountain of around 2,000 toys had piled up in a room set aside for them.

Kiri seemed in her element overseeing events. She took to the microphone to announce the winner of the best fancy dress prize, then introduced Max Cryer to recite a suitably risqué poem he had written about 'the butch kangaroo'.

A few weeks short of their twenty-fifth wedding anniversary, Kiri and Des appeared as indivisible as ever. 'If you'd have gone to that birthday party you'd have sworn that this was the ideal couple,' said Bob Sell.

Kiri had used the opportunity to catch up on old friends. Teresa Cahill and her partner, the composer Robert Saxton, did not even have Kiri's up-to-date address. They too saw a couple who had survived all that had been thrown at them.

'I feel sorry for anyone who's married to a superstar. They inevitably get treated like Mr Te Kanawa. Des was free of that. He had a very strong personality,' said Cahill. 'You need a certain strength to cope with the people who think, "Oh, he's only the husband." You need to have a very compatible relationship to weather the storm, and I thought they had it. She's actually managed very well and I think Des helped a lot. There are so many unscrupulous people who want to make anything out of you. He wouldn't take any old bullshit. He carved through all the problems.'

Only one subject seemed to threaten their long-term future. For all her public statements about her career being at its peak, Kiri had shown few signs of winding down. Jasper Parrott had made bookings as far ahead as 1997. If anything, Kiri regarded retirement as something of a running joke. As often as she talked about it in principle, she could never face up to it seriously. During the party she talked to her old employer Bob Sell. 'She said to me, "I'm going to quit at fifty, Bob. I want to enjoy my kids, and I want to enjoy my money." But of course she hasn't.'

Des, on the other hand, had already begun to look forward to quieter times. 'I don't think he wanted her to carry on working,' said Teresa Cahill. Des was soon contemplating the place where he would while away his retirement years.

Kiri climaxed the afternoon by unveiling a birthday cake, a model of Des's fiftieth birthday present, a rambling home in the Dordogne in southern France. 'The cake even showed the rubble from the alterations,' said Bob Sell.

Kiri's response to the snootier of her critics generally consisted of two fingers and two lines in particular. 'If you count the purists and the audience, the purists lose,' went the one she had first used back in 1990. 'When I'm feeling unloved and unpopular I look at my record sales,' went the other. Not long after Des's birthday, as she sat with a journalist in the lobby of the five-star Vier Jahrzeiten hotel in Hamburg, Kiri offered a rare glimpse of her real feelings towards some of those who inhabited the profession she now called a 'zoo'.

'You're being shot down by so many arrows so much of the time it's hard to keep up,' she said. 'You've got to be very self-contained in order to ride the storms, because there are all sorts of crazy things going on. I know there are many people who try and find a way of pulling me down. Well, you see, I don't need them. That's the problem. I don't need anybody, except my family, and it drives them crazy to think they can't get to me. I can walk away from it any time I want and it doesn't matter what they say. They can slash at me but they can't take away what I have – they can't physically remove it. They like people to think they can really pull me down. It's a hate factor, an envy, if you like.'

Kiri was not specific about the target of her tirade, but there were clues. 'You find that so many people have attached themselves to the circus, paid or unpaid, that I don't want any part of it. I like to be alone and unencumbered. A lot of top singers are different. They have someone to make the cup of tea, another to get the newspaper, a third to open the door. After a while these stars can't do without it. For me, my Australian husband and our children come first, and they are the only ones who get close to me. If anyone's going to make the tea, my daughter will. I don't need all the glamour.'

In many respects, Kiri's popularity was now at its apex. On 12 September, draped in a sequinned dress in the colours of the New Zealand flag, she led the singing of 'Rule Britannia' at the Last Night of the Proms. Later that month she even drew Princess Diana to Covent Garden. The Princess's tastes generally ran no deeper than Dire Straits. Her public appearance at a gala performance of *Otello* with Domingo and Solti at Covent Garden was one of the last she made at Prince Charles's side.

A memorable few months ended in October when she was named Artist of the Year at the Gramophone Awards at London's Dorchester Hotel. Sir David Attenborough presented her with the prize. She shared the headlines with her old mentor Solti, who collected a Lifetime Achievement award at the same time.

Kiri's ever-broadening appeal pleased no one more than Mark McCormack. Yet it was her massively lucrative marriage with IMG that was drawing down many of the arrows Kiri had spoken of that year.

The odd couple had remained close personal friends, despite what Kiri saw as the IMG chief's frequent philistinism. McCormack had upset Kiri after she sang at a Nobel concert with Georg Solti in Oslo that year. He had been baffled by her anguish at having missed a note in a Mozart aria. 'How many people in the hall knew you missed?' he had asked.

'Well, Solti knew, because he looked at me,' she said tearfully. 'And I knew. But very few others.'

As far as McCormack was concerned her mishit note was no more a matter for agonising over than a fluffed putt. 'In an objective thing like golf, you finish a round with sixty-five and everybody sees it,' McCormack remembered telling the singer when he recounted their meeting to Norman Lebrecht in a *Daily Telegraph* interview. 'When you play a tennis match and you have lost, everyone sees that. But in singing, how the heck do you know? More often than not, Kiri, you're the only one who knows, on a scale of one hundred, whether you have sung a ninety-five, or an eighty-two or a seventy-one.'

Far more worrying, however, was the occasional rumbling that now greeted some of her IMG-organised events. An open-air concert at a vineyard in Mitchelton, near Melbourne, in 1990, had drawn the first serious hints of disillusionment. The best seats for the concert had been priced at an extravagant A$400. The suspicion that such musical mega-events were now grotesquely over-priced was only strengthened by the organisers' attitude when a torrential rainstorm turned the arena into a mud bath. Kiri's arrival had been delayed by an hour because of gales which had grounded her helicopter. As the thousand-strong audience began booing and slow-handclapping, an MC arrived on stage to suggest that the delay was an ideal opportunity to buy more Kiri souvenirs. Many later said they had considered asking for their money back.

Even worse, a stadium concert planned for Adelaide in February 1993 had been cancelled after only 2,000 tickets, priced between A$77 and A$47 were sold in two months. 'You could call it a spectacular lack of interest,' one organiser admitted. The underwhelming response would be repeated less than a year later when a non-IMG concert planned for Leeds in England was cancelled due to poor ticket sales.

The impression that Kiri was becoming music's most visible diva-for-hire was underlined early in 1993. Kiri had come a long way since the days when, as a teenager, a jingle she recorded for an Auckland crockery firm was rejected because the firm's ad men decided it 'wouldn't sell'. Three decades later it emerged that she had been paid an estimated A$200,000 to sing at Melbourne's State Theatre in front of 2,000 guests hand-picked by the car company Nissan. The reason for the celebration was the launch of the Japanese manufacturer's new A$130,000 luxury car – the Infiniti. Kiri's audience was a select gathering of executives, car dealers and potential car buyers.

Kiri gave her all in the concert. 'She really worked so hard to reach that audience because they were obviously not a classical music audience,' recalled John Hopkins, who conducted the performance. 'Her eyes were moving across the audience, embracing them all and making them all feel part of a very important occasion. It was quite extraordinary. I just thought, "Well, you are the ace of communicators to people who may not want to be communicated to. You manage to reach them."'

She needed those communication skills afterwards as she faced a barrage of questions over the concert. 'Even rugby matches and football matches are now including classical music, so I think that the people who are presenting this product also appreciate classical music,' she said, mounting a stout defence.

Her opinion was that in the modern musical world pretty much anything was now acceptable. 'If you were trying to sell peanut butter I suppose you would not necessarily use one of my arias, but it might be put in a different sort of mould if you did,' she said when asked whether there were any other products her voice might be suited to selling.

Despite these criticisms, her appeal remained immense. Another outdoor concert at a natural amphitheatre at the Mission Vineyard in Hawkes Bay, New Zealand had pleased more than 15,000 paying customers. Then in early September Kiri's first open-air concert in England, in the setting of the Regency Royal Crescent in Bath, drew another sell-out 12,000 audience.

Yet the sense that Kiri's career was losing its focus was confirmed by the public discord she and McCormack displayed soon afterwards. In the interview with Norman Lebrecht in the *Daily Telegraph*, McCormack had boasted of the benefits he had brought Kiri's career.

'We had Kiri do a concert in the Outback. We had her singing in vineyards in Victoria. We had concerts in Tokyo,' he said. 'We got sponsors for these things, we got public acceptance. We made Kiri more money than she'd ever made before, and made money for ourselves as well.'

Kiri's aversion to talking publicly about her wealth had been inherited from Nell. 'She told me never to talk about money.' Well aware, as she had protested in 1977, that publicising her earnings might make colleagues 'unhappy', she dashed off a letter to Lebrecht's editor complaining that it was 'completely inappropriate' to talk about her art in such a materialistic manner. She should, perhaps, have been addressing the letter to McCormack.

As 1993 drew to a close, Kiri, Des and the children spent Christmas together at Pachesham Park. The celebrations conformed to what was, by now, a well-oiled routine. As usual the present opening began in the early hours of Christmas morning after a midnight Mass nearby. Even the cats, Flinty and Shady, had been left neatly-wrapped parcels under the tree.

Christmas Day itself began late in the morning. Kiri often joked it was the only day of the year she felt able to enjoy a lie in. By early afternoon, however, she was hard at work in the kitchen, a glass of champagne on the go and a favourite piece of music filling the air.

Amid the grisly greyness of the English winter, Kiri and Des liked to remind themselves of home with a 'sunny' Christmas meal. A whole fresh salmon, served with boiled potatoes and salad followed by Kiri's speciality pecan pie for pudding had become the traditional centrepiece of their Christmas Day. The family sat down together midway through the afternoon. As they did so, like families the world over, they took stock of the year gone and the year to come.

Toni could feel particularly proud of herself. That summer she had justified the decision to complete her education in England by getting six grades As, one grade B and two Cs in her GCSE exams. Like her father, her strength lay in the sciences and she had already started talking of becoming a marine biologist. At Des's suggestion she had agreed to continue her studies at Brisbane Girls Grammar School, the sister to his alma mater, Brisbane Boys. He had enrolled her for what he called 'a finishing year' to be completed the following November.

If Toni was closer to her father, Tom was his mother's boy. Like her, and his grandfather before him, he shone on the sports fields. He had an eye for tennis, golf and rugby. 'We're waiting for lightning to strike,' Kiri liked to say, seemingly wishing a career as a professional sportsman for her son.

Kiri's career and the children aside, Des's major interest centred on a vineyard he had his eyes on in France. He had long harboured an ambition to begin producing his own wine. He had already come up with the idea for the label: Château Des Park.

The fruits of Kiri's labours that year were visible on television over the holiday season. On Christmas Eve she appeared in *The Sorceress*, a fantasy based around seven Handel arias with Christopher Hogwood, the Academy of Ancient Music, the Scapino Ballet and Opera Atelier. The following Tuesday a recording of her San Francisco *Capriccio* was broadcast, also on the BBC. As she shared Christmas with her family, no one had more cause to look ahead than Kiri. The string of celebratory events to mark her fiftieth birthday was already dominating her thoughts. Kiri had admitted that she viewed her impending birthday with deeply mixed feelings. 'Fifty is nifty,' she joked in the interviews she had given to coincide with her busy Christmas. In reality she was approaching the landmark with a thinly disguised panic. 'You know, the weirdest thing of all is that, in my head, I still feel like I am fifteen,' she told Jan Moir of the *Observer*. 'How can I be fifty? Life suddenly seems so much shorter. It's a tough one and I still have to come to terms with it.'

At 3 p.m. that Christmas afternoon Kiri watched the traditional Queen's Speech on television. For the Royal Family, too, it had been a positive year. The events of the previous twelve months, and the

330

Queen's *annus horribilis*, had been put behind them. Kiri's, however, lay directly ahead of her. She would not refer to it in Latin. Instead she would simply call it 'the worst year of my life'.

Paradise Lost

In the English spring of 1994, the world seemed more divided than ever about the soprano now entering the autumn of her career. There were those who barely regarded her as a serious singer at all. 'A kind of upmarket Cilla Black,' the cerebral Hugh Canning of the *Sunday Times* called her. For Prince Charles and the full house who paid upwards of £100 each to join in the celebrations for Kiri's fiftieth birthday at the Albert Hall on 10 March, there was no question, however. Kiri was the most loved singer of her generation.

Two days after the actual anniversary, the qualities that had endeared her to so many were all on display as she took to the stage for her official, birthday gala. The faithful had arrived at their seats to find a small box of chocolates from Kiri. She then treated them to a medley of her 'greatest hits', moving seamlessly from Rodgers & Hammerstein to Andrew Lloyd Webber, Mozart to Kurt Weill. At the end, the flowers rained down in appreciation once more. 'Tonight I've encountered nothing but love,' she said, losing her battle to fend off the tears.

Asked to reveal her age by the *New York Times* in 1971, Kiri had replied coyly, 'I'm not telling exactly, so no one will know when I turn fifty.' Two decades later, however, Kiri, and IMG, seemed determined to let the entire world know the landmark had arrived.

The concert, sponsored by Lloyds Private Banking and planned by IMG Artists, had been sold as a television special around the globe. In the run-up, Kiri checked into a nearby hotel where she conducted a barrage of interviews, most of which left her complaining wearily, 'I've been asked every question 5,000 times before.'

Among those invited to the party were the Waihirere Maori Choir who had travelled to England under the leadership of Kiri's old friend Bill Kerekere. They were invited to a reception at Pachesham Park where Des handed each of them a gold watch as a memento. The formalities were all forgotten a month after the Albert Hall concert, as Kiri gathered a collection of eighty close friends and colleagues in New Zealand for an epic, three-day party held at Rawhiti.

Rumours about the grandeur of Kiri's party had flown all around New Zealand in the days beforehand. As a succession of limousines and helicopters delivered the first guests on the evening of Friday, 8 April, pockets of paparazzi photographers and curious locals lined the estate's electrified perimeter fence hoping for a glimpse of Luciano Pavarotti, Tina Turner or even Prince Charles – each of whom were, erroneously, rumoured to have flown out to New Zealand for the fun.

Des had risen to the challenge of outdoing his own fiftieth party with ease. Rawhiti had been transformed into a tented village of marquees and gazebos. A small army of waiters and maids, cooks and chauffeurs catered for the party's every whim. A stage had been erected among the pohutakawa and punga trees. A team of security men patrolled the rim of the estate to ensure there were no unwanted guests. Gatecrashers apart, Des's biggest worry had been the building work still under way on the eve of the party. He and Kiri had been determined that the occasion would mark the official unveiling of their four years' work remodelling Kura Beale's old kingdom. The finishing touches had been applied only that morning.

On a glorious autumnal evening none of the guests could fail to be impressed by what they saw. Inside the single-level, wooden house, vast, panoramic windows looked out over the dreamscape of the Bay of Islands. The ten-acre estate now boasted a caretaker's house, a guest house, a boat house complete with a twenty-three-foot launch, a speedboat for water-skiing and a small fleet of jet skis, a tennis court and a gleaming new indoor swimming pool.

It was difficult to tell who loved Rawhiti most. To Kiri it represented her version of Tom's cabin at Hatepe, a refuge from the trials of her professional life, a place to pick and cook mussels and watch the porpoises swimming off the headland. To Des it was a symbol of the success he and his wife had worked so hard for, a monument to their twenty-seven-year journey from stony broke newlyweds to members of New Zealand's Millionaire's Row.

The party got under way with a traditional Maori hangi, cooked by the local Rawhiti marae. At the end of the evening, guests were driven to accommodation on the estate or with friends along the coast. The revellers returned the following day to be given the run of the estate. On offer was a day's jet-skiing or water-skiing, clay pigeon shooting or simply sightseeing around the Bay of Islands on a specially hired catamaran. Needless to say the boat was equipped with 'free drinks all the way'. Once more a small team of security guards ensured the local paparazzi, moored off the jetty in Parekura Bay, were denied the pictures to feed the New Zealand media. Throughout the weekend Des oversaw proceedings with his customary rotweiller tenacity. To some, however, it seemed obvious he was trying a little too hard to make his wife feel happy. 'He was very actively running the show. It was almost over the top because she was out to have a good time anyway,' said one guest.

Des had always been protective of Kiri's public image. Over the years many journalists had been surprised by his gruff interventions and controlling manner. After conducting a perfectly pleasant interview with Kiri, one well-known New Zealand writer, Virginia Myers, had rung Des to check a fact only to be told that she was forbidden to describe Fairways and their life there in any way at all. 'I found the Svengali act a bit odd,' Myers later wrote, ignoring the demand as she did so. Des's paranoia over photographs only reflected Kiri's own, deep-seated insecurity about uncensored images of her. Two years earlier, as she had sung in Seville, shortly before Des's fiftieth, the leader of the New Zealand Expo delegation, broadcaster Ian Fraser, had witnessed Kiri in full flight. A female New Zealander had fired off two or three frames of Kiri in full cry just before the interval. Kiri had headed backstage incandescent, summoning Max Cryer.

'I thought we were not going to get Kiri back on stage,' said Fraser, who sympathised with her. 'She was in a state of absolute icy fury. She vented it at Max and Max went into a kind of Catherine wheel type spin.' After a heated argument backstage, a promise was extracted that the pictures would never be published. Radiant once more, Kiri returned to the stage to earn her ovation.

Des had originally hired a local photographer, Frank Habicht, to record the events of the birthday weekend. The German-born Habicht had worked in London in the 1960s. He had collaborated with, among others, Lord Lichfield before sealing his reputation with three books of his photography. He had worked with celebrities the world over. Even he had not encountered a man as paranoid as Des. 'I had taken Kiri's portrait a year or so before the birthday when she was publicising the Bay of Islands Festival and what happened then should have been a warning to me,' he said. 'I went out to the house and was met by Des and Kiri. He was very strange. He told me, "You can't take a picture with the trees in it. You can only take pictures looking out at the water, not in at the shore." Then I turned round and saw him looking through my camera bag. In all the years I have taken pictures of famous people that has never happened before. I was amazed. I asked him, "What are you doing?" He said, "I have to check for security reasons." I don't know if he expected to find a bomb or what?' Habicht smiled.

Kiri had been delighted by the results of Habicht's work. A year later he received a phone call from IMG's Paul Gleeson asking if he would like the commission to shoot her fiftieth birthday. As ever, the bargain was a hard one. 'He was only willing to pay $300 for the whole day, but he insisted that a lot of photographers would do it for free for the prestige,' said Habicht. Soon the photographer had been sent a letter informing him that everything to do with the job was confidential. The headed notepaper bore the logo 'Kura's Fiftieth', Des and Paul Gleeson's far from effective codename for the operation.

Such was Des's hyper-anxiety that even the guests had received notes saying, 'Media interference is expected. Please talk to nobody.' Inevitably, however, the press were fed morsels of information by workers inside the Rawhiti complex. Habicht had read a *New Zealand Herald* story based on the limited information it had of the events planned for the following weekend.

On the morning of the party, Habicht was preparing to leave for the function. 'I was all dressed up in my suit when I had a call from a local radio station asking whether I was looking forward to the job and what I would be photographing. I just told them what was in the *Herald* and that maybe I would do something of Kiri cutting the birthday cake,' he said. 'Well, within one minute I had a call from Des who said, "You have just lost your job. That birthday cake should really have been a surprise for Kiri!"'

Before Habicht had a chance to defend himself, Des had hung up.

'He was very abrupt and brief and I didn't even have a chance to reply,' said Habicht. 'I tried ringing back but Kiri's manager wouldn't have anything to do with me.'

Another leading New Zealand photographer, Rob Tucker, was hired at the last minute. As Tucker arrived at the party Des demanded he hand him his mobile phone.

Tucker's role was to photograph the events of all three days. On Saturday night his subject was the party to mark the official unveiling of the centrepiece of the new Rawhiti, the $400,000 indoor swimming pool Kiri had commissioned as her birthday present to herself. The ten-metre pool had been built at the end of a secluded woodland track and into the side of the hill on the peninsula. Its features included a waterfall and a sauna. Its huge cathedral windows looked out along the spectacular coastline towards Russell. 'It's the most amazing view you'll ever see,' said one of the party guests.

Part of the second evening's entertainment was provided by a game in which guests had to predict the number of bottles of Moët et Chandon champagne that would be consumed over the weekend. As she joined the festivities the newly appointed Governor General of New Zealand, Cath Tizard, half jokingly jotted down an estimate of 340 bottles. As her country's party of the year slipped into full swing, there were times when that estimate looked rather frugal.

Des and Kiri made speeches declaring the pool officially open. Guests were invited to test the waters before another lavish meal, this time a formal, black-tie dinner. A three-piece band played all night long. As the party drifted into the small hours, a group of die-hards, including Kiri and Des, stripped off and swam naked together. 'Everyone was drunk and got carried away. Kiri and Des and about half a dozen of their friends were naked in the pool,' said one guest. High on the atmosphere and the ever-present champagne, Kiri seemed utterly uninhibited. 'She was in brilliant shape for a fifty year old. It was just a natural thing, the sort of thing that happened at a party. It was just swimming. They weren't running round the garden.'

According to one guest the bathers were too relaxed even to protest when someone captured the scene on camera, although the pictures are unlikely ever to be seen publicly.

By the end of Sunday afternoon the official announcement was made that 296 bottles of champagne had been consumed that weekend, an average of three and a half bottles per person over the three days. No one was happier than the senior executive from Moët et Chandon with whom Kiri had become friendly in France, where he was a neighbour. Des then signalled for Kiri's birthday cake to be brought out. It had been made in the shape of the Rawhiti peninsula and decorated with scale models of the house and all its outbuildings. A local Maori theatre group performed a specially-written musical in which one of them played Kiri as a little girl. An old friend of Kiri's, Dot Paykel, wife of a New Zealand whiteware tycoon, brought the show to a close with a version of 'Pokarekare-ana'.

Inevitably, Kiri was asked to sing for the gathering. She politely waved each request away. 'Dot and the whole party were asking Kiri to get up and sing but she wouldn't,' said Bob Morgan, there for the weekend with his wife Sharon. 'A lot of people were surprised, but I knew she wouldn't; she never does. Twenty-four hours before a concert, any concert, she goes into concert mode and it's a different state of mind. She had had a few drinks and she hadn't prepared. She doesn't work like that.' Morgan was one of the few to know the strains Kiri and Des were facing behind the scenes. 'Things were very touchy between them at the time, not openly enough for the average guest to have noticed because they kept up a very good front for everyone, but behind that it was bad.'

'I heard that Kiri treated Des appallingly behind the scenes,' said another friend of the couple. 'They fought like cat and dog.' As the last glasses of champagne were drained, Des shared a quiet moment with his old friend Bob Morgan. Morgan was as impressed as everyone else by Kiri's and Des's achievements at Rawhiti. But at times he wondered whether, on their journey from blissful penury in Kensington, his friends had somehow lost track of their priorities.

Morgan had known Des almost all his life and he had never been an ostentatious man. 'He had never given any outward sign that there was a lot of money being made in that family. He never wanted to drive a Rolls Royce. He never wanted to display anything other than being himself,' he said. 'I don't think he's ever owned more than one suit. Sometimes I wonder whether they went a bit too far. They have both probably pushed a little too hard.'

As he talked to his friend, Morgan sensed that Des was ready to return to a simpler, happier life. He knew Des saw Kiri's retirement as their only hope of remaining together. Using a company named after the children, Antom Holdings Ltd, Des was close to completing the purchase of a NZ$895,000 section of land in Brookfield Street near their apartment in St Heliers where he hoped to build a large home. He seemed already resigned to the fact that it would never be built. As he and his friend surveyed the Bacchanalian scene around them, Des stared into his glass. It would be some time before Morgan understood the real significance of his friend's words. 'This is the last thing I'm ever doing for her,' Des said with a rueful shake of his head.

The strain between Kiri and Des was equally apparent in August when they retreated to France for a holiday with an Australian dentist, Kerry Lusk and his wife. Bob and Sharon Morgan, who had been due to arrive to celebrate Sharon's fiftieth that August, arrived later, after Des, Kiri and the Lusks had headed back to London. In England later, Lusk told Morgan they had timed their arrival well. 'He said, "You're lucky you didn't get to France, because the two of them were just squabbling the whole time,"' said Morgan.

Morgan had got to know Des's and Kiri's neighbour from Moët et Chandon. As he and Sharon spent time talking to him, they heard a familiar story. 'He said it was a terrible time because Kiri used to run across to him bawling all the time. Obviously Des was being very cool and the whole situation wasn't that good,' said Morgan.

By then Kiri had headed to New York where she was to climax her fiftieth birthday year with a new *Arabella* at the Met. After the traumas of working with Kathleen Battle in 1983, her return to the role was one of the happier experiences in recent years. The company of her old compatriot Sir Donald McIntyre, cast in the role of Arabella's father Waldner, only added to the more relaxed atmosphere. McIntyre proved as familial a figure off stage as he was on it. He joined Kiri as she began a new fitness drive, taking a Callanetics class in a gym above Carnegie Hall and learning to rollerblade in Central Park.

As they socialised together that season, McIntyre had introduced Kiri to a number of attractive women he was friendly with in New York. 'People make the wrong assumptions all the time,' said the singer, whose marriage to his wife Jill was – and remains – one of the most unbreakable. 'One day after coming out of one of these Callanetics classes, walking up the street from Carnegie Hall, Kiri gave me a sisterly talk about how men could go astray.'

Amused by the ticking off she had delivered, he later made a joke of it while having dinner with Kiri and a group of colleagues near the Met. 'I started to pull her leg and she wasn't happy,' he remembered. Over the years, he had come to know Kiri well enough to know where Des figured in her life. 'I don't say she didn't have difficulties with the children and him along the way. But I don't think she thought there was anything as important to her as her family and her husband. She idolised him.'

Kiri left New York to discover she was on the verge of losing the man – and the life – she so adored. Arriving back at Pachesham Park she made a worrying discovery. Through an accountant she learned that Des had been discussing details relating to the ownership of their properties. 'That's when she put two and two together,' said one friend. When Kiri challenged Des about the matter he revealed the shocking truth. He had been talking to the accountant with a view to dividing up their properties. Not only did he intend leaving Kiri, but he planned to do so with a woman with whom he had been conducting a lengthy affair.

Kiri's regular absences had left Des at a loose end in London. It had been there that he had met a vivacious, dark-haired woman. The two moved in the same circles and found they had much in common. She too was experiencing difficulties in her marriage as her husband spent the bulk of his time working overseas. She was left in London to raise their children alone. They found themselves being drawn together.

Kiri's reaction was instantaneous. 'Kiri is a warrior. She took immediate action,' said one friend.

Kiri would, of course, have been within her rights to throw Des off the Pachesham Park estate. Utterly shell-shocked by the deception, she opted to offer him another chance instead. Provided Des never spoke to or saw his lover again, she told him she was prepared to give their marriage another try. 'She told him that he must never speak to her again in his life,' said one person.

In the days that followed Kiri would discover how close she had come to losing her husband. Had she not learned of the deception when she did, her first knowledge of the affair may well have come in the form of a letter from Des. 'The tickets were booked,' said one observer. 'Apparently, Des was going to fly away and set up a new life with her.'

For years, friends and colleagues had wondered whether Des and Kiri had 'come to an arrangement' over their lengthy separations. Kiri's enjoyment of male company had never left her. Even among those who knew her capricious nature well, the answer to the question of whether she too had affairs is unequivocal. 'No. Definitely. I don't think she ever did that,' said Barbara Brown. Brown, like everyone else, had seen Kiri cast her spell over colleagues in pursuit of a professional end. 'But she was a very good businesswoman. If there was something she wanted, if she wanted to work with a particular conductor then, well, you butter them up a bit and you're very nice to them. I dare say there are some people around who would interpret more into that, knowing full well that that is not the case.'

The discovery that Des had been unfaithful left Kiri shattered. She confided the news to a small, inner circle of friends. Even those aware of the strains imposed by the increasingly separate lives Kiri and Des had been living were stunned at what they heard. Their questions echoed those Kiri was asking herself.

Like any betrayed wife, or husband, Kiri was consumed by an amalgam of anger and despair, guilt and shame. Only months earlier, at the end of 1993, she had once more paid glowing tribute to Des. 'If I didn't have the husband I have got and a normal happy family life, my career would not be worth all the sacrifices,' she told an interviewer. 'Des is so supportive, just in being a steady person at the other end of the phone when I'm down. He is always there for me.' In the aftermath of her discovery she chastised herself for being so stupid.

How could she not have seen what was going on? What of her own contribution to the affair? How had she failed him and their marriage? Was this the true price of her fame? At times the questions overwhelmed her. In the end, however, only one really mattered, of course. Could she ever forgive him?

As she spoke to her friends, Kiri seemed certain that their relationship could be salvaged. It would take many more months of pain before she saw the irretrievable reality of her situation, however. 'Everyone goes through it,' she would come to say. 'You are incredibly happy and you do something really stupid and you make yourself incredibly sad and then you try and retrieve the happiness and you can't.' For now, however, she had to try.

Kiri's views on the importance of family life remained simplistically – and, no doubt, sincerely – homespun. 'People should be as one. They have lost their sense of family and it must be refound,' she said in an interview that reverberated with personal significance that year.

Elsewhere in the same interview, perhaps with the events in her own life in mind again, she declared, 'I am proud of myself and what I have done in that I have not hurt a single human being.'

Neither statement carried the ring of truth as far as her family in Auckland were concerned. It had been while Kiri was preparing for the opening night in *Arabella* that she received the news that her sister Nola had died of cancer at Green Lane Hospital on 16 October. The end had come quickly. Doctors had diagnosed the cancer only ten days earlier. Her husband Bill and daughter Judy had been with her through her final days. As she sat at her mother's deathbed, Judy had healed the wounds of an often difficult past with her mother. At the same time Nola revealed the true depth of the hurt she had felt at her estrangement from Kiri years earlier.

In the immediate aftermath of the row, Kiri herself had shown little willingness to live by the credo she spoke of in public. Asked in 1992 whether she had any contact with her brother and sister, she replied negatively. 'We're not really in touch,' she said, before adding dispassionately, 'I'm not even sure how old they are.'

When, that same year, she learned from her niece Judy that Nola had undergone a quadruple heart by-pass operation, her half-sister's reaction to the flowers she sent had gone a long way towards building bridges.

'This huge bouquet arrived from Kiri. Mum said, "But I told you not to call her,"' recalled Judy. 'But secretly she thought it was absolutely wonderful. She was so thrilled, her face lit up.'

Nola's attitude towards Kiri remained much the same at the end. As she talked to her daughter during her final days, however, she could not disguise the pain she had felt years earlier.

At one point Judy mentioned the album of photographs of Kiri that Nola had painstakingly collected over the years. Her mother told her that she had destroyed them in the wake of the argument over Tom's will. 'I asked her where all the photos were and she said then she had got so bloody wild that she had cut them all up,' said Judy. 'I think the will had been the final insult.'

For years, Judy had remained Kiri's staunchest defender within the family but even her loyalty had now withered. She too could no longer forgive Kiri's coldness.

Despite a life led largely estranged from him, Judy had regarded her adopted father, Tom Webster, with the kind of awe-struck respect with which Kiri held her Tom. 'I idolised him,' she said. The roots of Judy's difficult relationship with Nola lay in the battle her mother and father had fought over her. Judy had blamed Nola for the way Tom had turned his back on her when she was nine, ending their regular weekends together. When Tom Webster died in 1992, Kiri had passed on her condolences to Judy personally. 'She had written me a lovely letter,' Judy recalled. When Webster's will was read out, Judy was deeply hurt by a reference to her not having attempted to make contact with him after the break-up of his marriage to Nola. In fact, Judy had wanted her father to be given custody. She had told him so in a letter written with Kiri's help at Mitchell Street.

In her distressed state after seeing the will, Judy wrote to Kiri asking her to confirm that she had helped compose the earlier letter. 'I just wanted her to put in writing that she had helped me do that,' she said. 'She never ever replied and I wrote back eventually and told her not to bother.'

In Kiri's defence, it seems possible that Judy's letters were read by Des. Subsequent events would suggest that they may even have been kept from Kiri altogether. After the second letter Des visited Judy's home in Mangere. 'He came round and had a chat, not about the contentious issues, and off he went,' she said. 'We've never heard from them since.'

Judy had been quietly devastated by Kiri's unwillingness to act. 'I've never asked for money or anything that would have taken her more than three minutes. That was the one thing I asked her to do,' she said, tears welling up. 'I can't understand why she wouldn't have done it.'

The incident marked a watershed in her relationship with the girl she had for so long regarded as her 'sister'. 'If Kiri walked in here tomorrow I'd make her a cup of tea, and we'd have a chat and I'd tell her exactly why I feel the way I do. I don't begrudge Kiri anything. Every family has their ups and downs but I feel she could have done more for Mum, and my grandfather,' said Judy.

Judy's fears for her aunt are very real. 'No money will buy real friendship, and you never ever forget where you come from and you never forget the people who were there right from the very beginning when you were on the bones of your bum,' she said. 'If you've got to hurt people or trample on them to get where you're going, is it worth going? No way.'

The pent-up feelings her family had suppressed were finally released in the days following Nola's death. Nola's second husband, Bill, had maintained a tactful silence over Kiri while his wife was alive. He made his feelings plain when the family were composing a death notice to be published in the newspapers. 'He absolutely refused to allow Kiri's name in that death notice,' said Judy. 'I said to him, "What about Kiri?", and he said, "Definitely not." He said, "After what she has done to your mother, definitely not."' Bill would not allow the flowers Kiri sent to Nikau Street to remain in his home.

Kiri could not attend the funeral because of her commitments in New York. When her old friend Betty Hanson arrived at the service claiming to be 'Kiri's representative', the family bit their tongues. 'If it wasn't a funeral, I would have turned round and said, "Who asked you to represent her?"' said Judy.

By then Judy had made her point rather eloquently in any case. For those who chose to read between the lines of the 'in memoriam' notice she placed in the local newspapers, the message was unmistakable. 'At peace and painless at last. Where God has taken you. You stand in no one's shadow now. You'll shine forever.'

After spending Christmas in England, Kiri began 1995 back at the Met in a new James Levine production of *Simon Boccanegra*. Her performance reminded many of her glorious debut in the role in the 1970s. 'She is just about perfect,' James Melick wrote in *Opera News*.

For both her and Des, however, life remained deeply imperfect. Des had confessed his affair to his old friend Bob Morgan. As far as Morgan was concerned, it was the first time Des had strayed within the marriage. 'Des was not the kind of guy who was after every girl and looking under every bush. He just wasn't like that. That was the first time Des had looked around. Kiri had always had the opportunity to be away doing her thing,' he said.

Kiri's constant travelling had left Des feeling isolated. 'I'm on my own for eleven months of the year. What does a grown man do?' he told Morgan.

His friend was convinced Des's relationship was not a serious affair. 'I didn't think it had any longevity. I just think he'd had enough of the other situation and felt this was a good avenue out.'

The strains on Des and Kiri's marriage were not helped by the extensive touring Kiri once more faced during the early part of the year. There were short-range trips to Berlin, Oslo and Copenhagen. At the same time there was an extended visit to the heat of South Africa, where Kiri had been invited as a personal guest of Nelson Mandela for the rugby World Cup.

As he accompanied her on a tour of Pretoria, Cape Town, Sun City and Johannesburg, where she sang at a fundraising concert for Mandela's President's Trust Fund, Des played the part of the Svengali spouse to the hilt. By the end of the summer, however, his reign as Kiri's most trusted advisor was over. He had become increasingly disillusioned by the constant travel. At the same time Kiri's trust in him had been severely undermined by his affair. A London-based company, Nic Grace Management, was engaged to take over the role Des had performed assiduously for the last fifteen years.

By the end of the year, with Nic Grace already at work on Kiri's behalf, Paul Gleeson was fending off the press's demands to know why Des was no longer in charge of his wife's career. Rumours of problems in the marriage had drifted around New Zealand and London. 'Des has just had enough of managing and has decided to pull back from that role,' Gleeson assured one Kiwi writer.

As the year drew to a close Des seemed almost relieved at the escape. Early in 1996, the Morgans joined Kiri and Des for a holiday at Rawhiti. Outwardly the marriage seemed happier than it had been for years. 'It was a terrific holiday. We would play boule and collect our own oysters and have our meals outside.'

Kiri, for her part, seemed at ease in her old homemaker role. 'Kiri still cooks every night for guests rather than go to restaurants. As long as everyone pulls their weight she doesn't mind,' said Morgan.

Her competitive urges were never far from the surface. 'Kiri loves tennis,' said Morgan. 'She wanted to play me most days – always early in the morning when we had been drinking the night before.'

She, Des and Morgan also took part in high-speed jet ski races across the expanse of Parekura Bay. 'We had a competition to see who could get to 100kph on the jet skis,' said Morgan. 'We had to get up really early to get the best flat water. Kiri was fearless but Des won with 108kph.'

Unknown to Morgan, Des and Kiri's daredevil exploits on their jet skis had already become a bone of contention in the local community where there were deep concerns about the noise and the damage inflicted on the local marine life. 'We came here because it is so peaceful and natural and we would like to keep it that way,' said one of Kiri's neighbours, Christine Hall. 'They ride all over the shellfish beds not realising that they are destroying all the juvenile stock. They are totally insensitive to the breeding patterns of the fish that live in the shallow waters that they like to use. They break all the rules of the sea. They go too fast within the designated areas. It's like me going to a concert of hers and roaring up and down the street on a motorcycle to piss her off.'

The community had circulated a diplomatically worded pamphlet, suggesting, as Hall put it, 'that this place wasn't appropriate for those kind of toys'.

Kiri's opinion of her neighbours had become obvious in her interviews. 'I don't want to talk about me, which makes conversation fairly limited. You've got to try and turn on to someone whose big thing is the garden shed they've been building for a year,' she said on one occasion.

She was equally dismissive when Hall finally approached her about the jet skis. 'Most people are sort of in awe and don't want to have a confrontation, which I didn't either, but there comes a point when you've had enough,' said Hall. 'I called her on the phone. She said that if I couldn't tell what was the problem within two sentences then there was no point in talking to her. They weren't really willing to listen and she kept on calling it "her" bay.'

Hall was appalled by her treatment. 'We approached her in a very simple manner and were told that we were spoiling her rights. We said, "What about the rights of us and the rights of the wildlife?" but that doesn't seem to count. It seems a shame for a person of her profile to have such a superficial attitude. They are only here for a short time so they think it's alright.'

As they spent time with their old friends, the Morgans were shown the blueprints Des had commissioned for the home he and Kiri intended spending the bulk of their time in in future. They had christened the unbuilt home Park House. 'They were asking my opinion about retaining walls and access points,' Morgan remembered. Des clearly saw the home as their future. 'Everything was pretty happy at that stage and they were looking to their retirement and the rest of their lives together.'

As Kiri headed back to work, however, Morgan had a sense too that despite the ending of Des's affair nothing in the marriage had really changed. 'Kiri got rid of the symptom, but not the underlying problem.'

Out of Reach

The Kiri who reported back to work at the beginning of 1996 was a new and defiantly independent one. Her colleague John McKay could not help noticing she seemed a solitary and rather sad one too.

In the five years since he had first worked with Kiri on *La Bohème* in his home town of Auckland, the avuncular McKay had become among her and IMG's most trusted professional advisors. That season he had been hired to produce a series of three outdoor concerts and act as director of production on her long-awaited appearance in a new Opera New Zealand production of *Don Giovanni* due to open in March.

The sense that her world had been transformed was obvious from the moment Kiri arrived for the first of her open-air concerts, at the smart Millbrook Country Club near Queenstown on the morning of Saturday, 14 January 1996. For the first time, in New Zealand at least, Kiri insisted on having autocues installed. To avoid being too obvious, the prompters and their wiring were skilfully disguised with flowers at the front of the stage. Kiri also seemed unwilling to take part in any publicity and had to be persuaded to do a television interview with the prominent New Zealand journalist Susan Wood. 'I got the job of driving her to and from the interview on a golf buggy and she sat in almost stony silence on the way back. She didn't want to do it,' explained McKay.

Even her rapport with the most loyal subjects in her troubled kingdom, her fans, seemed to be fading. 'She just sat there and didn't acknowledge these people. That was absolutely different from two years before at the Mission Vineyard concert where I had to do exactly the same thing, get her to and from an interview, and it took us three quarters of an hour to get back because she kept wanting to stop and talk to people that she saw or who wanted to talk to her.'

The most striking difference of all, however, lay in her relationship with Des. 'The difference was astounding. Des had turned into a guy who walked three paces behind and carried the suitcases,' said McKay. 'He did not look comfortable in that role at all.'

Des's demotion had made both him and Kiri deeply unhappy. Kiri seemed lost in a state of grim isolation. 'She's somebody who needs to have somebody with her almost twenty-four hours a day,' said McKay. Without Des, she seemed rudderless. With her new, full time manager Nic Grace in London, Kiri's decision to remove Des from his role as her ever ready right hand had left her effectively in control of many of the day to day decisions. 'Kiri drove herself to and from rehearsals. In the past if there were problems with anything, however big or small, Des would deal with it. Now Kiri was her own first line of defence.'

The strain this was placing on her had been obvious even earlier this, when she visited Auckland to meet the creative team planning *Don Giovanni* towards the end of 1995. On an unseasonably warm evening, a seemingly relaxed Kiri had invited executive producer Stephen Dee and director Simon Phillips, along with the award-winning husband and wife design team of Iain Aitken and Tracy Grant, to St Heliers to present their plans. For Phillips, Aitken and Grant it was their big moment. Aware *Don Giovanni* might well be Kiri's final full operatic performance in New Zealand, all three wanted it to be a production to remember.

In advance of the meeting the trio had briefed Stephen Barlow on the concept they had in mind, a transposition of the story to a 1930s North African hotel where the aristocratic principals had arrived on holiday. Kiri's affection for Barlow had grown in the four years since they had first worked together on *Capriccio* in San Francisco. He had, with her former favourite's blessing, replaced John Hopkins as her conductor of choice. 'I remember her writing to me about Stephen Barlow,' said Hopkins, with whom Kiri had shared many of her southern hemisphere highlights in the previous decade. 'There was a concert in Hawkes Bay in '93 which I couldn't do because I was doing *Traviata* with Malvina Major. She wrote to me about a young conductor who she'd like to help and spoke very warmly of him.'

Hopkins happily handed the baton to Barlow.

Kiri and Barlow had spent much of the last two years working together. In 1994 he had conducted her with the Auckland Symphony Philharmonia Orchestra in January and the London Symphony Orchestra at the Albert Hall in March. He had then done two nights at the Hampton Court Palace Festival in June, then toured with Kiri in Canada, the USA and the Far East. His hectic schedule had done little to ease the strains on his marriage. The previous year Joanna Lumley had complained publicly at the lack of time she had spent with her husband during Kiri's hectic 1994. Lumley had been capitalising on the runaway success of her hit comedy 'Absolutely Fabulous'. She had, among other projects, spent time as a castaway on an island off Madagascar for her TV documentary, 'Girl Friday'. 'We hardly saw each other last year because of work,' she sighed. 'It was horrible. At one point we were on a nineteen-hour time difference. Thank God for the fax.'

Barlow himself had complained of feeling overshadowed by his wife's heightened fame. He said he hated being referred to as 'Mr Lumley' or, even worse, 'Miss Lumley's guest'. Kiri's patronage had done much to lift his profile. 'She was, more than any other person, responsible for reviving his somewhat stagnant career by picking him up,' said his friend Stephen Dee, then general manager of Auckland Opera. 'Since then of course his career has picked up because he's a very good conductor, but he had been really languishing for a while.'

Kiri's dislike of modernistic treatments of opera was well known. She had also been badly burned by her experience with Versace in *Capriccio*. Barlow said he would sound out Kiri in advance of the formal presentation. 'He duly claimed that he had and that it would be okay,' said Stephen Dee. 'That was where the problem lay. When we finally came to present the thing to Kiri, we were presenting on the understanding that she knew what we were coming to her with, broadly speaking.'

Barlow, says Tracy Grant, had 'implied that Kiri was a traditionalist but certainly was not averse to putting a new twist on an old story as long as it was not too outlandish.' A winner of the Winston Churchill Memorial Fellowship in Europe, Grant was regarded as the rising comet of her country's artistic community. She had designed sets for Kiri's 1993 Mission Vineyard concert and had worked with Placido

Domingo the same year. While Phillips and her husband Aitken put together an elaborate presentation featuring models of the hotel, she assembled drawings, sketches and swatches of the material she intended using for the costumes. All four travelled to St Heliers full of optimism. 'We had done a big presentation for everyone at Opera New Zealand the day before and it had gone very well,' said Grant.

No sooner had they begun their presentation than that optimism was dissipating. Paul Gleeson and Des were in the room but kept a discreet distance. It was clearly Kiri's show now. Kiri poured coffee and asked the team to explain the ideas behind the models and drawings laid out on the living-room floor.

'I suppose we knew instinctively about fifteen or twenty minutes into it that she certainly was not bubbling over with enthusiasm,' said Grant.

Eventually a surly Kiri picked up Grant's costume sketches and in the bluntest terms announced she would not wear them.

'From that point on it was very, very difficult to have a discussion with her,' said Aitken. Grant had come up with designs in which the male chorus would wear Ivy League-style blazers and boaters. 'Kiri told us it was all wrong. She didn't think New Zealand men could wear it. She said, "They'll never look good in that."'

As the meeting degenerated, Kiri's tone became more imperious. 'It was almost like we were being told off for being naughty children, that we should not have been so presumptuous to have come up with a new angle on the opera, and that after all we were only inexperienced New Zealanders,' said Grant. 'She was very patronising. We were speechless. We were the best that her country could offer and she was dismissing us, more or less, with a sweep of her hand.'

In the past Des would have intervened to calm the situation. Instead he and Gleeson remained seemingly sworn to silence in the background throughout the meeting. 'Stephen Dee stepped in when he realised things were going dreadfully wrong. It was his baby and he had been confident that we could take the production out of the normal. He stepped in to say that obviously we could rework things. But it was never a discussion. I think we were all too terrified, stunned,' said Grant.

Dee had been brought in by Opera New Zealand as executive producer because of his long and trouble-free track record working with

Kiri at the Victoria State Opera, Auckland Opera – at both of which he had been general manager – and with IMG. Dee knew of Kiri's personal problems and that Des had, as he put it, 'gone bush'. The sympathy he felt for Kiri waned as he witnessed her treatment of his young team, however. 'She had the most patronising ideas about what we could and couldn't achieve and that was the insulting thing,' he said. 'Kiri can be quite lovely and she can be completely difficult. She is a mixed bag, and not ever completely irrationally. There is always some kind of motive to it but she can get quite bloody minded, and when she decides to become resolutely opposed to something or somebody, then nobody, not even Des, can shift her.'

Kiri's outburst left Grant, in particular, reeling. As she headed out of the flat and into the lift her emotions took over. 'I thought my career was over. I felt that, professionally, I had been given a huge kick in the guts. I found it very difficult to hold back the tears in the room,' said Grant. 'It was only in the lift on the way down that I gave in.'

'We came out totally stunned, crushed. We sat in the car knowing we were in for a very long haul,' said Aitken.

Deflated, the foursome headed for a meal at a fashionable waterside restaurant, Mikano, where Stephen Dee vainly attempted to console his colleagues. He was convinced they would have to scrap their design and bring an existing, ready-made production over from Australia. Within minutes, however, Dee was fielding a mobile phone call from Paul Gleeson. The IMG man explained that Des had intervened and persuaded Kiri to have another look at their ideas. By the following morning compromise design work was already under way.

The incident proved what many suspected when the news of Des's departure from the managerial role emerged. Kiri was simply ill-equipped to deal with the myriad new demands placed on her. The pattern became increasingly familiar in the fraught months that followed. 'Probably, we would have been better advised to pull the plug on it there and then,' said Dee. 'But, you know, often you only realise these things in retrospect.'

As if the pressures in her private life were not enough, Kiri felt her career being scrutinised more closely than it had been in years. Everywhere she travelled now she was asked about her retirement. 'I'd hate to put a nail in it and say the twenty-fifth of blah blah,' she

351

said in January that year. 'I think of these poor bank managers coming up to sixty-five, when they can see retirement looming down on them – I'd feel very depressed about that.'

Her non-committal responses did little to dampen the *fin de siècle* atmosphere now encircling her. Nowhere was the pressure greater than in New Zealand, of course. As she began working more closely with Kiri on *Don Giovanni*, Tracy Grant's anger softened into a genuine and heartfelt sympathy. After their disastrous first meeting, Grant had begun liaising with Kiri by fax at Rawhiti and then London. As she talked to her she realised the immense strain she was under.

'She was terrified of being made a fool of and terrified that we were taking a risk and she would carry the can,' said Grant. 'It was her one opportunity to come home and do something magnificent and it was just not what she dreamed it would be. Her costumes were seriously reworked, although I knew that was compromising the concept even more. My heart went out to her. I did my damnedest to give her exactly what she needed so she would not feel vulnerable.'

In the end, Kiri and Grant arranged for the three costumes to be made not in Auckland, but in London by the singer's long-standing costumier, Gary Dahms.

The new-found optimism was soon fading as Kiri began rehearsals with Opera New Zealand early in February. John McKay and his colleagues understood the sensitivities of dealing with stars. The rest of the cast and company were briefed on how – and when – they should address Kiri if they needed to. 'We made it clear to the rest of the cast that they were not to approach her prior to a performance. We indicated how they should address her, that she likes to be called Dame Kiri. It was in our interests to have the woman who had sold all the seats in the best frame of mind possible,' he said. It was soon obvious, however, that Kiri's spirits remained worryingly low. 'By the time she came to start rehearsals for *Don Giovanni* in Auckland she was clearly a quite unhappy lady. Kiri almost locked herself away. She'd arrive at the theatre, walk straight down the stairs and go into her dressing room.'

Kiri had decisively influenced the casting of the principal singers, including Michele Bianchini, Jean Glennon, Jonathan Veira and Maldwyn Davies. The chorus was made up of a combination of experienced company members or young graduates. Kiri's first appearance

at rehearsals sent a frisson of excitement through the ranks, particularly ·
the younger members, to whom she represented the nearest thing
New Zealand had to a living legend. 'Let's welcome Kiri Te Kanawa,'
announced a production assistant as Kiri joined Simon Phillips and
Stephen Barlow at the podium on her first day of work. As the applause
rippled around the room, Kiri smiled and mouthed 'thank you'.

Kiri's earliest intervention was unremarkable enough. During her
first rehearsal she insisted that the audience's initial glimpse of her was
more dramatic. 'I make an entrance,' she insisted.

'She changed it just like that, did a grand entrance, and did it very
well,' said one chorus member.

The junior members of the cast had been drawn from the musical
colleges to whom Kiri was a living inspirational force. 'Most of the
chorus were young first timers, deliberately, as they were playing varsity
students,' said one member of the production team. Many of them
had lived with the public image of the down-to-earth diva all their lives.
To some, the contrast between her public and private personalities was
a jarring experience.

Kiri would chew gum, often until the moment she arrived on stage.
'She would just hand it to whoever was closest,' said one member of
the production. 'She would chew up to the last minute and expect
someone to take it.'

Three days before the opening night, the production was ready for
its general dress rehearsal. By now Kiri's unhappiness was even more
obvious. 'Kiri missed her entrance, missed her call, came on late and
just started singing four or five bars behind the orchestra,' said one
member of the team who was present. Kiri was soon covering up for
her error. 'Stephen Barlow called it all to a halt and she walked to the
front of the stage and called to Simon Phillips, "Am I supposed to
be wearing this frock?"' said the staff member.

Even the more experienced members of the production had never
witnessed a scene quite like it. 'I think it was the only time we have
ever stopped a general dress,' said John McKay.

Kiri, as ever, chose attack as her means of defence. 'She was advised
by her dresser which frock to get in and chose to ignore that advice.
When she found out she was in the wrong one she came back and
suggested to the dresser that it was her fault – fairly loudly and upset-
tingly for the dresser,' said one chorus member.

'She laid into Karen Kouka, her dresser, in front of several people in the corridor, which was really uncalled for,' said another member of the production who witnessed the incident.

As an experienced producer, Stephen Dee knew singers were capable of deliberately making mistakes at dress rehearsals, either through superstition or as a ploy to keep their colleagues on their toes come opening night. He saw other motives at work here, however. 'It was deliberate sabotage,' said Dee. 'She quite consciously and intentionally stuffed up. She had gone round some of the younger singers in the cast trying to get them to follow her rather than the conductor. She disagreed with Stephen's tempi and really ground the whole thing to a halt. It was terribly humiliating. She really behaved very boorishly.'

Relations between Kiri and her conductor had become increasingly strained since, to Barlow's fury, he discovered Kiri was being paid a five figure fee to appear in Auckland's 'free' outdoor concert, Opera in the Park. Barlow, who had been hired to conduct at her insistence, had at first negotiated a much smaller fee – then angrily demanded parity.

'I couldn't say that their relationship disintegrated over that period, but it was difficult,' said Dee. 'I know that Stephen had a terribly hard time trying to deal with it all and I think to a certain extent she took out a lot on Stephen.'

As the rehearsal resumed, however, there were even more worrying signs. As Barlow directed proceedings, Kiri delivered a perfunctory, 'marked' performance of Elvira that was barely audible even at the front of the auditorium. 'I think everyone gave her the benefit of the doubt, thinking that she was saving her voice for the opening performance,' said John McKay.

On 24 February, however, it was clear she had not. 'The opening performance was exactly the same as the general dress, as was every other performance after that,' said John McKay. Kiri joined Des, Stephen Barlow and a visiting Joanna Lumley at a sponsors' party afterwards. Kiri's relationship with Barlow was strained. 'I know there was a conversation between Barlow and Kiri about the level of the performance, bits and pieces she had missed and this kind of thing. Barlow is a gentleman. He does not shout and scream. He was pretty annoyed by the end of the season.'

Not for the first time, Kiri's performances declined through the run. Her occasional musical lapses came as no great surprise to anyone. 'She didn't know her work and came in wrongly – wrong time and wrong rhythm – and put other people off,' said one member of the chorus. 'There were sudden moments of almost panic on stage where you know someone's gone wrong and you don't quite know in a flash how it's going to be resolved musically. What the rest did was in fact ignore her, they kept on singing. She had to come back to everyone else.'

More problematic was her lack of co-ordination with the rest of the cast. Kiri's absence from the earlier rehearsals had presented a problem as soon as she joined the company. 'Because she hadn't been to any of the rehearsals until we got into the theatre, she had no direction, she had no placement, therefore she just wandered about,' said one fellow singer. 'You never knew where the hell she was and then she would glare and tut and humph because you were in her place, when you were just going to the position where you were actually meant to be.'

A tightly choreographed dance sequence created the most serious problem. Matters came to a head during one performance when a female singer placed her foot on the corner of Kiri's dress. 'She turned her back on the audience to face her, yanked it out and said, "You're standing on my fucking dress!" I heard it, clear as a bell,' said one chorus member. 'The singer was in total shock. She was crestfallen and disbelieving that she had said this and at the implication she was at fault, when all she had done was go through her dance routine. Kiri had been in the bloody way, simple as that.'

The scene shocked John McKay, who had always admired Kiri's co-ordination. 'We used to joke about artists we would get here who, it didn't matter how well you directed them, they were going to end up walking to centre stage and singing their aria regardless of everything around them,' he said. 'Kiri had never been like that.'

The poor reviews the opening night attracted left the entire company rattled. Even the normally even-tempered John McKay boiled over at one point. McKay had been involved with an argument with another singer in the production and had bumped into Kiri as she complained to Paul Gleeson of IMG in a corridor.

'What am I doing here, Paul?' Kiri had been asking her agent.

Without thinking, McKay interjected. 'Well, it's the money, darling, that's what you're here for,' he snapped, before storming off. As he walked back into his office, McKay realised he had probably signed his own death warrant. 'I thought "This is it. This is going to be terminal."'

Instead he was soon greeted by the sight of a subdued Kiri passing his door. 'She just smiled to me and said, "Perhaps it is, John. Perhaps it is."'

McKay's anger gave way to a deepening sympathy for Kiri. 'There were points where I felt desperately sorry for her. My office was directly opposite her dressing room and we couldn't help but notice when she was coming and going that although it was relatively friendly she just seemed to be so unhappy.'

McKay tried all he could to help Kiri but to no avail. She had retreated into her inner island self. 'Unless you work with artists it's really hard to realise the amount of effort and energy that they have to put into getting out a performance and we could forgive almost any kind of behaviour if you got that performance out at the end. You support them, you help them, you guide them, you talk to them. But with Kiri we couldn't really reach her. There didn't seem to be any way we could help her feel comfortable enough to reach that point in terms of performance.'

Her unhappiness was obvious to everyone within the cast. 'If ever you met her in a doorway or you were entering as she was, she wouldn't look at you. She would look anywhere other than your face, because if she looked at your face she had to acknowledge you, or you her, and she particularly avoided doing that. It was very, very noticeable. It was very studied and deliberate,' said one chorus member.

Some saw it as unnecessary grandeur, of course. 'Right through the chorus there was a feeling of, "Who the hell does she think she is?"' said one senior singer.

'She had chosen to keep herself completely removed from the rest of the company and that to me didn't fit in with the public persona she puts across with the media where she's the local girl come home, and is just as ordinary as she ever was, with no airs and graces.'

By the end of the run, however, it was clear that even Kiri felt an apology of sorts was in order. On the evening of the final performance of the season, as the chorus went through their regular half hour warm-up, a nervous-looking Kiri appeared accompanied by a member of the administration.

'She was introduced by one of the production team who said, "Miss Te Kanawa would like to say something to you." And she then made this statement,' said one chorus member. 'She came in and said, "When you are an international star and you have a high reputation, there is an enormous expectation on you to always perform at the highest level so that you can't ever allow yourself to relax or not concentrate fully, totally, on what you are doing." She was saying that was the reason why she had kept herself aloof. Then she walked out.'

For a moment the chorus looked at each other in silence. 'We said nothing, but then turned to each other in disbelief and said, "What a load of crap!" It left a sour taste in everyone's mouth. The general feeling was, what a bloody up-herself prima donna she is. Which is the exact opposite of what she portrays in public.'

For more than twenty five years now, Kiri had occupied a position at the peak of her profession. It had often felt like the loneliest place in the world, never more so than now. Coupled with the burden of expectation always placed on her in New Zealand and her problems with Des, that loneliness had brought out the worst in her. To those who had known Kiri over the years it was a depressingly familiar picture. Rodney Macann had been in Auckland during the production and had friends among the cast. The horror stories confirmed all he knew of his former girlfriend. 'She came in at the last moment and then started telling people what to do, and I think people are just not prepared to accept this,' he said.

More than ever, however, Macann felt sadness for his old girlfriend. 'When everyone is worshipping you and you're getting all this adulation you have got to be quite a big person, a smart, intelligent person to be able to deal with that, otherwise it could destroy you,' he said. 'It hasn't destroyed Kiri but I think it has come pretty close to it.'

Stephen Dee left Auckland, never to deal with Kiri again. He maintains his admiration for her voice was undimmed. 'I've got a great deal of respect for Kiri, but I'm not one of these silly goggly-eyed fans,' he said. 'I do know how good a singer she is and she is an absolutely brilliant singer and amongst the very best, if not *the* best, in the world.'

On a personal level he knew her to be capable of acts of great kindness. Professionally, he was now less enamoured, however. 'She's a bloody minded woman who's prepared to make grand statements and be totally forthright and take no responsibility for ever thinking things through to their ultimate consequence,' he said. 'No one's ever had the guts to say "no" to her. Nobody's ever told her, "Go away you stupid cow and, you know, get your head together." She's always just had people saying, "You're gorgeous, you're wonderful, you're lovely." So she's never had any expectations of having to be intellectually responsible.

'This is the weird thing about opera singers. from time immemorial, they have this particular fascination where even intelligent men and women just fawn over them as if they are kind of precious baubles and they can do no wrong. It's a very strange thing. They put away their standards when they encounter someone like Kiri.'

Others found it hard to condemn her in the face of the extenuating circumstances Kiri was clearly facing. '*Don Giovanni* didn't gel, and I don't think for any other reason than there was something else going on with Kiri and she wasn't able to concentrate properly on it. She was clearly unhappy in herself and that ran right through the work,' said John McKay. 'We had always seen the haughtiness in Kiri. She is a regal lady, but the kindness and friendship and fun had gone, so that all that was left was the "I am the diva" attitude. I'm sure that had to do with the situation with Des.'

Kiri's increasingly strained relationship with Stephen Barlow had done little to ease her unhappiness. Barlow had remained a loyal ally throughout the difficulties of the last two years. In the wake of *Don Giovanni*, however, even his patience was now running out.

Kiri's performance in Auckland seems to have marked the turning point in their relationship. 'By the time of the Wellington show there was almost a state of war between Stephen and Kiri,' said one colleague.

When her former boyfriend, Rodney MaCann, rang her in her suite at the James Cook Hotel, he found her 'extremely stressed'. Kiri confessed her nervousness at the forthcoming concert and hinted at the differences she was encountering with Barlow. 'She felt she was having to do far too much singing the day before the concert, and if you're apprehensive about how you're going to perform then you're not going to perform as well,' said Macann who, by the end of the conversation, was sure Kiri was on the verge of quitting singing for good. 'So much of singing is a mental thing.'

Matters came to a head in a rehearsal at the Michael Fowler Centre on the morning of the concert, when Kiri was interrupted by a voice in the darkness.

'Somebody in the entourage was sitting in the back of the theatre and said, "We can't hear you",' said a witness.

A furious Barlow finally issued Kiri with a blunt warning. 'Stephen basically said to her, "If you behave like this tonight we are going to get junked",' explained a friend. 'It was his reputation as well as hers on the line.'

That night Barlow went out for dinner with his friend Iain Aitken at a fashionable Wellington restaurant, the Boulcott Street Brasserie. He had clearly been driven to the point of no return. 'He said he had had enough and had told Kiri that he wouldn't pursue any more contracts with her,' said Aitken. 'He didn't show a lot of anger or emotion about it but I think he was highly pissed off.'

Aitken, like everyone else in the New Zealand musical world, had heard rumours of an affair between Barlow and Kiri. Joanna Lumley's appearance at Barlow's side in Auckland only added fuel to the stories that had, by now, flown around New Zealand and then London where at least one newspaper would hint at an 'intimate friendship'. The most colourful version was being born that night, as rumours began to circulate that an enraged Lumley had stormed into Kiri's dressing room. 'Keep your hands off my husband, you b****,' she supposedly warned Kiri.

If the fact that Lumley had not even travelled to Wellington with her husband was not conclusive enough proof, Barlow's response when asked directly about the rumours put paid to the notion, in Iain Aitken's mind, at least. When he broached the subject with Barlow, the maestro's face had become a blank canvas. 'He looked totally bemused,' said Aitken.

As predicted the concert was one of the most disastrous of Kiri's career. Wellington's reputation as the great citadel of her support had been born in the 1960s. Publicly, at least, the romance lived on as a full house paid up to NZ$100 for tickets to the concert. Once more her delivery was sorely underpowered, however. Without microphones to amplify her voice, many complained they could not even hear Kiri.

The Wellington media had long since learned to speak its mind as far as Kiri was concerned. This time its critics penned some of the most poisonous reviews she had ever received in her homeland. 'This performance will be remembered as the Festival flop,' the *Wellington Dominion*'s critic Ivan Patterson wrote, opening the most damning review. 'Grumblings of "refund" resounded through the Michael Fowler Centre foyer after what must surely rate as the most unsatisfactory shortchanging of an audience in this Festival,' he added. 'Hopefully she was not well, as there is nothing sadder than a diva on the downward spiral.'

'Has Dame Kiri just left it too long – her fire dimmed and her audience tired of waiting and disappointed,' wrote another critic, Lindis Taylor of the *Evening Post*.

Many felt cheated. 'If you have a publicity machine that hypes you up and absurd programme notes then you are asking for a fall,' said Radio New Zealand's Roger Flury, referring to the huge PR build up that had preceded the concert and the adoring prose prepared for the glossy souvenir guide to the concert.

Kiri left Wellington for Brisbane and then London the following morning, the criticism still ringing in her ears. The condescending tone of her agent's official response only added to the distinctly sour atmosphere she left behind her. 'Your problem is that some people went there waiting for "Climb Every Mountain". It was a purely classical concert . . . everyone knew what they were buying,' said Paul Gleeson.

Three months earlier Kiri had playfully suggested this may be her final tour of New Zealand. If it was, it had hardly been the fondest of farewells. Indeed, several senior figures with the board of the Aotea Centre and Opera New Zealand were opposed to any return. 'Never again,' muttered one executive.

At the beginning of February 1997, she arrived in New York to once more sing the Countess in *Figaro* at the Met. Her performances in the role that made her famous would alternate with none other than Hei-Kyung Hong, who was making her debut in the role. Even in her fifties, Kiri's competitive edge remained undulled. Kiri could have been forgiven for mouthing 'I told you so' as Hong was utterly overshadowed by her elder. While Hong's Countess was roundly panned,

Kiri's remained as regal as ever. Of Hong, *Opera News* wrote, 'She has neither the vocal weight nor the physical presence to sing the Countess, and her "Dove sono" skirted disaster.' In contrast, when Kiri stepped into the role, the same critic thought 'she had the stage presence necessary to pull the opera back into dramatic balance'.

The victory was soon seeming painfully hollow, however. Kiri returned to London and a confrontation that had, by now, become inevitable. Kiri had continued to sign contracts that would keep her working up until 1999 and beyond. The 'new life' she spoke of publicly did not appear to be happening. Des's patience had finally run out.

As Kiri prepared to head off on a tour of South America Des announced he was going to stay in Brisbane for the foreseeable future. With Antonia studying there, he felt he could be of more use there than in London where he now felt more and more isolated. His decision sparked what Kiri later described as the most serious row they had ever had. It turned out to be their last.

Over the course of the previous two years Kiri and Des's friends had watched with an increasing sense of helplessness as the once happy couple had endured an emotional rollercoaster ride.

The optimism of Rawhiti in January 1996 had quickly proved a false dawn. Within a few months Des had been unveiling a new blueprint for his future. Kiri had shown few signs of fulfilling her promise to wind down her career. As he visited Brisbane for Christmas alone that year, Des had all but given up on their dream home. 'Everything had changed again and he told me, "I'm a Brisbane boy born and bred and I'm going to live my life in Brisbane",' said Morgan.

By now, however, his position had hardened further and it was clear that he would return to Australia without Kiri. 'It's all over,' he told a startled Morgan in the wake of the final, tumultuous row. 'It seemed to be an impulsive, sudden decision.' Des began looking for rented accommodation and took a modest house on Stradbroke Island.

In March Kiri set off for South America on a brief concert tour that included visits to Argentina and Brazil. On 11 April, as she rehearsed at the Teatro Municipal in Rio de Janeiro she was handed a telegram from Des in London. She read the brief, typeset message then broke down in tears. She spent the concert that evening fighting not to do so again. Des was now formally asking for a divorce. He had become involved with a twice-divorced Brisbane socialite he had met at a party over Christmas. Unlike two years earlier, when Kiri had discovered his previous affair, there was little hope of retrieving the situation. The woman had already become something of a fixture at his rented home on Stradbroke Island.

When Kiri had met and married Des only months after breaking off her 'engagement' to Brooke Monks, the media had turned a blind eye to the complexities of her personal life. Now, even in Brazil, backstage rumours were soon being transformed into headline news. It was left to one of Rio's cerebral arts commentators Antonio Hernandez of the *Globo* newspaper to claim the scoop. Hernandez's article ran under the headline, 'Tears illuminate the voice of the beautiful singer'. It included an explanation for the alterations Kiri had made to her planned recital. 'The reasons for the change in the programme are worth a short history,' Hernandez wrote. 'Among the causes was recent pain which was later discovered, according to rumours during the interval of the concert, to be due to a telegram from the soprano's husband which she received a few hours before the recital. According to rumours Kiri's husband had requested a divorce.'

To Kiri's relief the news was not picked up outside Rio for almost a month. By the time it had reached London's *Mail on Sunday*, however, there was no need to deny it. The newspaper reported the break-up on its front page. Inside a 'close friend' of the family confirmed a few bare bones of truth.

'She was very worried about the effect it would have on their children and wanted to get home before the news reached Britain,' the friend said. The associate made no attempt to deny the story. He or she knew that the legal wheels were already turning. The closing line of the carefully worded statement summed up the simple sentiment that would soon be echoed all around the musical world. 'It's very sad. It seemed an idyllic marriage.'

Freefall

On 30 May 1997, Kiri returned to one of the roles that had made her name. As part of the Royal Opera's Verdi Festival, she sang Amelia in *Simon Boccanegra* in a revival of a recent Elijah Moshinsky production.

The opera failed to capture the imagination of either the public or the critics. 'Every opera season has its troughs. This was simply dire,' wrote Tom Sutcliffe of the *Evening Standard*. Sutcliffe, like others, thought a drawn and slightly haggard looking Kiri sounded 'severely out of voice . . . She has never acted seriously. Her disengagement from everything around her on stage and total focus on the audience, suggested real anxiety.'

Only those close to Kiri knew the true depth of that anxiety, and the irony that lay behind it. By night she sang the bittersweet arias of the lovelorn Amelia. By day, in the office of a leading London divorce lawyer, she set about the business of ending the marriage that had dominated her life. Emotionally, as she later put it, she was in 'freefall'.

Kiri returned to London from South America in mid-April to the first of what would be a series of meetings with her lawyers. Des had made it clear he wanted the divorce to be as amicable as possible, primarily for the sake of Toni and Tom. Kiri shared his concern over the children. Remaining amicable was another matter.

Kiri had reconciled herself to the fact that her marriage was over. She admitted the pain was, at times, overwhelming. 'It's like tearing your heart in two – like Velcro being ripped apart,' she said later. She opted for immediate surgery. Rather than going through a protracted divorce, Kiri petitioned for a divorce on the grounds of Des's admitted adultery. As in all divorces, her despair was heightened by the pain of the practical realities she now had to endure. With her lawyers, Kiri began the process of dismantling and dividing what she sardonically referred to as 'the empire', the life she and Des had spent thirty years building together.

The previous year, Kiri had once more featured in New Zealand's *National Business Review* and its annual survey of the nation's highest earners, the Rich List. Her personal wealth had been estimated at NZ$10 million, around £4 million at the time, an outrageously conservative estimate when one considers the value of her properties alone. In England, in addition to Fairways, they had acquired a luxurious apartment in Cleveland Square, Holland Park. The two homes were worth £1 million or more. As well as these, there was the house in the Dordogne and the Bergerac vineyard, the apartment on the Algarve in Portugal, their properties in Brisbane, St Heliers and New York. The jewel in the crown, of course, was Rawhiti, worth well in excess of NZ$2 million alone. In addition there was their forty per cent interest in Kiwi Pacific Records International, their interest in Classic FM and the trusts in Switzerland and Lichtenstein. Des was also entitled to assorted royalty rights as manager or executive producer on various recordings, films, books and videos.

In the eye of the media storm, Des had retreated to the villa in Portugal and the golf course. He had originally hoped that he and Kiri might be able to work the principles of their settlement out between them. As Kiri arrived back in England, however, it was soon clear she had no intention of even talking to him. When Des attempted to speak to her he was instructed to talk to her lawyers instead. 'If she carries on like this is it is going to cost us both a lot of money,' an exasperated Des was soon telling a friend. When he received notice of a claim under New Zealand's Matrimonial Property Act, barring him from selling the St Heliers apartment, which had been bought solely in his name, it was clear the bond of trust he had once shared with his wife had been broken forever.

In London Kiri maintained her distance from the media. She installed Nic Grace at Cleveland Square where he fielded the flood of calls from newspapers and magazines in Europe and the Antipodes. His response to callers was brusque. 'Dame Kiri is not here and won't be here,' he would say before hanging up. Kiri stoically refused to cancel any of her engagements. On 6 May, as the story began to break in London she attended a gala opening of Belfast's £32 million new venue, Waterfront Hall, home to Opera Northern Ireland and its new artistic director Stephen Barlow. Extra security had been organised to protect her. She did not turn up for a civic banquet afterwards.

At Covent Garden, too, she kept a low profile, slipping in for her *Boccanegra* rehearsals as inconspicuously as possible. When the news broke days later, friends and wellwishers were greeted with a philosophical face. 'Things change, people change,' she told one friend from New York when she called to sympathise.

Others, however, glimpsed the agitation and natural anger Kiri found hard to contain. Echoing a view she expressed on her friend Prince Charles's divorce, Kiri seemed to expect the friends she and Des shared to fall into separate 'camps'. 'Kiri rang me after the separation and told me I could either be her friend or Des's, but not both,' said Bob Morgan. 'She said, "If you're going to be a friend of Des's you can't be a friend of mine." I told her that was ridiculous and that after thirty years I was a friend to both of them.'

As the divorce settlement was sorted out, a concerned Morgan remained in close contact with Des. In many respects, Des seemed relieved to be free from the world he had inhabited for three decades. 'I think he's happy now in the sense of the freedom. He wanted to do his own thing for once in his life,' said Morgan. He told his friend he wanted the ending of his marriage to be as painless as possible. 'He said he just wanted enough to live on for the rest of his life and Kiri could have the rest.'

The greatest cause of friction was, predictably, Rawhiti, the property both Des and Kiri valued above all others. 'I created a monster,' Des told Bob Morgan, referring to the hideaway he had invested so much time and money in developing.

'Des desperately wanted that house,' Morgan said. In his heart, however, he knew he had little chance of persuading Kiri to give it to him. Morgan asked his friend whether he thought he would ever see the place again. 'No,' he said with a shrug of resignation. Eventually Des capitulated. 'They both wanted it in the settlement, and she got it,' said Morgan.

The divorce settlement was thrashed out in less than a month. The process of disposing of the properties was already under way. Both Rawhiti and Cleveland Square would remain Kiri's, while most other assets were to be liquidated. By the time Kiri completed her run in *Simon Boccanegra* in mid-June, the paperwork was moving towards the Family Division of the High Court of Justice in London. Nine weeks short of their thirtieth wedding anniversary, on 15 June, the marriage was dissolved. What had begun as a whirlwind romance, ended in a 'quickie' divorce. Apart from the bare bones, the press were given few details. Kiri's office confirmed that Des had admitted to adultery. The rest remained 'a private matter neither party wishes to discuss'.

In the past Kiri would have retreated into her island state, adopted her emotional siege mentality and waited for the clouds to clear. This time, however, even Kiri could not deal with the heartbreak in solitude. Alone at Cleveland Square at night she found the tears hard to staunch. 'There were terrible times at night, five o'clock at night was about the worst, until about seven, just as the sun sets when you should be the happiest,' she said later. She looked for help wherever she could find it. 'I went to a psychiatrist. I read every single book that I could do, everything on marriage, why it breaks up, Mars and Venus.'

As she worked through the bewildering collection of emotions unleashed within her, Kiri inevitably vented her rage at Des. She had never truly forgiven his infidelity. Instead, in the three years since discovering his first affair, she had felt her faith in her husband and her marriage replaced by a deepening sense of distrust and disillusionment. By the end, she admitted later, even his insistence that she give up her music seemed suspect and somehow symptomatic of their troubles. 'A lot of things contributed but this was one of the things that was the mainstay of the problem,' she said.

As she raked over the ruins of her personal life, Kiri could at least take solace in the knowledge that she had, understandably, placed her faith in her career rather than her flawed marriage. With Des now gone and the children grown up, music, more than ever, represented her one real raison d'être. 'I feel like I have to sing until I can't sing any more. It's my life. And it's good for me. If I stopped singing I would die,' she said.

Slowly but surely, however, Kiri saw that the key to her new life lay outside even music. 'It's only you who pulls yourself out of it,' she was soon explaining to friends. As her spirits revived, she began to see the pain of the past as something to be boxed up, packed away and forgotten. 'I'm determined to put the past four years in the background and say, "Right. All that was pretty awful – now let's put it away",' she said. She began the proces of constructing a new life.

At Cleveland Square she exorcised the ghosts of the past. She called in the decorators for a major refurbishment. Photographs and obvious reminders of Des were removed. A photograph of the children climbing an old pohutakawa tree at Rawhiti and a framed shot of Kiri collecting an honorary doctorate at Cambridge University were given pride of place. On the walls hung a pair of paintings by Antonia and an oil portrait of her and Tom as little children in the mid-80s. Along with her favourite painting, a landscape of Hatepe by the New Zealand artist Peter MacIntyre, given to her in San Francisco in 1980, they reminded her of the positive parts of her past. Out too went the old image, replaced by a sleek new haircut and a new wardrobe of black-dominated Armani clothes. 'When everyone gets divorced they go to Armani,' she joked later. 'I had a personal dresser come to clear out my wardrobe completely. All the shoes went, all the clothes went. The whole lot went.'

Soon, a personal trainer had been hired to aid the reinvention now under way. 'The gym was a great healer,' she said. Even the loneliness was dealt with. Her old Blockhouse Bay sweetheart Robert Hanson, a longtime London resident, had moved in as a companion. 'Nothing romantic,' she told friends. 'When I want to I can say he's my boyfriend and when he wants to he can say I'm his girlfriend.'

Generally, they preferred to stay in. 'We have a policy here. We don't cook. We just send out or we go to Marks & Spencer and just throw it all together,' Kiri laughed.

Music, of course, provided the most healing therapy of all. Soon Nic Grace was tiring of the insistence in her voice. 'Now, work me,' she kept telling him. 'Keep me working.'

Kiri was committed to sing Madeleine in *Capriccio* in New York at the end of the year, and at Glyndebourne the following summer. Not for the first time, her new projects raised eyebrows. In September, rather than joining the New York Philharmonic as one of its special guests at a 150th anniversary concert at Carnegie Hall, Kiri agreed to return to the red dust of Yalkarinha Gorge and a reprise of her 1988 Opera in the Outback in Australia. In the wake of the ill-fated events of the previous year in New Zealand, Stephen Barlow had been replaced on the podium by Robin Stapleton, an old colleague from early Covent Garden days. She also spent time on the French Riviera, at the Cap Ferrat home of Andrew Lloyd Webber. Amid much secrecy, the most successful musical theatre composer of his generation was at work on a new show, supposedly a sequel to his *Phantom of the Opera*. 'It's a new lease of life for him and I just happened to be there at the right time,' Kiri said later as she recorded and performed the first song to be released from the secret project, 'The Heart is Slow to Learn'.

By the autumn she was beginning to feel like the decline had been arrested. 'I'm freer and more in control, and I was not in control before,' she was soon telling friends. 'I'm in charge.'

Kiri arrived in Australia in August to prepare for a series of concerts and her trip up to Beltana and the new Opera in the Outback. In Brisbane, she arrived for dinner with Bob and Sharon Morgan with a muscular, ex-British serviceman bodyguard called Kevin. Kiri managed to smile at Bob Morgan's jokes about Kevin Costner and his film *The Bodyguard* in which a pop diva falls in love with her minder. 'He said he was very happily married,' smiled Morgan. 'I think it was a combination of company and security which she misses with Des not around.'

Publicly Kiri claimed that she and Des had remained close friends for the sake of Toni and Tom. In reality Morgan knew relations remained strained. Des told his friend how, while staying at the Mirage Hotel on Australia's Gold Coast, Kiri had called him on his mobile phone to discuss something relating to the children. Coincidentally, Des was not only on the Gold Coast, but within 400 yards of Kiri's hotel. 'He could actually see the hotel,' said Morgan. When he suggested they met face to face, Kiri refused. 'I don't want to see you,' she told him. To no one's surprise Kiri did not mention Des once during the dinner. Morgan knew his relationship was ongoing. It was to fizzle out within a year, however. Kiri's only, indirect, reference to her ex-husband came when she declared that if she ever decided to remarry, it would not be to a man who had reached fifty-five and 'given up'.

Far more startling was the manner in which she dropped into the conversation the meeting she had organised for the following week. 'She told us she was going to meet her long lost brother,' said Morgan. 'She seemed quite cool about it.'

Kiri's composure was, more than ever, a mask. For years Des's controlling influence had extended to vetting Kiri's mail. He had increasingly taken on the role of judge and jury in deciding what correspondence she should and should not be exposed to. It had been in the heat of his fateful, final confrontation with Kiri in February that he had shared the secret he had kept from her for two years. According to the version of events Kiri later related, Des stormed out of their row with one parting shot. 'By the way, your brother in Australia is trying to reach you,' he had told her. Kiri had been so angry that she had slapped him across the face.

As the tears flowed, Kiri read and re-read the letter that had been kept from her. Addressed from a suburb of Sydney it was signed 'Jim Rawstron'. Since her discovery of her father at Gisborne in 1987, Kiri had made slow but certain progress in her search for her real identity. The little she could learn of her tribal background was revealing. 'My natural tribe is Ngati Porou, the most aggressive tribe in New Zealand, especially the women,' she proudly proclaimed in 1991. 'And somehow in the blood is the fighter, the female. It's very strong.'

In 1996, accepting an honorary degree from Waikato University, she alluded to both her Maniapoto and Ngati Porou heritage. From the latter she 'got the fire' she told the assembly. She had continued to talk to Bill Kerekere, the interpreter who had sat with her at the Gisborne marae when she first heard of Jack Wawatai. When Kerekere had joined the Waihirere Maori Choir at Fairways after Kiri's fiftieth birthday concert at the Albert Hall, Kiri's growing fascination with her real story was more obvious than ever.

Midway through the evening, Kiri sat childlike at Kerekere's feet. Her meaning was obvious. 'She was trying to ask me, "Do you know who I am now?" I knew what she was sitting there for, but there was no way I could say who she was,' he said. He could not help but feel for her. 'I could never satisfy her curiosity, even at her home.'

As Kiri read, and re-read Jim Rawstron's letter, however, she finally saw the door to the past opening.

Jim Rawstron had spent the first forty years of his life oblivious to his connection to New Zealand's most famous daughter. When Noeleen had married Rex 'Tubby' Williams after Kiri's adoption, Jim had moved in with his new stepfather. He grew up with Noeleen and Rex in New Plymouth before heading for Australia in the 1960s.

Jim, like every other member of his family, had never heard Noeleen discuss Kiri or their true relationship. It had only been after his mother's death during a visit to his home in Sydney in 1979 that he had discovered the truth from his stepfather.

Williams seems not to have known of Noeleen's affair with Jack Wawatai. As far as Jim was concerned Kiri was, like him, the product of Noeleen's relationship with Jim Collier. For years Jim resisted making contact. 'Some things are better left alone,' he frequently told his second wife, Ann Hargreaves. By the mid-1990s, however, his curiosity could not contain itself. In 1995, Jim sent Kiri a letter through his solicitor. When he received a reply from her own lawyer explaining she was not 'emotionally ready' to meet him, he had decided to let matters rest.

After her last, tearful fight with Des, however, Kiri had taken Jim's letter with her to South America. Adrift in the most turbulent emotional waters of her life, she had clearly grasped the lifeline he now offered.

In early April Jim received an unexpected letter, postmarked Buenos Aires, Argentina. The handwritten note, on hotel headed notepaper and dated 27 March, began: 'My dear brother Jim. I just want to say how pleased and proud I am to know that I truly have a brother, so long talked about, but never knowing who or where.' To his utter astonishment, it was signed Kiri Te Kanawa.

Soon Kiri and Jim had begun corresponding and talking to each other on the telephone. During the stormy months that followed, Kiri began to see Jim as one of her closest confidants. She would begin her letters lovingly: 'Dear Brother', 'My Darling Brother' and end with a kiss and a scrawled 'Sister K' or 'Your Warrior Sister'. The tone of her letters hint at the depths of the emotional turmoil she passed through.

Kiri began writing frequently, at times daily. 'My dear brother Jim . . . just to say that word is like a whole new world opening up to me,' she wrote on 28 April. A day later she wrote again, saying, 'I have cried over your letter so many times. I have re-read it just to get used to having a brother.' Kiri even wrote on 11 May, the day the news of her divorce broke in London. 'As you may know, my life has changed,' she told him. 'In a few days, when everything calms down, I would love to speak to you. At the moment I'm having a most awful time.'

She wrote too as the divorce argument reached its climax. 'I have been with a band of lawyers all day. All is well. I am now just going to bury myself in my work and start my new life,' she wrote early in June. By August, after three months of exchanged letters, Kiri had finally summoned the strength to arrange a meeting with Rawstron. The meeting was set for a hotel in Sydney. Kiri had asked that Jim come alone. She wanted their meeting to be a private affair between the two of them.

As Jim walked into the room, Kiri opened her arms and embraced him. Both of them cried openly. They spent hours sitting together talking about their separate lives. Kiri naturally wanted to know all Jim could tell her about Noeleen. Back home afterwards Jim told his wife Ann how much Kiri looked like their mother. At the same time the gentleness of her touch reminded him of their grandmother, Thelma.

Kiri asked Jim to join her at her second Opera in the Outback. Along with around 12,000 others, Jim and Ann, accompanied by a group of friends, travelled out to the Flinders Ranges for Kiri's 21 September concert. They met and shared a meal afterwards at which Kiri invited Jim to spend some time with her at Rawhiti.

Rawhiti's importance to Kiri was unmistakable. As they walked the shore, Kiri showed Jim the spot where she wanted her ashes scattered. At one point it had begun raining. 'She gave me a hug and said the sky was crying Maori tears because our ancestors were so happy we were together. It was terribly emotional, and I will never forget that time with her. The time that I spent with her was absolutely wonderful,' said Jim Rawstron. 'Nothing to do with the fact that she was a famous person. She was my sister, and that's the way it was.'

Both trod carefully. Rawstron did not want Kiri to believe he was out to exploit her. Kiri, by the same token, did not want their relationship to become public. The irony was that without the removal of Des's protective veil, Kiri may never have known of her brother's existence. With Des around, however, it is tempting to think matters would not have played out as they did.

Almost inevitably, word of the relationship Jim and Kiri were forming leaked out. Jim had done all he could to honour Kiri's requests that they 'keep it in the family' and avoid turning their reunion into what she called 'a circus'. The Chinese whispers had reached the city of New Plymouth, where Jim had spent his early years. In November he was contacted by a reporter from Auckland's most downmarket tabloid newspaper, *The New Zealand Truth*. The reporter, Mathew Lo Ho-Sang, was the son of an ex-girlfriend of Jim's in New Plymouth who had heard the rumours at a school reunion.

On 21 November 1997 *The Truth* ran a front page story headlined 'Kiri Turns To Lost Brother'. Despite being littered with mistakes – Jim was called Rawstorn, and was described as having been born in Tolaga Bay – the story was essentially correct. Jim's alleged conversation with Lo Ho-Sang became the root of the controversy that followed. 'You can imagine how stunned I was when I found out exactly who my blood sister was,' he was quoted as saying. According to the report, he had guessed that Kiri had reached out as a reaction to her marriage break up. 'Kiri obviously felt alone and upset,' he was quoted as having told the journalist. He was reported as being 'certain that a need for support and comfort inspired Te Kanawa to seek out her long lost family'. Rawstron does not deny that he was telephoned by Lo Ho-Sang. He remains adamant, however, that he told him he did not want to discuss the matter. 'He never spoke to me. He made it all up. Everything in that article he made it up.'

When Jim next called Kiri, the warmth of the previous three months was replaced with a stone wall. He called several times. Each time he was greeted either by the voice of Robert Hanson or Nic Grace. Their message was unequivocal. He was told Kiri never wanted to speak to him again.

As 1997 drew to a close, Kiri travelled to New York for a new production of *Capriccio*. The strains of the hellish half year she had been through were obvious. 'There had been a lot of anguish. One of the things she kept saying was that she hated living in New York in the winter because she had to take such care to stay well all the time. I think that was an extension, a projection of how vulnerable she was feeling,' said the Met's former publicist Johanna Fiedler, who often met Kiri socially that season. Ironically Kiri was now having to work hard to undo the talk of retirement she had begun in the years before her divorce. She had been 'furious' when the New York press began suggesting that this was to be her farewell to the Met. Far from it, she intended singing the Marschallin in 1999 and had never felt more committed to her schedule, she countered.

To the surprise of those who had seen her at her under-prepared worst, Kiri arrived for the first day of rehearsals note and word perfect. 'She had lost a lot of weight and was discussing the merits of personal trainers. She looked very beautiful,' said Johanna Fiedler. The sheer burden she felt at returning to the grindstone was clear, however. 'She told me that the strain of having to be as good as you were before is what wears her out,' said Fiedler.

Her reviews for *Capriccio* were mixed. The *Wall Street Journal* singled Kiri out for criticism while John W. Freeman in *Opera News* thought her 'poised singing and deportment gave us Countess Madeleine to the life'. By March back in London there were even surer signs that she was emerging from her trauma as she joined a glittering array of musical talent at a memorial concert for Georg Solti at Westminster Abbey. The maestro's remarkable life had come to an end on 5 September 1997, a few weeks before his eighty-fifth birthday. Kiri was among a crowd of familiar faces there to pay homage to the musical genius who had been so important to her success. Kiri had agreed to sing one of his favourite Strauss pieces.

The Abbey was filled with faces familiar and familial. Many carried their memories of Kiri too. Solti's most trusted aide, Joan Ingpen, recognised the same maddening, magnificent creature she had first seen in *La Donna del Lago* thirty years earlier. When Ingpen's husband, the actor Sebastian Shaw, died, Kiri had upset her old mentor by failing to turn up to sing at his memorial. 'On the morning there was a message that she'd got an emergency and had to go to the airport. At the time I was jolly annoyed. I thought she could have rung me herself. That was Kiri, she's always been scatty,' she said.

As Kiri took centre stage at the Abbey, forgiveness was not hard to find. 'I thought it was some of the greatest singing I have ever heard. Better than ever,' said Teresa Cahill, another who performed at the Abbey that day. 'I've never seen anyone do as poised a performance under those circumstances. He did so much to help us. She was very special in his life. They did some wonderful things together. To stand there coolly and do that; for me she reached new heights of real artistry that day.' Slowly but surely, the new Kiri was emerging. She was ready to provide audiences with a taste of what might lie ahead musically. She appeared on the BBC's Parkinson show to sing Lloyd Webber's 'The Heart is Slow to Learn'. Afterwards, in the first of a few, carefully controlled interviews, she talked publicly about the divorce for the first time.

Kiri did not deny the depths of despair she had gone through. 'Hell is being out of control in freefall, I think. I could say it lasted for three years, I could say it lasted for two weeks. You know what happens? You actually forget the hurt, so it's better just to move on, which I have done,' she said. She laid most of the blame at Des's door, insisting that he had tried to force her into retirement. 'He desperately wanted me to stop, I desperately didn't want to. That destroyed it in the end,' she told Parkinson.

She also blamed Des's fiercely protective personality for isolating her from friends. 'Des was not a very warm person so of course people were frightened to be around him,' she told a New Zealand chat show host, Paul Holmes. Kiri claimed that she had precipitated the end. 'He was not content, and so that made me discontent. I engineered the end. I decided that this is what I wanted. I wanted to be free, and I'm very happy about that.'

Hard as she tried to focus on the future, however, the past still had a nasty habit of returning to haunt her. In the wake of his alleged interview with *The Truth* in November, Kiri had continued to ignore her brother's attempts to contact her. In April Jim Rawstron let her know how hurt he had been. In return for a fee believed to be A$30,000, Rawstron shared the story of his brief relationship with Kiri with the readers of Australasia's biggest selling magazine, *Woman's Day*. At first glance the cover photograph of him cuddling Kiri, taken by his wife Ann at Rawhiti, looked charming enough. The headline, 'Rejected Brother Tells: "Kiri Broke My Heart"' hinted at another, more sinister story, however.

'When I met Kiri I was over the moon and the relationship we had was that of a true brother and sister,' he told *Woman's Day*. 'But I could never forgive her now for the way I have been treated and if anybody asked me today what I wished for I would say, "I wish Kiri were a nobody, flat stony broke and in need of help so I could look after her."' The article continued in the same splenetic vein.

Rawstron knew his action would bring his relationship with Kiri to an end forever. In the aftermath of the *Woman's Day* article he has heard nothing from Kiri or her organisation. 'Kiri's never going to have anything more to do with me as long as she lives. That's her choice,' he said. 'Quite honestly, the worst thing I ever did in my life was get in contact with her. The agony and the pain of it all has been horrendous for my family,' he said. 'Now we just want to be left alone.' At the end of their brief relationship, at least, brother and sister agreed on something.

Kiri treated Jim Rawstron just as she treated the divorce. He was an unwanted memory. She had packed it and dispatched it, 'put it away'. If she had a male sibling, she was soon telling whoever wanted to listen, he was Robert Hanson. 'He's like a brother to me – and he's wonderful,' she said. In the weeks that followed Kiri only referred to the Jim Rawstron drama elliptically. 'Unfortunately there have been people in my life in the last year that have taken advantage of my isolation, of my being without the protection of Des,' she said in May. The experience had provided her with another lesson, she admitted. If she could not trust anyone she did not already know, then so be it. The door would remain closed from now on. 'Now I just don't ever let anyone that's new in my life come in.'

'Being an opera singer is a desperately lonely life,' Kiri said once. Perhaps the key to her success and, even more, her longevity lies here. No singer has been so attuned to solitude, so hardened to existence in this artistic island state. The die was cast at the very start of her life. She has never truly rid herself of the rootlessness and the relentless drive to prove herself she felt as Nell Te Kanawa's adopted little girl.

'I was not given much of a chance at birth but, oh, by gosh, I was going to give, give it everything I had, until the time comes when I can't do it any more,' she said once. The rewards have been beyond even her mother's wildest imaginings. So too has the personal price her time at the peak of her profession has demanded.

For more than two decades she has reigned as the soprano supreme. In an era of revolutionary upheaval, she has – perhaps more than any other female classical singer – remained in tune with the ever-changing musical mood. Now she faces the final challenge of her career. How she copes with her departure from the stage, and the retirement that follows, will, perhaps, define her more clearly than anything that has gone before. More than three decades earlier, as she became the *Auck-land Star*'s Miss Entertainment of 1965, Kiri had made her ambition plain. 'I want to do all the things I should plus a few I shouldn't,' she said. 'Then when I reach sixty, there will be only one thing I want to do – flake out completely.'

That landmark will loom into view soon. She has made no secret of her wish to sing at the opening of the Sydney Olympics, in 2000. 'The dates are coming in for the year 2000,' she said recently. 'I didn't think I would go on until then, but now I don't know. We'll see.'

If she does decide to leave the stage earlier, one potential date resonates with more significance than any other. On 31 December 1999, New Zealand will be the first country in the world to welcome in the new millennium. Hours later, on the East Cape and its easternmost point, the historic Mount Hikurangi, overlooking Tokomaru Bay, crowds will assemble to witness the first sunrise. Plans for a concert on the mountaintop are already at an advanced stage. Kiri has been invited to usher in the new millennium.

It was in the parched hills around Mount Hikurangi that the ill-starred romance of Jack Wawatai and Noeleen Rawstron began more than half a century ago. It was from the community below that the unborn Kiri was taken by her mother, never to return. The road she has journeyed since then has been an extraordinary one. Her voice has reached out across the Pacific Ocean, stirred the spirits and the hearts of millions in the farthest corners of the world beyond. There could be no more fitting a time or a place for her to begin the final chapter in her story than amid the hope of a new dawn in the landscape where it all began.

NOTES AND SOURCES

The principal sources for *Kiri: Her Unsung Story* are the more than one hundred and fifty interviews conducted by its authors in New Zealand, Australia, the United Kingdom and the United States. In addition, it draws on numerous public documents and private correspondences, family scrapbooks and photograph collections as well as a vast archive of newspaper and magazine articles, biographical works and television documentaries spanning Kiri Te Kanawa's three and a half decades as a public personality. The bulk of these sources are acknowledged within the text itself and need no further explanation. The notes below refer to significant quotes and other material for which no specific source is given in the text. In some instances, particularly relating to family cuttings and scrapbooks, precise publication details are unavailable.

Chapter 1: The Road to Gisborne

pp. 6ff. Account of Noeleen Rawstron and Jack Wawatai's affair: Official records and author interviews with the following members and friends of the two families: Noeleen Rawstron's sister Donny, daughter Sharon, niece Jennifer, brother Ken, son-in-law Bill and son Jim, Jack Wawatai's former wife Apo, sister Huka, sister-in-law Ona and children 'Bubba', Lynne and Jason. Help on this section was also provided by Ira Haig, Pahoe Mahuika and Ngati Porou genealogist Phil Aspinall.

p. 8 Birth of Noeleen's baby: Registered in Gisborne and in the national register no. 2492 of 1944. The child's name is misspelt as Claire Mary Teresa Rawston.

Chapter 2: 'The Boss'

pp. 11ff. Genealogical background to the story of Nell Te Kanawa: Interviews with her granddaughter Judy Evans-Hita, information provided to her biographer David Fingleton by Kiri herself and the following official records: p. 11 Emily Sullivan's birth: registered at Christchurch, no. 990 of 1871. Emily and John Leece's wedding: registered at Buller, no. 2160 of 1887; Nell's birth: NZ Births Deaths & Marriages Central Registry certificate, folio RC 14/ 17–3959; p. 13 Nell and Tom's marriage: District of Gisborne, marriage certificate no. 1939/ 10373.

pp. 13–14 Description of Tom Te Kanawa's life at the family marae: drawn from the sub-tribe's own book of genealogy, *Whareangaaga*

Te Kanawa: He Whakamarumaru Mo Te Whanau, published privately in 1992. Other details are taken from author interviews with Kiri's cousin, Kay Rowbottom, in June 1997. Other sources include: '... basically rejected the Maori side' and 'My father would not speak Maori' from the 'South Bank Show', television documentary hosted by Melvyn Bragg, London Weekend Television, 1991.

p. 16 Purchase of Grey Street: Land Sales Court. Gisborne registry no. 44/383.

p. 19 'I was given two marvellous gifts ...': *North and South*, Auckland, January 1990.

p. 20 'They sent me home because I was the Maori girl': *Woman's Day*, 8.11.89.

p. 20 'Maori children were considered to be dirty': *Vogue* (English edition), 1.9.79.

p. 21 'You grow with this capacity to cut off': *New Zealand Woman's Weekly* (*NZWW*), 9.11.92.

p. 21 'It turned me into a survivor': Fingleton, David, *Kiri: A biography of Kiri Te Kanawa* (Collins: London & Auckland, 1982), p. 17.

p. 21 Descriptions of Kiri's punishment: Harris, Norman, *Kiri: Music and A Maori Girl* (A. H. & A. W. Reed: New Zealand, 1966), p. 14–15.

p. 22 Arthur Sullivan as Kiri's great uncle: Fingleton, p. 15, and others. Nell's mother, Emily Beatrice Agatha Leece, neé Sullivan, was, according to Nell's birth certificate, born in Canterbury around 1871. Sir Arthur Sullivan's only sibling, an older brother Frederic, was born on Christmas Day, 1839, and married Charlotte Lacy in 1862. Their eight children were, in order of birth, Amy, Florence, Edith, Herbert, Maude, Frederic Richard, George and in 1877, William, who was born after his father's death.

p. 22 Jeremiah Sullivan's marriage to Emily's mother, Sophia Kennedy, registered at Christchurch, no. 1033 of 1869; Jeremiah Sullivan's death: registered at Hawera, no. 1910 of 1895.

p. 22 'She used to be a real tomboy': Unmarked cutting, September 1965.

p. 23 'My mother had had a dream ...': 'Magic Kiwis', television documentary, Communicado/TVNZ, 1991.

p. 23 'I can see Mummy constantly kept the music going': Fingleton, p. 17.

p. 24 'I'll speak to you when everyone's gone': *High Fidelity*, undated.

p. 24 'I was not an extroverted child': *ibid*.

p. 25 'My mother was rather secretive ...': *NZWW*, 9.11.92.

p. 25 Judy Evans-Hita: Author interview, July 97 onwards.

p. 27 'She didn't move ...': 'Magic Kiwis'.

p. 29 'What was wonderful about him ...': *Listener & TV Times*, 5.8.91.

p. 29 'Always, whenever anybody came': *NZWW*, 9.11.92.

p. 31 Kiri on Foley: *Vogue* (English edition), 1.9.79.

p. 32 'All the books tell you ...': 'Magic Kiwis'.

Chapter 3: 'The Nun's Chorus'

p. 33 Sale of Grey Street: Memorandum of transfer. Gisborne District Land Registrar no. 54952.

p. 33 Purchase of Mitchell Street: Certificate of title. Auckland District Land Registrar no. 570129.

p. 34 'There is nothing I like about myself . . .': *NZWW*, 13.4.92.

p. 37 Historical details of St Mary's and biographical details of Sister Mary Leo are taken from author interviews with St Mary's archivists, Sister Mercienne and Sister Patricia. Also from *New Zealand Weekly News*, 1.12.65; *NZWW*, undated; an obituary written by St Mary's previous archivist, Sister M. Veronica Delany; St Mary's College Annuals 1963 and 1973; *NZWW*, 25.10.93. Other details were gleaned from a speech made by Kiri at the opening of St Mary's College new music school, 10.3.96.

p. 38 'I was brought up a Catholic . . .': *NZWW*, 5.7.82.

p. 39 Sister Mercienne: Author interview, February 1998.

p. 39 Sister Dora: Author interview, February 1998.

p. 40 Elsa Grubisa: Author interview, December 1997.

p. 41 Gillian Redstone: Author interview, February 1998.

p. 41 'She seemed enormously old to me . . .': Fingleton, p. 20.

p. 41 Diana Stuart: Author interview, September 1997.

p. 42 Hannah Tatana: Author interview, January 1998.

p. 44 'Now tell me, Kiri. Next term, would you like . . .': Harris, p. 21.

p. 46 'Other nuns quivered . . .', 'Magic Kiwis'.

p. 48 Terry Nash: Author interview, April 1998.

p. 48 '. . . so I slammed down the receiver': Kiri's first boyfriend, Fingleton, p. 28.

p. 50 'I thought it was quite fun – rather a good floor show . . .': 'Magic Kiwis'.

p. 51 Thelma Robinson: Author interview, April 1998.

p. 51 Maori Education Foundation: details extracted from Hoani 'John' Waititi's research paper, 'Understanding The Maori', 1962.

Chapter 4: Wicked Little Witch

p. 54 Neil McGough: Author interview, November 1997.

p. 55 Lindsay Rowell: Author interview, November 1997.

p. 56 Vincent Collins: Author interview, November 1997.

pp. 56ff. Beverley Jordan: Author interview, January 1998.

p. 62 Kiri in *Uwane*: *NZWW*.

p. 62 Press coverage of *Uwane*: *New Zealand Herald*, 11.4.62; *NZWW*, 9.4.62; *Auckland Star*, 8.3.62.

p. 63 Kiri's telegram to cast: Private collection.

p. 64 Tony Vercoe: Author interview, January 1998.

Chapter 5: A Princess in a Castle

p. 67 'You're in!': Harris, p. 29.

p. 68 'That night all of the streets were sprinkled . . .': *ibid.*

p. 68 Susan Smith: Author interview, February 1998 onward.

p. 69 Rodney Macann: Author interview, January 1998 onward.

p. 71 Clifton Cook: Harris, p. 34.

p. 72 'I'm part Maori, so I feel I should learn . . .': *Auckland Star*, 27.9.63.

p. 72 'If a baby tries to walk too young . . .': *ibid*.

p. 73 Pettine-Ann Croul: Author interview, January 1998.

p. 74 Bob Sell: Author interview, December 1997.

p. 78 John O'Shea: Author interview, January 1998.

p. 78 Colin Broadley: Author interview, January 1998.

p. 79 Don Hutchings: Author interview, February 1998.

p. 82 Nerida Nicholls: Author interview, February 1998.

Chapter 6: Now is the Hour

p. 89 Brooke Monks: Author interview, August 1997 onward.

p. 92 Les and Sonia Andrews: Author interview, February 1998.

pp. 93ff. Barbara Brown: Author interview, February 1998 onward.

p. 95 Account of the Melbourne and Sydney Sun Aria contests and the accompanying tour of Australia: Based on interviews with Barbara Brown, Joan Aronsten and Lynne Cantlon.

p. 96 Lou Clauson: Author interview, February 1998.

p. 98 'The only thing I have ever wanted . . .': 'Magic Kiwis'.

p. 99 'Well, Miss Te Kanawa . . .': Harris, p. 49, and others.

p. 100 'Kiri is a very attractive girl . . .': Fingleton, p. 39.

p. 102 Donald Perry: Author interview, January 1998.

p. 103 Kiri Te Kanawa Trust and the Arts Council grant: *New Zealand Herald*, 19.10.65, 25.10.65, 25.11.65.

p. 105 John Thompson: Author interview, April 1998.

p. 108 'For the second time in my life . . .': Magic Kiwis.

p. 108 'I felt as if I had this sort of cocoon over me . . .': 'South Bank Show'.

Chapter 7: Apprentice Diva

p. 111 '. . . black and dead': Private collection, unmarked cutting, October 1966.

p. 111 Jeremy Commons: Author interview, March 1998.

p. 113 Sheila Thomas: Author interview, February 1998.

p. 113 'The warlords': *Listener &TV Times*, 5.8.91.

p. 114 Sir Donald McIntyre: Author interview, January 1998.

p. 115 Teresa Cahill: Author interview, March 1998.

p. 115 'I am a typical Piscean . . .': *NZWW*, 17.1.83.

p. 116 John Kentish: Author interview, February 1998.

p. 116 Osvalda Robertson: Author interview, March 1998.

p. 117 June Mengennis: Fingleton, p. 47.

p. 117 Rosalind Plowright: Matheopoulos, Helena, *Diva: Great Sopranos and Mezzos Discuss Their Art* (Victor Gollancz: London, 1991), p. 139.

p. 118 'Without boasting . . .': Private collection, unmarked cutting.

p. 118 'We used to eat people like you': *New York Times*, 14.12.74.

p. 118 Norman Harris: Author interview, January 1998.

p. 119 'share my mushrooms': Fingleton p. 46.

p. 120 'I was twenty-two at the time which is quite late . . .': 'Magic Kiwis'.

p. 120 'I hurt her terribly': *Woman's Day*, 8.11.89.

p. 121 'There is only one . . .': Unmarked cutting.

p. 123 Kiri on London fashion: *Auckland Star*, 27.1.67.

p. 123 Tom Hawkes: Author interview, February 1998.

p. 124 Kiri criticised by judges: *New Zealand Herald*, undated.

p. 124 Thelma Robinson: Author interview, April 1998.

p. 127 'Miss Davies made more comments about me . . .': Unmarked cutting, February 1967.

p. 129 'She's very much in love': Unmarked cutting.

p. 131 Lou Clauson: Author interview.

Chapter 8: Mr Ideal

p. 132 Osvalda Robertson: Author interview.

p. 132 Kiri and Des's blind date: Fingleton, p. 51.

p. 133 'That night was really quite terrible': Des, unmarked cutting, August 1967.

p. 133 'I had found my Mr Ideal': Fingleton, p. 51.

p. 133 '. . . deprived of sunshine and good food': Unmarked cutting.

p. 133 'They are such gentlemen': *Auckland Star*, 27.1.67.

p. 134 Adolf Lacis: Author interview, August 1997.

p. 134 Bob Morgan: Author interview, August 1997 onward.

p. 137 Des's 3 a.m. proposal and father's absence: Unmarked cutting.

p. 137 'We were unofficially engaged': *Auckland Star*, undated.

p. 138 '. . . Mum's cooking and care': *Auckland Star*, 4.8.67.

p. 139 'I had heard that Kiri was popular in New Zealand . . .': Unmarked cutting, August 1967.

p. 141 Billie Trillo: Author interview, February 1998.

p. 144 Donald Perry: Author interview, January 1998.

p. 145 John Lesnie: Author interview, May 1997.

pp. 145ff. Descriptions of the wedding: Author interview, from Fingleton, *NZWW* 11.9.67, and several *New Zealand Herald* and *Auckland Star* articles.

p. 146 'It was a mess. People who thought they should have been invited . . .': Magic Kiwis.

p. 147 Kay Rowbottom: Author interview.

p. 147 Kiri on Des being 'very drunk': Magic Kiwis.

p. 148 'I thought he meant another bottle . . .': Fingleton, p. 59.

Chapter 9: Tamed

p. 149 Bob Morgan: Author interview.

p. 150 Tom Hawkes: Author interview.

p. 150 Rodney Macann: Author interview.

p. 151 'Silly girl': Aquarius, BBC TV, 1975.

p. 151 'I suppose because I . . .': *Listener &TV Times*, 5.8.91.

p. 151 'She said I should give up': *Sunday Telegraph*, Sydney, 3.5.81.

p. 152 Florence Norberg: 'Voice Production for Singers', *Journal of the College of General Practitioners*, 1967, Vol. 13, no. 377.

p. 152 Mary Masterton: Author interview.

p. 153 John Matheson: Author interview, April 1998 onward.

p. 154 Teresa Cahill: Author interview.

p. 161 John Thompson: Author interview, April 1998.

p. 162 Richard Campion: Author interview, January 1998.

p. 166 Joan Ingpen: Author interview, March 1998.

p. 168 'I've discovered that . . .': Unmarked cutting, Christchurch.

p. 170 'I just couldn't believe my ears . . .': Colin Davis, *Today*, 1982.

p. 171 'I felt totally convinced . . .': *Musical America*, June 1983.

Chapter 10: A Pearl of Great Price

p. 172 'I have only one desire . . .': Lebrecht, Norman, *The Maestro Myth: Great Conductors in Pursuit of Power* (Simon & Schuster: London, 1991), pp. 169, 173.

p. 173 'I decided I didn't like anything . . .': *ibid.*, p. 173.

p. 175 Judy Evans-Hita: Author interview.

p. 176 'I'm getting along fine': *Auckland Star*, undated.

p. 178 'A singing teacher is like a psychologist . . .': *Listener & TV Times*, 5.8.91.

p. 178 'I recognised in Kiri a free spirit': *ibid.*

p. 180 Kiri on Boris Christoff: Fingleton, p. 91.

p. 181 'I believe very much in the principle, when you're down . . .': *Weekly Telegraph*, Issue 71.

p. 182 'The best directors are gay': *Musical America*, June 1983.

p. 182 'Don't talk stupid. I'm only a student': Fingleton, p. 95.

p. 184 'If I'm asked when my career took off . . .': Magic Kiwis.

p. 186 Kiri's fights with Rosza and Copley: Fingleton, pp. 120–21.

Chapter 11: New Worlds

p. 188 'Which one was it?': Fingleton, p. 102.

p. 188 Sale of Mitchell Street: Memorandum of transfer. Auckland Land Registry no. A616393.

p. 189 'All my life, my mother wanted to see me . . .': *New Zealand Herald*, 25.2.72.

p. 189 Nell's will: New Zealand National Archives.

p. 190 'It was not my plan to hurt her': *Mail on Sunday*, London, September 1985.

p. 193 Sister Margaret Browne: Author interview, February 1998.

p. 193 Donna Awatere: Awatere, Donna, *My Journey* (Seaview Press, Auckland, 1996).

p. 195 'I should have done more of the priestesses . . .': *Opera*, London, July 1981.

p. 196 Colin Davis on wrestling: 'This Is Your Life', TVNZ, 1991.

p. 197 'Our work is very passionate . . .': interview with Anne Barrowclough, *Daily Mail*, reprinted *NZWW*, 13.4.92.

p. 197 'They are both Hungarian Jews . . .': Matheopoulos, p. 215.

p. 198 'I did my usual bitchy thing . . .': Fingleton, p. 120.

p. 200 'The people in charge will say . . .': Te Kanawa, Kiri, with Conrad Wilson, *Opera For Lovers* (Roeder Publications Ltd: 1996), p. 39.

p. 200 'Chinese, Chinese': *ibid.*, p. 38.

p. 201 'She enjoys a rather dangerous edge . . .': Matheopoulos, p. 211.

p. 202 'If it's the Met . . .': 'Magic Kiwis'.

p. 203 'The loneliest person in the world': *Newsday*, 15.3.74.

p. 203 'My taxi driver was from the Bronx': *Interview*, New York, September 1986.

Chapter 12: Fallen Angel

p. 206 Norman Kirk's memorial: *New Zealand Herald*, 27.9.74; *Auckland Star*, 28.9.74.

p. 208 John Matheson: Author interview.

p. 214 Sharon Walsdorf: Author interview, August 1997.

p. 215 'I had reached the stage where I wasn't thinking . . .' *Woman's Day*, Sydney, 14.8.78.

p. 217 'I turfed that life in': Fingleton, p. 147.

p. 217 'I have set myself a limit': *New Zealand Herald*, 31.8.75.

p. 218 Terry Valentine: Author interview, March 1998.

pp. 218ff. Kura Beale: Interviews with several members of her family, and with Christopher DeLautour, Mabel Kewene, Madge Malcolm, Claire Jones and Eva Brown. Other details are taken from an undated interview in the *Russell Review*.

p. 223 'Beautiful voice, tart tongue': John Yeomans interview, unidentified publication, 14.9.76.

p. 224 'Failed to excite?': Bernard Levin, *The Times*, London, reprinted *New Zealand Listener*, 11.12.76.

Chapter 13: Lost Souls

p. 226 Barbara Brown: Author interview.

p. 227 'Drifting around the world like a couple of lost souls': interview with Marcia Russell, *The New Zealander*, 1979.

p. 227 Kiri on X-rays: Interview with Anne Barrowclough, *NZWW*, 13.4.92.

p. 227 'I was never actually told that I could not . . .': Interview with Paul Valelly, *Today*, 1982.

p. 228 'Certainly no difference . . .': Fingleton, p. 154.

p. 228 'Oh, one day . . .': Interview with Rosalie Horner, *Daily Express*, London, reprinted in unmarked NZ cutting.

p. 228 Lynne Newman: Author interview, May 1998.

p. 229 'She's quite at home in hotels . . .': *Woman's Day*, Sydney, 14.8.78.

p. 229 'The best operatic administration . . .': Te Kanawa/Wilson, p. 223.

p. 229 Kiri on money: Interview with David Fingleton, *Bristol and Bath News*, March 1977.

p. 230 'I want Toni to have a normal upbringing . . .': *New Zealand Herald*, 27.5.78.

p. 230 'I was lucky. In those moments of despair   ': *Today*, 1982.

p. 231 'Look, I was given everything else . . .': *Guardian*, London, reprinted *Sydney Morning Herald*, 28.12.93.

p. 231 'There is a lot of me in her . . .': Matheopoulos, p. 214.

p. 231 'I'd like some eggs . . .': *Evening Post*, Wellington, 16.7.77.

p. 232 Joan Ingpen: Author interview.

p. 233 '. . . fans crowded into my dressing room': Te Kanawa/Wilson, p. 38.

p. 233 Kiri's blonde wig: *The Bulletin*, Sydney, 4.9.76.

p. 233 'One young man . . .': *Interview*, New York, reprinted *More*, New Zealand, September 1986.

p. 234 Moffatt Oxenbould: Author interview, May 1998.

p. 235 'There are just no facilities . . .': *Auckland Star*, 8.10.77.

p. 235 'New Zealanders deserve to see me . . .': Interview with Marcia Russell, *The New Zealander*, 1979.

p. 235 'I'm only looking for an opera house . . .': *New Zealand Herald*, 8.9.78.

p. 236 'I think to get a high profile throughout the world . . .': 'Magic Kiwis'.

p. 236 'Opera in Europe is largely subsidised . . .': *Don Giovanni* location report by Roland Gelatt, *American Film*, April 1979.

p. 236 'As a stage performer I could not really get used . . .': 'Magic Kiwis'.

p. 237 'It brings me to the brink of madness': Matheopoulos, p. 213.

p. 237 'I had this man coming into my dressing room . . .': Te Kanawa/ Wilson, p. 44.

p. 238 Piero Cappuccilli: Fingleton, p. 167.

p. 238 Graeme and Lurene Lindsay: Author interview, March 1998.

p. 239 'If New Zealanders want to hear me . . .': *NZWW*, 7.4.80.

p. 239 Eva Brown. Author interview, *ibid*.

p. 240 'We didn't want Antonia to be an only child . . .': *NZWW*, 16.6.80.

p. 240 'To know they are in such capable hands . . .': *ibid*.

Chapter 14: '250,000 Covent Gardens'

p. 243 'If Kiri had not been . . .': Tooley in Fingleton, p. 167.

p. 243 Colin Davis: 'Why don't you take this job . . .': Lebrecht, p. 174.

p. 246 'Charles who?': *NZWW*, 5.7.82.

p. 248 'There was no time': Television interview with Paul Holmes, TVNZ, April 1998.

p. 249 'It was so hot and stuffy . . .': *Evening Standard*, London, reprinted *Christchurch Press*, 12.10.81.

p. 249 Tom on Royal Wedding performance: 'Magic Kiwis'.

p. 250 'Prince Charles later asked me . . .': *ibid*.

p. 250 'I had a lot of proposals . . .': *Evening Standard*, London, reprinted *Evening Post*, Wellington, 3.10.81.

p. 250 'A puzzle that had to be put together . . .': Matheopoulos, p. 215.

p. 250 Chris Doig: Author interview, May 1998.

p. 252 'Don't you ever do that to me . . .': *New Zealand Listener* 15.1.83.

p. 252 Sir Donald McIntyre: Author interview.

p. 253 'Bloody words': *Today*, 1982.

p. 253 Terry Valentine: Author interview.

p. 257 'This biography has an ulterior motive . . .': Interview with Robert C. Marsh, *Chicago Sun Times*, 1982.

p. 257 'I had so many approaches . . .': *NZWW*, 7.5.82.

Chapter 15: A No-win Situation

p. 259 'Why wasn't it me?': *NZWW*, 17.1.83.

p. 259 '. . . if I go to the States, I will take five days . . .': *NZWW*, 13.4.92.

p. 260 'I was just thinking, How can I do all this?': 'South Bank Show'.

p. 260 'like a boxing ring': *NZWW*, 30.8.82.

p. 260 Dame Catherine Tizard: Author interview, March 1998.

p. 260 David Stubbs: Author interview, March 1998.

p. 261 John Hopkins: Author interview, May 1998.

p. 262 'I had to work out if...': *New Zealand Listener*, 15.1.83.

p. 264 'I sat through the dinner grinning': *Interview*, New York, September 1986.

p. 264 Kiri's investiture: *NZWW*, 7.2.83; *New Zealand Herald*, 7.1.83.

p. 266 Johanna Fiedler: Author interview, January 1998.

p. 267 '... The music continues like an echo': *Sunday Mail*, Brisbane, 19.5.85.

p. 267 'I believe in knives...': Memento, television documentary, Channel 4, London, May 1993.

p. 267 'It's alright while she's small...': *Woman's Day*, Sydney, 14.8.78.

p. 267 'I had a lack of mucous...': *Listener & TV Times*, 5.8.91.

p. 268 'I sang through. I kept going': 'South Bank Show'.

p. 268 'I tingle all over': *Musical America*, June 1983.

p. 269 'Everyone wants you to sing, forgetting...': Colin Davis, 'South Bank Show'.

p. 269 'It was like a snake pit': *Observer*, London, reprinted *New Zealand Herald*, 22.6.89.

p. 269 'It was the only time I have ever...': Matheopoulos, p. 216.

p. 270 'You cannot imagine how many people...': *ibid.*, p. 217.

p. 270 'I'm sure he tried to get me fired': *Observer*, London, reprinted *New Zealand Herald*, 22.6.89.

p. 270 '... reassess where I am going': *NZWW*, 17.1.83.

p. 271 Kiri and McCormack: Lebrecht, Norman, *When The Music Stops* (Simon & Schuster: London, 1996), pp. 348–9.

p. 274 'Don't talk about money': *New Zealand Herald*, 29.3.84.

p. 276 'I have never been so angry...': *Today*, 1982.

p. 276 'The sooner the snob factor...': *Observer*, London, reprinted in *New Zealand Herald*, 22.6.89.

p. 276 '... didn't leave me for a year...': 'South Bank Show'.

p. 277 'She is a real woman...' 'quite a few bumps...': Matheopoulos, p. 215.

p. 277 'I thought I'd got through': *Listener & TV Times*, 5.8.91.

p. 280 Kiri on Nelson Riddle: *Interview*, New York, September 1986.

p. 281 'Why do they always ask me...': *The New Zealander*, 1979.

p. 281 'Instead of saying...': *Christchurch Press*, 11.7.81.

p. 282 Kiri's routine on Long Island: *Sunday Mail*, Brisbane, 19.5.85.

Chapter 16: Home Truths

p. 284 Kiri in Gisborne: *New Zealand Herald*, 29.8.87, 1.9.87; *Gisborne Herald*, 28.8.87.

p. 286 Kiri at Te Korapatu: 'Return Journeys', television documentary, accompanying article in *New Zealand Listener*, 14.5.88.

p. 286 David Baldock: Author interview, January 1998.

p. 286 Pahoe Mahuika: Author interview, March 1998.

p. 287 Bill Kerekere: Author interview, January 1997/March 1998.

p. 288 'Why go through that old tragedy?': *Daily Mail*, 6.3.98.

p. 288 Jack Wawatai's death: Death certificate. Auckland District Registrar and author interview with Apo, Lynne and Jason Wawatai.

p. 289 Tom's will: New Zealand National Archives.

p. 290 Stuart Comber's affidavit: New Zealand National Archives.

p. 291 'The person who goes overseas now had to have . . .': *Auckland Star*, 20.8.87.

p. 292 'Not even Maria Callas . . .': *Evening Post*, Wellington, 3.8.87.

p. 294 '. . . now and again there are hiccups . . .': *Daily Telegraph*, London. 30.4.83.

p. 297 Ian Fraser: Author interview, June 1998.

p. 297 John Thompson: Author interview.

p. 299 Moffatt Oxenbould: Author interview.

p. 299 'They have an attitude problem': *Courier Mail*, Brisbane, 29.8.87.

p. 299 Opera in the Outback: *Sunday Star*, Auckland, 21.8.88, 11.9.88; *New Zealand Herald*, 5.9.88, 24.8.88; *NZWW*, 3.10.88.

p. 300 John Hopkins: Author interview.

p. 301 '. . . I loved it for its daring . . .': NZPA report, *New Zealand Herald*, 17.4.89.

Chapter 17: A Gift to the Nation

p. 303 'I don't think I will get round to that now': *Observer*, London, reprinted *New Zealand Herald*, 22.6.89.

p. 304 'I'm permanently hungry . . .': *Radio Times*, London, December 1993.

p. 304 'I'm not sure whether . . .': *NZWW*, 10.8.87.

p. 304 'The children hate music . . .': Interview with Janet Watts, *Observer*, London, reprinted *Evening Post*, Wellington, 16.1.88.

p. 304 'Let me out of this prison': *NZWW*, 15.7.91.

p. 304 *Land of the Long White Cloud*: *New Zealand Herald*, 16.9.89; *Dominion*, Wellington, 16.9.89; *NZWW*, 27.11.89.

p. 305 Bruce Rowbottom: Author interview.

p. 306 'I suppose I am Anglicised . . .': *NZWW*, 27.11.89.

p. 306 Kura Beale's will: New Zealand National Archives.

p. 307 'She passed it on from one woman . . .': *New Zealand Herald*, 8.1.94.

p. 308 'Bubba' Wawatai: Author interview, May 1997.

p. 309 'You don't get the feeling . . .': Helen Brown, *Sunday Star*, 14.1.90.

p. 309 'Dame Kiri is far too much . . .': Peter Shaw, *Metro*, Auckland. March 1990.

p. 309 'Whenever I visit New Zealand . . .': *North and South*, Auckland, January 1990.

p. 310 'If you count the purists . . .': *New Zealand Listener*, 20.1.96.

p. 310 'I feel that by advancing my own personal glory . . .': *North and South*, Auckland, January 1990.

p. 310 Rodney Macann: Author interview.

p. 313 St Heliers apartment: Certificate of title. Auckland Land Registrar no. C048708.

p. 314 Shares in Kiwi Pacific: National Business Review, Auckland, 1996.

p. 318 'For two days I just swamped

myself . . .': *Opera Now*, March 1991.

Chapter 18: Pop Goes the Diva

p. 319 'Do you realise how much . . . ?': *Dominion*, Wellington, 9.1.91.

p. 320 Rolling Stones fantasy: NZPA/ *New Zealand Herald*, 23.3.91.

p. 321 'Before, I had to do it . . .': *NZWW*, 15.7.91.

p. 321 Classic FM bid: *New Zealand Herald*, 2.10.91.

p. 322 Keith Foote: Author interview, 1998.

p. 322 Patrick Power on Mimì: *Evening Post*, Wellington, 7.9.91.

p. 323 'Photographers always want to get me . . .': *ibid.*

p. 323 John McKay: Author interview, February 1998.

p. 326 'If you count the purists . . .': *New Zealand Listener*, 20.1.96.

p. 326 'When I'm feeling unloved . . .': *Observer*, London, reprinted *Evening Post*, Wellington, 16.1.88.

p. 326 'You're being shot down . . .': Interview with G. Barrett, *Sunday Mail* magazine, Brisbane, 1.11.92.

p. 327 'How many people . . . ?': Lebrecht, p. 355.

p. 327 Kiri at Mitchelton: *Courier Mail*, Brisbane, 12.2.90.

p. 328 Adelaide cancelled: *New Zealand Herald*, 28.11.92.

p. 328 Leeds cancelled: *Yes*, Auckland, 26.6.94.

p. 328 Nissan show: AAP report, 13.8.93.

p. 328 'If you were trying to sell peanut butter . . .': *Dominion*, Wellington, 13.8.93.

p. 330 'We're waiting for lightning . . .': Interview with David

Gillard, *Radio Times*, December 1993.

p. 330 'Fifty is nifty': *Financial Times*, London, reprinted *National Business Review*, Auckland, 25.3.94.

p. 331 'The worst year of my life': *Daily Mail*, 6.3.98.

Chapter 19: ParadiseLost

p. 332 '. . . Upmarket Cilla Black': Hugh Canning, *Sunday Times*, 8.12.91.

p. 332 'I've been asked every question . . .': *Evening Post*, Wellington. 7.9.91.

pp. 333ff. Kiri's fiftieth birthday party at Rawhiti: *New Zealand Herald*, 8.1.94, 7.4.94, 9.4.94; *Dominion*, Wellington, 15.1.94; *Sunday Star*, 10.4.94

p. 333 'Everyone goes through it . . .': Holmes.

p. 334 'I found the Svengali act a bit odd': *Listener & TV Times*, 5.8.91.

p. 334 Ian Fraser: Author interview.

p. 334 Frank Habicht: Author interview, October 1997.

p. 338 Purchase of Brookfield Street: Certificate of title. Auckland Land Registrar no. 7c/1262.

p. 340 'If I didn't have the husband I have got . . .': *NZWW*, 27.12.93.

p. 341 'We're not really in touch . . .': *NZWW*, 9.11.92.

p. 343 Nola's death notice: *New Zealand Herald*, 17.1.94.

p. 344 'Des has just had enough . . .': *New Zealand Herald*, 20.12.95.

p. 345 'You've got to try and turn on . . .': *New Zealand Listener*, 20.1.96.

p. 345 Christine Hall: Author interview, June 1998.

387

INDEX

408

ACKNOWLEDGEMENTS

'Here is Kiri of the Lovely Voice, whose singing and whose love of song have led her to the threshold of a great career in music,' read the dust jacket notes for the first biography of Kiri Te Kanawa, written by the New Zealander Norman Harris, when she was just a twenty-two-year-old London Opera Centre student in 1966. In the thirty years since its publication, as Kiri Te Kanawa has more than fulfilled the promise of her youth, she has been the subject of three more biographical and semi-autobiographical books: *Kiri: A Biography* by David Fingleton (1982); *Land of the Long White Cloud* (1989) and *Opera for Lovers* (1996). Each publication, like Harris's initial effort, has offered a portrait as carefully choreographed as any of Kiri's operatic productions. *Kiri: Her Unsung Story* offers a new and alternative view of a remarkable life.

Ours is the first biography to have been researched and written without the co-operation of Kiri or those people currently associated with her. It is a wholly independent and unauthorised portrait. For that reason, we believe, it is the most exhaustive, truthful and revealing. While the lack of Kiri's stamp of approval inhibited some – most significantly Desmond Park, who in conversation with Stephen d'Antal said he preferred not to talk to us without his ex-wife's blessing – the vast majority of those whom we approached were ready and willing to share their memories. They have provided a multi-faceted portrait of a complex and compelling human being. Each placed in us the trust that we would present as honest a picture of her remarkable life as possible. We hope we have repaid that faith.

It was the American writer Bernard Malamud who best defined the thankless task that faces all biographers. 'One cannot make pure clay from time's mud,' he wrote. Few public lives can have been mired in such uncertainty, particularly in early years. The fact that we have been able to shape so much of Kiri's poignant and powerful story is largely down to the help and encouragement of a number of individuals to whom we owe a particular debt of gratitude.

Primary among these is Kiri's niece, Judy Evans-Hita, a lynchpin in our research, who is owed more thanks than we can muster. Similarly Bob Morgan, Barbara Brown, Susan Smith, Tony Vercoe, Rodney Macann, Kay and Bruce Rowbottom and Brooke Monks have shown a generosity that cannot be repaid. Time and again they have enabled us to piece together events that would otherwise have remained impenetrable. Time and again we would have been lost without them.

No area of our research was more demanding than that relating to Kiri's origins, a subject of controversy among those connected to the events of 1944 for more than half a century. Here again we were fortunate. Noeleen Rawstron's sister Donny, daughter Sharon, brother Ken and niece Jennifer patiently and gracefully permitted us to unravel a traumatic episode in their family history, as did Jack Wawatai's ex-wife Apo, sister-in-law Ona, daughters Lynne and 'Bubba', son Jason and sister Hukarere. We are indebted to each of them.

Special thanks for their patience and trust are also due to Don Hutchings, Stephen Dee, Iain Aitken, Tracy Grant, Tom Hawkes, Neil McGough, Vincent Collins, Mary Masterton, Pettine-Ann Croul, Lynne Cantlon, Peter Downes, Lindsay and Madeleine Rowell, Teresa Cahill, Hannah Tatana, Beverley Jordan, Jeremy Commons, Adolf Lacis, John McKay and John Matheson, Joan Ingpen and Sir Donald McIntyre.

For contributions great and small, we would also like to thank the following people: Jean Wishart, Michael Willison, John Lesnie, Felix Donnelly, Donald Trott, Sally Williamson, Lloyd Williams, Bill Denholm, Catherine Reed, Brian O'Connor, Selwyn Rogers, Mabel Kewene, Bob Sell, Elsa Vujnovich, Harry Hall, Cherry Raymond, Les and Sonia Andrews, Lou Clauson, Trish Cornish, Rosemary Barnes, Johanna Fiedler, Norman Lebrecht, John Kentish, Osvalda Robertson, Sheila Thomas, Diana Stuart, Murray Khouri, Patricia Price, Keith Foote, Sisters Mercienne and Patricia, Billie Trillo, Nerida Nicholls, Sister Margaret Browne, Graeme and Lurene Lindsay, Dame Barbara

Goodman, Dame Catherine Tizard, Professor Ranginui Walker, Logan Brewer, Richard Campion, Jill Palmer, Hugh Walzer, Cyril Brown, Ulric Williams, John O'Shea, Constance Kirkaldie, Donald Perry, David Baldock, Colin Broadley, John Thompson, John Thompson, Ian Fraser, Madge Malcolm, Frank Habicht, Claire Jones, Eva Brown, Christine Hall, Bill Kerekere, Phil Aspinall, Jim Rawstron, Bill Walsdorf, Julie Ferris, Kahu Bullivant, Allan Andrews, Ira Haig, Stan Green, Pahoe Mahuika, Marie Landis, Christopher DeLautour, Patricia Payne, Gillian and Barry Trott, Myra Webster, Bob Alp, Terry Valentine, Malcolm McNeill, Bob Parker, Margaret Lovell-Smith, Dame Mira Szaszy, Terry Nash, Simon Mehana, Beverley Simmons, Tony, Kelvyn and Klynton Alp, Ricky Evans-Hita, Bobby Webster-Kerr, David Stubbs, David Park, Harvey Joyce, John Hopkins, Rachel Bridge, Ross Land, Frank Thorne, Moffatt Oxenbould, Tony Williams, Thelma Robinson, Joan and Max Aronsten, Dr Charles Nalden, Peter Godfrey, Louise Wright and Simon Shields. Other names must remain unwritten but not forgotten.

Condolences go to the family of Elaine Hegan, for so long the doyenne of Auckland's theatrical agents, who died shortly after giving a very useful interview to the authors.

Gratitude is also due to the staff at the Gisborne Museum and Auckland City Library's research centre, the British Library, British Film Institute and National Sound Archive in London.

The book could not have been completed without the limitless generosity of Simon Runting in Auckland, to whom Stephen d'Antal owes particular thanks, along with Simon Bassett-Smith, B. J. Brown, Ken Cooke and Virginia Leonard for their help and support, Tim Willcox for his ideas, and Paul Scott and Alison Bowyer for their extraordinary resources.

In London we are deeply indebted to Mary Pachnos, our agent at Aitken & Stone, who was the first to grasp the book's potential while at HarperCollins we were particularly fortunate to benefit from the editorial brilliance of Val Hudson and Andrea Henry. Without their cool, calming wisdom we would never have met a deadline that seemed utterly impossible until the very end. Thank you both, very much.

Lastly, to Kim Parkinson and Eva d'Antal, Cilene and Gabriella

Jenkins, who endured great neglect cheerfully, go much more than thanks. They were all the inspiration we could wish for.

Garry Jenkins and Stephen d'Antal,
LONDON & AUCKLAND, JULY 1998